Case Studies in Behaviour Therapy

Case Studies in Behaviour Therapy

Edited and introduced by
H. J. Eysenck

Routledge & Kegan Paul
London and Boston

First published in 1976
by Routledge & Kegan Paul Ltd
Broadway House, 68-74 Carter Lane,
London EC4V 5EL and
9 Park Street,
Boston, Mass. 02108, USA
Text set in Times Medium Roman by
G. A. Pindar & Son Ltd., Scarborough,
N. Yorkshire, England,
and printed in Great Britain by
Redwood Burn Ltd.,
Trowbridge & Esher
Copyright Personality Investigations Publications and
Services 1976

ISBN 0 7100 8164 2

Contents

Figures

Notes on Contributors

L. MICHAEL ASCHER is Assistant Professor at the Behavior Therapy Unit, Department of Psychiatry, Temple University, Philadelphia.

TEODORO AYLLON is Professor of Psychology and Special Education at Georgia State University, Atlanta, Georgia.

ANNE BROADHURST is Lecturer in the Department of Psychology, University of Birmingham and Honorary Principal Psychologist for the Central Birmingham Health District.

JACQUELINE BROCKWAY is Counselor at the University of Oregon Counseling Center.

T. W. BUTT is Clinical Psychologist at Lynfield Mount Hospital, Bradford, Yorkshire.

EDWARD CHESSER is Consultant Psychiatrist to the Department of Psychiatry, Middlesex Hospital, London.

ROBERT S. DAVIDSON is Clinical Research Psychologist at the Veterans' Administration Hospital, Miami, Florida.

H. J. EYSENCK is Professor of Psychology at the Institute of Psychiatry, University of London.

EDNA B. FOA is a Psychiatrist attached to the Department of Psychiatry, Temple University, Philadelphia.

H. GWYNNE JONES is Professor and Head of the Department of Psychology at the University of Leeds.

R. S. HALLAM is a Research Worker at the Maudsley Hospital, London.

R. HODGSON is Research Worker at the Institute of Psychiatry, University of London.

HENRY KANDEL is Professor of Psychology at Georgia State University, Atlanta, Georgia.

ROBERT PAUL LIBERMAN is Director of the Program in Clinical Research at the Camarillo-Neuropsychiatric Institute (UCLA) Research Center, Oxnard Mental Health Center, UCLA School of Medicine, Oxnard, California.

W. CHARLES LOBITZ is Assistant Professor of Clinical Psychology at the School of Medicine, University of Colorado.

GRETCHEN K. LOBITZ is Post-doctoral Fellow in Clinical Psychology at the School of Medicine, University of Colorado.

JOSEPH LOPICCOLO is Associate Professor in the Department of Psychiatry and Behavioral Science at the School of Medicine, State University of New York, Stony Brook.

MALCOLM J. MACCULLOCH is Senior Lecturer and First Assistant in the Department of Psychiatry, University of Liverpool.

VICTOR MEYER is Senior Lecturer in the Department of Psychiatry, Middlesex Hospital, London.

S. RACHMAN is Reader at the Institute of Psychiatry, University of London.

R. W. RAMSAY is Reader in Experimental Psychology Personality Research at the Psychological Laboratory, University of Amsterdam.

JOHNIE ROBERTS is Supervising Mental Health Nurse at the Oxnard Mental Health Center, Ventura County Health Services Agency, Oxnard, California.

JEAN E. SAMBROOKS is Roche Research Fellow at the Department of Psychiatry, University of Liverpool.

ROBERT SHARPE is Clinical Psychologist at the Department of Psychology, Middlesex Hospital, London.

JOHN D. TEASDALE is Principal Clinical Psychologist at the University Hospital of Wales.

JOSEPH WOLPE is Professor of Psychiatry and Director of the Behavior Therapy Unit, Temple University School of Medicine and Eastern Pennsylvania Psychiatric Institute, Philadelphia.

Abbreviations

AA	Anticipatory avoidance aversion therapy
CAPS	Computer assisted psychometric system
Cattell 16 PF	Cattell 16 personality factor test
CR	Conditioned response
CS	Conditioned stimulus
ECG	Electrocardiograph
ECT	Electro-convulsant therapy
EPI	Eysenck personality inventory
FR	Fixed ratio
MAOI	Monoamine oxidase inhibitor
MMPI	Minnesota multiphasic personality inventory
MPI	Maudsley personality inventory
OSI	Oregon sex inventory
S^D	Discriminant stimulus
S^R	Reinforced stimulus
PACE	Programmable automatic conditioning equipment
SIL	Sexual interest latency
SOM	Sexual orientation method
VR	Variable ratio

Introduction

H. J. Eysenck

The use of single cases in experimental psychology and in psychiatry has a long and chequered history; there are many curious and almost certainly erroneous notions regarding it floating about. Much of the abuse that has been heaped upon those who publish single-case histories probably derives from the way psychoanalysts have used this device in order to *prove* their theories; Freud derived his theories from single-case studies ('Little Hans'; 'The Wolf Man'), and attempted to prove them by appealing to such cases. He explicitly denied the need for more experimental proof, using proper designs and control groups, in his famous postcard to Rosenzweig. Rosenzweig had sent Freud an account of his attempts to study repression experimentally, and Freud replied: 'I cannot put much value on these confirmations because the wealth of reliable observations on which these assertions rest makes them independent of experimental verification.' Few modern writers would so cavalierly dismiss the need for proof, particularly as history has shown that the 'wealth of reliable information' Freud appealed to was by no means as reliable as one might have wished.

Such proof is now usually taken to mean the use of groups, one of which is administered the treatment under investigation, while the other(s) is given placebo treatment, or no treatment. Such an experimental design, usually followed by some kind of analysis of variance or co-variance, makes assumptions which are not necessarily correct. Averaging over groups may lead to the summation of incommensurables; it is well known that different learning curves often differ so strikingly in shape that averaging them produces a mean growth curve which is unlike the majority of individual curves. Even more relevant is a possibility raised by Bergin (1966) who presented 'a curious and provocative finding' in his re-analysis of a number of outcome studies, namely that the variance of change scores for groups of patients in individual therapy far exceeded the variance of change scores for an untreated group. He took this as evidence for a 'deterioration' effect, to take its place beside an 'improvement' effect; some patients are greatly helped by psychotherapy, others are made considerably worse. On the whole, there is no overall effect (which is the usual finding in outcome studies — Rachman, 1971). This effect might be considered only a more extreme example of the absurdity of averaging dissimilar curves. Whereas normally learning curves differ in shape (sigmoid, linear, positively or negatively accelerated) they are usually monotonic; in the case suggested by Bergin they would not only differ in shape, but also in direction, some going up, others down.[1]

The realization that statistical treatment of group differences and group effects has many weaknesses is not new; the early German experimentalists were well aware of the dangers of averaging, and often worked with a sample of one (or at least, with samples so small that every individual was analysed separately). The epoch-making work of Ebbinghaus on memory, using only himself as the experimental subject, is of course too well known to need more than a mention, but this attitude was quite general. In Kraepelin's series of studies (published under the title of *Psychologische Arbeiten*) results are usually presented for individuals, not for groups; the same is true of G. E. Müller and many other pioneers. Pavlov furnishes us with another outstanding example; in his book on *Conditioned Reflexes* the typical documentation is a table setting out what one particular dog did on one particular occasion, under one particular set of experimental conditions. Pavlov never averaged results in the modern manner.

The years between the wars almost eliminated this single-case approach, until it was brought back into experimental psychology by B. F. Skinner and his followers (Sidman, 1960b). Typically, they demand effective experimental methodologies, based on single-organism research; their fine-grained behavioural analysis is predicated on complete experimental control over the behaviour of the animal (or patient). Effects which demand statistical analysis of

---

[1] Actually, as Gottman (1973) has pointed out, Bergin's interpretation of the observed increase in variance is not necessarily the only possible one; there are at least two alternatives. The variance of change scores can be affected by the initial and final variances, and the test-retest correlation. In the example analysed by Bergin, the pre-test variances of the two groups were already significantly different; furthermore, as Schofield (1950) has shown, test-retest correlations on the MMPI are considerably reduced for some treatment groups when compared with a non-treatment group. Thus for statistical reasons the conclusion does not follow. There is also another possibility, of more interest to therapists, namely a regression effect. Therapy is often designed to help patients at one extreme or the other of a distribution, for example, patients may be manic or depressive. If a given drug treatment brings these extremes closer to the mean, then automatically the variance of their scores on the continuum going from mania to depression would be reduced; this would be compatible with all-round improvement. Thus clearly analysis of treatment effectiveness requires considerable statistical sophistication.

group results to make them significant would be regarded by them as too unstable, weak and lacking in experimental control; the looked-for results should be demonstrable with every single case submitted to the experimental procedure in question. This demand links up with Pavlov and the other early investigators mentioned above; it restores to psychology a paradigm of considerable power which had been lost under the attack of the statistically-minded experimentalists. It is not necessary to decide that one approach or the other is 'better' in some metaphysical sense; both have their strengths and their weaknesses, and both complement each other. It is sad that psychology seems to be split into two 'schools', each almost exclusively advocating the use of a methodology regardless of conditions which make it applicable or not. What is needed in psychology is clearly an improvement in experimental control *and* improved statistical treatment of data; conditions and state of development of knowledge usually dictate whether we can rely more on the one or the other of these two methods. The ideal of gaining such absolute control of experimental conditions that no mathematical analysis is necessary has not even been approached in physics; it is certainly not in sight in most parts of psychology. That is not to say that it is not desirable; unfortunately what is desirable is not always feasible. And did not Peter Medawar call science 'the art of the possible' — suggesting that if we require perfection, then we will never be able to practise science?

In behaviour therapy, Shapiro (1961, 1966) has always urged the applicability of single-case study to research in psychotherapy, neatly inverting the Skinnerian approach. Skinner would regard the single case as an exemplification of demonstrated experimental control; Shapiro would regard the single case as an experimental problem to be attacked in the usual manner by means of the hypothetico-deductive method. Yates (1970) has gone so far as to make the single-case study the corner-stone of behaviour therapy (p. 18):

> Behaviour therapy is the attempt to utilize systematically that body of empirical and theoretical knowledge which has resulted from the application of the experimental method in psychology...
> and to apply that knowledge to the treatment or prevention of those abnormalities by means of controlled experimental studies of single cases, both descriptive and remedial.

This statement is incorrect for two reasons. In the first place, psychotherapy and psychoanalysis would also claim to apply psychological knowledge to the individual case, and to regard the individual patient's reaction to specific stimuli as support or disproof of their particular formulation of his case. Indeed, this is a standard practice in psychiatry, and does not distinguish behaviour therapy from psychotherapy. In the second place, behaviour therapists have certainly not practised what Yates preaches. As Leitenberg (1973) points out, 'between 1963 and 1968 of 258 articles published in the first major journal in this area, *Behaviour Research and Therapy,* only 36 provide controlled evaluations within individual cases' (p. 88). It was not until the publication of the Skinnerian journal, *Journal of Applied Behaviour Analysis,* in 1968, that in three out of four cases controlled experiments within individual cases were presented. In the other journals which now publish work on behaviour therapy, individual cases are usually published not in order to prove anything, but rather as examples of techniques which can be used, or of difficulties which may be encountered. Behaviour therapy is not distinguished from psychotherapy by its reliance on individual cases, but by the fact that the methods of treatment used are deduced from modern learning theory, and from laboratory studies on both humans and animals. When individual cases are used, controls and deductions are usually more rigorous than is customary in psychiatry, but this does not alter the principle.

However we may have to qualify Yates's definition, it is clear, as Leitenberg (1973) points out (p.88):

> That a large and vital segment of behavior modification research adheres to controlled investigations of single cases. The major thrust of this research has been to verify experimentally in individual cases that observed changes in behavior are really a function of the therapeutic procedures applied to produce these changes.

It is here that behaviour therapy parts company from psychotherapy; psychotherapists typically *assume* that the methods and approaches used by them are responsible for the changes observed in their patients (Rachman, 1971), while behaviour therapists are concerned to *prove* that this is so. The experimental conditions which make such proof possible have been discussed at some length by Gottman (1973) and Leitenberg (1973), and statistical methods applicable to single-case studies have been elaborated by Edgington (1967), Holtzman (1963), Namboodiri (1972), Revusky (1967) and Shine and Bower (1971); we will not make any attempt to duplicate these discussions here. It may, however, be of some interest to spell out just how a single case can provide proof for any scientific statement at all; many psychologists would consider deductions from a single case meaningless. That, however, is not so.

Consider a famous 'single case' study in cosmology. Herschel had discovered (by lucky accident) the planet Uranus; its observed path did not coincide precisely with the theroretical one calculated from Newtonian principles. LeVerrier in France, and Adams in England suggested that these deviations might have been caused by another planet, hitherto unobserved, and calculated its position and orbit; when astronomers looked in the postulated directions, they discovered Neptune. It would be idle to deny that this 'single case' greatly helped in establishing the value of Newtonian physics, even though a second attempt to use this method failed. (LeVerrier postulated an inferior planet to account for Mercury's perturbations, but this has never been found). It was not even held against Newton that the calculations which led to the discovery of Neptune were in part based on 'Bode's Law', which is not a law but simply an empirical statement of regularities in the successive increases in the distances of the planets from the sun, and which cannot be explained in terms of Newtonian physics at all. In fact, it does not apply to Neptune at all well; LeVerrier and Adams were lucky that they had their astronomers look at what happened to be the right time — six months later they would have found nothing in the predicted direction!

Not every 'single-case' study gives us acceptable information; the great mass of published material, particularly the cases exemplifying psychotherapy and psychoanalysis, must be regarded as scientifically useless. If this sounds a trifle harsh, we may perhaps point to the reanalysis of Freud's famous case of 'Little Hans', which is supposed to have started child analysis, at the hands of Wolpe and Rachman (1960). These authors point out, not only that Freud did not make deductions from factual observations, but imposed preconceived notions upon very recalcitrant facts in this case; furthermore, there are alternative and much more plausible interpretations of the facts in terms of simple conditioning principles. This 'case' illustrates beautifully the need for discipline and for proper design in single case studies; without these two characteristics the study may be of literary interest and value, but it cannot be used as proof in a scientific context. What sorts of methodologies do we have at our disposal?

One of the most important designs is the 'reversal design'. Such a design has four main sequential phases. First, we observe the occurrence of the two relevant behaviours: that is, that which we wish to decrease and an alternative, incompatible behaviour which we wish to increase. Having established this operant base-line, the therapeutic procedure is introduced for a period long enough to produce some substantial and stable change in the frequencies of the behaviours under investigation. In the third phase, therapeutic intervention is reversed and the behaviour which was being increased is now decreased, and the behaviour which was being decreased is now increased. Given that this reversal is successful, we would then go on to phase 4, which is a repetition of phase 1, that is, base-line behaviour. If behaviour changes each time in the predicted direction (that is, incrementing in phase 2, decrementing in phase 3 for the desirable behaviour, and vice versa for the undesirable behaviour), and if behaviour returns to the base-line frequency in phase 4, then clearly we have gained experimental control over the behaviour in question.

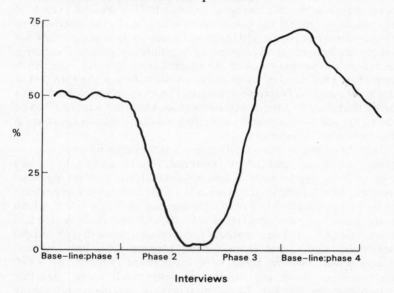

FIGURE I·1 *Percentage of interview time occupied by paranoid talk before (phase 1), during (phase 2) and after (phases 3 and 4) introduction of aversive noise as negative reinforcement*

Figure I·1 illustrates the application of this design to a particular paranoid persecution idea in one of our patients. The graph shows the percentage of time that the patient talked about this particular idea during a non-directive interview with the experimenter under base-line and experimental conditions. During phase 2 the experimenter would press a button which caused white noise to occur in the headphones worn by the patient, until he changed his topic. During phase 3, the experimenter would press the button whenever the patient did not talk about his fixed idea. Clearly a reversible effect is produced by this procedure. In itself, of course, this effect is of no great interest; however, concomitant with phase 2 the patient ceased to talk about his fixed idea in the ward, and with the nurses. After phase 4 was finished, a lengthened phase 2 was reinstated, and the patient was permanently cured of his habit of talking about his paranoid ideas. The reversal procedure makes it unlikely that this success was merely a case of spontaneous remission. Note that we can conclude that the therapeutic procedure was effective in this case; we cannot conclude that it would be equally successful with other cases of paranoid persecution mania. Such a conclusion would require a much extended group comparison. There are several designs of this kind in the literature, for example, Allen, Hart, Buell, Harris and Wolf (1964); while it may seem to impose a cruel burden on the patient, it does reassure us that in continuing with the treatment we are in fact benefiting the patient. This is an important thing to know.

The withdrawal design takes second place to the reversal design, and has some similarities to it. The difference consists in the absence of phase 3; instead of introducing an alternative treatment method which reverses the effects of the original treatment, we omit phase 3 and simply withdraw the treatment. As Leitenberg puts it, 'in the withdrawal design the major concern is what happens to a *single* clinically relevant behaviour when a single therapeutic procedure is instated, then withdrawn, and then reinstated' (p. 91). He quotes as an example a study by Ayllon and Azrin (1965); I shall recall an example I have given elsewhere (Eysenck, 1965). This is the case of a patient who suffered severe asthmatic attacks; these could be abolished completely by turning the portrait of his mother-in-law, which was hanging in his bedroom, to the wall. Returning to the phase 1 conditions (that is, with the portrait right side up) consistently reinstated the asthmatic condition. No phase 3 is possible in this experiment because we have no method of increasing the undesirable behaviour; we do not know how to increase the asthmatic attacks in this patient (except perhaps by actually introducing his mother-in-law into the experiment!).

A third research design has been called by Leitenberg (1973) the multiple schedule (stimulus discrimination) design. This design is based on discrimination learning principles; treatment of a given behaviour is different depending on the presence or absence of a given differential stimulus (S^+ as opposed to S^-). A study by O'Brien, Azrin and Henson (1969) is used to illustrate this design; the number of suggestions made by hospital patients is the dependent variable, and conditions of following these suggestions or not following them is the discriminant behaviour. This is a complex and difficult design, and it has not been much used. Probably more frequent, and also more useful, is what Leitenberg calls the multiple base-line (response discrimination) design. It can best be illustrated by one of the Maudsley studies using aversion therapy. Marks and Gelder (1967) attempted to decondition a fetishist, using electric shock; they used a penis plethysmograph to measure the success of the treatment. They started out with five different stimuli, all of which produced an erection (nude photos, panties, slips, skirts, pyjamas), and then proceeded to decondition each one of these in order, leaving out the nude photos. Response was extremely discriminative; only target behaviour was extinguished, without having any effect on non-target behaviours. Leitenberg argues that this demonstrates quite clearly the absence of non-specific effects (expectancy, patient-therapist relationship, etc.). This deduction is perhaps a little optimistic; the patient's expectancy after his usual briefing would surely be that the effects would indeed be specific! In spite of this objection, the method is clearly important and interesting.

Perhaps the simplest, most direct and most general value of the single case lies in its use as disproof of a general theory or hypothesis. The observation of a single black swan disproves the hypothesis that all swans are white. A single planet whose orbit was circular would disprove Kepler's Law — and Newton's as well. A single case successfully treated by behaviour therapy, and not showing either symptom substitution or relapse, would disprove Freud's generalizations about 'symptomatic treatment' (Eysenck and Wilson, 1973, have discussed this point at some length). In this, and the various other ways mentioned, case histories can be of scientific relevance and importance, provided we do not ask of them what they cannot give us; for wider knowledge, they must in all cases be complemented by larger-scale clinical studies and group comparisons. But equally, such larger-scale studies are not enough; they in turn must be supplemented by careful individual case studies in order to see whether important factors have not been left out of the statistical comparisons.

Consider as an example of the possibly misleading outcome of group comparisons a study reported by DiLoreto (1971). He compared the therapeutic effectiveness of three different techniques of behaviour therapy (Wolpe's method of desensitiza-tion, Ellis's method of rational-emotional therapy, and Rogers's method of client-centred therapy) on patients randomly assigned to these treatments; each treatment was practised by two therapists, in order to assess the importance of therapist variance. Looking at the overall figures, Wolpe's method was the most successful, with the other two rather less successful. Fortunately DiLoreto, in order to test a specific theory, had divided his patients into extraverts and introverts, with equal numbers being assigned to each treatment. He showed that while Wolpe's method of treatment was equally successful with these two groups, Ellis's treatment was much more successful with introverts than with extraverts, while Rogers's treatment was far more successful with extraverts than with introverts. This study illustrates beautifully the moral that averaging over dissimilar members of a sample can give meaningless results; effects for one person may cancel out effects for another, when the two are arbitrarily combined and averaged. Sometimes we can avoid this by relying on explicit theories, as DiLoreto did; sometimes we simply have to keep our eyes open and look carefully at individual cases — not in the hope of proving anything, but rather in the hope of learning something!

In addition to their purely scientific contribution, case histories have other important functions which should not be overlooked. Textbook discussions of behaviour therapy, even though correctly describing theories and procedures, usually give quite the wrong impression of what actually goes on in the treatment session. The reader easily gains the impression that the therapist puts a coin marked 'desensitization' or 'aversion therapy' into the apparatus, and out comes the 'cure'. Experienced therapists of course know that this is not so, but for training purposes it may be useful to eradicate this wrong impression, and instead introduce the student to the kind of thing that actually goes on during the treatment of a case. He will see that nothing is as cut-and-dried as he may have imagined from reading the textbook, and that often hypotheses about the dynamics of the patient's disorder, leading to one set of therapeutic procedures, have to be given up when these procedures do not work, and another set of hypotheses developed. This inevitably leads to other procedures being tried, until hypotheses and therapeutic success are in equilibrium. Each patient constitutes an experimental problem, and the first hypotheses suggested by the therapist may turn out to be inapplicable, and in need of replacement — very much as in experimental psychology generally the first, faltering hypotheses the scientist puts forward are not equally adequate for the purpose of explaining and bringing under experimental control the phenomena in question. One of the major purposes in producing this book was to illustrate in some detail this give-and-take, this development of better and more successful generalizations about the dynamics of the patient's disorder as treatment proceeds. It is my hope that this book will be found particularly useful in the training of behaviour therapists; one of the most important things which they have to learn is that nothing is simple, and that rigid, stereotyped methods of treatment are quite inappropriate to the complexity of the problems presented. Behaviour therapists must be aware of all the different methods; only then will they be in a position to make appropriate choices in the treatment of individual cases.

The cases here presented may also serve the purpose of killing stone dead the widespread notion that behaviour therapy cannot deal with anything but simple phobic disorders; most of the cases reported are clearly of a complex kind, and only one or two involve phobic elements. In fact, in the practice of behaviour therapy phobias of a simple kind play a very small role, and their complete omission would not materially alter the situation. Why has this legend grown up? The answer must lie in the fact that *experimental* studies, using analogue patients, have often concentrated on specific phobias (fear of snakes, fear of spiders, fear of public speaking) for the simple reason that these present a unique opportunity for measuring precisely the degree of fear elicited by the phobic stimulus; this enables us to measure with equal precision the change that is brought about by behaviour therapy. This is an important experimental paradigm, and it would be true to say that we owe much worthwhile information to its application. However, the fact that phobic disorders are exceptionally useful to the experimentalist interested in behaviour therapy is not to say that therapists are confined to using patients of this kind. Anyone using this false idea in criticism of behaviour therapy is clearly ignorant of what is going on in countless clinics and mental hospitals where behaviour therapy is being used in connection with all the various types of neurotic disorders, simple or complex — as well as many psychotic disorders, too!

It is in relation to these analogue studies that the notion of 'simple' cases originated; in practice, very few if any neurotic disorders that come to the attention of the behaviour therapist are 'simple' in any way. Their complexity may not be immediately apparent, of course — several examples are given where this apparent simplicity overlays a considerable complexity. Sometimes it is only the failure of a recommended therapeutic procedure based on an overly simplified hypothesis of the dynamics of a case which allows the therapist to discover these further complexities; again, several examples will be given to illustrate this point. Beginners (and textbooks) inevitably underestimate the degree to which the apparently simple symptom presented at the initial interview interacts with other, apparently irrelevant aspects of the patient's behaviour; experience (and good teaching) are required to alert the practitioner to these facts.

If things are so complicated, then, and if the presenting symptom may only be the tip of an iceberg; if we must look at the dynamics of each case in detail, and disentangle its complexities by noting response to each method of treatment tried — are we not back in the same position as the psychoanalysts, and does this not detract seriously from the proud claim that behaviour therapy is the application of *scientific* generalizations and laws? To argue thus is a mistake; it implies a misunderstanding of what applied science means in practice. When a new motor-car is being designed, the people concerned with its construction certainly base themselves very much on established scientific facts; that much is obvious. Yet the finished product also shows evidence of artistic flair, of inventive genius, of innovative departures from established practice. Even the most knowledgeable designer may have great difficulties in predicting whether the test car, once it has been built, will show oversteer or understeer, or whether the rear wheels will break away in a tight turn. There will be any number of faults to iron out which could not have been predicted; the notion of the gremlin originated with users of hard-science products, not with psychologists! 'Bugs' are inevitable in any new construction; they even appear in computer programmes where theoretically at least perfect mastery is possible. The complexities of real life are beyond the simple application of scientific principles, however firmly established these may be; such application requires good knowledge of these principles, but it also requires something more — experience, insight, originality, a 'nose' for successful departures from practice. Applied science (except in the most traditional aspects) always presents new challenges, requires new adaptations, demands new solutions. Behaviour therapy is no different to other applied sciences. We have a certain, limited amount of scientific knowledge on which we may draw and on which we must rely; in most cases we have to supply in addition a subjective, evaluative element, the value of which can only be tested by actual experiment — that is, by the success or failure of treatment based on it. In applied science there is no way of avoiding this personal contribution, or this acid test. Our bridges may be built with the most fastidious concern for scientific principles, but if they fall down in the next storm this will be a poor defence! We may treat our patients according to the best available principles, but unless they get better they are not likely to thank us. Each treatment is an experiment; only a quick cure is acceptable as proof that our hypotheses regarding the dynamics of the case were along the right lines.

It is this concern with proof that most clearly separates behaviour therapists from psychoanalysts. The neglect of the outcome problem has been the most culpable fault of the psychotherapists (Rachman, 1971); marked concern with it has been the most obvious virtue of the behaviour therapists. Psychoanalysts have been more concerned to make their theories inviolate from attack than to test them (Eysenck and Wilson, 1973); they resemble Father Clausius who tried to reconcile Galileo's discovery of mountains on the moon with the Aristotelian belief that all the heavenly bodies were completely spherical. His solution was to state that the moon was covered with a transparent, crystalline substance which covered all the valleys up to the highest mountain peaks, and which thus made the moon completely spherical. Galileo's reply is classical: 'Neither demonstrated nor demonstrable.' If a person presents with a severe obsessional complaint which makes it impossible for him to earn a living, or to live a happy and contented life, our only way to prove that we have some understanding of the aetiology of his disorder is to cure him of it, quickly and permanently; if we can do that the truth of our principles is both demonstrable and demonstrated. Psychoanalysts have always avoided this challenge; until they take it up their writings will inevitably be outside science, as ordinarily understood.

The complexity of neurotic disorders is often used to decry the statement that neurotic 'symptoms' are not symptoms of some deep, underlying complex but are simple conditioned responses (Eysenck and Rachman, 1965). This is not a reasonable criticism. Conditioned responses can themselves act as reinforcers, and as unconditioned stimuli (Eysenck, 1968); this is particularly true of anxiety and sexual responses. We can build up whole chains of conditioned and unconditioned responses and stimuli, in a very complex pattern; the complexity of the pattern is no argument against the conditioning theory. When we talk about 'dynamics' in this book, it is this network of conditioned responses we are referring to, not some speculative, hypothetical set of Freudian concepts. The concept of 'dynamics' is too useful to be abandoned because it has been abused by some earlier schools.

The case histories here reproduced do not invariably show a successful outcome. In putting together this book, it was far from my mind to try and prove the value of behaviour therapy by quoting a handful of successful treatment outcomes. It is too well known that spontaneous remission is extremely frequent in cases of neurotic disorder, and sometimes even in the most distressing psychotic illnesses, to make such an argument convincing. In real life, complete success cannot be guaranteed, even though the theory on which treatment is based may be perfectly adequate. Treatment of impotence may depend on the co-operation of the wife, and this may not be forthcoming — thus a sound method of therapeutic intervention may be impracticable. We do not, and obviously cannot, control the environmental forces which act on the patient to a sufficient extent to obtain optimal results; we have to make do with whatever may be available to us to try and manipulate the patient into a better and, to him, more satisfactory condition. Again, ingenuity is needed; the application of our scientific principles is not feasible on a penny-in-the-slot-machine kind of principle. Hence some of the authors have reported cases in which apparently well-designed treatment schemes fell short of complete success, for reasons beyond the powers of the therapist to control. Such partial failure, too, the budding behaviour therapist must learn to expect, and live with; even then he should always ask himself the question — is the fault mine, or does the patient's behaviour show that my interpretation of the dynamics of the case was correct?

The answer to such questions should of course by preference be objective, just as the assessment of the success of the treatment altogether should be objective. Therapists are only too likely to take a lenient view of their own mistakes, and an over-enthusiastic view of their successes; objective recording of the events which occur during the course of treatment, particularly changes in symptomatology which follow therapeutic innovations, is desirable, and should indeed be obligatory. Several authors have supplied such detailed documentation, and its usefulness will be apparent to anyone who has tried to see some design, darkly, in the changing behaviour of his patients. Such detailed recording for each patient, for each session, may not always be possible in the hurly-burly of the busy practitioner's clinic; it nevertheless presents an ideal state toward which we should strive. We are dealing with men's happiness, and no trouble should be too great to improve our chances of giving them a maximum amount of help. Mankind, by giving clinical psychologists and psychiatrists too heavy a work load to make the adequate performance of their work possible, would appear to hold the achievement of happiness in low esteem; we must try and alter this view.

I have used the term 'manipulation' advisedly a few paragraphs ago; this may seem to give support to those critics of behaviour therapy who feel that patients are being 'manipulated' — presumably against their better judgment, and to their own disadvantage. All methods of therapy involve manipulation, in the broad sense in which the term is being used; so does any form of social interaction. The crucial questions to be asked are these: Is the manipulation done with the full understanding of the patient? Is it being done with his full, informed consent? Is it being done to achieve aims set by the patient himself, rather than the therapist? Is it being done in the most humane, painless, dignified manner compatible with success? Is it likely to be successful after a reasonably short time, and without involving an unreasonable expense on the part of the patient? If these questions can honestly be answered with an unqualified 'Yes', then I suggest that the 'manipulation' involved is justified. The reader will have a chance to ask himself in relation to each of the cases recounted here whether he would answer these questions with a 'Yes' or a 'No'; I believe that the answer will overwhelmingly be in the affirmative. The reader may also ask himself what answers should be given in each case if psychotherapy, in particular psychoanalysis, had been the method used. I think the outcome of this comparison would be salutary and interesting.

One final word concerning the style in which these various reports have been written. As editor I sent to each contributor a general outline of the book, suggesting the type of case that might be of interest, and the sort of write-up I would like. I could have asked for conformity to a general scheme, going well beyond this, but I thought it better to leave each contributor to present his case(s) as he saw fit; uniformity for its own sake has no appeal to me in this connection. It will consequently be found that writers have adopted very different methods of presentation, and many different styles; in view of the fact that the cases selected by them differ profoundly in symptomatology, in type of treatment adopted, and in the appropriate mode of monitoring the effects of treatment, this does not seem unreasonable. It also makes the book more interesting; unity in variety may be the underlying principle of art, but variety is too often missing in edited books of this kind. The unity will be clear enough without stressing it; all the writers are experienced practitioners of behaviour therapy (using this term in its widest meaning), and have used the principles of modern learning theory in their attempts to modify the maladaptive behaviour of their patients. Their successes and failures should give the reader a more intimate understanding of what precisely it is that behaviour therapists do; such an understanding is not always gleaned from a reading of textbooks, or even relevant journals like *Behaviour Research and Therapy*. It is my hope that the reader will agree with my evaluation that here are a number of people devoted to the service of those of their fellow men who, through no fault of their own, are suffering from various maladaptive behaviours; that these therapists are trying, under considerable difficulties, to apply scientific principles to their therapeutic task; and that sometimes at least they succeed in formulating the dynamics of the case correctly, and in applying the right kind of 'manipulation' to cure the patient. The reader may also agree that the techniques used are of considerable interest in their own right, and that further work on clarifying and extending these techniques is likely to prove a worthwhile service to society. The identity of all patients in the case-histories has been disguised.

1 The Modification of Compulsive Behaviour

R. Hodgson and S. Rachman

The three cases[1] to be described all suffered from some form of compulsion: compulsive cleansing rituals in the first case, compulsive self-care rituals in the second and compulsive masturbation in the last. In each case the successful modification programme was derived from a learning theory approach to the problem behaviour and the three programmes share some common features. In each of them the patient was brought into situations that provoked the compulsive behaviour and then encouraged to refrain from carrying out the compulsion. *In vivo* exposure featured largely in all of the programmes.

Although the clinical outcome was ultimately satisfactory in each case, the successful modification programme was not always the first to be tried. In the first case, for example, a number of alternatives were explored and then discarded for lack of success, before we worked out an effective approach. It is by no means true that behaviour therapy (or modification) is sensibly applied in an automatic style, patient by patient. Often, careful experimental analyses are demanded before success can be achieved, particularly when one is faced with unusual or intractable problems.

The three cases were selected from a large pool of treated cases in order to illustrate two major points. In the first place, we hope that they are convincing examples of the successful application of a behavioural approach to undoubtedly complex, serious cases. Behavioural methods are not successful merely with mini-phobic undergraduates. Second, they should show the progression from single-case study to uncontrolled trials with selected patients and finally, to controlled trials carried out on randomly allocated

[1] We wish to thank Dr P. Slater of the Institute of Psychiatry, University of London, for analysing the grid data on the Medical Research Council programme, and Dr I. M. Marks and Mr J. Marzillier, also of the Institute, for their helpful collaboration. Part of the work described here was supported by a research grant from the Medical Research Council, London.

patients. Our experience with the first case, Mr A, led to the development of a therapeutic technique which has now been subjected to a controlled trial (Rachman *et al.,* 1971 and 1973; Hodgson *et al.,* 1972). The second case, Mr B, led to an experimental study of obsessional slowness and an uncontrolled trial of monitoring and pacing (Rachman, 1974). The next stage with this method will be a controlled trial. The third case required the introduction of a new treatment method which is now being subjected to clinical trials.

Each of the patients had a severe and lasting disorder. For each of them it was a source of considerable distress and misery. Two of the patients had become unemployable. All three were socially isolated and all were in serious conflict with their close relatives – usually the only people left who retained any regular contact with them. Two of them had undergone psychosurgery but in neither case was the improvement significant. Both of them had in fact been offered repeat operations.

In all three cases the modification programmes were developed after carrying out some behavioural analysis and in each instance the approach to treatment was exploratory (sometimes we made false starts, as in Case 1). In each case we planned the behavioural analysis and at least parts of the treatment in a way that permitted us to quantify the data produced. In the best of worlds one would subject each aspect of the patient's problem behaviour to behavioural analysis and quantify all of the data.

The main elements in the three modification programmes were: *in vivo* treatment (mainly), exposure to key types of provoking stimulation and encouragement to refrain from executing the compulsive behaviour despite the provocation.

In all three cases we had some help from other therapists and nurses and in Case 1 Mr J. Marzillier acted as a co-therapist.

Case 1 (Mr A)

The patient had developed some obsessional-compulsive behaviour patterns during adolescence but did not seek psychological assistance until the age of twenty when he was admitted to a psychiatric hospital suffering from a marked obsessional disorder. His request for treatment had been precipitated by dismissal from his job as a result of excessive washing rituals which interfered with his working capacity. At the time of his admission to the hospital, the washing rituals occupied the greater part of his day. He also complained of persistent and intrusive fears of contamination by dirt and displayed extensive avoidance-behaviour patterns. After largely unsuccessful treatment by drugs and supportive therapy he was discharged only to be re-admitted later in the same year. On his fourth hospital admission, a modified leucotomy was carried out and the operation was followed by a reduction in tension. The obsessional and compulsive behaviour was not improved. Six months later he was transferred to the Maudsley Hospital with a request that he be considered for a second leucotomy. This was felt to be inadvisable and instead he was given supportive therapy and a course of desensitization treatment in which he was asked to imagine aversive, contaminating stimuli while relaxed. Some slight improvement was observed but he was still considerably disabled and clearly in need of help. The 'modelling plus response prevention' treatment was carried out during the succeeding $4^{1}/_{2}$ months.

Prior to the commencement of this treatment, he was spending approximately $4^{1}/_{2}$ hours per day on his compulsive activities. He experienced particular difficulties over elimination. For example, he had to undress before urinating or defecating. After elimination he had to wash intensively and frequently take showers or baths (up to five per day). He also displayed extensive and elaborate avoidance behaviour (for example, he never touched the floor, or grass, or door handles, etc.). The flavour of the washing rituals is conveyed in an extract from a description written by the patient:

> In the toilet I wash my hands once under the tap with soap then wash the sink out then fill it up with hot water. I then wash my hands and arms, rinse them, then wash my face. Then I wash my hands again, dry my hands and face, undo the toilet door with a paper towel then pull up my trouser zip then wash my hands and arms again taking about the same time. At all cost I must not contact any item of the toilet or sink-basin or door-handle or any part of clothing after washing my hands for fear of contamination. If clothing becomes in contact with any of the above items, anything this item becomes in contact with also becomes contaminated, and so it carries on. As a rule I use my own soap. Back at the bedroom I wash my hands again, the periods before going to the toilet and after cause great worry and quite often upset me for the rest of the day.

Investigations and treatment

The aim of the treatment was the extinction of maladaptive autonomic responses to dirt and excreta, and the extinction of the motor avoidance responses (for example, excessive washing). The behavioural effects of possible methods of treatment were investigated by administering an avoidance test before and after each session. The test items consisted of a number of specimens of substances which the patient could not touch prior to treatment. The test distance scores, given below, indicate the closest point reached by Mr A in his attempt to approach and handle each of the contaminating items (prior to treatment):

1 Small dish of marmalade   7·5 cm.
2 Jar of cigarette ash   10·0 cm.
3 Tin of mud   15·0 cm.
4 Small bottle of urine   150·0 cm.
5 Smear of dog excrement   210·0 cm.

In the first investigation, we tested the effects of implosion and of non-specific emotional arousal. The second investigation tested the effects of participant modelling and the third, the effects of response prevention.

In the first session, information was obtained about the exact nature of the situations which would lead to excessive washing. Subsequent sessions were designed to assess the effects of implosion (sessions 2-12), participant modelling (sessions 13-23) and response prevention (sessions 24-8). After this experimental phase, the patient was given two months of 'modelling plus response prevention' treatment.

Phase 1: implosion
From the information obtained in session 1, a 40-minute tape recording was made of an implosion session in which disturbing images were presented. These images ranged from stepping in dog excrement to messing himself whilst in bed. Since, at this time, we were also interested in the effects of non-specific arousal (Hodgson and Rachman, 1970) we decided to investigate the effects of a 40-minute tape describing horrific scenes of accidents, torture, etc. Finally a number of control sessions were included in which the patient simply listened to a story lasting for 40 minutes. Three sessions of each condition were given in a balanced order followed by two 2-hour implosion sessions. In this phase of the investigation, the effects of the three conditions were assessed by comparing the proportionate change scores which were calculated in percentages as follows:

$$\text{Proportionate change score} = \frac{\text{actual change in distance}}{\text{possible change in distance}} \times \frac{100}{1}$$

These scores, given in Table 1·1, indicate that there is very little evidence of change resulting from any of the treatments except for the first implosion session which appears to have had an adverse effect (hence the negative scores). During this phase of the investigation there was no noticeable change in the patient's behaviour outside the experimental situation. The scores on the avoidance test were relatively stable throughout the first eleven sessions; although this was not a promising result it was useful in establishing a stable base-line.

TABLE 1·1 *Proportionate change in distance scores for implosion, horror and control sessions (in percentages)*

	Implosion					Horror			Control		
	40 min.	40 min.	40 min.	2 hr	2 hr	40 min.	40 min.	40 min.	40 min.	40 min.	40 min.
1 Marmalade	−33	0	0	0	0	0	−33	0	25	0	0
2 Ash	−50	40	0	0	25	0	0	0	0	33	17
3 Mud	0	0	0	0	0	0	33	0	−33	33	25
4 Urine	0	22	0	0	0	−25	−14	0	0	−33	0
5 Excreta	−14	−7	0	0	0	0	0	0	0	0	0

Phase 2: modelling

In this phase of treatment the patient was asked to watch while the therapist touched the items in the avoidance test and then to attempt to touch them himself. This was a gradual process: for instance, the mud and the excrement were initially touched through a piece of paper. After watching the therapist touch the item, the patient was encouraged, but never forced, to imitate this approach behaviour. Inevitably, these sessions incorporated some period of response prevention.

After session 15 the patient was touching the marmalade, ash and mud; during session 21 he touched the urine and during session 23 he touched the smear of excrement (Figure 1·1). After session 19 the patient began to report, for the first time, that he was noticing an improvement outside the experimental situation. During subsequent sessions he reported the following signs of improvement:

1 Showering once a week instead of twice a day.
2 Washing after urination was reduced from 20 minutes to 6 minutes.
3 Swimming for the first time in five years. Previously he was put off by the thought of dirty water.

4 Played croquet and touched the dirty ball.

5 Stroked a cat.

6 Didn't worry when the sole of another patient's shoe touched him during his meal.

7 Sunbathing on the grass. Previously he worried about the possibility of dogs having messed on the grass.

In each of the five sessions the patient spent half an hour touching the smear of excrement and then he was told not to wash his hands. The period of response prevention was progressively increased over the five sessions (¹⁄₄ hr, ³⁄₄ hr, 2 hr, 3 hr, 3 hr). Improvement outside the experimental situation was maintained over these five sessions.

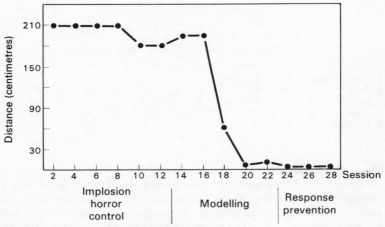

FIGURE 1·1   *Avoidance test behaviour*

During the implosion and control treatment periods, the patient showed no increases in approach behaviour. A marked improvement was observed after the fourth session of modelling.

Treatment phase

During the next two months, the treatment procedure of 'modelling and response prevention' was carried out in and around the ward. Each day between 10 a.m. and 12 noon the patient observed the therapist touching and handling dirty objects, participated himself and was required to refrain from washing his hands or any part of his body or clothes. The following activities were undergone by the patient and therapist-model:

Rubbing both hands into the floor.

Kneeling and sitting on the floor.

Rubbing coffee, chocolate, orange juice into his hands and then touching his face and clothes.

Touching a variety of dirty objects.

Sitting and lying on the grass.

Sitting on dirty chairs.

These activities were followed by normal behaviour, such as smoking, eating, conversation and playing games, with the aim of facilitating extinction. During the afternoon the patient worked at the Rehabilitation Centre, and before he left for work, modelling the therapist, he dirtied his hands with soil from the garden, and did not wash them until he returned to the ward, $2^{1}/_{2}$-3 hours later. All these activities produced discomfort and anxiety in the patient, but he was able to perform them once the therapist had acted as a model. After two weeks of intensive treatment (total time = 20 hours approximately), the therapist began leaving the patient to his own devices in the morning, initially for half an hour increasing to $1^{1}/_{2}$ hours. The patient found he could resist washing his hands until lunchtime if he was engaged in some task. He usually went to the art room.

Progress

A subjective assessment of progress during the treatment was the patient's increased tolerance for dirt on his body or clothes. At the end of each session the patient reported a decrease in discomfort and anxiety. Over the treatment period as a whole, he reported that he found the tasks increasingly easy to perform. A more objective measure is the amount of time spent washing and in the toilet each day, and particularly the number of times the patient washed. He meticulously kept a record of the times, and this record was converted into graph form (Figure 1·2).

Figure 1·2 shows the amount of time spent in the toilet, in washing and in both toilet and washing. The points represent the amount of time spent each day, averaged over a seven-day period. There is a steady decline for both washing and toilet times over the whole treatment period. (The sharp rise in toilet times over the week beginning 17 July was due to stomach trouble.) Figure 1·3 shows the frequency of washing and visits to the toilet over the treatment period. There is a marked and consistent decline in washing frequency, while the frequency of his going to the toilet showed an initial increase, stabilizing at 8-8·5 times a day. A clear change in washing and toilet behaviour can be seen when the figures at the onset and at the end of treatment are compared (Tables 1·2 and 1·3).

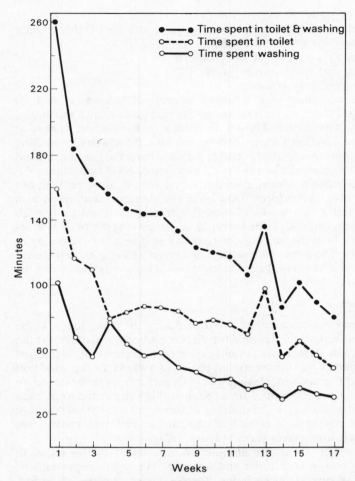

FIGURE 1·2   *Time spent on ablutions during treatment period (Mr A)*

The most marked and important decrease was the reduction of his washing frequency from 15 times a day to twice a day, as this reflects the total elimination of compulsive washing following chance contact with 'dirty' or 'contaminated' objects. At the end of the treatment the patient washed 87 per cent less frequently than before treatment, and spent 70 per cent less time on this behaviour. Toilet times also decreased partly because the patient spent less time washing his hands, after going to the toilet – over the last month of treatment he never took longer than 2-3 minutes – and

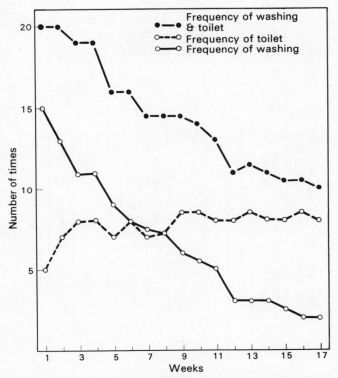

FIGURE 1·3   *Frequency of ablutions during treatment period (Mr A)*

partly because he used less lavatory paper. The number of sheets was reduced from 30 to between 8 and 10 on each occasion.

Washing
In the last month of treatment, the patient was given a washing schedule, on which optimal goals were written, and washing and toilet behaviour broken down. The patient listed times in the appropriate column and row, and additional items and times were written down separately. Each day his times were compared with the optimal times and specific goals were chosen for the next few days. For example, the optimal time for the morning wash was 15 minutes. If the patient recorded 30 minutes, a goal of 20-25 minutes was aimed at for the next few days. The effect of this schedule was to give the patient clear feedback on his progress, and to encourage him to make further efforts to reduce the time spent washing.

TABLE 1·2 *Amount of time spent in toilet and washing*

	First week of treatment	Last week of treatment	Difference
Amount of time spent in toilet, per day	2 hr 40 min.	49 min.	−1 hr 51 min.
Amount of time spent washing, per day	1 hr 41 min.	31 min.	−1 hr 10 min.
Totals	4 hr 21 min.	1 hr 20 min.	−3 hr 1 min.

TABLE 1·3 *Frequency of toilet and washing*

	First week of treatment	Last week of treatment	Difference
Frequency of toilet, per day	5 times	6 times	+ 1
Frequency of washing,	15 times	2 times	−13
Totals	20 times	8 times	−12

Discharge

At the time of discharge, the patient's compulsive washing had been almost totally eliminated, and the amount of time spent on washing and toilet behaviour as a whole was not considered to be unduly excessive. During the treatment, he spent sixteen days at home, and no recurrence of obsessional behaviour emerged. On the contrary, his washing and toilet behaviour showed the same pattern of steady reduction. On the ward, he no longer avoided 'contaminated' objects, such as door-knobs, certain chairs, objects dropped on the floor. In general, he expressed satisfaction with his progress and showed an improvement in mood. He returned home in an optimistic frame of mind.

The behavioural avoidance test was repeated shortly before discharge and at the 3-month follow-up. The patient was able to touch all the items, including urine and fæces. He experienced some discomfort but did not need to wash before or after contact.

Follow-up

The patient was interviewed three months after discharge. Because his washing and toilet behaviour had deteriorated slightly, we asked him to supply a list of toilet and washing times at monthly intervals, up to six months after discharge.

Analysis of these figures (cf. Figures 1·4 and 1·5) shows a tendency towards relapse after three months. In particular, there is a marked increase in washing frequency (from 2 to 7·6 times a day) though this does not approach the pre-treatment level (15 times). There is also a less marked increase in the amount of time the patient spent going to the toilet and washing. During the interview, the patient confirmed an increase in washing frequency, which was due to persisting discomfort following chance contact with dirty objects. However, he did not report any extensive or repetitive washing, as had occurred before treatment. His washing behaviour did not interfere with his life. He was able to hold a job satisfactorily, and did not avoid places because they were 'dirty' or 'contaminated'. Although experiencing some problems of adjustment to working life in his home town, Leeds, he had settled in sufficiently well to contemplate marriage within the year. He stated that he felt his washing behaviour to be under control, and was confident that his obsessional behaviour would not return.

The patient's optimism at 3 months follow-up was confirmed at 6 months. The amount of time he spent going to the toilet and washing, and their frequency of occurrence, all decreased compared to the figures at 3 months (Figures 1·4 and 1·5). The 6 months figures are very similar to those at discharge, and suggest that the

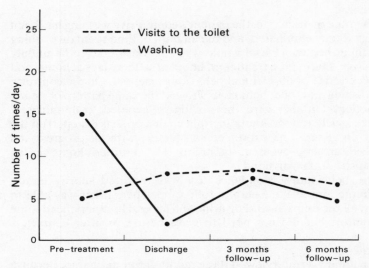

FIGURE 1·4   *Frequency of ablutions during follow-up period (Mr A)*

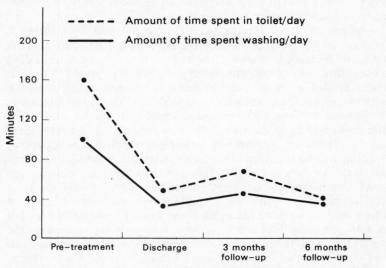

FIGURE 1·5   *Time spent on ablutions during follow-up period (Mr A)*

patient's obsessional behaviour has not returned.

Two years after treatment a letter of thanks was received from the patient's mother, which concluded:

He was married last September and has bought a house. He and his wife have settled in well, and it is a pleasure to call on them and see him gardening and doing various odd jobs around the house. This is a thing we would have thought impossible a few years ago.

Case 2 (Mr B)

Mr B was unmarried, aged 45, and had a 30-year history of obsessive-compulsive problems. He first saw a psychiatrist when he was 15 years old and treatment since then has involved psychoanalysis (3 times per week for 3 years – age 26), psychotherapy and drug therapy, including LSD (10 months – age 34); during the ten years prior to his present admission he consulted a number of psychiatrists and was finally given a leucotomy (age 43). According to the patient these interventions produced little change in his obsessional behaviour.

Mr B's basic problem was a compulsion to be slow, meticulous and ritualistic especially when dressing, washing, shaving, cleaning his teeth and combing his hair. As a consequence he was unable to work since most of his day was spent in ritualistic behaviour. In the two weeks prior to admission he was rising at about 8 o'clock and would not complete his washing and dressing rituals until late afternoon. For instance, cleaning his teeth involved 192 slow meticulous brush strokes for each application of toothpaste and for each rinse, the whole ritual taking about half an hour; shaving took one hour every morning, the whole ritual being frustrating (even for the watching therapist) and involving numerous slow repetitive circular movements of his electric razor. Bathing would take him up to three hours with half an hour spent in rinsing the bath before filling it and half an hour rinsing the bath afterwards. Every action was performed in a slow meticulous manner reminiscent of the care taken by a bomb disposal expert.

With the patient's help a number of goals were determined, namely:

1 Brushing teeth in two minutes.
2 Combing hair in two minutes.
3 Shaving in ten minutes.
4 Bathing in twenty minutes.
5 Dressing in five minutes.
6 Washing hair in fifteen minutes.
7 Washing neck and ears in two minutes.
8 Washing up crockery quickly.
9 Completing jobs without excessive planning.
10 Untidying room, clothes, etc.

During our initial investigations prior to treatment (also during treatment), there was no evidence of any emotional disturbance when his rituals were interrupted (see also Rachman, 1974). The idea proposed by Walton and Mather (1964) that compulsive behaviour of long duration becomes functionally autonomous (in the sense that it is not maintained by anxiety-reduction) is consistent with our clinical observations of this particular case. In contrast, Mr A had only a five-year history of compulsive handwashing and became very disturbed when handwashing was prevented. Cases 1 and 2 differ also in one other important respect. Mr A was troubled by compulsions which could be triggered by a large number of environmental stimuli. Mr B's main compulsions, on the other hand, were specific to his daily dressing and washing routines so that treatment progressed, not by exposure to environmental situations, but by interrupting his daily rituals.

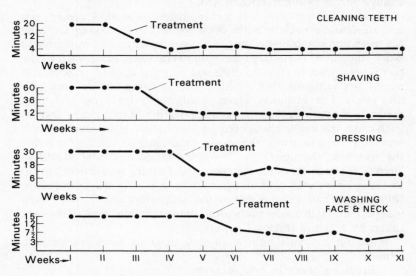

FIGURE 1·6 *Changes as a result of treatment (Mr B)*
Notice the specificity of the treatment effect, indicated by the stepwise change.

Treatment

Most of the therapeutic sessions (approximately 1 hour per day for seven weeks) were directed towards speeding up his daily rituals (that is, the first seven targets in the list of behaviour problems given). Mr B had been performing his intricate rituals for so long that he had forgotten the 'normal' way of brushing his teeth, washing, dressing, etc. Consequently, the first step involved therapist modelling of the desired behaviour; wherever possible the therapist demonstrated relatively normal routines of shaving, brushing teeth, washing ears, armpits, etc. The patient reported that he found this step to be helpful although we have no evidence that observational modelling alone effected a change in his behaviour.

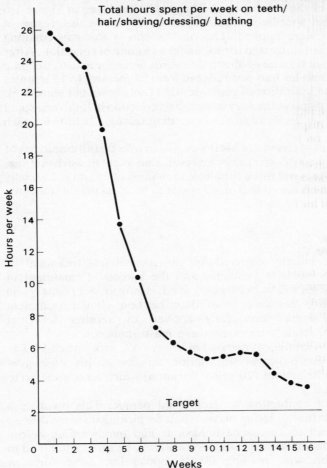

FIGURE 1·7 *Total time spent each week, during treatment, on daily rituals – i.e. teeth, hair, shaving, dressing and bathing (Mr B)*

Therapeutic modelling was always followed by close observation of the patient's performance during which he was given detailed advice about which segments of his ritual could be dropped out, along with encouragement, prompting and pacing. Each of the targets was modelled twice and then followed by close supervision of the patient's daily rituals. It should be noted that the treatment involved only 15 hours of the psychologists' time and that the treatment programme could not have been completed without the assistance of the nursing staff. The graphs displayed in Figure 1·6 indicate that specific changes occurred only when the treatment procedures were applied. The one exception was hair-combing which was left untreated for six weeks as a control condition. After one month of treatment directed towards his other rituals, the time taken to comb his hair was reduced from 25 minutes to 15 minutes giving some indication of generalization (not shown in Figure 1·6). Figure 1·7 displays the very substantial reduction in total time spent each week on his daily rituals (including taking a bath twice each week).

As a result of treatment Mr B was able to take up full employment and two years after treatment he is still able to get to work on time. Certainly, he is still more ritualistic than most of us and still socially isolated but his life style is much closer to his ideal than it was three years ago.

Case 3 (Mr C)

Mr C was initially referred for the behavioural treatment of obsessive-compulsive problems and the successful treatment of these problems will be briefly described. However, our primary aim in presenting this case is to describe how similar treatment procedures were successfully applied to another form of compulsion, namely his compulsive masturbation.

Mr C is an intelligent married man aged 43, with one child. The following list indicates the major aspects of his obsessive-compulsive behaviour (20 years' duration) which he considered to be abnormal:

1 Fear of contamination from bald people. This involved a specific fear of losing his own hair by picking up some disease and lead to avoidance behaviour and handwashing before touching his hair or comb. For instance, he often attempted to stop his wife reading library books lest some form of contamination might be transferred from the books to his hair.

2 Fear of contamination by poisonous substances. Any speck of white on his clothing was considered to be suspect, and

consequently he often brushed his clothes repetitively for up to two hours.

3 Fear of contamination from a schizophrenic. He feared that schizophrenia could be transmitted by physical contact. His anxieties about library books were partly determined by the possibility that they might have been handled by a schizophrenic.

4 At work part of his desk was out of bounds since it was contaminated by his colleagues who often leant upon it. This was a 'danger area' and only the remaining half of his desk could be used.

5 In his view, he was excessively concerned about order and tidiness. He considered his bookshelves to be an 'inner-sanctum, like an altar, pure and clean'. Every morning he would glance at his books to make sure that they had not been moved ('like a shepherd checking his flock'). If one was slightly askew he would shout at his wife, wipe it with a tissue and put it back in position.

These and other obsessive-compulsive problems were success-fully treated by modelling and flooding (Rachman *et al.,* 1971 and 1973) both in the hospital and in the home environment. This treatment produced no change in his masturbatory behaviour which he regarded as a major problem since, in his opinion, it was abnormal, interfered with his work and with sexual intercourse. Masturbation usually occurred either at work, or when alone in the house, or late at night when his wife was in bed. The major stimuli and situations which were associated with his masturbatory urges are listed below but one eliciting stimulus in particular will be mentioned here since it was abnormal and disturbing to him. Ever since adolescence he had been preoccupied with a fantasy of Christ on the cross. One of his earliest sexual memories involved a sculpture of the crucifixion which elicited an erection and subsequently, throughout adolescence, this fantasy was repeatedly linked with masturbation. When alone in the house he would often lie on his bed, picture the crucifixion scene and masturbate. The patient regarded masturbation as normal under certain cir-cumstances (for example, in the country, 'when overwhelmed by nature') and therefore the major aims of treatment, as determined by the patient, were to eliminate masturbation to the crucifix fantasy and to pornography, and to control masturbation in other situations. In other words, to eliminate the feeling of compulsion. Treatment of this compulsion began five months after the termination of treatment for his obsessive-compulsive problems.

Our behavioural model of masturbatory compulsions underlying the present treatment is essentially a simple one. The assumption is made that repeated masturbation positively reinforces a chain of antecedent responses linked to particular stimuli. The eliciting stimuli are both external (for example, sexually provocative, situational) and internal (for example, mood states) and involve response-produced stimuli (for example, fantasies, proprioceptive sexual stimuli). This model predicts that elicitation of this complex chain, without masturbation, will result in extinction of the compulsive urge.

Treatment

Masturbation occurred mainly under the following conditions:
1 When made to feel small at work.
2 Arriving home after seeing an attractive girl in the street.
3 When feeling depressed.
4 Alone in the country on a summer day.
5 In the house alone.
6 Back home after walking through Soho.
7 Any situation which elicits a slight erection.
8 Crucifix fantasy.
9 Watching neighbour in garden.
10 Looking at pornography.

The aim of treatment was to encourage confrontation with eliciting stimuli, situations and fantasies without masturbatory behaviour leading to ejaculation.

Mr C was told that treatment would be aimed at developing self-control in all those situations which provoked compulsive masturbation. To this end he would be encouraged to obtain an erection in many different situations and, in order for the treatment to be successful, he must resist masturbation both during a session and between sessions. He was told that exercising self-control would become easier as the treatment progressed.

During the first two weeks the patient received four treatment sessions (each of 1 hour duration). Each session consisted of approximately 40 minutes browsing through pornographic literature and 20 minutes maintaining crucifix imagery. The presence of a therapist made self-control much easier and consequently the patient was left alone for the major part of sessions 3 and 4. After session 4 Mr C felt that the treatment might be helping but that self-control was much more difficult at home; the crucifix imagery, in particular, was more compelling in the home environment. Sessions 5 to 10 were therefore completed in the patient's home. These sessions focused upon pornography, crucifix imagery, watching the woman next door in the garden and imagining attractive girls who had recently caught his eye. The aim was to confront him with situations likely to provoke compulsive masturbation and then inhibit masturbation and prevent ejaculation. To this end the therapist began leaving the patient alone for increasing lengths of time. Up to this stage Mr C was told to resist masturbating between sessions but not to deliberately tempt himself. Sessions 11 to 14 were similar to previous sessions with the exceptions that the therapist initiated and ended the session by telephone and the patient was additionally told to deliberately tempt himself between sessions (for example, walking through Soho, looking at attractive girls and provoking crucifix imagery). Treatment was ended after the fourteenth session (6 weeks of treatment) but Mr C was contacted during the next year. The one-year follow-up assessment, although encouraging, is confounded since a number of sessions of assertive and marital therapy were given in the intervening period.

Results

I Changes in obsessive-compulsive behaviour

(a) Behavioural avoidance test

Mr C was asked to attempt the following tasks:
1. Touch dirty scrubbing brush and then hair.
2. Touch canister of scouring powder and then hair.
3. Touch toilet seat and then hair.
4. Drop comb on floor and then comb hair.
5. Touch cigarette ash and then hair.
6. Walking in hospital corridor with bare feet.
7. Leaving clean clothes in an untidy pile.
8. Touching dustbin lid without washing.
9. Touch bleach tin and then fill pipe and smoke.
10. Touching a strange hair on his pillow.

The results of this test were unambiguous. Prior to treatment all 10 items were failed (that is, score of 10) but after three weeks of treatment all items were successfully completed. This change was maintained at follow-up and throughout the treatment of the compulsive masturbation.

(b) Self-ratings

Mr C was asked to estimate the degree of discomfort that he would experience in the threatening situations listed below (8-point scale, 0=no uneasiness; 8=panic):

    A Putting 'dirty' and 'clean' books on the same shelf at home.
    B Dropping comb on floor and then combing hair with it.
    C Wife untidying clothes in drawers at home.
    D Going for one week without brushing overcoat.
    E Contaminating desk drawer and desk top at work.
The mean changes in these ratings are displayed in Figure 1·8.

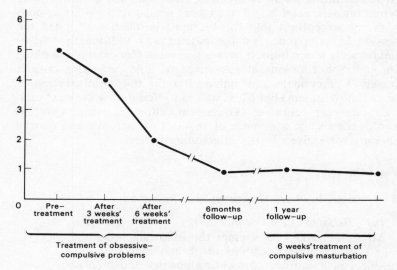

FIGURE 1·8 *Mean changes in 'obsessional-discomfort' ratings (Mr C)*

II Changes in masturbatory behaviour

(a) Frequency

Mr C kept a diary which was inspected by the therapist, prior to each treatment session. He was told to make a record in the diary at least twice each day and that accurate records would facilitate treatment. He was also warned against giving a false impression in order to encourage the therapist. Figure 1·9 displays graphically the changes in frequency of masturbation, urge to masturbate and sexual intercourse throughout the course of treatment and at the one year follow-up.

(b) Self-ratings

Other evidence of change was obtained by asking the patient to rate each of the conditions listed previously (p.34) on the following seven constructs (7-point scale):
    1 Strength of urge to masturbate.

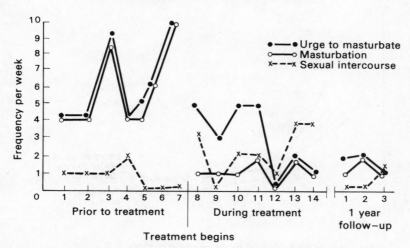

FIGURE 1·9 *Changes in frequency of masturbation, urge to masturbate, and sexual intercourse throughout the course of treatment and at 1-year follow-up (Mr C)*

2 Ability to control masturbation.
3 Guilt resulting from masturbation.
4 Abnormality of masturbating behaviour.
5 Frequency of masturbation.
6 Behaviour is like other men.
7 Behaviour is like ideal self.

A principal components analysis of these data gives a good summary description. An analysis of the matrix of scores prior to treatment indicated two major components accounting for 46 per cent and 24 per cent of the variance. The constructs loading highly on component 1 (abnormality of behaviour) were in the order 4, 6, 7, 3. Those constructs loading on component 2 (frequency of masturbation) were in the order 5, 2, 1. Changes occurred on both components as a result of treatment; the mean changes on the major constructs (4 and 5) are displayed in Figure 1·10. The change in the matrix of scores as a result of treatment is indicated by the low correlation (0·38) between matrix 1 (prior to treatment) and matrix 2 (post-treatment). On the other hand the high correlation (0·79) between matrix 2 and matrix 3 (follow-up) indicates that the treatment effect is maintained at one-year follow-up and also attests to the reliability of the ratings.

Both behavioural assessments and self-ratings indicate a change in compulsive masturbation as a result of treatment which has

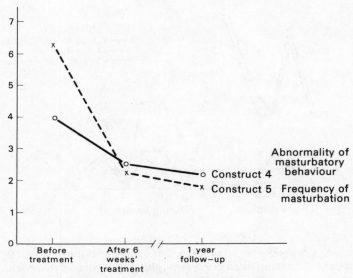

FIGURE 1·10   *Ratings on major constructs (Mr C)*

persisted up to a one-year follow-up. The patient pointed out that his behaviour has fluctuated during this period. He has occasionally masturbated compulsively but never to the extent that was evident prior to treatment.

A number of points of theoretical and practical importance emerge from a consideration of the specific changes which resulted from treatment. First, Figure 1·9 indicates that our treatment procedures and instructions had an immediate effect on frequency of masturbation. However, frequency of the urge to masturbate remained relatively stable until the sudden drop after five weeks of treatment. It appears that Mr C was exercising a high degree of self-control during the first five weeks of treatment and only then was there any appreciable treatment effect upon his compulsive urges. Our work with obsessive-compulsive disorders has led us to believe that self-control between sessions is an essential element in the treatment of compulsive rituals. Similarly, it is probable that excessive masturbation between sessions may counter the beneficial effects of treatment.

A second point of interest emerged from Mr C's observations when followed up one year after treatment. He noted that eliminating compulsive masturbation to the crucifix image had led to a reduction in the spontaneous occurrence of this image. An analogous finding was reported by Meyer (1966), in treating an obsessional patient whose rituals were triggered by blasphemous thoughts. Meyer noted that a reduction in the frequency of compulsive rituals was followed by a reduction in the spontaneous occurrence of the intrusive thoughts. These observations suggest that when a thought or a fantasy is divested of its significance as a trigger or signal for compulsive behaviour then the probability of its spontaneous occurrence is reduced.

Discussion

The first two patients were afflicted with obsessive-compulsive rituals; we considered these rituals to be active avoidance responses since, in the patients' view, failure to carry out a ritual could be followed by a catastrophic event and/or an unpleasant emotional state. The third case suffered from compulsive masturbation and non-performance of this compulsion was also followed by an emotional state, namely, frustration. There are, of course, differences between obsessional and masturbatory compulsions but, in our view, both types of compulsion can be viewed within one framework. Obsessive-compulsive rituals avoid discomfort (avoidance of discomfort being positively reinforcing) and non-performance of a ritual is followed by discomfort (that is, is punishing). Compulsive masturbation produces gratification (that is, positive reinforcement) and resisting the compulsion is followed by a feeling of frustration, also punishing.

Thus we are suggesting that avoidance of discomfort and achievement of sexual gratification constitute positive reinforcements whereas discomfort and frustration of sexual gratification are negative, that is, punishing events.

Considering both types of compulsion within the same framework gives rise to the possibility that similar treatment methods might be effective in eliminating them. Both obsessional compulsions and sexual compulsions are associated with certain discriminative stimuli and our theoretical conception implies that exposure to these stimuli, followed by prevention of compulsive behaviour, should lead to extinction.

In the first case we included an attempt to test the efficacy of participant modelling and response prevention in the treatment of an obsessive-compulsive handwasher. The positive outcome encouraged us to complete a series of controlled trials on further groups of patients (Rachman *et al.*, 1971; Hodgson *et al.*, 1972; Rachman *et al.*, 1973).

The second case suffered from an obsessional disorder characterized by excessively slow, meticulous and ritualistic behaviour. Treatment was directed towards increasing speed and encouraging behaviour which was neither meticulous nor ritualistic. The relative success of this simple treatment plan was repeated in some later cases (with one or two failures as well) and consideration of these individuals provoked an experimental investigation of obsessional slowness (Rachman, 1974).

The treatment of the third case (compulsive masturbation) was sufficiently successful to encourage us to initiate the controlled investigation on a larger group of patients which is now in progress. The third case shows also that the effects of treatment within a hospital environment can fail to generalize rapidly to other situations. It is, therefore, advisable to continue treatment outside the hospital and particularly in the home environment. Failures of generalization can be largely avoided by using *in vivo* treatments.

Behavioural procedures must always involve non-specific factors, for example, supportive discussions, nursing supervision, a non-threatening hospital environment, etc. These non-specific factors, although of importance, were not the crucial variables in producing the main therapeutic changes since, in all three cases, specific and predicted behavioural improvements were only obtained after the introduction of the specific behavioural procedures.

In concluding, it seems worthwhile comparing our approach to the case-study method with those of the psychoanalysts and Skinnerian-minded psychologists. We share with them the belief that useful information can be obtained from single-case studies but part company with those who argue that information of this character is sufficient for either drawing general conclusions or that it can serve as a basis for large-scale theorizing. In other words, we differ in that we regard single-case studies as part of a chain of information-gathering and hypothesis-testing – but incomplete and insufficient in themselves.

In matters of style we are closer to the Skinnerians and share their enthusiasm for *experimental* analyses and manipulations – even in the single case. Unlike many of them, we favour the statistical analysis of case data wherever necessary (see Maxwell, 1958, Gottman, 1973 on this subject). In so far as their rejection of statistical analyses is based on a belief that there are no appropriate techniques available, the Skinnerians are mistaken.

Our differences with the psychoanalytic style of case study are numerous. As we have shown, our style is to emphasize *experimental* analysis and quantification and our approach is to regard case information as useful but inadequate. Among others, there are also differences in the weight placed on the patient's verbal reports (we greatly prefer to supplement them with other sources of information), their reliance on dream material and on symbolic interpretations. When it comes down to it, the only common element is our shared belief that patients are a source of valuable and usable information about themselves and their problems. Today this statement is a truism, but it is worth remembering that there were times in the history of psychology when it was a matter for debate.

2 Multiple Behavior Techniques in the Treatment of Transvestism[1]

Edna B. Foa

A brief review of the literature on behavior therapy of sexual deviations introduces the presentation of treatment in a case of transvestism, where a sequence of behavioral techniques was successfully applied. First, anxiety to social interaction and to heterosexual overtures was reduced by assertive training, desensitization and behavior rehearsal. Suppression of deviant habit was then hastened through the application of covert sensitization and electric shocks. Seven months after the completion of treatment there was no recurrence of the deviant sexual behavior and normal heterosexual activity was maintained. The order of application of the different techniques is considered in relation to the sequence of behavioral problems presented by the patient.

A few years ago the movie *Clockwork Orange* presented to the lay public a negative image of behavior therapy, as a mechanistic and anti-humanistic, if not altogether cruel treatment. The core of the criticism seems to be imbedded in the fact that inappropriate behaviors of the 'hero' were suppressed, but no attempt was made to replace them with acceptable ones, thus leaving him helpless and unprotected. Curiously enough, exclusive concern for the needs of society, as opposed to the welfare of the patient, led ultimately to socially undesirable consequences.

Although the movie was biased against behavior therapy it artistically raised problems which we encounter in the clinic. The sexual deviant finds himself in a conflictual situation: on one hand his behavior has intrinsic reinforcement value; on the other hand it

[1] The preparation of this paper was facilitated by postdoctoral research fellowship MH 52831-01 from the National Institute of Mental Health, Bethesda, Maryland.

provokes social disapproval and even legal sanctions, which often bring him to seek treatment. As *Clockwork Orange* implicitly suggests, more socially acceptable avenues of reinforcement should be provided; thus elimination of deviant behavior is only a part of therapy; let us begin by considering it.

The vast experimental literature available to the therapist who is engaged in response elimination rests on two main paradigms:

1 Extinction — removal of reinforcements contingent upon the response to be eliminated.
2 Suppression — pairing of the response with aversive noxious events.

Faced with a sexual deviant who requests a fast, efficient and permanent removal of his undesirable behavior, what course should we take?

At first sight aversion therapy seems to be superior to extinction for two reasons. It requires minimal information on the case; all we need to have is a list of the stimuli which immediately precede the critical behavior (if the classical paradigm is used), or the specific behaviors which constitute the habit (when the operant paradigm is applied). Furthermore, by the application of aversion techniques suppression is achieved rather rapidly. Conversely, techniques aiming at removal of reinforcements require not only identification of reinforcers, an information which is often not readily available to the patient himself, but also present problems in the development of adequate removal procedures. The most obvious reinforcement value of the deviancy is the sexual gratification it provides. In addition, it often acquires negative reinforcement properties by serving to reduce anxiety generated by sexual as well as social inadequacies. It seems that the compulsive nature of some sexual deviances is due to the fact that a state of anxiety is terminated upon their emission. A relapse, then, is more likely to occur when anxiety rises. Indeed, Bond and Hutchison (1964) reported relapse in an exhibitionist after increase of social stress occurred.

When such chain of events is found it becomes advisable to employ an anxiety-reduction technique; lower anxiety decreases the value of sex deviancy as negative reinforcement. Nevertheless even after anxiety reduction, this behavior pattern will continue to possess positive reinforcement properties as provider of sexual gratification, and particularly so when no other sexual outlet is available to the patient. Reinforcement, then, cannot be removed unless an alternative, more adaptive channel for sexual gratification is acquired by the patient. However, anxiety is often attached to such alternatives (Barlow, 1973). Whether this anxiety precedes or follows development of the deviant response, its successful elimination may again require the use of anxiety reduction techniques. Stevenson and Wolpe (1960) and Edwards (1972) employed assertive training in the treatment of sexual deviants. In both reports the removal of social anxieties and of inadequacy feeling was, by itself, sufficient to extinguish the deviant habit. Systematic desensitization to heterosexual experiences was successfully used by Kraft (1967a and 1967b), Lazarus (1968a) and Wickramasekera (1968).

Judging from published reports, treatment based on aversive techniques has been used more frequently than the anxiety reducing procedures which have just been mentioned. Following Raymond's report (1956) on suppression of fetishism by chemical aversion this technique became quite popular (Barker, Thorpe, Blakemore, Lavin and Conway, 1961; Clark, 1963a; Glynn and Harper, 1961; Lavin, Thorpe, Barker, Blakemore and Conway, 1961; Oswald, 1962). For practical and theoretical reasons (Lavin *et al.,* 1961) chemical aversion was later replaced by electrical aversion (for example, Blakemore, Thorpe, Barker, Conway and Lavin, 1963a; Kushner, 1965; Marks, Gelder and Bancroft, 1970). More recently cognitive elements have been introduced in aversion therapy of sexual deviants: covert sensitization (Cautela and Wisocki, 1971) and shame therapy (Serber, 1970). According to several reports (for example, Blakemore *et al.,* 1963b; Clark, 1963b; Freund, 1960) initial success in suppressing deviant sexual responses by aversion treatment was followed by relapse, particularly when stressful conditions intervened. These reports are in line with experimental results regarding the temporary nature of suppression (Azrin and Holz, 1966; Church, 1963; Solomon, 1964).

A possible solution to this problem was proposed by Eysenck as early as 1960; his suggestion to combine aversion techniques with therapy by reciprocal inhibition was adopted in some later studies. Fookes (1968) paired relaxing music with heterosexual slides after administering a series of electric shocks. Levin, Hirsch, Shugar and Kapche (1968) replaced the music by systematic desensitization. Cooper (1963) combined chemical aversion with desensitization *in vivo.* Covert sensitization was used in conjunction with assertive training by Cautela and Wisocki (1969) and with desensitization *in vivo* by Gray (1970).

Concern for enhancement of alternative sexual outlet, in addition to suppression of deviant habits, was later shared by many authors (for example, Marks, Gelder and Bancroft, 1970; Serber, 1970; Ullmann and Krasner, 1969, p. 488) and was manifest in the wide utilization of aversion relief treatment; pairing of heterosexual stimuli with relief from a noxious stimulus. This technique became quite popular, perhaps because it conveniently lends itself to combination with aversion therapy (for example, Abel, Levis and Clancy, 1970; Clark, 1965; Feldman and MacCulloch, 1965. 1971: Gaupp, Stern and Ratliff, 1971; Larson, 1970; Solyom and Miller, 1965). In all these studies deviant behavior was punished while appropriate sexual material was reinforced by terminating an aversive stimulus upon its presentation. The rationale for the use of aversion relief treatment is that it increases the reinforcement value of heterosexual stimuli. Feldman and MacCulloch (1971) stated that this technique also reduces heterosexual anxiety; however no experimental evidence to this effect is available.

Among the studies reporting on the combination of suppression and extinction techniques, a recent one by Hallam and Rachman (1972) is of particular interest. These authors treated seven sexual deviants with shock aversion; out of three patients who showed good improvement, two received desensitization in addition to aversion therapy. An attempt to carry the combined use of different techniques a step further, and to integrate their respective application into different stages of the treatment, is described in the remaining part of this paper. In this case both suppression of deviant behavior and facilitation of satisfactory heterosexual relations were achieved.

Description of the patient

The patient, C, an unmarried 25-year-old male, came to therapy under pressure of the court. He was caught by the police several times approaching young girls while dressed in female clothes. The judge was willing to discharge him on probation provided he sought effective help. Group psychotherapy in which he had participated for two years was not found helpful. C came to the clinic on 8 September 1972, quite reluctantly. Five years prior to this date he approached a behavior therapist in another city who upon hearing of his problem for about 10 minutes started electrical aversion therapy. The patient did not return for additional sessions, because he resented being treated in a 'mechanical rather than a humanistic manner.'

Life history

C was born on the West Coast in 1947, has one full brother two years older than him, two stepsisters (one his age and the other three years older), and one half-brother twelve years younger. His mother, a very strict Methodist, died of cancer when he was ten, after two years of being confined to bed. Until his mother's death the atmosphere at home was extremely prudish; sex and related topics were not to be mentioned and were regarded as sinful. For them mankind was divided into 'worldly' people who were sinful, and 'we' — the people who obeyed God's laws. His father did not partake in the religious and ideological beliefs of his wife; yet, being a non-assertive person, he did not express any opposition. C never saw his mother's underwear nor had he ever seen her less than properly dressed. Shortly after his mother's death C's father married again, this time to a 'worldly' woman whom C describes as just the opposite of his mother. She had two daughters from a previous marriage who joined the family with her. Within the first month of her arrival C learned from his stepmother that she had had sexual relations with his father for several years prior to their marriage. He could still remember the overwhelming effect that this information had upon his value system. Now, with three 'worldly' women at home (the daughters were 11 and 14 years old) the atmosphere suddenly became loaded with talks about sex, and female underwear were scattered all over the house. C's father, being a passive person, went along with this new atmosphere as much as he had accepted the strict Methodist practices imposed by his previous wife. He never took an active role in raising his children or found it necessary to express his own values. It was around this time that C developed his habit of cross-dressing.

C was always a top student at school. He enrolled in one of the Ivy schools with a full fellowship. All through his life he felt lonely and outcast by his classmates. He did not participate in sport events and had no friends. His lonely feeling increased at the university where most students belonged to a different social class. The more depressed he was the more his cross-dressing practices increased in frequency. He left this school at the end of the first year and went to his hometown university. He refused to live with his parents since they had asked him to pay rent for his room — a request which made him feel alienated and resentful. It was then, at his second year of undergraduate education, that he started to develop friendship with peers for the first time in his life. At the end of the academic year he moved back to the Ivy school for another academic year. When he applied for treatment C was registered at a state university, needed only a few more credits to complete his undergraduate work, but was not motivated to do so.

Three years ago C started to work in an agency for community development where his intellectual abilities are highly respected. The atmosphere in this agency was friendly and intimate and C acquired a great number of friends, spent every evening with them and almost 'compulsively' added new people to his 'list of friends' until he became overburdened with social responsibilities. At the beginning of treatment C was temporarily suspended from work with full salary, following two consecutive arrests for cross-dressing. His employers, although understanding and compassionate, felt that the agency, being leftist-radical oriented, could not afford the damage to its reputation that might be inflicted by his arrests. They urged him to seek help and thus provided an additional source of pressure for therapy.

Sexual development

The earliest sexual experiences C can recall involved mutual exposure and penis manipulation with his brother, starting at age four. (His brother is an exhibitionist.) At about age five they were caught by their mother, while exposing, were spanked and threatened with God's wrath. Half a year later they were caught again while indulging in the same activity. This time C has a vague recollection of being brought to a doctor who examined his penis. This experience frightened him to the extent that all his sexual activities stopped.

When C was 11 years old he became involved, for about half a year, in light petting and kissing as well as mutual exposure with the younger of his stepsisters. He does not remember how and why these heterosexual activities terminated. For the next nine years he did not have any heterosexual contact. At age 20 he had his first coital experience. The girl was a classmate with whom he had been friendly for several months prior to that. He never felt sexually attracted to her but went along with her initiative. She took him to her apartment and bluntly asked him to have intercourse with her. He complied, experienced no difficulty in completing the coital act but does not recall any special pleasure. This relationship lasted for about three months. He was not assertive enough to terminate the sexual contact although the amount of pleasure he derived from it did not increase.

For the next few years he was in love with a girl who refused to have any sexual relationship with him but reciprocated his friendship. About two years before treatment he lived with a girl, who again took full initiative for their relationship; again he felt trapped, but unable to terminate it. They separated after eight months, upon his refusal to marry her. When C came for treatment he maintained platonic relationships with several girls including the only one he really loved. He had no heterosexual activities for fourteen months.

In summary C had heterosexual relationships with two girls to whom he was not particularly attracted; he did not enjoy intercourse with them and felt manipulated and trapped, being chosen rather than choosing. He was in love with only one girl with whom he maintained a chaste relationship for several years.

Development and nature of the sexual deviancy

At age eleven C started to develop special interest in women's underwear, to which he could then have easy access. A year later these garments, especially bra and underpants, became sexually arousing. For the next six years his sexual activities consisted of holding or wearing women's underwear while masturbating to ejaculation.

At age 18, in his freshman year, C developed more elaborate sexual habits, as cross-dressing in privacy became unsatisfactory. He used to wear a bra and women's underpants under his regular clothes, go out and look for young girls, preferably a group of two or three. He approached them with a story about initiation rituals of his fraternity which required that he should be tied up to a tree or a pole, stripped of his outer clothes and remain there in women's underwear until his friends would come and untie him. He would then ask the girls to tie him at a pole, unzip his pants and open his shirt. He especially enjoyed when they noticed his full erection while undressing him and commented about it. He would then thank them and ask them to leave him tied as prescribed by the 'rituals.' After the girls had left, C would untie himself and masturbate on the spot. Within the last five years C used to indulge in this practice between three times a week to once in three weeks, with an approximate average of twice a week.

Treatment

C was seen in the clinic for a total of 48 sessions, starting in September 1972. His treatment was terminated in May 1973. In the first four months he came twice a week, then once a week for two more months and later on twice a month. He was further seen once in June 1973, once in September 1973 and again in November 1973 for follow-up sessions.

The first four sessions were devoted to collect the information given above and to define the goals to be achieved in treatment. We arrived at three major goals:

1   Enhancement of satisfaction from interpersonal relations in general.

2   Extinction of the deviant habit.
3   Enhancement of satisfaction from heterosexual relations and
    reduction of the apparent inhibition to fall in love with an
    appropriate sexual partner.

Enhancement of alternative social and sexual responses

(a) Assertive training

Because C complained about social anxiety and inability to
establish satisfactory intimate relationships I decided to explore
first the relationship between feelings of inadequacy and the sexual
deviation (Edwards, 1972; Stevenson and Wolpe, 1960). This
decision was also influenced by the negative attitude C had
expressed toward aversion techniques.

Upon a thorough inquiry about events precipitating C's urge to
perform his transvestite-exhibitionistic activity it was found that
being in places where he had accomplished his habit successfully
and the sight of women's underwear elicited sexual excitation and
urge for cross-dressing. Most of the times, however, C would feel
the same urge while being at home in absence of the above stimuli.
Since no more information regarding precipitating events could be
elicited from C he was asked to keep a detailed diary giving
particular attention to interpersonal encounters. From these notes
it became apparent that C's urges often occurred several hours after
a frustrating social encounter had taken place. A fairly common
sequence was that C was approached with a demand on his free time
at short notice and would comply. Several hours later he would
become angry and resentful, feeling exploited and pushed around.
He then would find himself with an urge for cross-dressing coupled
with the thought, 'To hell with everybody, I too deserve some fun.'
The discovery of this pattern called for assertive training. There was
however a barrier to a successful application of this technique: C
was not aware of his anger at the time frustrating events took place;
several hours later when he became cognizant of such feeling,
assertion was often inappropriate. By continuing to write a detailed
diary and by reading it every evening, awareness of anger came to
him progressively closer, in time, to the triggering encounter. We
then started to analyze the exchange of resources (Foa and Foa,
1973) which took place in events that made him resentful. This was
done by determining what, and how much, he received and gave.
Often a qualitative and quantitative imbalance was found between
his giving and his receiving, which accounted for his feeling of being
exploited. C was then taught to refuse requests which appeared

unfair to him as well as to formulate demands towards others; both behaviors were rarely emitted by him in the past for fear of being rejected. An example will illustrate this point: one of C's female friends, to whom he was sexually attracted, was hospitalized in a psychiatric ward for depression. Prior to her hospitalization she preferred the company of other men and was quite careful to make C aware of it. After being hospitalized she called C frequently, making long telephone conversations. She also asked him to visit her often. In the beginning of treatment C was visiting her at least twice a week. Any attempt by him to turn their conversation to his problems was discouraged with the excuse that she was the one who needed more attention. Often on these visits C would take the girl to restaurants or movies since he thought that entertainment would help her depression. One evening, on the way to a restaurant, they met one of her male acquaintances. The girl asked him to join them in spite of the clear messages of dissatisfaction sent by C. She flirted with this friend and ignored C all evening. From the analysis of C's relations with this girl it became apparent that all the giving — love, services and sometimes money — was done by him. What he got from this relationship was a vague feeling of being needed and of generosity; these sentiments, however, did not balance his giving nor did they fulfill his need to be wanted and loved. In addition, he was made to realize that he was dispensable when more appealing partners became available. On his next visit to this girl C expressed his anger, disappointment and unfulfilled expectations. It was then agreed between them that since the girl was not particularly interested in him she could not expect him to be available whenever she felt lonely. Her next request was met with a refusal and C felt extremely proud of himself.

At work, C started to refuse to cover up for the incompetence of his subordinates by taking over their assignments; he also initiated a confrontation with his supervisor. To his amazement these episodes of assertion did not result in rejection, as he had feared, but rather gained him increased respect.

During these twelve sessions, the frequency of urges to cross-dress dropped from an average of five times a week (in the first three weeks) to an average of twice a week (in the last three weeks). Both these incidents remained uncompleted: in the first instance the girl he approached got scared and refused to tie his hands; in the second occasion he was arrested by the police.

(b) Desensitization

At the beginning of treatment C's relations with women (mainly acquaintances from work) fell into two categories: with unattractive girls he mostly discussed politics and professional topics, treating them as if they were male friends; with attractive girls he repeatedly found himself in the role of a listener and a consultant to their love affairs and personal conflicts. This latter type of relationship resulted in frustration and resentment. Examination of C's behavior ascertained that expressing sexual interest to a girl was anxiety evoking for him and therefore he usually refrained from doing so in spite of the fact that he is handsome and attractive. However he did not experience anxiety in earlier or later stages of the relationship. C was able to ask any girl for a date with no difficulty; likewise he was not anxious once it was established that sexual activities would take place. It was the intermediate stage when he was to express sexual interest that was loaded with the expectation of being rejected. On the basis of this information a hierarchy was constructed, composed of situations which varied on three dimensions:

1   Degree of his attraction for the girl — the more attractive she was the more anxious he became.
2   Degree of explicitness of his approach — varying for less explicit ('I like being here with you') to more explicit ('I wish to feel your body close to mine').
3   The intensity of the rejection going from 'I feel we should know each other better before . . .' to 'I am not really attracted to you.'

Fifteen situations were devised, ranging from 'mild rejection to an indirect advance by a scarcely attractive girl' to 'strong rejection to an explicit invitation by a very attractive girl.' The first and the last items on the hierarchy were as follows:

You are driving with M (an unattractive girl). On the way you invite her home to listen to records. M says: I would love to do it but I am afraid it is too late. (This situation initially created 15 subjective units of discomfort (*suds*).)

You are driving with B (the girl whom C loved for years) and you say: would you stay overnight with me? B answers: I won't do it, you know I am in love with A (80 *suds*).

Treatment by systematic desensitization (Wolpe, 1958, 1969) was conducted for five sessions until all items could be visualized by C without anxiety. After the third session C met a girl, 17 years old and extremely attractive. We shall call her Jill (not her real name). This was his first contact with a girl who was not related to his work and therefore the sexual implication of the encounter was obvious. At this point C reported no anxiety in being with this new friend; yet he expressed feelings of being awkward and deficient in courtship repertoire.

(c) Behavior rehearsal of courtship

Role playing, in the office, of several courtship situations demonstrated that C had, indeed, a very limited repertoire of behaviors conveying sexual interest. This deficiency may be attributed to the paucity of his heterosexual contacts during adolescence, the age at which courtship behaviors are learnt and become refined through repetition combined with feedback.

Drawing from the literature of social psychology we rehearsed verbal and non-verbal behaviors connoting personal interest and intimacy: Eye contact, postures of body while standing and sitting, as well as tone of voice and verbal messages. By the twelfth week of treatment C reported being involved in heavy petting with Jill; for the first time in his life he took the intitative in developing a normal sexual relationship. However, the girl, being young and conforming to the conservative norms of her family, refused to have intercourse. Inability to obtain relief from the arousal caused by very heavy petting several times a week, resulted in frustration which led C to terminate this relationship.

Behavioral rehearsal of courtship was stopped after six sessions, when C reported successful sexual approaches to two girls, whom he had previously found attractive but did not dare to express sexual interest to them.

Suppression of deviant habit

In November, after eleven weeks of treatment, C reported another incident of cross-dressing. He went to a shopping center at midnight, wearing a nightgown; he was caught by a policeman before he could approach any girl. This relapse occurred after a frustrating day in which he handled situations at work poorly and failed to assert himself. C was not alarmed by this episode as he saw progress in the fact that for the five preceding weeks he did not have any urge to cross-dress. This was the longest period he had ever experienced of being free of this urge. Nevertheless, because this new episode ended with an arrest, we decided to employ aversive techniques, to hasten suppression of this habit.

(a) Covert sensitization

We started by pairing arousing settings with aversive imagery (Cautela, 1967). The scene used was as follows:

You drive in the car at night near the college. You see a bra and underpants on a clothesline. You stop the car, watch the garments and think: 'If I take them I can go out.' You start to feel sick in your stomach. As you walk towards the clothesline the pains get worse and worse. Now you are near the clothesline and a bitter nauseating juice comes into your mouth. You feel really sick now. You are almost touching the bra and food comes into your mouth. Just as you touch the bra you feel very sick and you vomit, soiling the bra, your hand that reached for it and all over yourself. An awful smell spreads around. You can see pieces of meat and vegetables, some red tomatoes and green peppers all over the bra which is wet and soggy. You look at your hand and at the bra and you feel even more sick. Now you throw away the dirty bra and you feel so much better.

This scene was taped and presented to C ten times each session for six sessions. C was also instructed to practice at home (using the tape) with ten presentations in the morning and ten in the evening. However, he neglected to do so, feeling quite sure that the last episode of cross-dressing was accidental.

Seven weeks passed with only one brief urge to cross-dress. For the first time in fourteen months C had intercourse, this time of his initiative, with several girls whom he liked although he felt no emotional commitment toward them. In general he was quite content until he met again a girlfriend whom he had not seen for a year. The old pattern of listening to her talking about problems she had with her boyfriend reappeared and C was unable to break it. It was at such time (January 1973) that the last incident of cross-dressing occurred after excessive drinking. C did not remember anything that happened since he was completely drunk. When he regained awareness he was in detention wearing a nightgown.

(b) Aversion by shock
This new episode indicated that the weekly ten minutes of aversive imagery during therapy sessions may not have been sufficient, in the absence of regular daily practice at home, to suppress the deviancy. Therefore covert sensitization was replaced by four sessions of electric shock. C was instructed to imagine himself being tied to a pole wearing a nightgown. When he raised his finger to signal that the image was clear, a painful electric shock was administered for five seconds. This procedure was repeated ten times in each session.

(c) Sensitization of urge
At this time C's motivation to invest more time and effort in

eliminating his deviant behavior appeared to increase. Predicting now a better chance for home practice it was decided to employ covert sensitization again.

Following the electric aversion treatment C reported the disappearance of all images involving cross-dressing and being tied to a pole. Moreover, it was extremely difficult to induce such images even in the office under explicit instructions. The imagination of any behavior related to his habit (for example, walking toward a clothesline where a bra was hanging; imagining himself wearing a nightgown) evoked negative reactions of pain and disgust which would cause C to involuntarily terminate the scene. However the *abstract thought* 'the hell, I wish I could go out' still crossed his mind for a split second; this happened usually when he was alone in his room, tired after a long day at his office, knowing he had some more work to do. Although these thoughts appeared rarely, took the form of short flashes and did not evoke any sexual arousal, C expressed discomfort at their existence. Hence covert sensitization was aimed this time toward elimination of the urge.

The following scene was then designed with the goal of attaching aversion to the thought itself:

You just came back from work; you are tired, it seems that everything is on your shoulders. You look at your desk and you know there is a lot of work still waiting for you there. Today things didn't go for you the way they should. You lay on your bed thinking: 'The hell with everything, I too deserve to have some fun.' As soon as this thought crosses your mind you feel sick in your stomach. You feel like vomiting and you get up starting to walk toward the bathroom but you can't make it and you vomit all over yourself and on your bed. You then say to yourself: 'The hell, I am never going to do it again.' As soon as you say that, you feel much better.

This new stage of covert sensitization continued for eight weeks, the image being presented ten times at each session. The scene was taped and C was requested to practice daily at home alternating it with the previous scene (which was also taped) regardless of the difficulties he encountered in imagining it. This time C practiced at home with considerable regularity. With this stage, aversion treatment was terminated.

Enhancement of feelings

As mentioned earlier, C had, since February, occasional sexual relations with a number of girls. He enjoyed intercourse but did not care to develop a deep relationship with any particular girl. Three weeks later, however, he achieved a satisfactory ongoing relation with a girl he liked, who was very much in love with him. By this time, he had no urge for cross-dressing, was appropriately assertive in his interpersonal relations and in general was quite content. Nevertheless, he felt that one important objective, ability to fall in love, had not been reached. The last stage of therapy turned to this problem.

During the last few years C had maintained occasional contacts with B, the only girl he loved but who rejected him as a sexual partner. He used to write her long letters sharing his feelings about events and thoughts; many of those letters contained statements of love for her. During therapy he visited her several times, although she lived quite a long distance away from him. In April, B became engaged to another man and mailed all his letters back to C.

C brought some of these letters to the session, said that he had spent many hours reading them. He displayed no affect and was emotionally detached. C himself was surprised and disturbed at his lack of feeling, which was dissonant with his recognition that further relations with B could not be expected.

It was hypothesized that unless he displayed behaviors expressing sadness and loss C would never 'get rid' of B's image as the only girl who deserved his love. This hypothesis rests on the observation that when a mourning process involves behavioral display of grief functional behaviors reappear more rapidly.

'Intellectual' discussion of the mourning phenomenon and its importance did not produce any emotional display. C was then instructed to read aloud some of the love-letters he had written to B. He was further instructed to close his eyes and to imagine the beautiful uplifting encounter with B which preceded the writing of these letters. When these images achieved clarity he was requested to repeat the sentence: 'B is lost forever.' This procedure resulted in deep sobbing and a process of mourning took place for about a month, during which C cried a lot reading his letters to B over and over. In the last two sessions the memory of B evoked only mild sadness. By then four months had passed since C had an urge for cross-dressing. Even fleeting thoughts of it had disappeared and it was decided to terminate treatment.

Follow-up sessions

June 1973

Six weeks after the last treatment session C reported no urges for cross-dressing. He maintained satisfactory heterosexual relations with one girl and had occasional intercourse with other girls, mostly when he was travelling away from home at meetings. It seems that he enjoyed his new skill to form quick heterosexual relations and was exercising it. He expressed interest in moving back to the West Coast and was planning to go there in the summer to enquire about job possibilities.

September 1973

About three months after treatment C was free of any urge for cross-dressing. In July (about seven weeks after treatment) he fell in love with a girl whom he described as attractive and intelligent, 'the girl of his dreams,' who reciprocated his feelings. Because of this new relationship (he now lived with this woman and her 3-year-old daughter) he postponed his visit to the West Coast. He had a very intense summer with pressures at work and in his personal life. Since he had no urge to transvest in spite of these stresses he felt he was 'really cured.'

November 1973

Five months after termination of treatment C reported a short single urge for cross-dressing, after heavy drinking. His last girlfriend moved to California for three months, to finish her undergraduate work studies. He found a job in the West Coast and planned to join her after training a person to take over his job. He encountered some problems in his relations with this girl, concerning mainly her daughter and his role as 'a father.' This problem, however, did not discourage him from exploring further the possibility of marriage. Occasionally he continued to have intercourse with other girls. He expressed amazement at the easiness by which he now seemed to form sexual relationships. C is not aware, anymore, of the particular behaviors he emits when interacting with attractive women. However he constantly receives messages of sexual interest on their part. This change (in the beginning of therapy none of his acquaintances showed sexual attraction toward him) probably reflects modification of his own conduct.

C registered at the university in the West Coast, planning to finish his undergraduate work and to continue at the graduate level. He was not alarmed by the last brief urge, the sole one in ten difficult months during which a lot of tension was generated by the move to the West Coast, struggling with new meaningful relations and by starting a new job.

A telephone conversation with C in December 1973 (six months after treatment) revealed no change.

Discussion

The sequence in which the techniques described earlier were used to eliminate cross-dressing, as well as to establish satisfactory heterosexual relations and a sense of general self-adequacy, is summarized in Table 2·1.

In the first three weeks no treatment manipulation was introduced; therefore this period can be considered as a base-line of C's sexual behavior. Examination of Table 2·1 indicates that assertive training alone was quite effective in reducing the number of urges as well as the episodes of actual cross-dressing, thus supporting previous reports (Edwards, 1972; Stevenson and Wolpe, 1960). This technique, however, did not affect courtship behavior which was still ineffective even when assertive behavior was achieved in other circumstances. Desensitization to rejection expressed by attractive females, and the actual learning of courting behavior, was then introduced to increase heterosexual encounters.

The decision to start treatment with techniques directed toward enhancement of adequate behavior followed Ullmann and Krasner's (1969, p. 488) statement that 'a sexual outlet should not probably be changed by a technique such as aversive conditioning unless (1) a better outlet is available; (2) one can teach and reinforce such an alternative outlet . . .' Accordingly, C was first taught ways to reduce general interpersonal frustrations which had been previously decreased by transvestism. He then learned to react with no anxiety to the various stages of courtship as well as to enrich his courtship repertoire. Only after some heterosexual outlet had been established (in the tenth week), aversion therapy was employed. The combination of covert sensitization and electric shocks resulted in complete suppression of the urge and of actual cross-dressing (nineteenth week).

It may be argued that the combination of assertive training, desensitization and behavior rehearsal would eventually have been sufficient to eliminate altogether cross-dressing. However, since C was on probation, and in order to decrease the probability of his being confronted again by the police, it was deemed desirable to employ aversion techniques rather than going through a process of gradual extinction.

One last comment about some cognitive aspects of the treatment described here. In behavior therapy we focus on behavioral changes. Indeed, the achievement of such modification provides the criterion of success. Often direct manipulation of the behaviors to be changed is sufficient. At times, however, it is necessary to induce appropriate cognitive changes before the modification of a certain

TABLE 2-1   *Sequence of techniques and of relevant sexual behaviors*

Weeks	Frequency of sessions	Interviewing	Diary	Assertive training	Desensitization	Behavior rehearsal of courtship	Covert sensitization	Electric shock	Feeling enhancement	Deviant (frequency) Urge only	Deviant (frequency) Actual	Normal (presence) Petting	Normal (presence) Coitus	Normal (presence) Love
1-3	2 per week	√	√							15	6				
4-6				√						6	2			
7-9				√						0	0			
10-12				√	√					1	1	+		
13-15				√		√				1	0	+		
16-18	1 per week			√			√			1	1	+		
19-21				√			√	√		0	0	+	+	
22-4				√			√	√		0	0	+	+	
25-7							√			0	0	+	+	
28-30	2 per month								√	0	0	+	+	
31-3									√	0	0	+	+	
34-5									√	0	0	+	+	
Follow-up After treatment										0	0	+	+	+
Six weeks										0	0	+	+	+
Three months										0	0	+	+	+
Six months										1	0			

NOTES: 1 Each row refers to a three-week period of treatment except the last one and follow-ups.
2 Treatment shown for a given period, by check mark, may have lasted less than the whole period. See text for details.
3 Presence of given normal behavior is indicated by +, its absence by —

behavior can be undertaken. C could not learn to respond assertively before awareness of his anger became contiguous to the frustrating event. Thus cognitive training had to precede behavioral training. Likewise C's continued expectation to establish a reciprocated love relationship with B constituted an obstacle to his falling in love with another girl. The first problem was overcome by the writing of a diary which enhanced the patient's awareness of interpersonal events. The second problem was solved through the introduction of a mourning process by which expectation of future relations with B was eliminated. It is of interest to note that these cognitive changes were induced through specific behavioral instructions. Thus, it seems, behavior altered cognition, and this change, in turn, opened the road to further behavioral modifications.

3 'I Hear Voices but There's No One There'[1]

(A Functional Analysis of Auditory Hallucinations)

Teodoro Ayllon and Henry Kandel

Introduction

Hallucinatory behavior has long been regarded as a major clinical index of psychopathology. Freud (1938) regarded hallucinations as unconscious manifestations of percepts which first satisfied a psychic need. As with dreams, Freud felt that hallucinations, when analyzed, could serve to uncover these long buried unconscious needs and conflicts. This analysis proved to be the cornerstone of psychotherapy throughout the twentieth century. As part of this psychotherapeutic method, the patient is asked to report his fantasies, dreams, slips or hallucinations to the therapist so that they can be discussed, interpreted and eventually resolved.

An alternative approach to the treatment of hallucinations is that of Rogers (1961). The non-directive therapist refrains from interpreting the patient's hallucinations and concentrates instead on the re-statement of the patient's feelings.

A behavioral approach to hallucinations has been largely limited since such clinical phenomena do not readily lend themselves to established recording procedures. There is, however, little question about the legitimacy and importance of developing a suitable behavioral analysis and treatment procedure for hallucinations. Indeed, a start has been made by identifying for study some delusional behaviors. For example, in paranoid schizophrenics (Ayllon and Haughton, 1964; Liberman, Teigman, Patterson and Baker, 1973), it has been dramatically demonstrated that social interactions with patients concerning their delusions often serve to exacerbate them. It has been further demonstrated that conditioned reinforcers such as tokens, when available on a contingent basis, can significantly reduce delusional speech (Wince, Lettenberg and Agras, 1972; Patterson and Teigman, 1973). These studies on

[1] With apologies to Irving Berlin.

delusions suggest strongly that the investigation and treatment of psychotic symptoms is within the realm of a behavioristic approach. However, to lend further experimental and clinical support to this conclusion, additional research must be performed on other 'bizarre' and clinically significant symptoms, such as hallucinations.

Hallucinations, unlike delusions, imply the apparent perception of sights or sounds, which are not actually present. However, to the person who experiences hallucinations, there is no question about their reality. Indeed, during clinical examination, the patient often vividly describes his hallucinations. Freud attempted to analyze these reports of hallucinations since he, naturally, could not perceive the actual hallucinations of his patients. Following Freud's lead, the therapists of today, whether they be psychoanalytical, client centered, or directive, treat hallucinations by focusing on the descriptions offered by the patient. Thus, if a patient reports to a therapist that he is suffering from constantly hearing far-off, high, squeaky male voices, the therapist might diagnose him as 'suffering from severe auditory hallucinations.' If the same patient, after treatment, reports that he no longer hears these voices, the diagnosis would be updated to exclude auditory hallucinations.

The following study represents an attempt to analyze and treat the auditory hallucinations of a chronic schizophrenic using a functional analysis of behavior.

Experiment I

Subject

The subject, Viola, was a 54-year-old female patient diagnosed as a paranoid schizophrenic with bizarre hallucinations. She had been hospitalized for a period of ten years prior to her admission to a ward where a motivational system was in force for 45 female patients (Ayllon and Azrin, 1968).

Symptom: hallucinations

Hallucinations, especially auditory ones, have posed a very difficult problem to therapists from the point of view of assessing their severity or complexity. There is, however, the matter of reports of hearing voices which can be recorded and thereby analyzed in terms of content and frequency. In Viola's case, these verbal reports were, after all, the criteria by which relatives, therapists, and nurses judged Viola's need for treatment. The same dimension was used here to assess Viola's hallucinations as well as to monitor and evaluate the relative effectiveness of her treatment.

Behavioral strategy

Unlike many psychotic experiences which appear to occur without particular circumstance, Viola's auditory hallucinations seemed to be experienced only when an audience was present and especially when she was interviewed by a mental health professional. It had been observed by the senior author that this audience usually met Viola's reports of hallucinations with either sympathy and understanding or disgust and mockery. Many of the therapists, nurses, and understanding patients seemed to feel that hallucinations were an important component of Viola's personality and that 'talking them out' would be highly therapeutic. Although this approach continued for some time, Viola complained endlessly of the 'voices in her head.' Since a token economy system was already in effect on Viola's ward and had been found to be effective in modifying a wide range of behaviors (Ayllon and Azrin, 1968), a decision was made to employ these techniques in an effort to arrest Viola's worsening condition.

Before treatment was instated, Viola's hallucinations were analyzed from a behavioral point of view. Since this view holds that behavior is a function of its consequences, it was hypothesized that Viola's reports of hallucinations were maintained by the attention she received for them from other people on the ward.

A behavioristic approach also holds that when a behavior is reinforced in the presence of a particular stimulus, that stimulus will gain control over the behavior. In Viola's case, reports of hallucinations appeared to be under the control of any verbalizing person or group of persons. For example, a nurse, asking Viola how she felt, usually triggered a long chain of reports of hallucinations.

Since stimulus conditions which prompted reports of hallucinations (that is, people verbalizing) are also the conditions which are requisite for 'normal behavior' (that is, talking to someone else), they could not be removed from Viola's environment. Thus, the strategy for eliminating the reports of hallucinations had to consider both the social conditions that prompted them and the consequences that maintained them. Social conditions for eliciting reports on hallucinatory experiences included a systematic set of verbal prompts in a therapy-like format. Reports of hallucinations were followed by token reinforcement, while other types of verbal behavior were inhibited by response cost procedures. The tokens accumulated by Viola under the system could be exchanged for a variety of reinforcers including sleeping accommodations, ground passes, and consumable items such as cigarettes, candy, coffee, etc. (for details, see Ayllon and Azrin, 1968).

Procedure

A 1·5m x 2 m room was used as the interview room where all verbal interactions between Viola and the therapist were recorded. The therapist in this investigation was a nurse who had been trained in the administration and supervision of reinforcement procedures conducted in a token economy ward environment (Ayllon and Azrin, 1968). Both Viola and the nurse were made aware that each session was tape-recorded.

Since Viola had been complaining of hearing voices for such a long period of time and had requested 'something to make the voices go away,' the nurse explained to her that individual psychotherapy was going to be made available to her. To insure voluntary attendance at the therapy sessions, Viola was paid ten tokens at the end of each meeting. Therapy sessions were conducted by the nurse, once a day for 50 minutes, five days a week.

Recording procedure

During the 50-minute sessions, Viola was asked questions regarding the hearing of voices every 3 minutes, for a total of 15 questions per therapy session. Throughout all the therapeutic conditions, the procedure for asking Viola questions was standardized to insure consistency. At the start of each of the 15 questioning periods of each therapy session, a timer was set for 3 minutes. From previous interviews, it was known that Viola had a tendency to ramble on endlessly about subject matters irrelevant to the presented stimulus question. It was felt that the 3-minute time period would minimize these digressions, because the temporal period between the stimulus questions was short enough to insure that Viola's rambling would be frequently interrupted. At the start of the 3-minute time period, Viola was asked if she heard voices. If she responded, 'Yes,' she was then asked to identify the sex to which the voices belonged.

Experimental design

The problem of demonstrating a functional relationship between the behavioral procedures used and the frequency of voices reported became apparent when deciding upon an experimental design for the present study. If Viola's auditory hallucinations were successfully treated using extinction procedures, it would not be clinically justifiable to reinstate them, through reinforcement, just to demonstrate that the variables in question are critical. It, therefore, became necessary to devise a methodological solution to determine the relative effectiveness of the variables in question. Thus, an attempt was made to keep her reports of hallucinations intact while studying the treatment effects on the specific content or gender of voices reported. Viola was asked to identify the gender of voice she heard during hallucination and, in so doing, it allowed analysis of hallucinations into two discrete categories: female voices and male voices. These dimensions could then be manipulated in a multiple ABA design, thus allowing a functional relationship to be demonstrated.

After obtaining an assessment of the patient's auditory hallucinations, an attempt was made to systematically influence the content of the hallucinations by differentially reinforcing one specific content over another. This procedure allowed one content of hallucination to remain unaltered, thus serving as a constant against which the relative effects of the therapeutic procedure could be evaluated.

The procedure used to influence the content of hallucinations (for example, gender of voices) involved first the nurse awarding tokens for a specific voice heard during the hallucinatory episode (for example, female) and concurrently withdrawing tokens for its opposite (for example, male). This procedure was reversed in the next condition so that male content was reinforced while female content resulted in losing tokens. Finally the first condition was reinstated (see Table 3.1).

TABLE 3·1 *Summary of the consequences applied to Viola's reports of auditory hallucinations under the three conditions in Experiment I*

Phase	Number of sessions	Number of tokens gained or lost for gender of voice heard during hallucinations[1]	
		Female	Male
Behavioral assessment	10	No tokens	No tokens
I	20	+5 tokens	—5 tokens
II	20	—5 tokens	+5 tokens
III	20	+5 tokens	—5 tokens

[1] Reports of hearing no voices received no consequences. Since each session consisted of 15 prompts, a maximum of 75 tokens were available per session.

Results

When hallucinatory experiences of a certain content are followed by token reinforcement, they increase in frequency. Conversely, when hallucinatory experiences of a certain content are followed by a loss of tokens, they are inhibited and decrease in frequency.

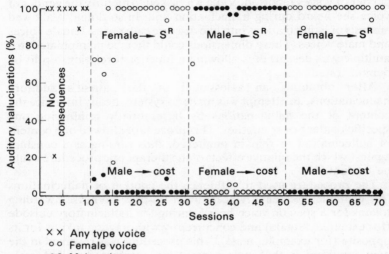

X X   Any type voice
o o   Female voice
● ●   Male voice

FIGURE 3·1   *Percentage of time Viola reported experiencing auditory hallucinations of a female and/or male variety*
The first segment (sessions 1-10) served as a base-line during which Viola's reports of auditory hallucinations were neither reinforced nor inhibited. During the second segment (sessions 11-30) reports of female auditory hallucinations were reinforced with tokens and male ones were inhibited through loss of tokens. In the third segment (sessions 31-50) the response contingencies were reversed: male auditory hallucinations were reinforced with tokens but female ones resulted in loss of tokens. The final, fourth segment (sessions 51-70) reinstated the conditions noted in the second segment.

Figure 3·1 shows that during the behavioral assessment, hallucinations were reported 100 per cent of the time in 8 of 10 sessions. No effort was made during this period to reinforce the patient's hallucinations. When hearing female voices was reinforced and statements of hearing male voices were followed by a loss of tokens, female voices were maintained at 90 per cent to 100 per cent per session. When the contingencies were reversed so that male voices were reinforced, they increased to 100 per cent, while female voices fell to zero. Finally, when differential reinforcement was reinstated for hearing female voices, they showed a dramatic and rapid increase from zero to 100 per cent.

Throughout all conditions, the percentage of unreinforced content of hallucinations reported ranged from zero to 74 per cent with a mean of approximately 2 per cent. The reinforced content ranged from 16 to 100 per cent with a mean of 96 per cent.

Discussion

The results of this study demonstrate that the content of auditory hallucinations can be effectively controlled through the use of behavioral techniques. A major feature of this study consisted of devising a methodological procedure that would allow a suitable experimental evaluation of auditory hallucinations by keeping one aspect constant while another aspect was under manipulation. In so doing, this study demonstrates that a functional analysis is a suitable experimental design to study complex clinical phenomena.

While hallucinations are difficult to detect from moment to moment, they may be prompted by interview procedures as was done here. It is important to point out that the patient was able to learn quickly that the consequences for certain types of hallucinations were such that she could seek the most advantageous opportunities to report them.

The major importance of this study is that it presents evidence indicating that the behavioral consequences of hallucinations prompt, generate, and maintain specific types of hallucinations. While these findings are impressive, they do not demonstrate that these same procedures will be effective in therapeutic treatment oriented toward elimination of such hallucinations. In effect, one could argue that in the present study the hallucinations were never affected, but that there was a simple shift from one content to another consistent with the notion of symptom substitution. Therefore, the question still to be answered is whether total elimination of hallucinations is possible rather than a mere shift of symptoms. The following experiment represents an attempt to answer this question.

Experiment II

This experiment was concerned with the feasibility of eliminating chronic and severe hallucinations. The best test of whether or not behavioral procedures can eliminate behavior would be if the behavior in question is occurring most or all of the time prior to the use of these procedures. Since the experimental procedures in Experiment I had shown that one of the contents (for example, female voices) of Viola's hallucinations could be maintained for long periods of time at a very high level, the strategy for Experiment II was to use this level as the criterion for effectiveness of subsequent behavioral procedures. Thus, female auditory hallucinations which were occurring 100 per cent of the time at the end of Experiment I were now subjected to extinction procedures. That is to say, any reports of hearing either male or female voices were followed by a loss of 5 tokens while reports of *not* hearing voices resulted in a gain of 5 tokens. The behavioral design used to evaluate effectiveness is known as an AB design wherein the major effects are to be seen by contrasting the level of behavior during the assessment period with the level of behavior during the period of treatment. Again, it should be remembered that a functional relationship between auditory hallucinations and the variables at issue had already been demonstrated in Experiment I and therefore Experiment II attempted, only, to apply these findings on a therapeutic basis.

To ensure continuity of previous therapeutic procedures the same therapist using the same room and consequences for attending therapy were maintained. The therapeutic procedure was in effect for 27 sessions.

Results and discussion

Auditory hallucinations were inhibited when therapeutic procedures were made contingent upon not experiencing them. The patient's reports of hallucinatory experiences were quickly reduced, and in a matter of three days, completely eliminated.

Figure 3·2 shows that the level of auditory hallucinations ranged from 85 per cent to 100 per cent per session for the 20 sessions prior to behavior therapy. This high level of auditory hallucinations fell immediately to 8 per cent, and within three sessions to zero. For the next 24 sessions, the patient reported having no more hallucinatory experiences.

These findings indicate that contrary to clinical expectations, the patient's content of hallucinations did not simply shift from one content to another as a consequence of therapeutic manipulations. Rather, the therapeutic procedures were instrumental in eliminating the patient's major symptom without untoward effects.

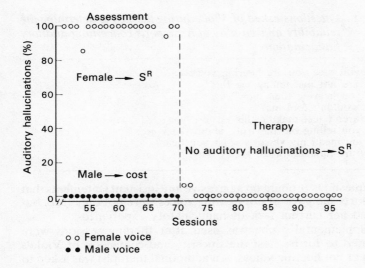

FIGURE 3·2   *Percentage of time Viola reported experiencing auditory hallucinations of a female and/or male variety during behavior therapy sessions*

During the assessment period (sessions 51-70), which served as a base-line for therapy, Viola's reports of female auditory hallucinations were reinforced with tokens and reports of male auditory hallucinations were inhibited. With the instatement of behavior therapy (sessions 71-97) reports of *not* hearing hallucinations (male and/or female) were reinforced, and reports of hearing hallucinations were inhibited.

An effort to estimate the degree of sincerity and awareness of the patient with respect to the hallucinatory experiences was made by conducting an in-depth interview whenever she reported hearing no voices. This interview consisted of eight questions (see Table 3·2) intentionally arranged in such a way that they could not be answered by all yes or all no answers. Rather, if the answers to the questions were to make any sense, some would have to be answered yes and others no. Thus, if Viola's answers were to be considered reliable, they would have to be answered without discrepancies. The questions also served to check on whether Viola's reports referred to the voice of the questioning nurse or to voices that were part of her auditory hallucinations.

TABLE 3·2 *Questions asked of Viola during therapy to determine the reliability and validity of her reports concerning auditory hallucinations*

1 Are you sure you are hearing voices?
2 You are not just telling me this?
3 Are you hearing them now?
4 You wouldn't fool me?
5 You aren't just making this up, are you?
6 Are you telling me the truth about the voices?
7 Do you mean my voice is what you hear?
8 They are human voices, aren't they?

These questions brought on aggressive and insistent statements that the reports she gave of not hearing voices were not only true, but reflected her current lack of hallucinatory experiences.

A supplemental probe was used after therapy sessions were completed to further test the sincerity and conviction of Viola's reports of not hearing voices. An additional therapist was asked to evaluate Viola's psychological condition in the therapy room. This interview was tape-recorded with both the patient's and the therapist's consent. The ostensible purpose for interviewing Viola was that a survey was being conducted regarding treatment in the hospital. The patient was told that she, along with others, would be asked a few questions and that she should feel free to answer them to the best of her ability. Embedded in routine questions regarding her stay in the hospital, Viola was asked a variety of questions within the general theme of auditory hallucinations. Her general composure and answers to these questions were very consistent: she denied hearing voices or experiencing hallucinations despite repeated efforts by the interviewer to elicit them.

Concurrent with the behavior therapy program conducted in the therapy room, the patient's statements regarding her auditory hallucinations were being monitored on the ward at large. These observations enabled us to determine that the patient's newly gained therapeutic improvement appeared to be limited to the setting within which such gains had been generated, namely the therapy room. These results are consistent with current findings indicating that learning which takes place in one setting may not ordinarily generalize to another (Lovaas *et al.,* 1973; Wahler, 1969). In respect to therapy, it is, of course, of the utmost importance that any therapeutic success be maintained beyond the limited confines of the therapy situation. It was this general background that led us to consider the possibility of extending these procedures that were effective in eliminating the auditory hallucinations in the therapy room to the world within which the patient lived, namely the psychiatric ward.

Experiment III

Experiment II demonstrated that reinforcement and response cost techniques could effectively control Viola's hallucinations in the therapy room. Because of the failure of therapy gains to generalize to the ward, an additional study was conducted. The focus of Experiment III was to determine whether the effectiveness of the therapeutic procedures used in Experiment II would carry over to the larger and more complex environment of Viola's ward.

Procedure

In an effort to obtain accurate and objective measures of Viola's hallucinations, nurses were instructed to record her reports of hallucinations on the ward. The nurses were to confront Viola once a day with the question of whether or not she was experiencing hallucinations. The recordings were initiated three weeks after behavior therapy was terminated, and were maintained for a 20 month period.

Generalization of hallucination-free verbal reports was assessed for $4\frac{1}{2}$ months with no contingencies placed on their occurrence. This condition served as a base-line against which the relative effects of two subsequent treatment conditions on the ward could be compared. Treatment condition A involved the administration of a fine in the amount of 50 tokens for reports of hallucinations made by Viola to inquiring nurses on the ward. This condition was in effect for a two-month period. Condition B involved the administration of a more severe fine of 75 tokens for reports of hallucinations during a $13\frac{1}{2}$ month period.

Results

When no consequences followed reports of hallucinations on the ward, they occurred approximately one-third of the time they were prompted. On the other hand, when a high cost followed auditory hallucinations on the ward, they decreased sharply and were virtually eliminated.

Recordings taken on the ward showed that during behavioral assessment, Viola reported having auditory hallucinations an average of over 8 times a month or about 27 per cent of the time she was asked. When a response cost of 50 tokens was put in effect,

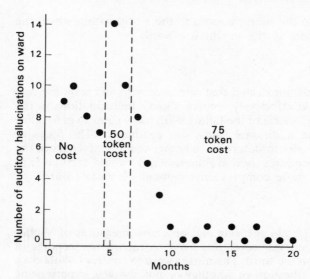

FIGURE 3·3   *Number of times Viola reported experiencing auditory hallucinations on the ward*
The first segment designates the period during which reports of auditory hallucinations were not followed by consequences. In the second segment response — cost of 50 tokens was introduced. In the final segment the response — cost was increased to 75 tokens.

Viola reported hearing voices an average of 12 times per month, or 40 per cent of the time she was asked. Finally, with the addition of a higher magnitude of response cost 75 tokens, the number of reports concerning hearing voices dropped to an average of less than one per month with no reports being recorded during the final three months despite all efforts to elicit them.

Discussion

Generalization of reports of the absence of auditory hallucinations can be assured by using contingencies similar to those used during the therapy situation. Without the transfer of contingencies from the therapy situation to the ward environment, it is apparent that complete generalization will not take place. This finding is in agreement with current literature which states that the behavioral effects produced through therapy are situation-specific; that is, they occur only in the situation where the consequences which generated the behavior are in effect. These findings have been so convincing that they have led Nordquist and Wahler (1973) and Ayllon and Skuban (1973) to treat patients within their natural habitat using natural consequences, thus eliminating the possibility of generalization problems from one setting to another. It is essential, however, that when the post-therapeutic environment is included in the planning of therapy, it makes use of the contingencies found to be effective in therapy sessions. The present findings support Baer, Wolf and Risley's (1968) statement that 'generalization should be programmed rather than expected or lamented.'

In the present experiment, a token cost of 50, then 75 tokens was used to attempt to inhibit auditory hallucinations on the ward. The results indicate that a 50-token fine did not lower the level of reports of hearing voices, but rather, it increased them from the previous base-line level. It was noticed during this time that Viola was becoming very aggressive and indignant to the questioning of the nurses. There are several hypotheses as to the reason for Viola's increase in reports accompanied by her emotional behavior. First, it can be assumed that Viola had more severe and frequent hallucinations at this time. Second, it can be assumed that reports increased as response cost increased because they were previously continuously reinforced on the ward by patients and staff. From a behavioral standpoint (Ferster and Skinner, 1957) when a behavior is put on extinction after having received continuous reinforcement it usually increases and is accompanied by emotional behavior before it is extinguished.

Finally, it can be hypothesized that 50 tokens was too weak an inhibitor to cancel out the strong social reinforcement present on the ward. It was for this reason that a higher magnitude of response cost was used, resulting in a decrease and finally an elimination of auditory hallucinations.

In summary, it seems that once auditory hallucinations are cured in the therapeutic situation, they will not occur in the patient's living environment if similar contingencies are used. It appears, however, that any contingencies used in the living situation will have to be strong enough to compete with the overwhelmingly powerful social contingencies which may be maintaining the behavior.

Conclusion

The first experiment in this study demonstrates that reports of hallucinatory experiences are a function of environmental consequences — that is to say, they follow the same type of analysis as do other less subtle behaviors. The influence of the environment in generating and maintaining such hallucinations has, to this date, been underestimated in clinical practice. This is unfortunate, since the procedures used by various schools of therapy include techniques which often call attention to the undesirable behaviors of the patient, thus supplying them with possible reinforcing environmental stimuli. With this in mind, it is possible that clinicians not only maintain, but also influence, the type and content of their patients' symptoms.

The second experiment demonstrates that behavioral techniques can be used in an effective therapy to totally eliminate reports of hallucinations in the therapy room. The experiment further suggests that therapeutic gains are only possible if hallucinations are reported by the patient and are occurring at a high enough rate to allow recording procedures and systematic behavioral consequences to follow. Conversely, no gains are possible if the auditory hallucinations do not occur during therapy sessions. The therapy room appears to be the most desirable setting to obtain such a high frequency of reports, since these reports can be intensively prompted here and hopefully they will eventually come under the stimulus control of the room and the therapist. At the same time, possible competing influences to the reporting of auditory hallucinations can be eliminated. Such desirable control of behavior for therapeutic gain is not initially possible in the patient's complex living environment.

The third experiment demonstrates that once the reports of hallucinations are under the control of contingencies arranged in the therapy situation, these same contingencies can produce similar effects in the patient's living environment. This finding suggests that some type of bridge must be built between the therapy room and the larger social environment to insure permanent remediation of hallucinations. In the present study, the stimulus properties of the nurse and the therapy room, which had, in the past, set the occasion for the patient to report on her hallucinations, were both transferred to Viola's living situation in the form of other nurse therapists and a larger room, for example, the ward. In addition to these stimulus properties, similar procedures were carried over from one setting to the other, the most obvious being the response cost procedure for reports of hearing voices.

Without this carry over of procedures from one situation to another, it appears that reports of hearing voices are stimulus bound. That is, the effects produced by behavior therapy may not automatically generalize from the therapy room to the ward, even if they have some similar stimulus properties.

It may be argued that the present study did not eliminate auditory hallucinations, but rather it only eliminated reports concerning these hallucinations. It may be further argued that the patient was deeply suffering from auditory hallucinations when, in fact, she reported that she heard nothing. These arguments are, of course, legitimate, but they remain academic. Hallucinations are, by definition, private events which cannot be observed by anyone other than the patient experiencing them, and, therefore, no one except the patient knows if the hallucinations are 'really' present or not. The only means of another person knowing that a patient is experiencing hallucinations is by the patient telling the person or signaling to the person through the use of body language (that is, holding their hand to their ear in a manner which would suggest they are listening for something) that they are occurring. At the present time, psychologists have no choice but to respect the reports and actions of patients as being true referents of what is actually happening to them. Reports indeed have always been the important signs by which clinicians have gauged the success or failure of their therapeutic procedures. The present experiment used this same trust in the patient's verbal reports, along with the observation of any accompanying actions, to assess the relative effectiveness of behavior therapy on auditory hallucinations.

It must be pointed out that researchers in applied behavioral analysis have been particularly reluctant, in the past, to deal with clinical phenomena such as hallucinations because of methodological reasons. Skinner (1969) has made it clear, however, that 'An adequate science of behavior must consider events taking place within the skin of the organism.' Indeed, a few researchers (Azrin, 1972, and Stuart, 1969) have realized the importance of dealing with such important but covert dimensions as joy and happiness.

The fact that a functional relationship could be demonstrated in this study indicates that hallucinations have no special properties which place them outside the realm of scientific study. This finding has major implications in that it suggests the possibility of analyzing and treating other covert behaviors such as troublesome thoughts, delusions, dreams and feelings. Further research along these lines is imperative in building a science which can treat all aspects of human behavior.

4   The Loneliness of the Long-distance Runner

John D. Teasdale

David had been arrested and charged with indecent exposure. A woman, while she was out walking one night, had noticed him, naked, masturbating, staring at her. She had subsequently made a complaint to the police. When charged, David claimed that he had no recollection of what had happened until he 'came to' and found himself naked, with his clothes beside him. He maintained that he had suffered some kind of 'fit', and described three other occasions on which he had experienced similar 'fits' and, on regaining consciousness, had found himself naked.

Before appearing in court, David was referred to a neurologist for investigation. The neurologist found no evidence for the presence of epileptic fits. Accordingly, David was sentenced to a period of probation, with the condition that he should receive treatment.

At interview with a consultant psychiatrist, David, for the first time, gave a true account of his behaviour. This suggested that his problem was in fact one of abnormal sexual habits rather than epilepsy, and he was referred to me to assess his suitability for behaviour therapy.

David was 19 years old and lived in a fairly close community in Yorkshire with his parents. They ran the local social club, which served the function of a public house and social centre. He was employed as an electrician. He was a good-looking, somewhat shy boy, who gave the impression of being younger than 19. After I had explained to him that I already knew something of the true nature of his problem, and assured him that everything he told me would be in confidence, he told me what had actually happened on the evening that led to his arrest.

He was a keen athlete and in the habit of going on a training run in the evening. That evening, as he was running, he caught sight of a woman, some distance away. He felt a shiver go up and down his spine, a thrill of sexual excitement, and had stopped and quickly stripped off his running clothes. This enhanced the sexual excitement further and, with his eyes fixed on the woman, he had started to masturbate. He had no intention of exposing himself, in the sense of wanting to draw the woman's attention to himself, but she happened to notice him, and subsequently complained to the police. David had never suffered epileptic fits, and admitted that his original explanation had been quite untrue.

David's sexual problem began when he was 13. He was an only child, and, as his parents were always busy running the social club in the evenings, he would be on his own at this time. He would spend the evening alone in the television room of the club, watching the television in the dark. He began to masturbate in this situation. To add to the excitement, he would stand, in the darkness, looking out on to the stairs along which women went to the toilet in the club. In this situation he could see women passing by without being seen himself. This pattern of masturbation rapidly became established as a regular evening routine. He would sit, clothed, watching the television in the darkness. He would hear women's footsteps coming up the stairs on the way to the toilet. As soon as they had passed the door of the television room, he would get up from his chair and hide behind the piano, waiting for the woman to reappear. When he heard the toilet door closing, and footsteps approaching, he would feel very sexually excited, take off his clothes as quickly as possible, and masturbate as he saw the woman pass the door and go down the stairs. He would then get dressed and return to watching the television. Middle-aged, motherly women were the most sexually arousing in this situation, although when David saw them in other situations they would leave him quite unmoved.

This routine continued nightly for over a year, until a woman passing the door of the television room noticed him with no clothes on. She took no action as a result of this, but David stopped this form of sexual behaviour for two months. He was then approached by a boy at school who said he had a photograph of him in the nude, and who began to blackmail him. He threatened that unless David paid him money, and participated in homosexual activity with him, he would make this photograph public. For two to three months, David stole money from the social club till to pay the blackmailer and had homosexual relations with him. David's father then discovered what was going on, and put a stop to it.

Two months later, one of the teachers at his school involved David in a homosexual affair which lasted six months.

When he was 15, David resumed his former practice of undressing and masturbating in the television room. This habit had continued ever since, mainly on Wednesday and Saturday evenings, when the club was busiest. Over time, the behaviour had generalised to a number of other situations. When asked why he continued to behave in this way, David replied that he found it sexually exciting and rewarding. However, the immediate effects of the behaviour were not always pleasant; sometimes he felt worried and upset at the awareness of what he had done. There had been an increase in the frequency of abnormal sexual behaviour up to the time that David was caught.

David used fantasies of the situations associated with his abnormal sexual behaviour when masturbating on his own in his bedroom.

A brief personal history was also obtained at this first session. David was an only child who had relatively little contact with his parents who were always busy running the pub and social club. His parents regarded themselves as somewhat superior to the other people in the community and discouraged David from mixing with the boys at school, whom they regarded as 'roughs'. David had led a lonely, isolated life, and was socially quite anxious and inept. He had never had any close friends except his current girl friend.

Early in his teens, David had become interested in athletics, and had spent most of his leisure time training for long-distance running. He had been extremely successful in this direction, frequently winning major events. To maintain this standard, David had to spend several hours a day training, usually on his own. His athletics brought him into contact with other young people, but David had difficulty in relating to them and remained quite solitary and isolated.

David's athletic achievements had made him quite famous in his community, and his parents gloried in the achievement of their son. He did not feel very close to his parents; he felt that they tried to show affection by buying him presents, or doing things for him, but that really they had little affection for him.

David had no girl friends until the age of 17; his spare time until then had been largely occupied by training, and he had also felt shy, embarrassed and inept when with girls. With the exception of his present girl friend, none of his relationships with girls had been very satisfactory. He had become rapidly bored in his relationships, and moved on from one girl to another. Sexual intercourse had not been very satisfactory with girl friends originally but, apparently, had improved over time. He had been going out with his current girl friend for 18 months, and they were thinking of getting engaged. David described their sex life as quite satisfying to both of them.

Before his arrest, David had been engaging in his abnormal sexual behaviour from twice a week to daily, and this had continued since his trial and conviction. Following his appearance in court he was tense and depressed. Details of the charges against him had appeared in the local newspaper so that his unusual sexual habits had become public knowledge in the small community in which he lived. This had made him anxious, self-conscious, and very reluctant to appear in public. He was also very worried about the persistence of his abnormal sexual behaviour, which he regarded as beyond his control.

From the information obtained at the first interview, it was possible immediately to formulate a plausible model for the development and maintenance of David's problem in learning theory terms. At a time when he was beginning to experience the sexual urges of adolescence, David found himself on his own every evening in the darkened television room. He began to masturbate in this situation. As an experiment, to see if it would enhance the sexual excitement of masturbation, David took his clothes off and, in the security of the darkened room, masturbated to the sight of women passing the doorway of the room on the way from the women's toilet. The membership of the social club was such that the majority of these women would be middle-aged, motherly types.

Masturbation in this way was repeated as it was sexually rewarding. Consequently, there would be repeated associations between that particular stimulus situation and sexual arousal. By a process of classical conditioning, sexual arousal would become attached to that particular stimulus complex. This would further increase the sexual reinforcement obtained from masturbating in that situation, which would increase the frequency of masturbation in that situation, thereby strengthening further the classical conditioning of sexual arousal to that situation and so on. An additional factor was that, in choosing a fantasy to use while masturbating in his bedroom, David would imagine a scene which had the power to evoke sexual arousal. Use of the television room scene for this purpose would provide for still more associations between that particular scene and sexual arousal.

Normally, sexual arousal might have become associated with more usual forms of heterosexual contact with girls of his own age. This would have provided an alternative form of sexually reinforced behaviour, which might have led to a reduction in the more deviant sexual behaviour. However, as a result of his general social isolation, David was anxious and inept in his social contact with girls. He consequently avoided the social contact with girls of his own age which might otherwise have provided the opportunity for the development of more normal heterosexual interests and behaviours. In addition to this, David's homosexual affairs may have increased his anxieties concerning normal heterosexual contact.

By the time David began to establish social and sexual contacts with girls, his deviant sexual behaviour was already firmly established so that it was not possible to simply substitute the more normal for the less normal sexual behaviour.

Once the original deviant behaviour was well established, stimulus generalisation occurred so that other situations which included the essential stimulus elements of being alone, seeing a middle-aged woman at some distance, being unseen himself, and removing his clothes, acquired the ability to evoke sexual arousal and masturbatory behaviour.

The formulation reached for the origin and maintenance of David's deviant sexual behaviour fits strikingly well into the general model for the development of such behaviour proposed by McGuire, Carlisle and Young (1965).

The initial formulation outlined suggested that the essential factor maintaining the deviant behaviour was the attachment of sexual arousal to inappropriate stimuli. Accordingly the aim of treatment was seen as stripping these stimuli of their ability to evoke sexual arousal. As the patient already had normal heterosexual behaviour with his girl friend, which he described as quite satisfactory, an alternative reinforced sexual behaviour was available to him. It was therefore considered that treatment directed at removing sexual arousal attached to the deviant stimuli would be sufficient to allow the patient to adopt a more normal sex life. Electrical aversion therapy was seen as the treatment of choice to achieve this end, and it was described in general terms to the patient at the end of the first session. It was stressed that his participation in aversion therapy was quite voluntary. He was told that if he declined aversion therapy this would not be considered a violation of the Condition of Treatment Order included in his probation. He was given a few days to make his decision.

The decision to embark on a specific form of treatment as a result of information obtained in only one interview, without further exploration of the problem, was made for two reasons. First, the deviant behaviour was occurring quite frequently, and there was a real risk that further complaints would be made about David, which might lead to more severe legal sanctions. Second, the information available was sufficient to allow a plausible formulation of David's problem in behavioural terms, and to suggest a specific form of treatment, for which there was some evidence of efficacy (Rachman and Teasdale, 1969).

Session 2

David agreed to participate in aversion therapy and more detailed descriptions of situations currently evoking the deviant sexual behaviour were obtained. As it was proposed to employ electric aversion therapy to imaginal representations of the situations eliciting the abnormal behaviour, it was necessary to check David's power of imagery. He was asked to imagine the situations he had described as if he were there and able to see them. His power of imagery appeared remarkably good, and he gave a commentary on what he was imagining which suggested that he could see the situation very clearly, just as if he were there.

After completing the test of imagery, David became quite upset. With tears in his eyes, and emotion in his voice, he spent some time complaining that he felt very lonely, had never had any friends, that his parents were only interested in him to the extent that he was successful athletically and that he felt strong pressure from them to spend many long hours training, to the exclusion of other activities.

Routine enquiry was made to ensure that David suffered no heart condition which might contra-indicate electrical aversion therapy.

Session 3

After the second session, David was seen again by the consultant psychiatrist, who prescribed a minor tranquilliser and handed over the rest of David's treatment to me. At the third session, David reported that he had experienced none of the abnormal sexual urges or behaviour since taking the tranquillisers, with the exception of one night when he had not taken the tablets and had had dreams related to his abnormal sexual practices.

The third session was used to write 'scripts' to be used to help David obtain vivid fantasies in the treatment situation. In addition, Semantic Differential ratings of concepts related to his abnormal sexual behaviour, to normal sexual behaviour, and of neutral concepts, were obtained. These were to be used to assess progress of treatment (Marks and Sartorius, 1968). However, David, whose verbal ability seemed to be in the dull average range, did not appear to fully grasp how to complete the ratings. These were considered to be of dubious reliability, and were not in fact used to monitor treatment. Assessment of treatment was largely by clinical report from the patient and his girl friend.

Sessions 4-8

The next five sessions were daily aversion therapy sessions, in which

David would be instructed to visualise one of the situations evoking his abnormal sexual behaviour and would be shocked at a predetermined, randomly varying, point in the fantasy sequence. The scenes presented included situations currently evoking the abnormal sexual behaviour, and the original situation in the television room. A scene was presented until imagining it failed to produce any feelings of sexual arousal. Shock was administered on every trial, and a total of 82 trials was given in these five sessions.

Session 9

Reviewing the situation after five sessions of aversion therapy, David reported that he had not indulged in his abnormal sexual behaviour for a fortnight and that currently he only had very occasional fantasies or urges related to it. It was felt that this was a remarkably rapid response to treatment, and David's report was taken with some caution in the light of his previous performance as an informant. There was also the possibility that the effects observed might have been a function of the medication he was receiving, and the psychiatrist was asked to withdraw this to help find out what had been responsible for the change observed.

At this session, David reported that twice in the previous two days he had been unable to get sexually aroused when he had tried to have sexual intercourse with his girl friend. As it was considered that successful treatment of his abnormal sexual behaviour might well depend on the availability of satisfying normal heterosexual behaviour as an alternative response, this problem was explored further, and a more detailed heterosexual history obtained.

He had first attempted sex with a girl nearly two years previously. He had never been very sexually aroused by this girl, and had failed to get an erection on each of the six occasions he had tried to have sex with her.

With his current girl friend, Mary, he had been sexually aroused, and successfully had an erection and ejaculation the first time he attempted intercourse with her. He had not had an erection or ejaculation on subsequent occasions, although he had been sexually aroused. He described himself as feeling comfortable during sexual foreplay, but he became very tense when he actually attempted intercourse. Lately, he had not only failed to get an erection and ejaculation, but also failed to get sexually aroused when attempting intercourse. Since first attempting intercourse with Mary, the main situations in which he had obtained an erection had been those related to his abnormal sexual practices. Imagining having sex with Mary did not produce any feelings of sexual arousal.

It will be recalled that at the initial interview David had described his sexual relationship with Mary as quite satisfactory.

The preliminary formulation of David's impotence was that anxiety was associated with heterosexual intercourse, and by the reciprocally inhibitory relation existing between sexual arousal and anxiety (Wolpe, 1958) led to failure to achieve erection and ejaculation. David was asked to bring Mary with him to the next session, both to obtain her account of the situation and also to enlist her help in David's treatment.

Session 10

Mary was a 20-year-old physiotherapist, whose personality was quite different from David's. She was warm, open, relaxed and much more verbally fluent than David. She appeared to be quite a strong person who did not particularly care what others thought of her. She essentially confirmed the heterosexual history David had given. She also added that in the period preceding his appearance in court and since David had been extremely tense, anxious and irritable. She described him as 'on the verge of a nervous breakdown' before he sought help; he would become extremely tense and shake all over

A treatment for David's impotence, based on Wolpe's (1958) method of desensitisation of heterosexuality *in vivo*, was outlined to David and Mary. This included the following elements:

1   David should only attempt any form of sexual relations with Mary when he felt the desire to, rather than when he felt he was expected to but did not feel any particular desire himself.

2   David and Mary should proceed through the sequence of kissing, caressing, foreplay, etc., gradually, and only so long as David felt sexually excited and comfortable. At the first sign that David felt any discomfort, they should not proceed further. This was established as an agreement between David and Mary so that David would not feel under pressure to meet Mary's expectation that he would proceed to intercourse.

3   Before attempting intercourse, David should drink two pints of beer to reduce his general level of tension.

4   After attempting intercourse once, David and Mary should attempt intercourse again the same evening.

David and Mary agreed to try this treatment régime.

At this session, David reported that he still had not indulged in his deviant sexual behaviour, and had not had the urge to do so in any of the situations which had been treated by aversion therapy. He had experienced urges to undress while making repairs to his car. Mary independently reported that David was afraid to go out on his own as he still had urges to take his clothes off.

Session 11

David reported that he had intercourse with Mary, after he had drunk two pints of beer. He had achieved an erection and sex had been satisfying both to him and to her. Fantasies of sexual intercourse with Mary still failed to arouse him sexually, and he reported rarely feeling sexually aroused by her.

He had masturbated daily to the fantasy of taking his clothes off while out training, and had in fact on one occasion taken his clothes off while running down a disused railway track, a scene that had actually been employed in aversion therapy. He had had no thoughts of the consequences of this action at the time. He reported that he was preoccupied with thoughts related to undressing while out.

It was stressed again to David that he should on no account use fantasies related to his deviant behaviour in masturbation, as this would only increase the tendency for him to actually perform the behaviour. The basis of this advice was the model which had been formulated to explain the origin and maintenance of David's sexual deviance, and the evidence presented by Evans (1968). This demonstrated that exhibitionists with masturbatory practice to deviant fantasies took much longer to treat by aversion therapy than exhibitionists with more normal masturbation fantasies. David was encouraged to masturbate to female pin-ups in newspapers, which he had done on occasion before, with the intention of providing an alternative masturbatory fantasy which would strengthen the attachment of sexual arousal to more normal heterosexual stimuli.

Session 12

David was seen a week later with Mary. David reported they had had sex twice, very satisfactorily, and Mary confirmed this report. Both agreed that in terms of his mood, David was feeling better than he had for six months, and that there had been an improvement in his relations with his work mates and with his parents. The latter had been recently told of the true nature of David's problem, for the first time.

David had not indulged in any overt deviant behaviour since the previous incident, but continued to be troubled by thoughts and urges related to the deviant situations.

It was apparent by this time that the original doubts concerning the efficacy of the brief period of aversion therapy had been justified. As the improved heterosexual behaviour with Mary now provided a more viable alternative rewarded sexual response, it was decided to resume aversion therapy to eliminate the sexual arousal attached to the deviant stimuli. It was felt that an intensive course of twice daily treatments for a fortnight would be appropriate. Arrangements were made for David to be admitted as a day patient for a fortnight to receive this treatment. Practical considerations meant that this admission could not start for another seven weeks. David was seen twice in the intervening period.

Session 13

At this session David's mood was still good. He had not indulged in any overt abnormal sexual behaviour but was still troubled by urges to undress, particularly while out training. He had had sexual intercourse satisfactorily with Mary. As instructed, he had been masturbating to pin-ups of attractive young women in newspapers, and reported that he had experienced slight sexual excitement at the sight of them. However, fantasies of sexual relations with Mary still failed to produce any sexual arousal. In an attempt to increase the sexual arousal associated with fantasies of Mary, and thereby provide David with a sexually exciting fantasy alternative to his deviant ones, and also to improve his sexual relationship with Mary, he was instructed in the technique of orgasmic reconditioning (Marquis, 1970). This is a technique designed to increase the sexual arousal attached to a set of stimuli by altering masturbatory practice. David was instructed to masturbate to pin-ups and, just before the point of ejaculation, transfer his attention to fantasies of Mary, naked in bed. When he had satisfactorily done this on five occasions, he was told to start moving the introduction of the fantasy of Mary backward in time towards the beginning of masturbation. This was to be done gradually, so that sexual excitement was never lost when the transfer was made, until masturbation occurred using the fantasy of Mary from beginning to end. Thus, by a process of classical conditioning in which sexual excitement would be repeatedly paired with fantasies of Mary, it was intended to increase the sexual arousal attached to such fantasies.

Session 14

David reported that he was moody and worried about his relationship with Mary. She had been seeing a number of boys she had gone out with in the past. He had felt very embarrassed and tongue-tied in the situations where he was together with Mary and these boys, and had not joined in on trips they had taken together. He felt extremely jealous of her friendship with these boys, and worried most of the time about the security of his own relationship with her. He reiterated that he did not know how to be friendly, did not know what to say, and that, with the exception of Mary, he had never had any friends. He reported feeling very miserable and thoughts of suicide had occurred to him.

Sexual intercourse with Mary continued to be satisfactory. However, he had undressed outdoors on two occasions. On both occasions, David had been walking through a field looking on to some houses, and had noticed a young woman, with something of a reputation for sexual promiscuity, through the window of her house. He had become sexually excited and undressed in the field.

Day Patient Treatment

David was seen twelve days later at the beginning of his fortnight's period of treatment, and reported no deviant thoughts or acts since session 14.

Reviewing the situations which were involved in the deviant thoughts and urges, and which had led him to the act of undressing, revealed that the situations which had been treated in the initial phase of aversion therapy no longer figured prominently. Rather, David now found that in a number of situations which would evoke 'normal' heterosexual arousal, for example, seeing a pretty girl, he experienced sexual excitement and the urge to undress. It appeared that treatment to date had been effective in altering the stimulus situations which would evoke sexual excitement but had not been effective in preventing this sexual excitement leading to the urge to undress. Three treatment sessions were devoted to electrical aversion therapy directed at fantasies involving the most recent situations where David had undressed. These fairly soon failed to evoke any sexual excitement in the treatment situation. However, David continued to report a number of occasions in which he had experienced 'urges' in a wide variety of situations. Careful examination of these suggested that they were situations where sexual arousal was not necessarily inappropriate; what was inappropriate was that such sexual arousal was frequently accompanied by the urge to undress. It was considered that further treatment using electrical aversion therapy to imaginal stimuli was of limited value, as there was a wide variety of heterosexual situations which might provoke sexual excitement and the urge to undress. It was not really possible to attempt to treat all such possible situations. Further, there was the danger that one might actually reduce some of the 'normal' 'desirable' element of heterosexual arousal associated with these scenes. The task of aversion therapy was reconceptualised in terms of the need to administer shock when sexual arousal was followed by the urge to undress in public, but not to administer it when sexual arousal was not followed by the urge to undress. It appeared very difficult to establish this discrimination by using aversion therapy to imaginal stimuli in the hospital situation, as the urge to actually undress as a result of imagining arousing scenes was by now fairly minimal. The solution to this problem was seen to be to provide David with a small portable shock device that he could carry around with him (McGuire and Vallance, 1964) and administer shocks to himself whenever he felt the urge to undress in public, but not when he felt sexually aroused when this was not followed by the urge to undress. Unfortunately, no such apparatus was available at this time. It was not practical to use the large shock box used in the previous aversion therapy sessions. The best that could be done pending the arrival of a portable shock box from the manufacturer was to instruct David to inflict pain on himself by pulling sharply at his hair whenever he felt the urge to undress.

At this time, a general review of David's problems was undertaken. One of the problems that had hindered the assessment of the efficacy of previous treatment approaches, in addition to the possible unreliability of David as an informant, was the variability in the frequency of the problem behaviour. This appeared to vary from one time to another over and above the effects that could be expected from the treatment procedures used. Re-examining the notes that had been made from interviews, it appeared that there was some relation between David's general mood and the frequency of his undressing and deviant urges. It appeared that when David was generally worried or depressed the abnormal behaviour increased in frequency, and when he was feeling generally well the behaviour decreased in frequency, for example, the initial rapid reduction in the frequency of the behaviour following the prescription of minor tranquillisers before the initial phase of aversion therapy, and the fact that the occasions of undressing before the phase of day-patient treatment coincided with a period when David was very worried, depressed, and jealous about his relationship with Mary, and generally concerned about his inability to make relationships.

Up to this point, the importance of David's loneliness and social difficulties had been seen mainly in terms of their significance in the development of his problem behaviour. They were seen as preventing the development of more normal heterosexual behaviour. However, it now appeared that these difficulties might also have had an important effect in maintaining the problem behaviour. The undressing, as well as providing direct sexual reinforcement, might also have provided reinforcement in the form of tension-reduction and temporary relief from the worries caused by his social difficulties (see Bandura, 1969, p. 466).

As a day patient, David found himself with people, some of his own age, whom he had never met before, and with whom he had the opportunity to make some form of social contact. In the first few days of his admission, David had reported difficulties in making contact with these people. It was decided to use the opportunity this situation provided to instruct David in assertive training (Wolpe, 1958) and provide advice on how to handle social relationships. Assertive training seemed particularly appropriate as David's social difficulties stemmed largely from a social anxiety related to his extreme concern about what others would think of him.

As a first step, David was told to:

1 Be himself, 'not give a damn' what others thought of him, and to use his brief stay as a day patient as an experiment in being himself.
2 Express his feelings and opinions, contradicting others if necessary.
3 Be spontaneous, rather than calculating the impression he would achieve.
4 Use facial expression to emphasise feelings.
5 Use the word 'I' as often as possible.
6 Accept praise, and not apologise.

David seemed to grasp the ideas very well, and set off from this session determined to put them into practice. He was subsequently seen twice daily for the remainder of his admission as a day patient, to obtain reports on his progress, reinforce his social successes, and provide further guidance and an opportunity for rehearsal of social situations.

This procedure had an immediate effect in improving David's relationships with other day patients. He was delighted with his immediate success in improving his social performance, which gave him added confidence, thereby improving his ability to relate still further.

David rapidly made a number of friends among his fellow day patients during the period of his admission, and met with them socially in the evenings and at the weekends. With the opportunity to give fairly intensive guidance and reinforcement for his social behaviour as a day patient, David was told to visit relatives at home and talk to them, and to talk more to his fellow athletes when he went training. A number of social situations were rehearsed and role-played with him. He accomplished these set tasks, if with some difficulty in the beginning.

By the end of his fortnight's admission as a day patient, David's social skills were much improved, and he reported feeling much happier. He continued to experience occasional urges to undress, however. At the last session of his admission, he was reminded of the principles of assertion training and told to coninue to expand the extent of his social contact. He was told that a portable electric shock device was on order and he would be provided with it when it arrived.

He was seen a fortnight later, when he reported that he was getting on much better socially with his workmates and with Mary's friends. He had, however, undressed on two occasions, at night in a corner of a field overlooking some houses where he could see young women through the windows. Both of these occasions had been at the end of days where thoughts related to undressing had been on his mind all day. He had felt the need to relieve them by actually undressing. He had tried pulling his hair and slapping himself to remove the thoughts, but this had had only a temporary effect.

After four weeks David was seen again, with Mary. He said that he felt everything had now changed; he had been feeling very much better since he was last seen, he had not had a single urge or deviant thought, nor undressed in this time, his relationship with Mary, his parents, and people in general were much improved, and he had regained weight that he had lost. He certainly appeared very well, and confident, and Mary independently confirmed that a great change had occurred, and that he now seemed to be over his old problem. I pointed out to David that he had in the past not always told the exact truth about his situation, and suggested to him that he might be painting a somewhat optimistic picture. Both David and Mary convincingly rejected this possibility. The portable shock device had arrived by this time, but David declined to take it with him as he was convinced that this problem was finished. I arranged to see him in six months' time to review the situation, but stressed to David and Mary that if there were any recurrence of the thoughts, urges or actions he should contact me immediately.

I saw both Mary and David at the six-month follow-up, when they both agreed in the face of my mild scepticism, that 'everything in the garden was lovely'. There had been absolutely no recurrence of the sexual problem in the six-month period. Sexual relations between them were fine, David was much less jealous, and they were planning to get married. David continued to relate much better to others, and now had his own circle of friends, with whom he would go out without Mary. David's running had improved greatly and he had in fact won the last three major races he had entered for.

Twelve months later. I saw David again. In many ways his improvement had been maintained and extended, but there were still a number of remaining problems. There had been no recurrence of David's deviant sexual behaviour since I had last seen him making a total of 18 months free of this problem. The urges related to the deviant sexual behaviour had not been totally eliminated, however, and recurred at a frequency of approximately once per week. The improvement in his general social relations had been maintained. David was now part of the social group of the boys who trained for athletics with him, and went to parties and dances with them. He was also talking more to his parents and workmates. Social contact still posed some problems and David was still somewhat shy. He and Mary had parted three months before I saw him. They had constantly argued and eventually decided to part. Much of the argument was related to sex, as David had had a recurrence of his impotence, and estimated that sex between him and Mary was only really satisfactory on about one-fifth of attempts. He had not been out with other girls since the break up of his relation with Mary. He felt apprehensive at the prospect of forming a relationship with another girl friend, both because he still felt somewhat shy and awkward with girls, and because he anticipated he might make a fool of himself because of his impotence. However, he was now sufficiently friendly with the boys he knew to consider seeking their advice and guidance as to how best to approach girls.

David's mood had in general been good, but on occasion he became worried by his social difficulties. His running had been consistently of a high standard.

Overall, David felt that his general situation was much better than it had been in the period when I had been seeing him regularly, and he felt optimistic that he would resolve his remaining problems.

Comment

It could not be said that David was a case where a thorough, accurate, initial formulation of the problem led immediately to the design of a treatment régime which was implemented flawlessly, and led rapidly to total therapeutic success. For that very reason, it may be instructive to examine David's treatment to see in what way it could have been improved.

The first point to note is that the success of a behavioural treatment probably depends to a large extent on the accuracy of the behavioural formulation of the problem. It is this which will determine the treatment régime employed. In any complex case where there are a number of problem areas, the difficulty of deciding the nature of the relationship between problem areas arises, for example, does problem area A have an effect on problem area B, does problem area B have an effect on problem area A, are problem areas A and B jointly affected by problem area C, or is there no relation between problem areas A and B? Usually, the choice of treatment régime will be powerfully affected by the decision as to which of these alternatives is actually true.

In David's case, the initial formulation placed most weight on sexual reinforcement as a factor maintaining the problem behaviour. The initial treatment plan, directed at removing the ability of certain stimulus situations to evoke sexual arousal, reflected this formulation. David's difficulties in social relationships, while recognised, were considered of importance in the origin of David's sexual problem, but were not ascribed major importance in its maintenance. With the benefit of hindsight, this formulation was in error. The most marked change in the sexual problem occurred when attention was directed at David's social difficulties. This observation suggests that the influence of these difficulties was much more important than the initial formulation recognised. Clearly, the sexual reinforcement obtained from the abnormal behaviour was one factor maintaining it, and treatment directed in this direction probably had some effect in determining the eventual outcome of treatment. However, it would appear that David's social difficulties may have been the most important factor in maintaining the problem behaviour. This may have been because there was an appreciable element of tension- and discomfort-relief in the reinforcement obtained from the abnormal sexual behaviour, so that David would experience temporary relief from the distress he suffered as a result of his social difficulties, by indulging in the behaviour. Alternatively, the distress occasioned by his social difficulties may have weakened David's self-control of his problem behaviour.

An additional aspect in which the initial formulation was in error was the assumption that David had available a normal, satisfying, heterosexual alternative to his problem sexual behaviour. For this reason, no treatment was initially directed at David's impotence as this was not recognised as a problem. This error in formulation arose from false information provided at the initial interview. When this information was corrected, treatment was changed accordingly.

David's case illustrates very well the link between the accuracy of the behavioural formulation and the success of the subsequent behavioural treatment. Is it possible to learn from his case how the errors that were made might have been avoided, and the most effective régime implemented at an earlier point in treatment?

There are two main steps in the search for an accurate formulation. The first is the generation of a number of alternative formulations. The second is the evaluation of the worth of the various alternative formulations.

The generation of a number of alternative formulations is likely to increase the probability of reaching a correct formulation. In David's case, the initial formulation appeared quite plausible and so little attempt was made to generate additional alternative formulations. Perhaps we should always, as a discipline, explicitly attempt to construct a number of rival formulations to account for a problem, however plausible the initial formulation may appear.

One obvious way to generate more formulations is to collect more information. A more lengthy initial investigation of David's problem might have provided the opportunity for alternative formulations to emerge.

Another way to increase the number of alternatives under consideration is to review the published literature on a particular problem. If, in David's case, a comprehensive literature search had been conducted initially, the therapist might have been reminded of the work of Bond and Hutchison (1964), which emphasised the importance of stress experiences provoking feelings of inadequacy in eliciting exhibitionistic behaviour.

Clearly, it would be too time-consuming to conduct a search of the literature for every new patient. Perhaps, instead, each therapist or group of therapists could assemble over time dossiers of the relevant publications for each particular problem area. Such collections have been found to provide a time-saving source of reference. They also make it possible for therapists to begin to construct flow charts in which they formalise the consideration of alternative formulations, and their associated treatments, and make explicit the criteria for deciding between rival formulations.

As well as reviewing published work on a particular problem area, the therapist, of course, will have to draw on his knowledge of experimental psychology and his accumulated clinical experience, in generating alternative hypotheses to account for a particular problem.

Having generated a number of rival hypotheses, we have the problem of deciding which, if any of them, is correct. In David's case, the initial formulation was simply assessed in a global way in terms of its plausibility in relation to the facts available. None of the implications or predictions of the model were explicitly tested out. In practice, this global approach to examining the plausibility of the model was not very fruitful.

If we regard the rival explanatory models of a problem behaviour as hypotheses which we wish to test, then clearly we could attempt to test these hypotheses by conducting a number of experiments on the patient. In these single case investigations, we could experimentally manipulate the variables of interest with a view to testing the predictions derived from the rival hypotheses. In general, manipulation of the variables of interest is often practically difficult, and the experiments required to reach reasonably definite conclusions are very time-consuming. While this approach might be the most elegant scientifically, it is in practice far too lengthy for the workaday clinician.

While we may have to abandon the use of intensive experimental investigations, we can still attempt to test predictions from rival hypotheses by making use of high quality clinical data.

A good data recording system is perhaps the most effective and practical means of examining the validity of rival formulations, and of avoiding therapeutic blind alleys. The method of data collection used with David was fairly crude, consisting of retrospective report of large samples of behaviour at a time. It is known that this is a procedure of dubious validity. A better recording system would have been to ask David to note every occurrence of a deviant thought or behaviour, the circumstances in which it occurred, its consequences, and any other information thought relevant to deciding between rival formulations, during an extended base-line period. This would have improved the chances of being able to make firm decisions between rival hypotheses, and might have generated new formulations. For example, this procedure most probably would have pointed up the co-variation of feelings of inadequacy and episodes of undressing. It would certainly have allowed a better evaluation of alternative formulations than a judgment based on their overall plausibility. Further, the continuation of such an improved data collection system after the base-line period would be expected to provide a more sensitive indication of the effects of the treatments used, allowing a more rapid rejection of ineffective treatments.

There is a tendency in behaviour therapy to be impatient to begin the treatment proper as soon as possible, and to regard time spent on lengthy initial exploration, measurement, and analysis, as a luxury which workaday clinicians cannot afford. To some extent, David is an example of what can happen with this approach. The right formulation and treatment are reached eventually, but the overall effectiveness and efficiency of treatment are less than if more care and time had been spent on the initial assessment and analysis of the problem. It is often a case of more haste, less speed.

5   A Complex View of Simple Phobias[1]

R. S. Hallam

The phobias are not the most obvious choice for case-study presentation. Behaviour therapy has developed reliable and effective methods for eliminating abnormal fears and so the author could be accused of lacking enterprise or a sense of challenge. In actuality a close examination of the treatment of phobias provides an opportunity to look at questions which have not yet begun to be asked in relation to other psychological disorders. The very success of exposure methods, such as desensitization and flooding, produces a situation in which the outcome of therapy is more likely to depend on the characteristics of the client and his environment than poor technique or misplaced therapeutic effort. This confidence in our methods renders more interesting the client who seems eminently suited to exposure treatment but fails with this approach. Equally interesting is the client who responds quickly with one method of exposure but not another. This individual variability with which case studies are concerned is often lost in the error term in the large, controlled group studies which have investigated the overall therapeutic effectiveness of these techniques. In any event this individual variation seems to be poorly correlated with the measures that researchers have sought fit to include in their battery of prognostic tests and remains to be accounted for.

The four cases for presentation in this paper will be discussed within the context of a theoretical model which the author has found useful in devising treatment programmes for phobic clients. This model incorporates variables which might conceivably throw some light on the problem of predicting individual outcomes. First, though, a few points of criticism directed at attempts to predict

[1] This article owes a great deal to discussions with Dr I. M. Marks and Dr J. Connolly of the Institute of Psychiatry, University of London. I would also like to thank the therapists in the Psychological Treatment Section for permission to write up their cases.

individual outcome in large group experiments. In the interests of 'good methodology' these experiments contain certain artificial features which make it difficult to obtain a reliable treatment effect in all cases. The first is the problem of finding groups of clients with identical behavioural problems. As a very poor approximation to this requirement clients are frequently grouped together on the basis of a similar diagnostic label. Where multiple problems exist the interaction between each problem and final outcome is often ignored. The second artificial feature is the inflexibility of standardized approaches (even assuming that the therapist can maintain this standardization). Length of therapy may be strictly curtailed or unheralded reversals in treatment strategy may occur at an inopportune moment. Put concisely, clients are tailored to the therapy rather than the therapy to the client.

Finally, group studies are interested in group effects and therefore ignore differences in the ongoing life events of each client. While this can be justified statistically (since the effects of these differences are assumed to cancel each other out in each group), they are quite likely to determine how the client finally fares in therapy. As an example, a car phobic may witness, or be involved in, a car accident during the course of treatment and thereby become resensitized. Other important events such as marriage, bereavement or change of employment are not uncommon during therapy. Many life events are not, of course, strictly independent of the treatment the client is receiving; conversely one cannot ascertain a 'pure' treatment effect unless the interaction between treatment interventions and life events can be disentangled. Therefore, in attempting to predict therapeutic outcome in an individual case it is necessary to measure variables which are not typically included in large-scale group experiments.

The case study comes into its own by portraying the detailed events of therapy, including the therapist's ingenuity in applying general principles. In this instance the description of cases will be preceded by a conceptual model of the treatment process, or rather, a small part of it. In this way it is hoped to systematize in an explicit form a rather intuitive process, and to take away some of the *ad hoc* nature of case presentation.

As an overall framework we might use the analogy of a management system in a business enterprise. The client, the therapist and the external environment can be viewed as a system of interrelated acts and processes with definable inputs and outputs. Some components of the system will be related by causal mechanisms and others by procedural rules depending on the nature of the interactions. The system will continue to function until the state of the components attain certain critical values – hopefully the client's degree of satisfaction rather than the therapist's degree of impatience. The description of such systems, some of whose features will be shared by all therapeutic schools, would require a very determined collection of data in the natural setting.

The most interesting part of the system from our point of view, and the one most difficult to plumb, is located somewhere in the clinician's brain. It determines the nature, order and timing of therapeutic interventions under the influence of inputs from a variety of sources including a general model of the psychological disorder in question. In the case of phobias the model might be concerned with the ways in which fears are currently maintained in the environment. The data derived from the client will then be fitted to the general model in order to make an informed guess at the contingencies and processes thought to maintain his irrational fear. It has to be accepted that the model will be based on a paucity of hard data and contain its own measure of speculative assumptions. This comes close to the actual situation of the clinician who is forced to act in the face of ignorance. Nevertheless, the consistent application of the model to actual problems should gradually enlighten the user as to its redundant or invalid assumptions. The dangers of this approach as a scientific method must, however, be guarded against. Such models may be used to validate in retrospect, rather than to guide prospectively; alternatively they may have no predictive power, if they are ambiguous. Finally, the model's predictions may be self-fulfilling if the client is persuaded to share its assumptions as a necessary part of treatment (for example, as in faith-healing), or if the therapist fails to use the consequences of his interventions as a source of corrective feedback. There are several elementary strategies which can be employed to obtain this feedback in single cases but they will not be discussed here.

To recapitulate, the model to be presented is one small component in the overall system of management of phobias. The implications for treatment will be of a general nature, and the specific solution will be determined by practical constraints such as the client's imagery ability or the availability of props if the phobic situation needs to be simulated. The case histories to follow will illustrate the use of the model.

A model of factors maintaining fear

The elements of the model (from left to right in Figure 5·1) are broadly classifiable into external stimulation, central processing and various response alternatives. Positive and negative feedback

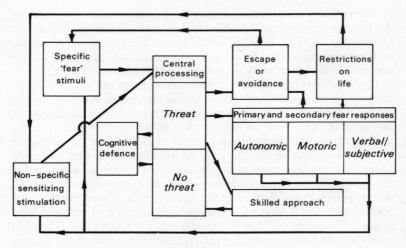

FIGURE 5·1 *A model of factors maintaining fear*

influences are denoted by the arrowed lines. The model is concerned with processes that *maintain* fear; the role played by past-learning and genetic influences has not been included. Two classes of external stimulus are distinguished:

1 Specific stimuli which have the potential to arouse fear. The characteristics of these stimuli have been described by Marks (1969) and Gray (1971).

2 Sensitizing stimuli whose non-specific effects influence the persons's sensitivity to specific fear stimuli. Examples are physical illness, the effects of disappointment, overcrowding in the home, etc.

The response to the fear stimulus will depend on the interaction of many variables at a central level culminating in an appraisal of the degree of threat the stimulus presents. The fear stimulus is defined as non-threatening if it can be approached and handled in an adaptive way, without disorganizing emotional concomitants. Skilled avoidance, although it may *not* be accompanied by emotional arousal (Grings and Lockhart, 1966), is seen as a response to threat-appraisal since it operates by by-passing the source of fear stimulation rather than coping with it. It is assumed that other threat-responses will be elicited if avoidance fails. Amongst the factors determining appraisal of threat will be the effects of previous experience with the fear situation, including beliefs about the likely consequences of approaching it and beliefs about the effects of fear itself.

The emotional response to threat (fear) has three main components (Lang, 1968):

1 Autonomic arousal (rapid pulse and respiration, sweating, facial pallor, etc.).
2 Motoric (trembling, freezing, disruption of skilled performance, etc.).
3 Subjective/verbal (awareness of somatic sensations, and statements such as 'I am panicking').

These components may appear together but their relative importance varies from client to client. Occasionally, components of the fear response itself appear to have acquired an escape or avoidance function. Some of the cases to follow will illustrate this point.

A number of authors have suggested that there are two positive feedback loops maintaining fear responses. The first (Lader and Matthews, 1968) assumes that the expression of fear can have *non-specific* sensitizing effects on subsequent exposure to the fear stimulus. Under certain conditions this leads to a spiralling panic attack terminated by exhaustion or fainting. It is not too uncommon to find that clients undergoing exposure *in vivo* suffer from a heightened state of nervousness following, or in anticipation of a treatment session. A variety of somatic symptoms are reported, such as unpleasant dreams, loss of appetite, diarrhoea and palpitations. In our experience these clients are less likely to be treated successfully by real-life exposure methods.

In the second mechanism, described by Eysenck (1968), *specific* feedback from components of the fear response (or its environmental consequences) is experienced as unpleasant and a secondary fear is conditioned to elements of the primary fear response. For example, palpitations may be thought to signal a heart attack, verbal statements such as 'I am going to panic' or 'I am going to blush' may trigger the self-same reactions.

There are additional feedback links which are more speculative. Escape from or avoidance of the fear situation may effectively provide relief in the short term but in the long term lead to a stressful limitation of daily activities. For example, the inability to go shopping may have consequences which sensitize the individual still further to specific fear situations. Similarly 'cognitive defensive strategies' such as intellectualization, or derealization (Lader, 1969), are usually only partially effective in transforming the appraisal of 'threat' to 'non-threat', and they may bring about difficulties in social communication. The maintenance of fears by rewarding contingencies has not been included in the model although this mechanism is not too uncommon. Ramsey (1971) has described how the needs of a marriage partner were satisfied by a client's agoraphobic behaviour.

It follows from this model that therapeutic intervention can take a variety of forms depending on which element of the system is attacked, for instance, reduction of non-specific stresses, manipulation of cognitive appraisal or self-statements, prevention of secondary fear, encouragement of skilled approach and so on. The following case histories illustrate how the model aids the therapist in devising treatment strategies.

Case histories

In the first example, our initial intervention failed. The problem was re-examined in terms of the model and subsequent treatment was rapidly effective.

Case 1

Mrs P was referred because she was unable to use the telephone. Up to this point her life had been free of problems and she had had no previous encounter with psychiatry. She was young, attractive, and married to a successful businessman. There had been a gradual increase of her difficulty in using the phone over a three-year period. It began with uneasiness, which worsened, until finally she was just able to make a well-rehearsed phone call to her husband. The first few words were the most troublesome; they would either be blocked altogether or come out as a stutter. Once the conversation got under way her dysfluencies disappeared, and in normal conversation Mrs P was well-spoken and articulate. The problem had spread to requests for fares on buses and asking for items in shops. On one occasion she had bought mince at the butcher's because she was unable to ask for steak. In these situations she was afraid of being unable to say what she wanted to say and appearing a fool. In restaurants she would point to items on the menu rather than ask for them.

The problem had unfortunate consequences on her style of living. She was forced to give up her secretarial job; in addition, she became more socially isolated because she would avoid travelling by bus to see her friends or calling them up on the phone. This was particularly distressing as she described her basic personality as extraverted and frivolous.

When first seen Mrs P was mildly depressed and suffered from sleeplessness, headaches and palpitations. She had lost any interest in love-making over the previous nine months although formerly sex had been frequent and enjoyable. We could not determine whether this depressive state arose in response to her telephoning difficulties (an example of feedback sensitization) or whether it was in some way causative. We hoped that it would disappear as her social life was returned to normal.

Our choice of treatment was determined by the simple notion that speech-blocking was a motor component of a primary fear response to certain kinds of social situation. Her response to a fears survey questionnaire indicated that social anxieties were present. For example, she reported being particularly uncomfortable if suddenly 'spot-lighted' by a question when in conversation with a group of friends. However, physiological and subjective components of fear were not prominent; she did not interpret her palpitations in social situations as a sign of anxiety. In the first two treatment sessions, totalling three hours, Mrs P was required to repeatedly initiate conversations on the telephone with the therapist and other co-operative persons. She found this task a little easier at the end of the first session but there was no carry-over of improvement to the beginning of the second session. When interviewed at the beginning of the third session it was apparent that no gains had been made in the home environment.

It was unusual to find this lack of improvement in such a specific problem, and so we assumed that our treatment strategy was incorrect. Her secondary fear of appearing foolish when unable to speak fluently had already been noted. In terms of the model, this secondary fear (of the consequences of her primary speech-blocking) could be seen as part of a positive feedback loop. This loop would be interrupted if speech-blocking was prevented. Treatment was therefore modified to eliminate errors. When using the telephone Mrs P was instructed (a) to *wait* until she felt able to speak fluently and (b) to speak slowly in time with a metronome. The opening statements were graded in complexity with progress dependent on fluency at an earlier stage, for example, (1) Hello, (2) Hello, Janet, (3) Hello, Janet, this is —, etc.

Fluency was rapidly achieved within three hours' treatment spread over two sessions. Subsequent progress was monitored by telephone as the client lived a long distance from the clinic. At home, she was able to produce slow and rhythmic speech simply by imagining the metronome or tapping her feet. Within one month she was phoning most of her friends with ease and she began practising in shops and on buses. Two weeks later she had taken a part-time job as a secretary and was using the phone all the time.

At the follow-up assessment three months after the last treatment session, Mrs P reported that there was a slight initial slowness in her speech at the beginning of a telephone conversation, but it was not noticeable to others. She was shopping regularly and making requests without stuttering.

The elimination of her specific problem was accompanied by an overall improvement in her mood and somatic symptoms. Scores on mood check lists returned to within normal limits.

Case 2

This client's problem could be seen as a complex interaction between avoidance behaviour, autonomic components and threat appraisal. The treatment intervention was relatively simple and improvement occurred as predicted.

Mrs D's problems dated back some thirteen years to the time just before her marriage. While on holiday and sharing a bed with a girl friend, she was told her breath smelled. Being a shy and reserved person the idea that she smelled preyed on her mind and grew in intensity. At the time of referral the idea had a delusional quality which hinted at a more serious diagnosis. Sometimes she thought she could smell the odour of her body ('like drains or BO'), but her conviction was not firm because she frequently asked her husband whether she smelled. She had not spoken to her neighbour for years ever since a certain conversation in which she thought smell was mentioned.

Previous treatment had been ineffective. Tablets had been prescribed to 'calm her nerves', and at one point she was admitted as an in-patient to a mental hospital. There she was resentful of the psychiatric interpretations of her symptoms and left after two days. On another occasion she became depressed but refused to see her local psychiatrist.

Her strange belief had extensive repercussions on her life and that of her husband and young son. The main consequence of her concern about smell was an avoidance of other people, but this did not apply to her family or to her mother who lived near by. She was unable to go out unless accompanied by a member of the family. In particular, she disliked the close proximity of other persons in shops, restaurants, churches or other enclosed places. She managed to visit the church (not the local one) but had to sit in the back row or stand away from others. If friends visited she sat away from them and would have to leave the room if smell was mentioned by them, or on the television. Naturally the effect of this behaviour 'enslaved' her husband because he could not bring friends home or visit them and he was constantly barraged by requests for reassurance.

At the first appointment Mrs D was interviewed with her

husband. She sat stiffly in her chair and was reluctant to give much detail of her problems. Mr D was more forthcoming and was clearly sympathetic and understanding towards his wife. The marriage appeared stable, although Mr D was anxious that his wife be treated. Mrs D was evidently less certain and kept her husband in check if she was cast in a bad light. Her quiet-spoken manner belied an obvious authority in the marriage. In her behaviour, she was markedly anxious, flushed, and blinked her eyes excessively. In the interview we looked for evidence of other obsessive ideas or compulsive behaviour but Mrs D denied them. However, her husband had informed the referring psychiatrist that his wife was very house-proud, sometimes washing the floor five or six times per day. She bathed frequently and often changed her clothing during the day.

It was decided to observe Mrs D's behaviour at close quarters and so she was accompanied to the local shopping area. As expected, she avoided joining a queue in a shop and her face was flushed most of the time. However, to our surprise, she was much less anxious in the crowded conditions of London than in her rural home surroundings. Complete strangers were tolerated much more easily than acquaintances, while doctors were no problem at all. This was unlike the typical fear of an agoraphobic which increases rather than decreases with distance from the home.

The choice of treatment strategy in this interesting problem depended on our conceptualization of the maintaining factors. Seeing the belief as primary would suggest a cognitive or attitude-change approach. Alternatively, there was the possibility of desensitization to social comments relating to smell, or to social situations in general. The method of approach was in any case limited by her difficulty in reaching the clinic. This entailed a long journey by car with her husband who had to take time off work.

Our view of the problem followed the line that the primary fear was related to social situations which demanded a moderate degree of intimacy, such as 'small talk' and close physical proximity. The autonomic component of this fear was excessive perspiration and flushing. This response had apparently acquired special significance in this client's system of beliefs. One might speculate that she was predisposed to obsessive concern about dirt and smells which led to ruminations about her own body-odour but it seemed more likely to us that the expression of her belief served as a means of escape from or avoidance of social situations. Certainly, this client avoided social situations far more effectively than most socially phobic individuals manage to do, though at great cost to herself and her family.

On the basis of this analysis it was decided to extinguish Mrs D's

anxieties by graded exposure to the avoided situations. In this way
the two factors thought to maintain her belief – the automatic
response of sweating, and the instrumental value of the belief in
terms of escape and avoidance – should slowly be eliminated. A
third mechanism which may have been maintaining the belief was
the reassurance provided by her husband in answer to her requests
to know whether she smelled. To be told that she did not could have
maintained requests for reassurance by providing some relief from
tension. Any response presumably gave her reason to infer that her
questions were meaningful. The husband was therefore instructed
to ignore all references to smell by saying nothing, and this strategy
was also adopted by the therapist.

The programme of exposure to the feared situation was in part
conducted in the therapist's company, but the greater part of the
responsibility for treatment was assigned to the client. Tasks were
set each week, first within the client's capabilities, and success or
failure was to be recorded on weekly record sheets which were
brought to therapeutic sessions or posted to the therapist. Due
praise was given for tasks successfully performed, either directly, or
by letter. The following tasks were suggested for the first few weeks
– waving to a neighbour in his garden, saying 'Hello' to
acquaintances in the street, following different routes when taking
her son to school (so that meeting someone was more probable),
going to the cinema and going shopping. She was instructed to stay
in the shop until any uncomfortable feelings of being hot and sweaty
had subsided, and definitely *not* leave because of these feelings. She
rated her discomfort (anxiety) and the intensity of her belief that
she smelled in these situations on a simple scale. In addition to her
task assignments the therapist spent 5 sessions (14 hours) with the
client giving her experience of crowds in shops, buses and other
situations in London (including a state royal visit) during the height
of summer. Mrs D felt hot, flushed and clammy much of the time but
each session was accompanied by a diminution of these responses.
Questions such as 'Do I smell?' were consistently ignored. Joining a
queue seemed to be the most difficult situation, although she was
not allowed to avoid doing so. Mrs D was persuaded to come to the
clinic alone by train for the fifth session and by this time she was
feeling greatly improved in many ways. She could enter shops
accompanied by her husband and stay there until shopping was
completed. Thoughts about smell were less frequent and of shorter
duration.

Her husband was acting in a therapeutic capacity at home on
instructions and in the sixth session the therapist withdrew, leaving
the client and her husband to make a prolonged shopping trip to

Oxford Street.

The improvement observed in London was showing further signs of generalizing to the home environment. For example, Mrs D had been able to shop alone on a few occasions. In order to consolidate these gains the therapist travelled to the client's home and spent three hours with her in the local shopping areas. In a variety of shops and restaurants, Mrs D tolerated her initial anxiety and discomfort, although the therapist had to exercise tact and persuasion to prevent her from leaving the sometimes hot, crowded conditions of the shops. Thirty minutes to an hour was usually long enough to see her unease dissipate. Awkward situations often crop up with *in vivo* treatment of this nature. On this occasion a prolonged sojourn in one shop aroused the suspicions of a floor walker who followed them. Mrs D was a regular customer of this particular shop and so the situation could not be explained. There was no alternative but to leave.

From this point on Mrs D managed her own problem and simply came to the clinic for the resetting of social targets, discussion of progress and praise for targets achieved. One-hourly sessions were scheduled monthly while record sheets were posted weekly. Progress was not always smooth and at times Mrs D became disheartened; nevertheless considerable progress was made, so that over a period of six months she learned to tolerate eating in restaurants, going to the cinema, shopping alone, visiting friends, staying with them overnight, and having friends visit her. She could go out anywhere if she bathed first, but could visit the clinic without bathing. Not all of these activities gave her enjoyment, nor did she make the suggestions to go out – these came from her husband. Nevertheless she was keen to continue her home tasks until she was free of all anxiety.

At a follow-up appointment one month later Mrs D's improvement had continued. She now looked forward to seeing her neighbours; the first time she spoke to her nextdoor neighbour she thinks she almost 'fell through the ground'. Naturally her husband was very pleased with this progress.

As predicted, thoughts about smell diminished in direct relationship to her social anxiety. Mrs D always rated both at the same level on her weekly record sheets. The observable signs of her anxiety in the interview situations had disappeared. She looked cool and relaxed rather than flushed and tense, and the eye-blinking was no longer present. However, the items on the fear questionnaire which related to social situations were still rated as moderately fear-provoking although there was some reduction in her fear of eating and drinking with other people. Mrs D is still a timid woman and it may require further behavioural gains before she changes her view of herself towards a more extraverted, socially adept image. The important consequence of treatment was the removal of gross limitation on her life and elimination of an erroneous belief that she smelled.

Case 3

This case illustrates how a very simple intervention rapidly eliminated a problem of six years' duration. Again, the model was helpful in understanding the sequence of events that maintained the problem.

Mr K complained of nausea and a fear of vomiting before and during his social engagements. Frequently he had to excuse himself from company in order to vomit in the bathroom. The problem was a relatively isolated social difficulty. In his job as a sales supervisor he told of his ability to deal with difficult customers, superiors and work people. His main concern was that through declining too many social invitations his advancement at work would suffer.

In the initial interview, Mr K presented himself as a quietly-spoken, diffident young man who talked frankly and freely. Although accepting that he was insecure, he was unable to account for the origins of his present problem. His mother had deserted her husband soon after his birth leaving his father and paternal grandparents to bring him up. This they did kindly but rather strictly. From 4-6 years of age he was fostered when his father became ill.

There had been no previous psychiatric encounters and the only difficulties of note were in the area of sexual performance. During his teens he suffered from partial impotence and delayed ejaculation but these problems largely disappeared after his marriage at the age of 20.

The history of the vomiting problem was as follows. At the age of 18, while in a station bar waiting for a train to take him to a holiday camp where his mother worked, he felt sick while drinking a glass of beer, and vomited. He recalled no unease at the time and attributed it to 'a bad glass of beer'.

The following evening he went out to dinner with his friend, his mother and several other people. It was an enjoyable evening but he became unwell during the course of the meal and left the table to vomit in the lavatory – he returned to enjoy the rest of the evening. One week later his friend phoned him to invite him to go on a blind date with two girls to the cinema. He felt nauseated throughout the day to follow but attributed this to indigestion left over from his experiences the previous weekend. He was not aware of any anxiety and was in fact looking forward to the date. The girls did not turn up, he and his friend went into the cinema and during the programme he felt increasingly nauseated and left before its completion and vomited.

For 18 months after this, although he went to work every day, he did not go out socially and thought that if he did go out to enjoy himself he would vomit. He entertained young women at home but could not escort them to the bus stop at the end of the evening. It was not until meeting his wife-to-be that he began to go out socially. On their first meeting he became ill, vomited and returned to enjoy the evening with her. This pattern remained constant ever since.

On receiving an invitation face to face, by phone or by letter, he would feel nauseous for perhaps a couple of hours. This also happened if it occurred to him to go out, even to events that involved no eating or drinking, like the cinema or a football match. The nausea usually faded only to recur an hour or two before the social engagement. He would resist the urge to vomit, become hot and sweaty and would appear unwell to others. Usually, at some stage in the evening, he vomited. This was accompanied by tremendous relief and he would return to the social situation to enjoy it and be very much part of the party. Often he made himself vomit before leaving home. Thus, although he did not necessarily avoid social engagements, he limited the invitations he accepted to those people who would be sympathetic to his unusual disability.

It is impossible to come to any definite conclusion about the origin of Mr K's phobia nor would this knowledge be an essential prerequisite to treatment. For example, it is probably insufficient to say that nausea was conditioned to social situations as a result of an accidental sickness in one such situation. Many persons become sick after eating or drinking but do not develop phobias. In this instance, Mr K was anticipating a meeting with his mother who, formerly, had deserted him and towards whom he had mixed feelings. The nausea subsequently returned when he finally met his mother the following evening for a meal. However, in retrospect Mr K denied any particular feelings of anxiety or unease in these situations. Similarly he did not refuse invitations on account of a lack of enjoyment of other people's company, and typically returned to a party after vomiting. The only item on a fear survey which warranted attention was a total avoidance of, and fear of, argument. Perhaps Mr K anticipated the possibility of expressing some resentment to his mother when the problem started which mediated his sickness.

It seemed most unlikely to us, and to the client, that the behaviour was a form of attention-seeking.

In terms of the model an autonomic response of nausea and vomiting appears to have become established (perhaps as a primary response to the threat of arguments) to specific social cues. A secondary fear presumably developed around the nucleus of nausea and vomiting. That is, he avoided situations in which he knew he would feel ill and where his subsequent vomiting would prove an embarrassment. With his close friends he was less likely to worry about his disability and would not avoid meeting them.

The question remained, why his symptoms persisted in spite of minimal avoidance of social situations. Our solution was to suppose that vomiting provided immediate relief from the unpleasant nausea that invitations elicited, that is, that technically speaking vomiting was an escape response. Mr K himself reported considerable relief after vomiting and it enabled him to fulfil his social obligations.

The remedy was to break into the chain of events which terminated in vomiting and relief. Mr K was, therefore, told to accept all invitations and to delay vomiting for as long as possible; ideally, he should prevent it altogether. He was warned that his discomfort would intensify in the short term, but we predicted that in the long term prolonged exposure to nausea without relief would lead to its gradual extinction. Mr K agreed to this self-treatment procedure. In addition the therapist arranged a treatment session in which he invited the client to tea in the staff canteen. Mr K vomited before his arrival at the appointed time, and his discomfort over tea was not great. He attributed this to the lack of a 'surprise element' in the invitation.

The next invitation was therefore 'sprung on' Mr K during his annual leave one month later. The therapist invited him, over the phone, to meet in a restaurant in half an hour's time. Mr K felt an instant desire to be sick and said, 'I shall never make it – not by car.' His wife rang 15 minutes later to say that Mr K could not drive and would certainly be sick. Tactics were then changed and the message was passed on to Mr K to further prolong his vomiting; meanwhile, the therapist would communicate again in a couple of hours or so. One hour later the therapist rang to ask for directions to his home. By this time the client's extreme discomfort had dissipated to unease and he had not vomited.

A visit to the client's home was not necessary. The afternoon's experience brought home the essential method of dealing with the problem and he felt better prepared to undertake his self-treatment in future. When contacted by telephone a week later he had not vomited and so a further six weeks of self-management was recommended. Contact was again by telephone and the client reported that he had been to the cinema and to a party in the preceding week without feeling nauseous or vomiting. In view of this improvement he was discharged and a follow-up interview arranged for six weeks later. At the follow-up the client claimed he was 'cured'. He had attended many social engagements including surprise invitations to drink with friends, all without nausea. He admitted to taking tranquillizing drugs (prescribed by his GP) on occasions when he foresaw difficulty. He readily agreed to cut these down and then leave off taking them altogether.

When interviewed again six months later he remained symptom free without the use of tranquillizers. He had vomited only once, before a football match, which he attributed to rushing his food and drink. Anxiety was not associated with this isolated incident. In all, he had received about five hours of the therapist's time including assessment and follow-up interviews.

Case 4

This case illustrates how an autonomic component of fear (an involuntary desire to micturate) became the nucleus for a secondary fear of appearing a public spectacle. Normal urges to micturate then became the cues for panic.

As is so often the case, Mrs T's problems began with an unexpected attack of panic. This happened on a tube train in London's Underground. She panicked suddenly, feeling a great wave of depression come over her. Then she wept bitterly in front of the other passengers.

At that time, Mrs T, single and in her early twenties, had come to London from the country to further her career. Her associations with London had never been pleasant; on a former visit she had been frightened by a scantily dressed man who had entered her room at night. Nothing untoward happened but since that night she has slept with her head covered and she never fails to lock the bedroom door.

Mrs T was also feeling lonely and she did not like the college she was attending. She had always been a timid person and as a child had been keenly aware of the poor financial state of the family. It was not too difficult to visualize Mrs T's vulnerability giving way to despair in the noisy, crowded conditions of the Underground.

The most significant event of her panic was a desire to void urine, although she did not do so. After the attack it gave rise to an increasing fear that she might void urine and become a spectacle. Any situation which did not present an easy escape route to a toilet, such as a lecture hall, cinema or train, could trigger a desire to void which was followed by panic and an attempt to find a toilet. Her relief was not complete until she found the toilet and voided. In these ventures she had always been successful, never once being 'caught short' in the attempt.

Events took a turn for the worse as she avoided more and more of the situations in which panic might occur. As a result she became withdrawn and depressed, and went to see a psychiatrist who arranged psychotherapy and prescribed anti-depressant medication. The treatment she received improved her self-confidence and lessened her fear of being a spectacle. However, the intensity of her fear associated with the desire to void did not diminish. Nor did marriage, at a later date, significantly change the problem.

When Mrs T sought help from our clinic, five years had elapsed since her original panic attack. Her freedom to travel by bus, train or air was extensively restricted. Even walking in the street was limited to districts in which the public toilets were known to her. At work, attendance at conferences or lectures was an ordeal. If at all possible she sat at the back nearest the door. Although she had never actually passed urine, she avoided drinking liquids before going out and would make a prophylactic visit to the toilet.

It was interesting to note that once she had escaped from the confining situation her desire to void and its associated panic passed away. Similarly, on the rare occasions that she had been unable to find a toilet her panic would build up and up until it too passed away.

This woman's problems were conceptualized as follows. The strong desire to void in the original panic was interpreted as a primary autonomic component of the panic. Spontaneous micturition in states of extreme fear is well recognized in man and animals. It should be noted that Mrs T had indeed become a public spectacle although she did not in fact void. Thenceforward, Mrs T anticipated the highly embarrassing possibility of voiding in front of others when she could not with ease escape to a toilet. Restricted and confined situations are in any case inherently capable of arousing fear, and together with her anticipatory fear of becoming a spectacle, she was presumably highly sensitive to feedback from her bladder. An awareness of a desire to void triggered further panic, completing a positive feedback loop, which was terminated by Mrs T's escape and subsequent use of the toilet.

The treatment intervention was therefore aimed at modifying the desire to void in confined situations when her bladder was partially full. A base-line frequency of micturition was obtained for 19 days before treatment began which showed a higher rate than normal – 8-9 times per day on average. A graded programme of prolonged exposure to the feared situation was constructed.

In the first session, Mrs T sat for 1½ hours in a small room with the therapist on the understanding that she would not leave. She was first asked to empty her bladder so that later, at the end of the session, she could be given feedback on the amount of urine which had accumulated over this period. Mrs T was moderately anxious at the beginning of the session, becoming extremely fearful after 35 minutes when she desperately wanted to leave the room. Ten minutes later the feeling left her and she felt fine. Several times during the session she thought she would wet herself; for this reason she avoided getting up or uncrossing her legs. When she did finally get up she checked the chair for water. This 1½-hour period was the longest time she had spent in a similar situation since her problem began. She was also surprised to discover how much urine her bladder could hold when she voided at the end of the session.

There was an immediate improvement in her ability to tolerate a full bladder in the following week. On one day she did not use the toilet for six hours, which she could hardly believe. Moreover, she travelled by tube to the clinic without using the toilet *en route.*

The second session was longer (2 hours) and a preliminary visit to the toilet was not permitted. In addition Mrs T drank two cups of coffee. Once again, the client was moderately anxious and after one hour felt that her bladder was bursting. At the end of the session she felt fine but was glad to get out of the room.

Only two further treatment sessions were required in which Mrs T sat alone for three hours while being plied with cups of coffee at hourly intervals. In the third session her anxiety and desire to void decreased to a negligible level. She passed 600 ml. of urine which had accumulated over a 4-hour period. In the fourth session anxiety was not reported, although a strong desire to void was present which she controlled for three hours. She then passed 800 ml. of urine.

Mrs T kept thorough records of her micturition frequency throughout treatment. In the week preceding the fourth session her frequency was down to between 4 and 5 per day. Mrs T had become confident in her ability to control her bladder and consequently she was able to attend two concerts and several long meetings. She felt quite bad in the first half of the concerts but delayed voiding until the interval. In the second half of each concert she was perfectly at ease.

Mrs T began to think less and less about her problem and when it arose her attitude changed to a desire to control it rather than escape from it. She attempted to form a toilet pattern based on a regular 3 to 4 hour interval which was relatively independent of the situation she happened to be in at the time. The therapist assisted her in working out a programme of social engagements which would test out her new-found confidence. Her progress was monitored by telephone.

Over the next month Mrs T put herself through some very exacting tests including a three-day conference at her old college, a place that had always evoked panic. Although at first anxious, she did not use the toilet unnecessarily and soon felt at ease. With practice, the main problem of travel by train and bus no longer presented any difficulty.

At the time of discharge Mrs T felt more confident, more vigorous and had widened her interests. Promotion had been offered at work which she felt had been helped by the fact that she no longer took days off. For the first time since her marriage she was contemplating starting a family.

Although we have not yet conducted a lengthy follow-up on Mrs T a relapse seems most unlikely. The one-month follow-up ratings of her treatment targets showed a modest increase of her unease in travel and social situations but no increase in frequency of micturition. These ratings coincided with a visit from her mother, which proved to be a trying experience. The visit apparently brought about an elevation of her general level of anxiety and this is likely to have mediated the changed ratings.

Concluding comments

In these four cases of phobia an attempt has been made to illustrate the use of a theoretical model in formulating a treatment rationale. The model is, of course, only a partial analysis of the therapist's clinical intuition. It needs to be supplemented by a set of rules to generate the goals of therapy and the nature, order, and timing of the interventions necessary to achieve them. The distinction between theoretical and practical solutions of psychological problems seems a reasonable one. A problem may have a theoretical solution with no practical means of implementing it or alternatively be solved empirically without a conceptual understanding of the underlying processes.

An analysis of the 'executive function' of clinical intuition is a daunting task and has not been attempted in spite of the speed and confidence with which many clinical decisions are made. Nevertheless, it is the author's contention that an understanding of therapeutic processes depends on attempts to unravel such intangibles as the therapist's 'realistic appraisal of feasible targets for the client', reasons for preferring one technique rather than another, and his behaviour when faced by a multitude of practical constraints such as his client's willingness to accept the method and comply with its demands.

It is unlikely that the basis of decision-making can be worked out *a priori* although its nature could probably be inferred from detailed observations in the clinical setting. Arguing on a related topic, Ferster (1972) has suggested that a behavioural description of the activities of psychodynamic therapists might uncover new phenomena for the behaviour therapist. Ferster's emphasis is on a behavioural description rather than the therapist's putative explanation of his actions. It is not contradictory to assume that a behaviour therapist's account of his transactions with a client will also differ from an observer's behavioural description of the same transactions. Both partners to the transaction may have a vested interest in misperceiving the stream of events.

At this point one might question the value of a systematic description of therapeutic behaviour. Ferster has stated several obvious advantages including communicability and replicability. Experienced therapists can train others if they can accurately describe what they do and the therapy can also be replicated in other treatment centres. Cross-comparison of therapeutic systems should also aid a cross-fertilization of ideas between different schools of thought and ultimately lead to a simplification of idiosyncratic languages.

To illustrate this point of view, we can return to the four phobic clients to point out some advantages of this approach. The first problem of research into therapy is the characterization of the client sample. It is well recognized that terms such as 'agoraphobic', 'alcoholic' and 'stammerer' describe only the gross manifestations of a behavioural disturbance. Although the conceptual tools for a more detailed and dynamic behavioural analysis of psychological problems are available, these behavioural diagnoses need to be stated in operational form before their heuristic value can be tested. For example, the model of factors maintaining fear described earlier could be used to generate different categories of phobic clients. Structured interviews, check lists or behavioural assessment situations could be used to operationally define the criteria for each diagnosis. The relevant criteria would probably include the nature of the eliciting cues, cognitive defensive styles, the relative importance of the components of fear and the significance of secondary processes, etc. Researchers, in any case, implicitly engage in typing clients when assessing their suitability as subjects. Case 4 was rejected for an agoraphobic treatment trial because she was not 'typical' in spite of fears of travelling and walking in the street. Clients in a highly sensitized state (highly anxious or depressed) are often excluded from research trials or given medication prior to inclusion. The aim then is to develop a diagnostic system based on a psychological model of the disorder which suggests a theoretical if not a practical solution to the problem.

A second area of concern in current research into therapy has already been mentioned in the introduction. This is the question of the standardization of treatments. It was argued that a reliable treatment effect may not be obtained with too rigid a specification of procedures. It can also be stated that most procedures are inadequately specified. Length of treatment is usually one feature which is rigidly controlled, yet of the four phobic clients described above, Case 1 required only a few weeks' treatment and Case 2 more than six months.

Moreover, therapists usually have to rely on rather massive generalization effects from the artificially contrived learning situation of the clinic (sometimes just a fantasy rehearsal) to the real-life situation. The client's attempts at generalization, even if dictated by homework assignments, is difficult to standardize in a scientifically respectable way, even though gradual readaptation between sessions may constitute the most beneficial aspect of treatment. In Case 2 and 3 it was the client who took on the major responsibility to expose himself to relearning experiences, the therapist taking a teaching and supportive role. On the other hand, it would be arrogant to state that every client is different and no standardization is possible. There is insufficient evidence to demonstrate the superiority of individualized client-tailored therapy over the standard treatment package, although this is the author's bias. Flexibility of approach within certain limits is quite capable of prior specification. The advantages of flexibility could be tested by programming the therapist in different ways, for example, by changing the basis for making decisions at various points in the overall management of the problem. Thus the output of the system when the therapist was permitted to use only fantasy exposure methods could be compared with the output when only *in vivo* techniques were employed. It could be argued, for example, that Case 1 and Case 3 would have responded equally well to systematic desensitization because this technique would have eliminated speech errors (that is, by fantasy rehearsal of fluent speech) in Case 1 and prevented vomiting (by very gradual elicitation of nausea) in Case 3. The outputs of the system under these two conditions could then be compared for success rate, hours of therapeutic time, percentage of drop-outs, or any other relevant criterion.

The experimental programming of therapists to investigate therapeutic processes would therefore take an intermediate form between the artificiality of many current experimental designs and the unconcerned freedom of practising clinicians. For example, a specification of treatment strategy would have to be sufficiently general to allow for the change in treatment tactics in mid-telephone conversation in Case 3. Here, the general principle of exposure to nausea cues combined with the prevention of vomiting was adhered to but the strength of the cues had to be reduced in order to guarantee the client's compliance with instructions.

Standardization of treatment procedures has usually been confined to the 'operations' performed on the client in the therapist's office and has often excluded such important variables as the modification of set, provision of reality-based information and discussion of changes in life-style which would facilitate the attainment of treatment goals. Case 2 is a good example of a client who rejected psychodynamic interpretations of her idea that she smelled and discharged herself from hospital, but at a later date accepted a learning theory formulation and persisted with treatment. (There are, of course, clients who reject a behavioural approach and seek insight psychotherapy.) In Case 2 it is useful to view treatment as part of a matrix of ongoing life events which must be incorporated into a complete description of the therapeutic process. The idea that she smelled was related to deficiencies in her social repertoire. In order to modify the presenting problem it was necessary to instigate a variety of useful social behaviours which could be reinforced in the home environment. At the termination of treatment the 'psychiatric problem' (the idea that she smelled) had been 'cured', but the client's repertoire of social behaviour, though much improved, was still to some extent deficient. It was fortunate that her husband encouraged her expansion of social activities, praised her for the progress she made and declined to give in to her requests for reassurance on our instructions. An attempt to predict this client's response to treatment would therefore have to include the following variables at least: receptivity to the treatment method, the favourability of the rewarding potential of the environment and the husband's co-operation. Conventionally, marital status, socio-economic level, social assets and other prognostic variables have simply been correlated with treatment outcome with rather disappointing results. However, if clients were given a behavioural diagnosis and received treatment with an explicit theoretical rationale according to a systematically formulated set of procedures, it should be possible to test specific hypotheses about the nature of the interaction between prognostic variables and therapeutic outcome. For example, the prognostic significance of marital status in the treatment of social fears of this kind will depend on the spouse's potential to reinforce appropriately and, in the case of a single person, the presence or absence of supporting social contacts. When the mechanism of treatment is conceptualized specific hypotheses can be drawn up relating these variables together.

Lastly it seems necessary to incorporate current life events into a description of the therapeutic process. In most cases, it would be false to assume that the therapist does more than provide the initial impetus in returning the client to a life situation which is more rewarding than punishing. It is usually events which have a detrimental effect on this process that particularly arrest the attention of the therapist although some of course are life-enhancing. The influence may be subtle. Mrs P (Case 1) described at the one-month follow-up interview how she had met some friends in considerable trouble, 'on the verge of nervous breakdowns'. This experience apparently changed the frame of reference in which she viewed her own problem so that it assumed lesser importance. Mrs P went as far as to claim that this event contributed as much to her improvement as treatment itself. We cannot be sure, of course, that clients do not have a tendency to pick on events such as these to explain to themselves rather rapid behavioural changes.

A good example of life events having an adverse effect on treatment is provided by Mrs T (Case 4). During the latter part of treatment she received several phone calls from her mother who was going through a crisis period with her adopted daughter. The daughter was rebelling against plans for her future and in addition she had been alienated by her mother's suspicions about her sexual behaviour. Mrs T also found her mother a difficult and domineering woman and she became rather upset following the calls. While upset the urges to micturate intensified which resulted in more frequent visits to the toilet. In the follow-up period Mrs T's mother became depressed and her father asked her to invite her mother to stay with them for a week's holiday. This visit imposed considerable stress and it coincided with an increase in Mrs T's unease in social and travel situations. Fortunately, the visit was short but we might speculate that a prolonged stress of this nature would have precipitated a relapse. In this case there is a fairly clear relationship between current life events and fluctuations in the intensity of the target problem.

To sum up, this article has described the treatment of four phobic clients to illustrate the following points:

1 That systematic naturalistic observation of therapists at work

would further an understanding of treatment processes.

2 That communicability and replicability of treatments would be facilitated if the theoretical formulation of a problem and its practical implementation were described with reference to explicit conceptual models. A model of factors maintaining fear was presented.

3 That typically, current research methodology (for example, the factorial experiment) ignores, or is unable to bring under control, many variables that are relevant to treatment outcome. In particular, the interaction between therapeutic procedures and environmental processes needs to be specified.

4 That a research strategy is feasible in which the output of a specified system of management is monitored when therapists are programmed to modify their decisions at different points in the system.

5 That prediction of the outcome of therapy will improve when specific hypotheses are produced relating client variables, environmental variables and theoretical formulations of the treatment process. We are probably closer to this point in the treatment of phobias than any other area of therapy.

6 Untwining the Double-bind

T. W. Butt and H. Gwynne Jones

Since the age of 10 Alice had been terrified of fainting or of seeing others faint. She had never actually fainted but a variety of situations evoked agoraphobic or claustrophobic reactions closely linked with sensations of dizziness and palpitations which convinced her that fainting was imminent. She would frequently panic, rush home and take to her bed.

In fact, home offered little in the way of sanctuary. Her father had never wanted children and was very hostile and often even violent towards her, the only child. He refused to believe her account of her symptoms or that she suffered at all. Sometimes he would not speak to her for weeks at a time. By contrast, her mother strongly reinforced her own conviction that she was ill and in need of treatment. However, Alice gained no comfort from her mother whom she described as two-faced and inconsistent, not only to herself but also to her father and, later, to her fiancé. Far from being sympathetic her mother regarded her as lazy, ungrateful and a failure. Alice, in accepting this evaluation, experienced considerable feelings of guilt.

Alice's phobic reactions interfered greatly with her life at school and later at work and prevented her from entering into many social activities. She had been unable to sit examinations in large rooms whether others were present or not. She had finally taken her 'O' levels in a small classroom with only the invigilating teacher present. Panic attacks forced her to abandon three successive jobs and she had been unemployed for several months before the treatment to be described was initiated.

As a young adult, Alice felt that she was fighting a losing battle at home. Although she occasionally responded to her parents' goading with outbursts of temper she considered that, in general, she was too sensitive and easily imposed upon. She saw her only hope in an escape into early marriage. She was 19 when things at home seemed worse than ever and an upsurge of panic attacks forced her to leave her current job as a shop assistant. She presented herself at the Psychiatric Outpatient Clinic and was later referred to a clinical psychologist as a candidate for behaviour therapy. She had been treated at a Child Psychiatric Unit during her schooldays by the administration of a variety of tranquillising drugs but with little beneficial effect.

Following assessment by interview, personality inventory, a fear schedule and other questionnaires, the psychologist concluded that, although Alice's tangled emotional problems might require further investigation at a later stage, her anxiety reactions were sufficiently clearly related to well-defined environmental situations to hope that she might respond favourably to a straightforward desensitisation procedure. As a preliminary she was taught to relax in individual and group sessions. She consistently failed to achieve any appreciable degree of relaxation in either situation and reported that thoughts of fainting could not be excluded and foiled all her attempts to relax. The group classes in particular terrified her to such an extent that she invented excuses to stay away. At this stage, the psychologist moved to another hospital and the first author took over and embarked on a more detailed assessment procedure.

A 50-minute relatively unstructured interview during which Alice was encouraged to talk about her complaints, symptoms and feelings was tape-recorded and 23 'illness statements' were later abstracted. These fell roughly into three categories:

1   Internal physical sensations which adumbrated fainting.
2   External situations (agoraphobic and claustrophobic) which evoked panic attacks.
3   Feelings of intense dissatisfaction with herself as a person and her home situation.

Exhaustive enquiry elicited no evidence of a traumatic event linked with the onset of the fear of fainting which, Alice claimed, 'came on very suddenly at the age of ten'. Her own explanation of her disorder was in terms of 'an illness' and she rejected any suggestion that she might resume relaxation training which she felt had no relevance to her condition. Nevertheless, she expressed a strong desire to 'talk things over', an apparent appeal for psychotherapy.

The relationship between the internal and external cues for anxiety were consistent with a conditioning explanation of the disorder, sympathetic activity, cognitively associated with fainting, having become classically conditioned responses to crowds, open and closed spaces and other common phobic stimuli. What was unclear, however, was the connection between the dissatisfactions of category 3 and the other two categories. Alice claimed that her panic attacks definitely increased when strife at home reached its periodical peaks. It is certainly plausible to suggest that at these times the basal level of emotional arousal was increased and therefore lowered the degree of additional cue-related arousal necessary to precipitate an attack.

However, the case of Alice could be looked at quite differently and would be by many clinicians. For example, her account of her family life fits very closely to the 'schismatic' and 'skewed' patterns described by Lidz (1973) and the intra-familial communication is certainly of the 'double-bind' type which is claimed by several writers to produce schizophrenic reactions in the recipient but which, in at least one of the authors' experience, is very often associated with the type of neurotic personality disorder displayed by Alice.

That author (Jones, 1971) has argued that human beings should be regarded as functioning at a number of hierarchically organised and complexly interrelated levels which may be conveniently divided into biological, social and humanistic realms. Behaviour therapy has tended to concentrate on change at the lower, biological levels. The complex interrelationships between levels usually ensure that change at one level produces related changes at other levels but the strategically optimal level for the initial therapeutic attack will vary from case to case.

Thus behaviour therapists are becoming increasingly impressed with the need to take cognitive and other 'higher level' functions into account. The work of Schachter and Singer (1962) illustrates how emotional phenomena cannot be adequately explained without reference to both physiological and cognitive factors. Bandura (1961) has criticised behaviour therapists for their focusing on only a few learning principles at the expense of others equally relevant.

A number of authors (for example, Norris and Jones, 1971; Ryle and Breen, 1971) have drawn particular attention to the importance of the self-image and, in particular, of the self/ideal self discrepancy in neurosis. Argyle (1967) has suggested that one's self-image is compiled from three sources:

1 From the feedback and reinforcement from others, particularly in childhood when behaviour is shaped and selectively reinforced.
2 From observation of one's own behaviour in the context of the behaviour of others.

3   From the roles a person has played in the past and is playing at present.

Thus an unworthy self-image could be thought of as resulting from neurotic behaviour. It might also play a part in the propagation of symptoms by positive feedback effects. Therefore, it is not surprising, as Beech (1969) has pointed out, that many behaviour therapy patients appear to require assertive training as well as desensitisation. In addition to the inhibition of anxiety, they need to learn new behavioural responses for use in stressful situations and to allow new facets of their personalities to emerge.

For all these reasons, it was considered desirable to explore further Alice's self-image and the cognitive framework from within which she viewed her world. This was attempted by use of the Repertory Grid Technique (Kelly, 1955; Bannister, 1965; Bannister and Mair, 1968) and it was hoped that the findings would provide a set of objectives at which a rational form of the verbal type of therapy which she appeared to be seeking might be aimed.

Thirteen grid 'elements' were selected, including members of Alice's own family and the family of her fiancé:

1 Self	8 Former best friend
2 Ideal self	9 Fiancé's mother
3 Mother	10 Fiancé's father
4 Father	11 Pitied male friend
5 Fiancé	12 Fiancé's sister
6 Grandmother	13 Fiancé's brother
7 Phobic friend	

Ten 'constructs' were elicited by Kelly's self-identification method:

1 Uncritically confiding	v independent
2 Too soft and sympathetic	v hard
3 Unfortunate and imposed upon	v hard
4 Rigidly organised	v free and easy
5 Takes life too seriously	v couldn't care less
6 Understanding	v not understanding
7 Easily upset	v takes life as it comes
8 Sensitive	v thick-skinned
9 Self-conscious	v over-confident
10 Self-sacrificing	v selfish

Four constructs were supplied, three others being derived from the 'illness statements' from the initial interview:

11 Psychiatrically vulnerable	v stable

12 Tense	v relaxed
13 Bad-tempered	v calm
14 Secure in the home	v insecure

Alice was asked to rate the elements in terms of each of these construct dimensions on a 7-point scale.

The grid was analysed into its principal components by Slater's (1965a, 1965b, 1967) INGRID Programme and four factors with latent roots >1 were extracted, as shown in Table 6·1.

TABLE 6·1   *Grid I: components with latent roots >1*

	% total variance	Characterising constructs	Appropriate labels
I	47·4	2, 3, 7, 8, 10, 11	over-sensitive, vulnerable
II	13·2	4, 13	rigid and bad-tempered
III	12·6	1, 14	independent, insecure
IV	10·1	no information in printout	

Component I is responsible for almost half the variance of the construct system, and may be thought of as a sickness factor. The vulnerability construct (11) is correlated ($p < 0.05$) with all the other constructs with high weightings on component I ($2 = 0.53$; $3 = 0.67$; $7 = 0.70$; $8 = 0.72$; $10 = 0.68$). Certain personality characteristics are seen as implying psychiatric illness. Being too sensitive implies weakness and misfortune. An inspection of the matrix of grid 1 shows that Alice sees herself as possessing all these unfavourable characteristics.

Following Slater's instructions, a map was drawn representing the positions of elements in construct space. Figure 6·1 shows the relationship between constructs and elements with respect to components I and II.

Component III was ignored for map purposes, for two reasons:

1 Alice gives herself a rating of 4 on construct 14, one of the only two constructs characterising this component. This suggests that she sees herself as out of the range of convenience of this construct.
2 Construct 14 appears to change its meaning during the course of ensuing treatment, which makes interpretation of component III difficult.

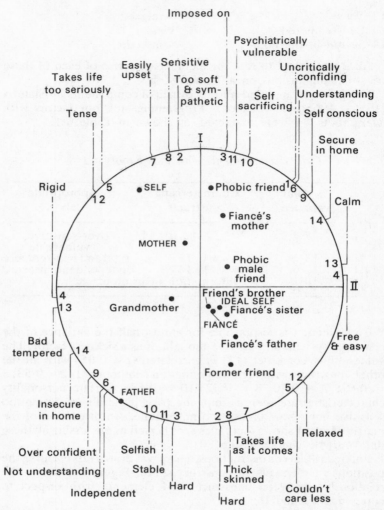

FIGURE 6·1 *Grid I: elements and constructs in space defined by components I and II*

1 Elements with the highest positive loadings on component I are 'self' and 'phobic friend'.
2 Elements with the highest negative loadings on component I are 'father' and 'former friend'.

3   Elements with the highest loading on component II are 'self' and 'father'.
4   The element 'ideal self' is near the origin of the map.
5   The elements 'ideal self' and 'fiancé' are positioned closely together in this two-dimensional construct space.

This grid structure suggested that initially therapy might be aimed at a loosening of the construct system and movement of the self concept in relation to the first and second components. If this could be achieved by a re-educative programme, it might then be possible to launch a more successful direct behavioural attack on the fear of fainting.

Alice wished to become less sensitive and vulnerable but not to become 'hard'. Father is seen as hard and as unlike the 'ideal' self as is the 'actual' self. Her fiancé, on the other hand, is seen as tempering assertiveness with sensitivity and, from the grid analysis, appears to possess many of the characteristics of the ideal self.

Consistent with this analysis, three formal objectives were established for the re-educative phase of therapy:

1   To encourage, enhance and reinforce those qualities of the ideal self which were already evident or could be shaped into Alice's behaviour.
2   To modify Alice's view of her father in the direction of seeing him as less 'hard'. Successful achievement of this aim would be likely to facilitate the desired changes in the self-image as well as improving relationships at home.
3   To bring Alice to a recognition that her fear of fainting was an acquired anxiety reaction, not an inevitable consequence of her basic personality or a realistic reaction to a physiological weakness.

A combination of modelling and assertive training techniques was adopted for the pursuit of the first aim. Her fiancé was presented as the model and Alice was encouraged to attempt consciously to react as she thought he would, especially when confronted with a domineering person. She would try to be more assertive but not to respond to goading and impositions with outbursts of temper which had previously not only proved ineffective but also resulted in strong feelings of guilt. A record was kept of her encounters with unreasonable demands and, in discussion sessions, her strategies were reviewed and reinforcement in the form of praise, couched in the terms of her own ideal characteristics, supplied as appropriate. Successful outcomes were presented as evidence that she had not been too 'sensitive' and that she was not 'taking life too seriously'. In parallel with this real-life training, it was also intended that assertive behaviour should be rehearsed in psychodrama sessions.

These procedures were seen as providing reinforcement of a new self-image, experience of new roles and an opportunity for more insightful analysis of the effects on herself and others of changes in Alice's behaviour in stressful situations. It was predicted that a consequent change in self-image would be evident from a post-treatment re-administration of the repertory grid. In particular, the location of the 'self' element was expected to shift in relation to constructs 2, 3, 5, 7 and 8, those with high weightings on component I. This shift would bring the 'self' nearer to 'ideal self', 'fiancé' and other elements near the origin in Figure 6·1.

The second objective was approached by a series of rational discussions of the father's behaviour and attitudes, aimed at better understanding of these and the planning of strategies to enable Alice to deal with him more objectively and effectively. Any success by these means should result in 'father' becoming less heavily weighted in a negative direction on component I of a second grid.

The first two objectives are concerned with both the social and humanistic realms of functioning. The third, although involving important cognitive re-orientations, has more relevance to the biological level. Nevertheless, the approach at this stage was through rational discussion. The physiology of fainting, conditioning theories of the genesis of phobias and the rationale of desensitisation techniques were explained and discussed. In this way it was hoped to pursuade Alice of the relevance of these matters to her own condition. It was also predicted that she would not continue to see her psychiatric vulnerability as an essential aspect of her personality and, therefore, that, in grid terms, construct 2 would decrease its loading on component I. A further expectation was that, if this aspect of the treatment was effective, a more favourable outcome should result from a second attempt at desensitisation therapy.

From this description of the treatment proposed it will be seen that rational verbal discussion plays a very major role. The fact that the discussions were to be based on a logically derived multifarious strategy would have been of little scientific or didactic value if the effects were not also to be carefully assessed in as objective a manner as possible and matched with those predicted. The single case nature of a therapeutic venture of this type does not imply an abandonment of experimental discipline (Jones, 1960; Shapiro, 1970). The conclusions drawn from the initial evaluation of a patient and his problems are of the nature of hypotheses to be tested. Too frequently, criteria of improvement are vague, subjective and holistic. A thorough evaluation of all the possible effects of a particular treatment is impossible but an attempt should certainly be made to measure changes along those dimensions related to the avowed aims of the therapist.

In the present instance, the more general behavioural and experimental predictions were given a type of operational definition in terms of specific predicted changes in structure between pre-and post-therapy repertory grids based on the same elements and constructs. However, the repertory grid has many deficiencies as a psychometric instrument. Even leading advocates (Bannister and Mair, 1968) have emphasised that the technique should be validated against external criteria of change if this is possible. For this reason, the course of change in Alice's symptoms was also followed by means of a personal questionnaire of the type pioneered by Shapiro (1964). This was constructed so as to collect series of self-ratings of symptoms from within the three categories already descirbed.

For each of the twenty-three original illness statements, an 'improvement' and a 'recovery' statement was constructed. Alice was then asked to rate each of the 69 statements on a 9-point hedonistic thermometer (Shapiro, 1964) such that:

All illness statements were rated as implying v. great displeasure or great displeasure.

All improvement statements were rated as implying 'moderate or slight displeasure'.

All recovery statements were rated as implying 'indifference or slight pleasure'.

The statements were then adjusted in consultation with Alice so that each class of statement had similar hedonistic implications. (All the statements are listed in Appendix 1 at the end of this chapter.)

Each statement was typed on a 12·5 cm. x 7·5 cm. index card. It soon became apparent that a comparison of all three cards in a set with every other one (procedure advocated by Shapiro) would be too time-consuming, as it was intended to administer the questionnaire at the beginning and end of each session. Instead, it was decided that Alice should be presented with the three statements applying to a particular symptom, and asked to indicate which one best described her mental state. If the 'improvement' statement were chosen, she would be asked to decide whether the 'illness' or the 'recovery' statement was most appropriate to her present state. This questionnaire was administered at the beginning and end of each treatment session.

A four-point scoring system was used, as shown in Table 6·2.

TABLE 6·2   *Personal questionnaire: scoring system*

		Score
Patient chooses	illness statement	3
Patient chooses	improvement statement	
Patient chooses	*then* illness statement	2
Patient chooses	improvement statement	
Patient chooses	*then* recovery statement	1
Patient chooses	recovery statement	0

Alice attended the clinic twice a week for sessions of about 50 minutes. In the very first session she discussed the possibility of seeking a clerical job which she had seen advertised, and was encouraged to apply. The remainder of this and the next two sessions were devoted to assertive training but several attempts to enact situations in psychodrama failed as she felt too embarrassed to take part in this activity. The discussions therefore centred around a rational appraisal of her behaviour when she felt she was being imposed upon. The successful application for her job provided a valuable opportunity for practising more assertive behaviours in her work situation. Although she felt able to cope at work, she was unable to be more firm with her mother, who appeared to assume more importance and become more of a difficulty as the discussions progressed. This at least had the result of enabling her to see the point of view of her father in a more understanding light.

Sessions 4 and 5 were spent discussing her relationship with her father, during which time she was encouraged to think of his reasons for acting the way he did towards her. She was also encouraged to think of more effective ways of responding to him. This strategy had some success, as she reported that she and her father developed more of a mutual understanding. This, she felt, threatened her mother and in session 6, Alice elaborated on how two-faced her mother was, first siding with her against her father, and then with him against her. She had experienced an increased incidence of panic feelings, and it was pointed out how her fainting fear and anxiety increased together.

In session 7 the fear of fainting was discussed further and, for the first time, Alice felt that relaxation might be of some use. This discussion continued in the next session and, in this and the last discussion session, the theory behind desensitisation was explained. At this point, Alice decided that she could profit from a course in desensitisation.

At this stage, as planned, a further repertory grid was applied to examine the changes in construing that might have resulted from the discussion.

Principal components analysis of this grid extracted three components with latent roots >1, as shown in Table 6·3.

TABLE 6·3 *Grid II: components with latent roots >1*

	% total variance	Characterising constructs	Label
I	52·1	2, 3, 5, 6, 7, 8, 11	over-sensitive, vulnerable
II	17·01	1, 9, 4, 13	rigid, independent, over-confident
III	8·89	10, 14	self-sacrificing, insecure

Component I can still be thought of as a sickness factor. The system had tightened rather than loosened, with construct 5 now more highly correlated with other constructs. Construct 11 (psychiatric vulnerability) still had significant correlations with all other constructs, implying sensitivity.

Alice assigned herself less extreme ratings on all constructs contributing to component I (with the exception of construct 7). Despite this, as can be seen from Figure 6·2, the element 'self' has a higher loading on this component in grid II than grid I. This appears to be due to the fact that the rating of 1 is very seldom used in the second grid, and Alice was not using the full range of the 7-point scale. It is difficult to assess to what extent the new self-ratings represent a real change in the self concept.

A large change in the predicted direction had occurred in the father's position in relation to component I (loadings of —1·3 and — 0·7 in grids I and II respectively).

Thus, although there had been some success in the change of construing of the father, there had been little success in changing the self concept, and none in loosening the system. However, the trend towards less extreme self-rating seemed to suggest that change was beginning to occur.

The Christmas holiday intervened at this stage and the second, desensitisation phase of treatment was started a fortnight after the first discussion phase ended. The desensitisation procedure, in imagination, was focused upon the fear of fainting and the associated physiological sensations. Less attention was paid to

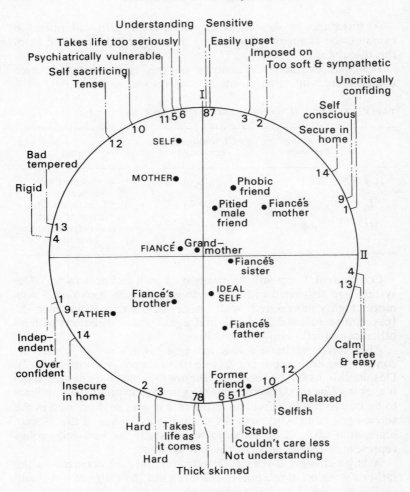

FIGURE 6·2   *Grid II: elements and constructs in space defined by components I and II*

environmental stimuli. Also, and linking with the previous phase of treatment, cognitive features were explored and any apparent progress was emphasised.

The procedure, involving relaxation training, the construction of a hierarchy and the presentation of successive levels of the hierarchy while Alice was deeply relaxed, followed the lines described by Wolpe and Lazarus (1966). Relaxation training occupied about twenty minutes in each of four sessions. Different sets of muscles were attended to in successive sessions, and Alice was encouraged to practise relaxation twice daily at home. She was also alerted to the state of tension in her muscles at various times and it was suggested to her that she might attempt to control any feelings of physical anxiety by countering with her relaxation. This she was able to do on one or two occasions and her resulting confidence after session 3 enabled her to go shopping in the market 'for the first time in years'.

The anxiety hierarchy presented a number of problems. Fainting, to Alice, was an all or none activity. To think of it terrified her. Asking her to imagine fainting seemed unreasonable as she didn't know what it felt like to faint. Maximum terror was inspired by her physiological reactions. Using a 'fear thermometer' (Wolpe and Lazarus, 1966) it was found that no situation involving dizziness and related sensations rated at less than 60 *suds*.

Imagining watching others faint was not quite so anxiety-provoking, and the hierarchy was extended downwards by using such items. The following dimensions were important in this part of the hierarchy:

1   Reality of the faint
2   Distance fallen
3   Situational factors
4   Suddenness

It was decided that there should be one hierarchy, the theme of which was fainting generally, and that this hierarchy should be divided into two halves:

1   Watching others faint
2   Subjective feelings of a fainting

In part 1, successive stimuli were presented while Alice remained relaxed. If anxiety was felt (signalled by raising a finger), relaxation was encouraged, and the stimulus presented once more. Each stimulus was repeated several times.

In part 2, a procedure closer to the operant paradigm was followed. Successively more severe anxiety-provoking situations were presented and, during each presentation, the experience of unpleasant physical sensations was suggested. Once these were aroused, Alice was asked to relax and thus control her anxiety. It was hoped to demonstrate that she had the ability to control her panic attacks even if feeling dizzy.

The actual sequence of situations worked through was as shown in Table 6·4:

TABLE 6·4   *Desensitisation hierarchy*

		No. of presentation
1	Watching an actor faint on TV	2
2	Watching somebody fall off a chair in a faint	4
3	Watching somebody faint, with warning, in a large crowded store	3
4	Watching somebody faint, without warning, in a large crowded store	3
5	Watching somebody faint in a crowded lift	3
6	Lying down and feeling dizzy	3
7	Feeling dizzy, etc., in waiting room	4
8	Feeling dizzy, etc., in crowded store	6
9	Feeling dizzy, etc., in small room in the hospital	5
10	Feeling dizzy, etc., in a crowded lift	4
11	Feeling dizzy, etc., in a crowded lift that was stuck between floors	6

Relaxation training and the construction of the hierarchy took four sessions, the desensitisation itself a further five. Progress was increasingly rapid and the treatment came to an end when Alice indicated on the personal questionnaire that 'the fear of fainting does not bother me at all'.

Five days after the last treatment session, a final repertory grid was applied. The principal components analysis extracted four components with latent roots >1, as shown in Table 6·5.

TABLE 6·5   *Grid III: components with latent roots >1*

	% total variance	Characterising constructs	Label
I	40·36	2, 3, 6, 7, 8, 9, 10	too sensitive
II	17·41	4, 5, 12	rigid, tense, bad-tempered
III	11·95	1, 13, 14	independent and insecure
IV	10·41	No information in printout	

A certain amount of loosening in structure is evident in this grid. Component I accounts for 40 per cent of the variance in the system, and the construct of 'psychiatric vulnerability' is only significantly correlated with 'tense' (construct 12).

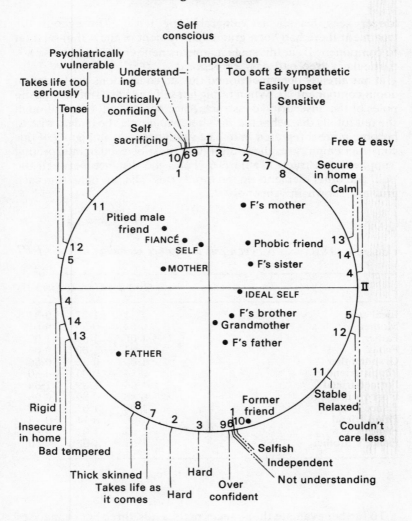

FIGURE 6·3 *Grid III: elements and constructs in space defined by components I and II*

Component I can still be labelled 'too sensitive' but, as can be seen from Figure 6·3, the self has moved appreciably along this dimension and in such a way that it is no longer seen as over sensitive, but neither is it seen as 'hard'. Also, apparently, Alice no longer sees herself as vulnerable or tense. Throughout the treatment there had been gradual movement of the self in relation to component II: at this stage it appears neither rigid and tense nor particularly free and easy or relaxed.

It has already been mentioned that no conclusions can be drawn about component III. When rating her self and ideal self at opposite poles of the 'insecurity' construct, Alice pointed out that, although she felt totally disenchanted with her own home, she had no wish to become more integrated in it. The vagueness and ambiguity of this construct emphasises the caution that must be used in interpreting 'supplied' constructs. Table 6·6 shows the distance between the 'self' and other elements on the three grids. The raw data from each grid are shown in Appendix 2.

TABLE 6·6   *Distances between self and other elements in grids I-III*

	Grid I	Grid II	Grid III
Ideal self	1·21	1·27	0·84
Mother	0·64	0·50	0·61
Father	1·06	1·04	1·02
Fiancé	1·02	1·00	0·06
Grandmother	1·00	0·92	0·86
Phobic friend	0·54	0·83	0·80
Former friend	1·05	1·09	1·04
Fiancé's mother	0·88	0·89	0·96
Fiancé's father	1·04	1·05	1·02
Pitied friend	1·00	0·74	0·73
Fiancé's sister	1·02	1·01	0·84
Fiancé's brother	1·01	1·03	0·80

To further evaluate the changes in the grids, three DELTA analyses (2-1, 3-2 and 3-1) were carried out (see Slater, 1968). An examination of the sums of squares of elements in each change grid indicates the amount of change each element has undergone, those with the largest sums of squares having changed most. Table 6·7 records the relevant sums of squares and Figure 6·4 portrays the first two components of change between grids 3 and 1. This shows a large first component (42·4 per cent of total variance) accounting for the change in usage of constructs and construing of elements.

TABLE 6·7 *Sums of squares of elements in the three change grids*

	2-1	3-2	3-1
Self	11·1	50·1	69·4
Ideal self	18·8	22·3	10·9
Mother	28·7	36·5	31·8
Father	47·2	51·6	51·4
Fiancé	48·3	28·4	52·3
Grandmother	19·6	20·8	27·3
Phobic friend	37·8	25·7	62·0
Former friend	20·1	44·9	37·4
Fiancé's mother	48·9	26·7	17·7
Fiancé's father	29·8	26·1	25·8
Pitied friend	24·5	14·3	33·4
Fiancé's sister	33·7	23·1	31·7
Fiancé's brother	33·8	14·8	32·2

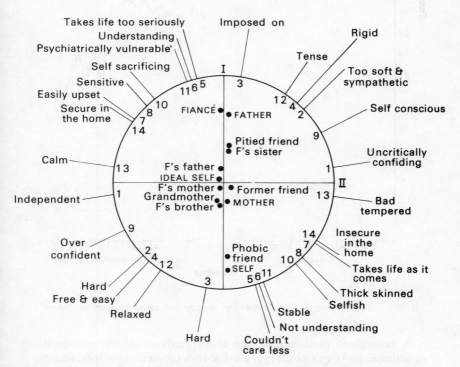

FIGURE 6·4 *Delta Grid (3-1): elements and constructs in space defined by change components I and II*

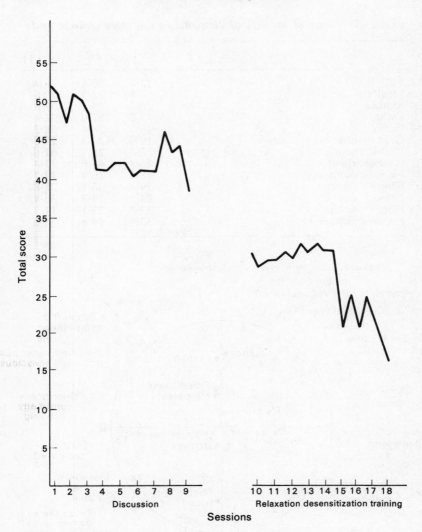

FIGURE 6·5   *Personal questionnaire scores on consecutive sessions*

A consistent picture emerges from analyses of the personal questionnaire responses. Figure 6·5 shows the decline in total score at each stage of treatment. To analyse this further, the symptoms were divided into three groups:

(a) Feelings of dissatisfaction with herself (symptoms 4-10)
(b) External cues for anxiety (symptoms 11-18)
(c) Internal cues for anxiety (symptoms 9-13)

Items 1-3 do not fall naturally into any of these groups. Item 1 (fainting) remained high through almost the entire treatment period but declined dramatically during the latter part of the desensitisation phase. Item 2 (feeling trapped at home) fell early to zero, but item 3 (can't stand home) remained at either score 2 or 3 to the very end.

Linear regression lines were fitted to the summed scores within each group of items for each of the three phases of treatment; discussion, relaxation and desensitisation. Table 6·8 shows the gradients for these regression lines and they are graphically displayed in Figure 6·5.

TABLE 6·8 *Gradients for linear regression lines*

	Discussion	Relaxation	Desensitisation
Feelings of dissatisfaction with the self	—0·06	0	—0·28
External cues for anxiety	—0·40	+0·37	—0·78
Internal cues for anxiety	—0·17	—0·13	—0·27

The changes from grid 1 to grid 3 were entirely consistent with the predicted effects of the discussion phase of treatment, but these were not evident in grid 2 which directly followed this phase. However, the personal questionnaire gradients of Figures 6·5 and 6·6 do suggest that some improvement did occur during the first phase but that this improvement was mainly associated with Alice's reactions to external cues evoking anxiety. It may be that the personal questionnaire is a more sensitive instrument than the repertory grid but it may also be possible that the effects of the verbal type of therapy of the first phase require something like an incubation time before they become manifest. The experiences of real life may play an important part in such an incubation. This incubation hypothesis is supported by the decline in questionnaire scores rather like the reminiscence effect in motor learning, which occurs over the Christmas period between the 'discussion' and

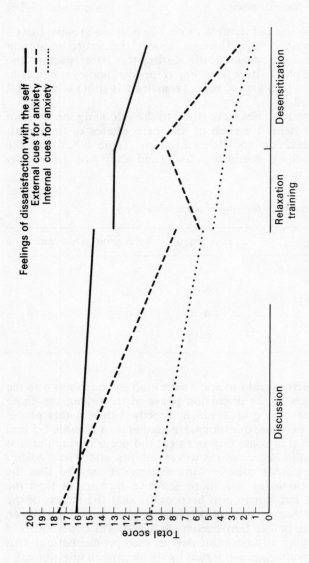

FIGURE 6·6 *Regression lines for personal questionnaire scores within categories during three phases of treatment*

'relaxation' phases of treatment. In fact, improvement generally is greater between sessions than within them, suggesting again the successful testing of strategies in real situations. The relatively larger improvement in agoraphobic symptoms may well be an effect of the job which required Alice to face this type of situation regularly.

The questionnaire gradients do demonstrate quite clearly the dramatic rapid declines in illness scores which occurred during the desensitisation phase. Grid 3 was applied at the end of this phase and it could be argued that the 'social' and 'humanistic' changes were a consequence of this, the only significant symptomatic improvement. The beneficial general effects of successful symptom-orientated behaviour therapy are well documented. However, in the case of Alice, the earlier phase of treatment was essential to her acceptance of desensitisation.

Agoraphobic symptoms actually increased during the relaxation phase. This is probably related to apprehension about the desensitisation which was to follow. A similar increase in anxiety was noted just before the end of the discussion phase when fainting and desensitisation were being discussed. During relaxation, as might be expected, the physiological symptoms did show some improvement but the feelings of dissatisfaction with herself were not influenced in either direction.

Despite the usefulness of the personal questionnaire in this study, the elaborate procedure for compiling the statements was laborious and time-consuming. A simple 'thermometer' scale, constructed for each symptom, might have served the purpose equally well.

The repertory grid is even more complex although the computer service provided by Dr Slater greatly eased the task of analysis. However, in this study, the labour was justified by the aid provided in the analysis of the problem and the specification of objectives for the therapy. Reciprocally, perhaps, the study has contributed to the construct validity of the technique. No statistical tests of significance were applied to any of the assessment data: none are available for the repertory grid findings. However, the changes measured by both assessment methods were systematic rather than random, were related comprehensibly to the therapeutic interventions and were consistent with observed changes in behaviour and spontaneous verbal report.

Follow-up is essential to any therapeutic case study. Owing to circumstances, no test or other formal follow-up data could be collected in this instance but contact has been maintained with Alice over the 18 months since the end of treatment and she has attended for periodical interviews at lengthening intervals.

After a month she reported that she still experienced anxiety in a variety of situations but found herself able to control any feelings of panic and was no longer terrified of fainting. Being able to go out without anxiety was a great boon as she still found home unbearable. She intended to marry in the near future and thus escape from the situation. However, her better relationship with her father had led to him offering to buy her and her husband a small house. She saw the referring psychiatrist five days later and he reduced her allotment of tranquillisers which she had used throughout her treatment and still considered a necessary precaution. Some days later, the following letter was received:

Dear Mr Butt,
    I felt I must write to thank you for all you have done for me during the past few months. Although there are still times when I could feel a lot better, I certainly feel I have benefited more over the past eighteen weeks than I ever did over the past nine years. Also I appreciate knowing that I can still get in touch with you if and when I need to.
    Thank you once again for all your time and understanding. I am very grateful.

Yours very sincerely,
Alice (M————)

Some five months later, a month before her marriage, family strife was making life very uncomfortable and she attended for five brief sessions to 'talk things over'. The wedding ceremony took place without hitch and she moved into the house purchased by her father. Soon after, she suffered something of a relapse in that she experienced dizzy spells at work, had three weeks off work, and ultimately changed her job to a nursery which she enjoyed. Nevertheless she continued to experience headaches and dizziness and some agoraphobic symptoms returned. These symptoms responded to the sympathetic treatment of a general practitioner who treated some possible physical causes of her dizziness and provided her with tranquillisers. However, even during this 'bad' period she had no greater fear of fainting than at the end of desensitisation.

She improved again and could make social calls, travel on buses and shop, even in large supermarkets. She would not like to tackle a lift but was not terrified by the prospect. She described desensitisation as 'like an insurance'. It had enabled her to go more confidently into situations in the knowledge that she could control herself.

Her marriage has been a happy one with a 'very understanding' husband and she says that she gets on 'marvellously' with her father. Her relationship with her mother has been less troublesome but only because she has left home. The parents have continued to quarrel bitterly but Alice now realises that she was not 'the cause of it all'.

She was last seen just before this chapter was written and after an interval of a year. Her condidtion has been stable throughout that year during which she has become pregnant. She still sees her general practitioner at monthly intervals but has considerably reduced her drug intake to two or three tablets a week. Her fears still recur but in relatively mild form and she says that she can cope with them. She visits her home once a week as a duty but still finds her mother almost intolerable.

Appendix 1

The personal questionnaire

In the following list, the statements concerning each symptom are in the order:

> illness statement
> improvement statement
> recovery statement

I am terrified of fainting and the thought of fainting.
I am no longer preoccupied with the thought of fainting.
The thought of fainting does not bother me at all.

Being at home makes me feel trapped.
Being at home occasionally makes me feel trapped.
I feel reasonably free at home.

I feel that I just can't stand home any more.
Sometimes I feel that I can't stand being at home.
I feel able to cope with things at home.

I am often imposed upon.
I am not imposed upon so often.
I am usually reasonably assertive.

I take life too seriously.
I still get upset, but not so often.
I feel more easy going.

I get upset very easily.
I am not upset quite so easily.
I am not easily upset.

I have a terrible temper.
I am sometimes able to control my temper.
Most of the time, I am reasonably calm.

I feel very depressed.
I sometimes feel depressed.
I rarely feel depressed.

I often feel like a failure.
I do not feel a failure so intensely.
I am no longer troubled by feelings of failure.

I feel guilty because I don't know how lucky I am.
I don't feel all that guilty.
On the whole, I'm not troubled by feelings of guilt.

I am terrified of panicking in a strange place.
I am able to control my panic to some extent.
I no longer panic in strange places.

I get acute feelings of claustrophobia.
The thought of enclosed spaces no longer terrifies me.
I am not unduly worried by enclosed spaces.

I hate large empty spaces.
I don't like large empty spaces, but they don't terrify me.
I don't mind large empty spaces.

I hate standing in queues.
I don't like queues, although they don't frighten me so much.
I don't mind standing in queues.

I feel anxious if I am in a crowd and restricted.
I don't feel quite so anxious in a crowd.
Crowds don't make me at all anxious.

I feel nervous in a room with closed windows.
I feel slightly uneasy with closed windows.
I don't mind closed windows.

Walking down a street on my own makes me extremely anxious.
Walking alone makes me anxious less often.
Walking alone does not worry me unduly.

Walking with other people makes me feel a fool.
Walking with other people does not bother me quite so much.
Walking with other people does not bother me at all.

I am often very tense.
I am sometimes tense.
I am rarely tense.

I often get dizzy spells.
I sometimes get dizzy spells.
I rarely suffer from dizziness.

I often get palpitations.
I am sometimes able to overcome my palpitations.
I no longer get palpitations.

My legs often feel very wobbly.
My legs occasionally feel wobbly.
My legs seldom feel wobbly.

My throat often feels very dry.
My throat occasionally dries up.
My throat never dries up.

Appendix 2

GRID I

	Self	Ideal self	Mother	Father	Fiancé	Grandmother	Phobic friend	Former friend	Fiancé's mother	Fiancé's father	Pitied friend	Fiancé's sister	Fiancé's brother
1 Uncritically confiding	3	5	1	7	1	6	1	3	6	7	2	3	7
2 Soft	1	2	2	7	4	2	1	7	1	6	2	5	2
3 Imposed on	1	4	2	7	4	5	1	7	1	6	3	1	5
4 Rigid	3	2	3	1	4	2	5	7	6	6	3	6	5
5 Takes life too seriously	1	6	4	5	6	5	1	7	5	7	2	7	6
6 Understanding	2	1	1	7	2	3	1	5	3	3	3	4	2
7 Easily upset	1	6	2	7	7	5	2	5	3	7	1	3	3
8 Sensitive	3	5	3	7	5	3	1	6	1	7	6	4	5
9 Self-conscious	3	4	6	6	3	3	1	6	1	2	5	6	7
10 Self-sacrificing	3	4	4	7	4	5	1	6	1	5	1	5	5
11 Psychiatrically vulnerable	1	7	4	6	7	7	2	7	3	4	4	6	6
12 Tense	1	6	3	1	6	3	3	3	3	4	6	7	3
13 Bad-tempered	2	6	6	1	3	4	5	7	6	6	6	5	5
14 Secure	4	2	4	4	3	2	5	4	2	2	5	2	2

Each digit represents a rating on a 7-point scale, such that a rating of 1 indicates an extreme rating on the emergent pole shown. A rating of 7 indicates an extreme rating on the contrast pole (not shown).

GRID II

Construct	Self	Ideal self	Mother	Father	Fiancé	Grandmother	Phobic friend	Former friend	Fiancé's mother	Fiancé's father	Pitied friend	Fiancé's sister	Fiancé's brother
1 Uncritically confiding	4	6	5	7	5	4	2	4	3	5	4	2	5
2 Soft	2	5	3	6	4	3	2	6	3	5	3	4	5
3 Imposed on	2	5	4	6	3	6	2	7	3	6	4	4	6
4 Rigid	3	4	4	2	4	4	5	7	3	6	4	4	5
5 Takes life too seriously	2	4	3	6	4	5	5	7	4	6	3	4	5
6 Understanding	2	3	2	4	3	4	2	6	3	4	2	4	5
7 Easily upset	1	5	2	5	6	4	2	7	2	6	4	4	5
8 Sensitive	2	4	2	5	5	4	2	7	3	6	3	4	5
9 Self-conscious	3	5	4	6	5	4	3	4	2	4	4	4	6
10 Self-sacrificing	4	7	3	5	3	4	3	6	5	6	4	4	3
11 Psychiatrically vulnerable	2	7	2	7	3	4	5	7	4	6	3	7	5
12 Tense	2	6	3	4	4	3	3	7	4	6	5	7	5
13 Bad-tempered	1	4	3	1	5	4	4	6	7	4	6	4	4
14 Secure	3	4	3	5	4	3	6	7	1	1	6	1	4

GRID III

	Self	Ideal self	Mother	Father	Fiancé	Grandmother	Phobic friend	Former friend	Fiancé's mother	Fiancé's father	Pitied friend	Fiancé's sister	Fiancé's brother
1 Uncritically confiding	3	4	2	6	3	5	1	7	6	6	4	4	4
2 Soft	4	4	6	5	5	6	3	7	2	6	4	5	6
3 Imposed on	4	6	4	7	3	6	5	7	3	6	3	2	7
4 Rigid	5	5	4	1	5	4	7	7	6	6	5	7	5
5 Takes life too seriously	2	5	4	3	4	5	7	7	6	7	3	4	5
6 Understanding	2	1	4	6	2	5	5	7	3	4	1	4	4
7 Easily upset	2	5	4	6	3	4	2	7	1	6	4	3	3
8 Sensitive	4	5	4	7	3	5	2	7	1	6	5	4	4
9 Self-conscious	5	4	3	5	3	5	2	7	1	6	2	3	7
10 Self-sacrificing	3	4	4	6	4	5	5	7	4	6	3	4	4
11 Psychiatrically vulnerable	5	6	3	4	2	5	3	7	3	2	2	6	5
12 Tense	5	7	3	2	4	5	4	7	3	4	3	6	6
13 Bad-tempered	1	6	2	1	3	6	4	1	7	6	4	6	5
14 Secure	6	1	5	1	2	3	5	7	1	1	7	1	2

7 Behavioural Analysis and Treatment of a Complex Case

Victor Meyer, Robert Sharpe and
Edward Chesser

Preamble

When dealing with relatively isolated symptoms, particularly in
cases where a patient's general adjustment to life is good, we may
often find it easy and advantageous to apply one or more of the
behaviour therapy learning techniques or treatment packages to the
problem. However, when we are faced with complex cases
involving, for example, multiple symptoms, depression and
personality disorder, the technique-orientated symptom by
symptom approach may be quite inappropriate. Very often
behaviour therapy technology may have no ready-made technique
to apply to a particular symptom or group of symptoms. Or even if
treatment packages are available the treatment of symptoms one by
one may become unwieldy and uneconomical for both patient and
therapist. And, perhaps most importantly of all, the treatment of
presenting symptoms individually may result in the omission from a
treatment programme of those underlying problem areas which
may be primary and causative and thus most relevant to treatment.
In this last case the inappropriate application of technological
treatment to presenting symptoms might reasonably be expected to
result in relapse or the emergence of other symptoms.

The main difficulty with complex cases such as these is in
ascertaining just what are the primary problem areas. A varied list
of symptoms and syndromes may not be difficult for a therapist to
collect. But in order to develop a full formulation of these
symptoms, determine the ways in which they may be related and
their possibly well-disguised primary causes, it is essential that we
carry out a more detailed behavioural analysis. This behavioural
analysis, which we would argue is as indispensable for relatively
isolated symptoms as it is for the most complex cases, may take
several hours of interviewing and cross-validating of information in
order to develop a coherent formulation. It is obvious that one must
ascertain the problem areas which the patient is presenting (often

called target areas) and the immediate factors involved in maintaining them. But then we would argue that this data must be set in the context of other relevant areas of the patient's life to become of use as a working hypothesis. For example, a thorough account of the development of the presenting problems may shed light on how the patient acquires behaviour and how principles of learning may operate on him idiosyncratically. Again, a knowledge of the patient's development of a life-style, ideals, aspirations, attitudes and self-image at the hands of parents, siblings, peers, school environments, work situations and marital relationship may enable us to see how the presenting problems might be seen as part of a more general problem of coping with life. From this body of information we attempt to develop a final formulation of the problems and a working hypothesis from which we can develop and evaluate a treatment programme (for example, Sharpe and Meyer, 1973).

In using such a behavioural analysis approach we can see that four general stages are involved. All of them are guided by principles of experimental psychology. Schematically they can be presented thus:

1   Collection of data concerning the presenting problems and maintaining factors. This is done by detailed questioning of the patient and people with whom he interacts and by observation *in vivo* of his behaviour.

2   Determination of any relationship between this collection of data and the development of the patient's life-style. Here we have to order the existing data into a coherent picture. As historical data emerge we may be developing new hypotheses concerning the patient's problems and using these to look for more historical or present data to confirm or refute them. Thus, we gradually modify our hypotheses in the light of new evidence until we arrive at a formulation which holds together the facts logically.

3   Development of a treatment approach from the formulation of the problem. Having ordered the data and historical development of the patient's life-style into a coherent formulation we then use our working hypotheses to predict a treatment approach which will modify the problem areas.

4   Implementation and evaluation of the treatment approach. The formulation and working hypothesis is tested at this stage by observation of the patient's response to the treatment approach. Depending upon this response we might modify the formulation and treatment approach or continue to use them.

Using such a behavioural analysis approach we may often discover important variables in the problem area which were never presented as part of the symptomatology. However, they may be induced by looking at a coherent body of facts and used in treatment — often as an essential component (for example, Sharpe and Meyer, 1973).

Thus, a behavioural analysis may result in a general formulation from which a relevant and parsimonious individualised treatment approach can be induced. This stage may often require an ability on the part of the therapist to innovate and evaluate experimentally a treatment approach which is not indicated at all in the literature. The case which we present here is one which we consider to be an example of the use, based on a thorough behavioural analysis, of a more relevant and economical treatment than had been tried unsuccessfully by a previous technique-orientated approach. A general formulation was made in the case which led to the treatment of quite different problems from the ones which had previously been treated.

Description of the presenting complaints

The patient, whom we shall call Jane, was a 31-year-old married woman who on admission to hospital listed the following complaints:

1 A fear of uttering, or hearing any curse words or 'bad' thoughts. This fear was exacerbated when there was any religious connotation. She reported that the fear was associated with the possibility that such words would put a curse on some part of her environment and that this curse might be fulfilled. She feared that her environment from individual people through to the whole universe might be adversely affected. In short, she feared she was a witch. However, she said that she realised that these fears and associated rituals were all nonsense, that she tried to resist them but was unable to do so.

2 Frequent and prolonged obsessional ruminations in which she performed rituals in her head. These rituals took place after she had uttered, or feared she had uttered, one of the curse words. If this happened she would repeat 'safe' words and sentences to cancel out the 'cataclysmic' effects of the curse words.

3 Marital problems which she described as an inability to relate to her husband socially or sexually. She said that she depended on her husband because she could feel safe with

him in regard to her fears and ruminations but that she resented this dependence on him. This resentment and later loss of respect had resulted in her loss of social and sexual contact with him.

4   Recurrent depressive moods.

5   Inability to speak freely, and on the few occasions when she could speak the appearance of frequent blocks.

6   Inability to eat on her own. Even when with others she could eat only very little and was considerably underweight. There was some debate over the question of whether or not she had some of the features of anorexia nervosa.

7   An extremely low self-image which manifested itself in such statements as 'I've never done anything in my life'; 'I'm no good as a mother or a wife'; 'I can't see anything in the future'.

8   Agoraphobia.

Psychiatric history

We include at this point the psychiatric history taken on admission. We feel it to be of importance that this history should be considered in comparison to the behavioural analysis which follows later. In particular the previous treatments and diagnoses are emphasised and we intend them to be contrasted with the treatment approach which we developed from our behavioural formulation.

Reason for referral

Jane was admitted for behavioural assessment and treatment in 1971 when aged 31 with a ten-year history of fluctuating obsessive-compulsive symptoms associated with secondary depression and phobic anxiety.

Family history

Her father was killed in naval action in 1940 when she was three months old. Mother, a forceful, lively person, is now a healthy 61-year-old. One older brother of 34, single, a Cambridge graduate, ordained and doing ecclesiastical research, whom she much admires for his academic and athletic success. The home atmosphere was described as secure despite the early death of father and some financial hardship. There was a strict moral code and regular Protestant church attendance. New clothes and cinema visits were rare events and holidays were spent with maternal grandparents. There were no family illnesses of note.

Personal history

Early development
Born in India, 1940. Birth, early development and health were normal. The family returned to England from India after the death of father and there were no separations from mother during childhood.

School and occupations
She was happy and academically successful at two private day schools but was unhappy in her first term at boarding school at 13. After this she made plenty of friends, did well at athletics and was average academically, passing four out of six 'O' levels at 16, failing French and maths at the second attempt. She left school at $17^{1/2}$ years and obtained a place for general nursing training at a London teaching hospital when 19. The year's interval was spent doing a secretarial course and three temporary secretarial jobs. She enjoyed her first year of nursing training but left before the first-year exam in order to get married. She did not work after her marriage except for part-time shop assistant work in the last year.

Sexual history
Menarche, age 13. Prepared by mother. Periods heavy, sometimes irregular. Casual boyfriends from age 15. No masturbation or premarital sexual intercourse.

Marital history
She met her husband when aged 19 and married a year later. Sexual relationship was good initially but has been affected by her illness. Husband joined RAF and was commissioned six months before marriage. Husband is described as a pleasant and capable man but less interested in social activities than she is. This had led to some deterioration in the marital relationship.

Children
Her son was conceived shortly after marriage and was wanted. Full-time, normal delivery. 1960. Two years ago she had a spontaneous miscarriage.

Medical history
There have been no physical illnesses of note except for two episodes of low back pain and sciatica attributed to disc lesion in 1971.

Personality

The premorbid personality was described as outgoing, gregarious, usually cheerful but variable in mood, enjoying sport and entertaining, and not unusually tidy or punctual. Until her marriage her religious faith was quite strong and she shared her family's moral attitudes concerning chastity, sanctity of marriage, gambling and self-indulgence.

Present illness

The first evidence of obsessional symptomatology was at the age of 13 when she heard a friend say that the only unforgivable sin was swearing against the Holy Ghost. She often used to think about the effects of swearing on other people and would spend a long time praying for forgiveness for having these thoughts. However, these ruminations could be fairly easily suppressed and concealed from other people. In 1960, at the age of 21, about one month after the birth of her son, she began to feel faint and nauseated. She had had a haemorrhage and was receiving stilboestrol to suppress lactation. She became anxious about carrying the baby or going out alone because of feeling faint and had an acute panic attack. Anxiety about being left alone persisted but in addition obsessional thoughts occurred. Predominantly the thoughts are concerned with swearing, evil and black magic. She is frightened that if she utters words such as 'curse', 'damn', 'evil' or 'Hell', something harmful will happen to other people. These thoughts may be triggered off by something she reads or hears but more often 'come out of the blue'. In order to prevent any possible harmful consequences she adopted several manoeuvres — hesitating before speaking; asking if she has spoken the words; distorting them if they cropped up in ordinary conversation, for example, 'evil' became 'ever' or 'eve'; avoidance of being alone in case she uttered the words in panic; fear of or avoidance of opening mouth to eat or clean teeth in case she uttered the word; repeating words that she fears may have been harmful to reassure herself they were not; after meals going to the toilet to repeat certain thoughts or do mental arithmetic or some other superstitious thought; avoidance of church services. At her worst she has had to isolate herself from other people, is frightened to talk at all and has lost weight because of her fear of opening her mouth. In addition to this she has been housebound.

Previous psychiatric treatment

She first sought psychiatric help soon after the onset of the phobic anxiety and ruminations in 1961. Initially treatment consisted of supportive psychotherapy and medication with phenothiazines. Later, both tricyclic antidepressants and MAOI's were given with little benefit. Three courses of ECT in 1967 and 1969 brought definite but only temporary improvement in depression and ruminations. In 1970 she had 11 months in-patient treatment at another psychiatric hospital. Treatment included flooding in fantasy and practice for travel by bus, tube, shopping or staying at home alone, uttering the 'evil' words, wishing for something impossible to happen, for example, preventing sunrise tomorrow. In addition she received a training programme in typing and some exploration of the marital attitudes and relationship was undertaken. At the time of her discharge a year before the present admission she was able to travel alone, her mood was much improved and the level of rumination considerably less. However, she was still unable to eat alone and was underweight. For a time after discharge she wished to be independent and continued a part-time typing course and part-time shop assistant work in London. She then developed acute lumbago which recurred after a holiday abroad with husband. There was a gradual relapse with increasing obsessional ruminations and avoidances.

Mental state

On admission she appeared pale and thin but otherwise no physical abnormality was noted. Mood was tense and depressed. Depressive preoccupations about her wasted life and how she had spoiled other people's lives, pessimistic thoughts about the future. There was considerable hesitancy in speech when questioned about obsessional ruminations and avoidances as described above in history of present illness. There was no evidence of formal thought disorder, delusions or hallucinations. Orientation was correct, intelligence appeared above average and insight was present.

Initial diagnosis

1 Obsessive-compulsive neurosis — predominantly fears, thoughts and ruminations.
2 Mild agoraphobia.
3 Secondary depressive reaction.

Behavioural analysis, formulation and tactics of the therapeutic relationship

The 'curse phobia'

The first major problem which we observed was that Jane blocked in her speech whenever she uttered any word which was similar to a curse word — for example, 'purse' (like 'curse') — or at words such as 'damn' or 'blast'. She showed very high anxiety reactions if she or anyone else uttered such words. She would immediately stop speaking and we discovered that she repeated 'safe' words to herself subvocally. Frequently she would leave us or the company in which she was involved and go to an isolated place, usually the toilet, where she could silently perform very complicated obsessional rituals. These would be entirely in thoughts and included the name of nice, 'safe' people repeated a certain number of times, multiplying and cubing numbers and using 'safe' sentences. At this time we were not clear as to what the safe people or sentences comprised but this was clarified later. It would take Jane approximately thirty minutes to complete her rituals unless she was interrupted, in which case she would have to restart the whole process. If she could not ritualise according to this pattern she became extremely anxious.

We also observed, during interviews and general ward activities, that Jane would often leave people after chatting to them and seek solitude. When we asked her about this she said that she would ask herself whether she had uttered any curse words. On occasion she would ask the therapist, before leaving an interview, whether she had said 'anything'. By observation again we found that Jane could not speak to anyone, including therapists, in the morning unless she had performed her ritual in advance.

These problems, which were obviously striking in the early stages of treatment planning, were naturally disruptive during interviews. If Jane had been allowed to continue her disruptive behaviour of leaving interview situations it is doubtful whether we could have gathered sufficient data for treatment planning. Thus we found it necessary to prevent Jane from leaving the interview situation to ritualise. We attempted to do this by reducing her anxieties about uttering curse words during interviews and by motivating her to stay in the interview situation.

This was done very effectively by using the interpersonal relationship which had begun very early on between Jane and one of us (VM). This relationship was one which was often based on sneering, jibing and cynical remarks from Jane and adroit verbal countering by VM. We found that if Jane was met on her own verbal battlefield and similar (but not necessarily aggressive — rather more humorous or rational) tactics employed she would stay for longer in the interview situation. In a short time a very strong relationship was developed on this 'sparring' basis and we were able to motivate the patient to start to resist her blocking and interview disrupting. It was not until later on in behavioural analysis that the full reason for the effectiveness of these tactics was obtained. At the time they were used on a purely empirical basis and we feel it relevant to describe them here to demonstrate how a therapeutic relationship can be used to prepare a patient for a treatment programme. As with many other of our therapy programmes the therapist was establishing himself as a potent social reinforcer and using his reinforcing qualities to keep the patient involved in the programme. We frequently find it of value to use the reinforcing qualities of the therapist in such a way and then fade them out at the end of the treatment. Having established with Jane a satisfactory interview behaviour pattern we were able to continue to gather more detailed data.

She went on to report that at home, before going to bed, she would ask her husband whether she had said anything wrong or harmed anyone with whom she had come into contact during the day. She would also go through a list of friends' names and ask 'Is Mildred, Mildred?' etc. To none of this was her husband required to answer but just to listen.

Eating, yawning and cleaning her teeth were also found to be difficult for Jane. The reason for this, she said, was that in opening her mouth a curse word might slip out.

The reason for her anxiety concerning the uttering of 'curse' words was not fully understood for the first few interview sessions. However, Jane was eventually able to tell us that her fear was that some disaster, possibly at a universal level, might be caused by her uttering curse words. Her later obsessional rituals were methods which she had developed to eliminate the possibility of the curses being fulfilled and if she was not allowed to carry them out she became extremely anxious. Thus, we were able to conceptualise her pattern of ritualistic and avoidance behaviour as being related to her fear of universal disaster brought about by her curse words. In this way we were able to look at, early on, several of her presenting problems as a coherent group: fear of curse words, obsessional ruminations, inability to speak freely, inability to eat — with resultant weight loss and inability to open her mouth in general — were all seen as a result of her curse phobia. More links were to be found with other presenting complaints, but these will be discussed at a later stage to preserve more accurate chronology of the formulation.

The marital, existential and depression problems

Having described how we began to gather data in our behavioural analysis — by exerting stimulus control over Jane through a therapeutic relationship so that she stayed and talked in interviews and also by observational methods on the ward — we can now look at her other problem areas and the way in which they related to her life-style and development from childhood. Here again, we were to find a coherent clustering of problems and a central causative factor.

At the basis of Jane's marital problem seemed to lie her very low regard for her husband. She said she considered him to be weak, submissive and unable to take decisions. She used phrases such as 'He's a fool and gets on my nerves' and clearly had little respect for him as a man. It was at the same time apparent, however, that she was very dependent on her husband as a safe support and indulged herself in his great attachment and affection for her. Thus, she had found herself in an approach-avoidance conflict concerning her husband whereby she was very dependent upon him as the only safe support in her life and very resentful of this dependence because at the same time she had no respect for him. His presence in her life had become a constant reminder of her failure and inability to succeed at life. She said that she could not imagine being sexually excited by her husband again and talked about a separation and divorce. Just prior to our seeing her Jane had spent some time in London living away from her husband and having an affair with a married man. Interestingly, she had met this man while in another hospital and had begun having intercourse with him to help him overcome his impotence problem. She had been successful in this undertaking which had obviously been reinforcing for her.

Her marital conflict had also provided her with a large source of guilt concerning her husband and her 10-year-old son. While she lacked respect for her husband and wanted to be able to be free from her dependency on him, she also realised that her extramarital relationship was making her husband very unhappy. She knew that she indulged herself in his permissive attitude and eventually would hurt him by going too far. As well as feeling that she was not the wife she should be she also felt that she was lacking as a mother. She felt that she was ruining her son's life through the unhappy marital situation and often cried while discussing her son. She said that she wanted to be with him at such an important stage of his development but could not bear to resume her marital ties.

As regards her existential problems, it was clear that she also held herself in very low regard. She was completely unable to envisage any future for herself and had no goals or even subgoals in her life. She was devoid of the sort of self-confidence necessary for gaining employment and because of her fear of curse words and thus inability to talk freely, her interpersonal relationships were completely crippled.

These areas together with her deteriorated marital relationship completed the picture of a person who had a total lack of behaviour from which she could gain any reinforcement. In view of this non-existence of reinforcing behaviour patterns it was not surprising, in behavioural terms, that she should suffer the bouts of depression which she reported. Thus at this stage her depression was formulated tentatively as being one possible consequence of her existential problems.

Pausing here for a moment, we might look now at the way in which these three major problem areas in Jane's life can be seen against a background of her early development and upbringing. When we look at this upbringing we can see more easily how her presenting behaviour patterns might have developed and been maintained. We will also see how important it is that such a historical overview is taken as it was from a combination of such historial data and present data that the eventual formulation was reached.

Jane was brought up by a Victorian mother who prepeared her for life in a religious, romanticised, rigid and punitive way which was unrealistic in terms of goals. The main principle which governed Jane was to be 'clean, good, Christian and do things well'. She was, in short, to be a perfectionist. She was regularly reinforced for achieving this perfection and punished for failing to reach it. She had no father (he died when she was three months old) and her mother created the atmosphere in her home of pushing her to achieve. The public schools which Jane attended were at the same time very over-protective and this general home and school environment resulted in her gradually acquiring a fear of taking responsibilities and failing. At school she had considerable problems with examinations and similar testing situations.

Thus it was possible to conceptualise Jane's development in terms of growing up in an environment where she was taught to achieve, but where attempting to achieve was dangerous in case she failed. On the other hand, though not attempting to achieve was not threatening, she never got anywhere in her life by using this approach. Thus she was in a conflict situation. In behavioural terms this would be called a double approach-avoidance conflict. Both choices have possibilities for punishment as well as reinforcement. If, as she had tended to do throughout her life, she did not attempt to achieve then she would be reinforced by avoiding the anxiety-producing result of possible failure. However, this choice also provided her with punishment in the sense that she could never get anywhere or achieve anything in her life. If she chose to attempt to achieve she might be reinforced by actually succeeding in this attempt. However, this choice also bore the possibility of punishment in terms of her extreme anxiety if she failed.

The double approach-avoidance model also pertained to interpersonal situations. It was typified by the interview situations which we described earlier. She would present herself as an attractive and intelligent woman who would get involved in the therapeutic encounter and then hit the therapist with very nasty, bitchy comments. Responded to appropriately this situation was used as we described to keep Jane in the interview situation. But looking once again at the double approach-avoidance model we would argue that developmentally she had learned that interpersonal relationships could be attractive but there was always a possibility of their leading to failure and rejection. Thus, to avoid this eventual failure, she would sabotage the relationship herself before she was rejected. On a great number of occasions she seemed to be doing this also in therapy. It transpired later that one of the reasons why the relationship between Jane and VM was so tenable in the early stages was because if she kept sniping at the therapist then the situation would be difficult already and there was no danger of losing a good relationship. Thus, her anxieties about failing in this relationship were low as she was already avoiding any attempt to form a good relationship. We can now see that a formulation of the presenting problems began to emerge from these details.

As the double approach-avoidance conflict developed, it became responsible for Jane's failure to achieve anything and the gradual development of a large discrepancy between her ideals for herself and her real self. That is, in her upbringing she was always taught to aim high; but because the goals were too high she failed and was rejected because of failure and thus received in reality very little encouragement or reinforcement from her environment. Jane, seeing this great discrepancy between what she had attained and what she felt she should attain, could not even develop subgoals to achieve and thus approach her level of aspiration. The fear of failure was even related to the smallest subgoal.

The discrepancy also made her extremely sensitive in that she related all that was going on in her environment to how it affected her. She was looking for any criticism and because of the ease with which she might be criticised her environment became threatening. It was clear in interview that she had great difficulty in being perceptive of others and was always defensive — particularly with people who were intelligent, of high status, and high achievement. The behaviour therapy approach, of course, had goals and even in the early stages of this goal-orientated situation Jane wrecked treatment progress by being unreliable and attacking with her therapists. This behaviour could be related to her fear of failure in therapy and consequent avoidance of therapy goals by unreliability.

The marital problem could be related to the same basic fear of failure and criticism. She was afraid of the responsibility which marriage involves and because she was afraid of being rejected she married someone she considered to be non-threatening and safe. She was in fact attracted by exciting men but did not trust them and opted instead for an indulgent man. However, he became a stimulus which reminded her of her failure. When she married this man she was safe but by avoiding life's challenges she did not do anything or achieve anything in her life. She became very dependent upon him but he also, because of his indulgent manner, became a stimulus which prevented her from getting on with life and highlighted her failure. She thus began to resent him as well as herself. Her low self concept led to her feeling such things as 'how can he love someone as useless as me?'. Her resentment of him grew as he indulged her uselessness more and more. The social interactions between them became impaired because she felt guilty that she was not acting as a wife should, and instead was languishing in hospital. He in turn felt insecure that he had been rejected by his wife and any slight disagreement between them became blown up due to each other's sensitivity and guilt about the marital relationship.

It is also interesting to consider her affair in the light of her double approach-avoidance conflict. Once again she had the opportunity to form a relationship and in this case she took it. But it should be remembered that the man was a patient with a sexual problem. To this degree he was a relatively non-threatening person and Jane was able to offer help to him — rather than being dependent as she usually was. In this case she accepted the challenge of the relationship and, in being able to give help, was reinforced. This tendency to look for situations where she could be of help was to be repeated and give an important clue to the vocational aspects of Jane's treatment.

The curse phobia in relation to existential problems

Thus far our formulation was quite firmly founded in factual data obtained and validated as far as possible from Jane, her husband and general observations. It was possible to speculate further on the development of the obsessional-compulsive behaviour and curse phobia in the context of this life-style. The reason for such speculation as follows was to help attack the problem and to give the therapists ideas for treatment approaches.

The patient was a perfect child with a religious mother. She believed very strongly in God, the Church and all the concomitant ideology. She heard one day that uttering swear words was an unforgivable sin — and this at a time in her life when she was becoming interested in such words. From that time, which factually occurred in her life, whenever she heard or thought of a swear word she became anxious that she might be punished (again for not being perfect) and prayed to put it all right. Anxiety was decreased by this praying and she learned a response which removed anxiety evoked by a stimulus (swear word) to which the anxiety was attached. Aetiologically, this anxiety and ritualising appeared to generalise to the extent that Jane developed a phobic anxiety state.

These symptoms all increased dramatically soon after she gave birth to her son. As indicated earlier, she had great problems taking responsibility in case she failed, particularly in terms of her discrepancy between ideals and reality. Bringing up a child was a great task to her and with the threat that she might fail as a mother as well as a wife the anxiety increased. Thoughts about curse words and ruminations increased. It seems possible that with increased arousal sensitisation occurred and with it the need to ritualise more and more. That is, she had learned to reduce anxiety by rationalising and with the additional anxiety at this point she began to ritualise more frequently. Predictably, when her husband was away the rituals became more and more pronounced as she was in the position of being totally responsible for the family.

Thus, we formulated that the curse phobia and associated rituals were precipitated by strong admonishments that swearing was very wrong. However, the later maintenance of these problems was probably due to her concern that she would fall short of her mothers ideals if she swore, and the final florid presenting symptomatology seemed to have been brought about by the birth of her son and the consequent responsibilities.

'Agoraphobia'

The so-called agoraphobia problem, which had formed the basis of previous treatmental approaches, was examined thoroughly. Jane reported that it was not primarily a fear of people or being outdoors *per se* which made her anxious but the fact that if she uttered a curse word there would be no safe refuge for her to go and ritualise. Thus, on closer examination, this problem became one of a fear of inability to find a secluded place where she could undo any curses by ritualising. It need hardly be pointed out that the treatment of this part of the problem as a fear of going out as such would not necessarily lead to any considerable or lasting improvement. In fact, such an approach would be an example of inappropriate emphasis in treatment on an area of symptomatology which is two stages removed from the major problem area. The fear of going out seemed to be based on the fear of uttering curse words which in turn was based on a fear of failure, imperfection and rejection.

Summary of the formulation

Using the facts which we gathered during the behavioural analysis we were able to formulate a coherent hypothesis of the development and maintenance of the various symptoms.

Of central importance in Jane's problems was her fear of responsibility, testing situations and possible failure, falling short of perfection, criticism and rejection. The discrepancy between her ideals, which were perfectionist and unrealistic, and the reality of her situation was very large. She was unable to formulate and attempt even the smallest subgoal between her ideals and reality as any attempt to achieve a goal, however small, put her into a double approach-avoidance conflict situation in which her fear of failure was dominant. The resultant lack of reinforcement from achieving anything of social, marital or career value in her life had led to her experiencing bouts of depression.

Her obsessional rituals and fear of curse words were probably initiated by severe warnings that swearing was evil and were exacerbated throughout her life by her fear of falling short of perfection. Because of this fear she had to ensure that any possible wrong she had done was put right by ritualising.

The agoraphobia seemed to have been a consequence of the curse phobia. Thus, it was not seen as a central problem but one which should disappear if the fear of criticism and imperfection and fear of curses were removed.

Treatment formulation

In terms of the present formulation — based on a fear of failure and responsibility — it is easy to understand why previous treatments, which were based on facilitating Jane's taking longer and longer walks and implosion of the ruminations, had no persistent effect. The basic fear of taking responsibility should indicate instead a treatment whose aims would be to decrease the discrepancy between levels of aspiration and reality, by enabling the patient to reach for and attain subgoals, and to improve, perhaps by these means, her self-concept.

Basically, the programme which was formulated was as follows:

1 To eliminate the most crippling problem behaviour — that is, the obsessional ruminations and related ritualistic behaviour. We considered this to be an expedient treatment stage because these problems were standing in the way of the therapists' relating to Jane and of her being able to eat which was resulting in her being underweight and lacking in energy.

2 To help Jane readjust to the extent that she would start to develop a better self-concept and relinquish her present bad one. This was to be accomplished by outlining and helping her to attain subgoals by which she could achieve a final goal commensurate with her assets and abilities. We predicted that in this way she would gradually achieve and accept responsibility and reduce the discrepancy in goals. We further expected that by enabling her to do this her marriage would no longer be a threatening and constraining situation. She should see her husband not as a stimulus which prevented her life from flourishing but as someone with whom she could stay and become productive or whom she could leave and divorce — but of her own free choice rather than because of a dependency problem.

Implementation of treatment programme

Jane was admitted to hospital on 25 November 1971. In this section we shall chart her progress over the two years which followed. We shall attempt to give a description of the general decisions which were made concerning her ongoing treatment during that time. Also, where appropriate, we shall give some detailed account of the treatment procedures which were developed from our formulation and continuous evaluation of the treatment programme.

1 The ritualistic behaviour

Although this part of the problem was considered to be a consequence of Jane's perfectionism and fear of doing wrong, it was also clear that it was now a problem area which had developed and generalised to become an autonomous, rigid behaviour pattern. In addition, it was a problem which was interfering with any treatment planning to the point where this was almost impossible.

Thus we decided that her ritualistic behaviour should be put under control as a first treatment goal. In terms of this single target area we decided that the most appropriate method of treating the problem was by response-prevention (Meyer and Levy, 1973). The object of this approach was to expose Jane to anxiety-provoking situations (swearing, opening her mouth, cleaning her teeth, eating, laughing, etc.) while, at the same time, preventing the rituals. She would, of course, become anxious in these circumstances, but would be encouraged to control her anxiety by waiting for it to extinguish rather than by ritualising.

Although we were moderately successful in this attempt in the first few days we were aware that response-prevention was by no means complete. Jane would ritualise before going to sleep and on waking up. Another problem with the response prevention was that Jane found it difficult to grade various situations in any hierarchy according to the degree of anxiety which they provoked. This latter problem meant that we could not introduce her gradually to the situations in any systematic way.

It was for these reasons that we then decided to use a flooding procedure with Jane. It had also transpired during interviews that she would be terrified of any interaction with a 'witch', a medium at a séance, or in any situation which pertained to space or the universe. She also said that any involvement of a priest in any of the anxiety-provoking situations would increase the level of anxiety.

Thus began Jane's period of flooding which we attempted to make as comprehensive as possible. In many interchanges between therapists and Jane we would express ourselves in terms of her feared swear words. The sight of a therapist preventing Jane's rituals by saying, 'If you use that bloody toilet to ritualise I'll discontinue treatment' was not uncommon at that time. We also had to spend nights in the ward over a period of a week so that a therapist could be present immediately on Jane's waking and before her going to sleep. She would be required to talk as soon as she woke up to prevent her rituals. Her eating, cleaning of teeth and many other daily routines were carefully monitored.

We also made trips to graveyards, planetaria, seances, churches, Hampstead Heath and other places of worship where swearing (on our part) was *de rigueur*. In the more public planetaria we would swear at a discreet level of volume; on Hampstead Heath we would shout the words lustily and with gusto. No arrests were ever made, but it is not possible to estimate the number of souls who, while walking their dogs, may have been traumatised to the point of becoming Heathphobes as a consequence of Jane's treatment programme.

We even enlisted the aid of a priest who read out in his church a prayer[1] which Jane had produced for us, saying that this would be the worst curse she could ever imagine. At the more irreverent passages his voice dropped in volume; but on a re-reading by VM this balance was redressed by a rise in volume at the appropriate passages. In this way we hoped to appease the gods of experimental psychology whose wrath may have been incurred by the lack of consistency in the priest's voice level. A second priest was later found whose voice remained constant — thus satisfying our rigorous scientific requirements without intervention from us.

Such exercises were performed many times by Jane and the therapists. We used methods varying from verbal coaxing, threat of discontinuing treatment, humorous diversions, modelling and many others to enable Jane to get through treatment. The light style of writing in the last three paragraphs typifies the way in which we approached the flooding — an approach to which Jane responded very positively. This régime continued for some three weeks and all our efforts were concentrated on eliminating the obsessional rituals. At the end of this time the rituals were under control while Jane was being supervised and she was sent home for Christmas (23 December). However, she started to relapse and ritualise after two days and returned to the ward after five days.

At this point she became very despondent and negative about treatment. Her main therapist (VM) was away at a conference and would not be returning for a week. It was apparent to Jane that she had become very dependent on VM and she said that she wanted to try to reduce her dependence on him. While he was away she felt that she could not go out of the ward because of her agoraphobia problem. Generally it was clear that VM was a discriminative stimulus for Jane's continuing to progress and in his absence her motivation had rapidly declined.

---

[1] *Prayer*
I pray to everything that has ever been and that is and that ever will be and everything more than that and everything else apart from that and everything more than that.
  At all times that have ever been and that are and that ever will be and everything else besides that and everything else apart from that and at everything more than that and at everything that has ever been and is and ever will be and more than that.
  That God, the Devil and all the Evil and everything else that has ever been and that is and that ever will be and everything more than that.
  Will Damn, Curse, Bugger, Blast, Blight, Bless, Loath, Love and Do everything that has ever been and that is and that ever will be and everything more than that.
  And everything that has ever been and that is and that ever will be and everything more than that; everything that has ever been and that is and that ever will be and everything more than that.
  To Dr Vic Meyer and to me and everything that has ever been and that is and that ever will be and everything more than that.
  And everything that has ever been and that is and that ever will be and everything more than that; everything that has ever been that is and that ever will be and everything more than that.
  And everything that could be more than that.
  I damn and I curse and I bugger and I do all the evil that has ever been and ever will be and may everything else do the same to the Holy Ghost.
Please Full Stop; Full Stop.

However, while discussing these points, Jane also began to demonstrate feelings of gratitude towards her therapists. She said that they had facilitated her going out of hospital and controlling her rituals (though blocks in speech were still occurring to some degree). She was also showing some insight into her sarcasm and nastiness and said herself that it was mostly used as a defence.

None the less, her despondency remained and on the day before VM returned (3 January) she said she might be dead before he came back. She talked about using razor blades and was watched carefully on the ward as a possible suicide risk.

On the return of VM (4 January) she agreed to restart the programme which had been so productive before Christmas. More flippancy was introduced into the situation and Jane's bitchiness turned more to flippant sarcasm. Her earlier activities were resumed under the supervision of therapists but as Jane became more confident we gradually faded out until she was exerting self-control and asking for help when she needed it. This was to continue during the rest of the treatment programme and, in fact, the ritualistic patterns gradually faded out from that point on. It is worth noting here that Jane's relapse at home was probably due to her going too suddenly into an environment which was very stressful for her. The fading programme which we instituted was a result of our experiences with a more abrupt ending of the programme and is a good example of the feeding back into treatment of the implications of an earlier treatment attempt which had not been productive. Again we would stress here the importance of continuous assessment and modification of a treatment programme.

2 Interpersonal relationships on the ward

During this period of response prevention Jane was developing relationships — both good and bad — on the ward. One very important observation was that she had a great facility for helping other patients who were in distress. She had an obvious leaning towards such a 'helping' capacity and it was thus not surprising that when she eventually admitted to having any career aspirations at all these were towards social work. This was a major point which was taken up around the end of her response prevention and gave a clue to the second treatment stage.

Another relationship was not so productive — but was used to demonstrate to Jane that adjustments could be made even in less than ideal relationships. A female patient had been admitted who was very difficult to manage and the whole situation on the ward, involving the staff, houseman and patients, was deteriorating. The situation was particularly bad between the houseman, Jane and the other patient. Eventually, vm arranged a confrontation between these people and a successful resolution of differences resulted. The ward situation started to ease and Jane learned an important lesson in handling interpersonal relationship problems. Equally, we learned a good deal about the necessity of intervention in the patient's environment as well as in the behaviour of the patient *per se.*

3 Agoraphobia and job-hunting

By the end of January the therapists had faded out sufficiently for Jane to be travelling for distances of five miles by bus. But it should be made clear that the agoraphobia symptom had not been treated directly. Jane's confidence had increased after putting her rituals under control and the agoraphobia seemed to be coming under control as a result.

We decided to maintain the travelling behaviour by giving Jane a series of instructions to go and find out more about a social work career and to try to get herself a post in social work as a trainee. In the latter part of February, however, she decided on her own initiative to get a temporary job and succeeded in obtaining a position as saleswoman in a local shoe shop. She had been encouraged in this by staff and by her husband on his weekend visits and her success was heavily reinforced by all. Jane herself was very pleased by it. During the next six weeks she lost this job, which she did not like very much anyway, and got another in a chain department store selling clothes. At the same time she was having interviews with social work departments and obtaining positive reinforcement, both from us and from her achievements in the interviews, for applying to them.

Her motivation was rising throughout this period. The gradual steps which she had taken to make herself independent and to put herself to the test in a job had been rewarding and she was now very hopeful of succeeding in a social work career. Her motivation soared higher when, early in May, she was able to leave hospital and move into a flat in London which she shared with two other people. Again, this was a positive step in attaining her independence. Her husband stood by her in this move and even helped to some degree, saying that he would wait for her to develop her independence to her satisfaction.

In June, she went for an interview at a social work department in a very difficult London borough. There were eighty applicants for twelve posts and the situation presented Jane with her biggest challenge so far in treatment. There were some fluctuations in her ritualistic symptoms and her relationship with her husband, which were probably related to the challenge. In fact, Jane was offered a post as ancillary social worker in this department two months later. With some trepidation but also a great deal of pleasure at her success in being offered the post she accepted and began work. We supported and encouraged her during this early part of her work, which she found quite demanding and difficult, while also living up to her expectations in terms of its interest. She held this job for just under a year until the following August and after working for a period with us in the treatment of obsessional patients has now gone on to work in a social work department nearer to her and her husband's home.

4 Marital, sexual and social relationships

At the end of the early period of response prevention in the February after her admission, Jane's husband was entering into her therapy and regular sessions were held with him as well as Jane. He obviously wanted his marriage to continue and said he would be prepared to wait until Jane felt she could come back to him of her own accord.

Jane was still very undecided about her marital future and found her husband both a likeable and stable person in her life but also a bore. She felt that she wanted to experiment with life for a while. We advised them that they should see what happened if Jane did experiment and they only saw each other for brief periods at weekends. Since home was another stressful environment for Jane she was not required to go there except for special occasions. We felt justified in taking this step as both Jane and her husband had indicated that they could adjust to the situation for a time.

One of these occasions, in March, was to organise her son's birthday party which she did very ably. This was one of the many small subgoals which Jane attained during this period. Over the next four months, with the absence of demands on her to succeed as a wife, Jane and her husband grew much closer together and developed mutual interests in their marriage again. During the time that Jane was staying in her flat, which was a period of about one year, she was able to compare the somewhat promiscuous lives of her flatmates with her own marriage and see the positive values of the latter for her. She was gradually able to spend longer and longer periods with her husband at their home and obtained a great deal of reinforcement from reinstating herself as a wife and mother again.

She went to parties and on holiday with her husband and finally, after about a year in her flat, she was able to return to her husband's home.

Just before her move into her flat, Jane began a relationship with a male patient which was to last for the next six months. Again, in many ways this was a relationship in which Jane was able to give and led to some pleasure on her part — as well as some accompanying complications. The relationship, which had had stormy moments necessitating an intervention at their request, ended when Jane began her job at the social work department. From then on she developed her relationship with her husband as described above.

It should be emphasised that the marital work which we carried out was extremely limited in extent and consisted mainly of teaching Jane and her husband how to increase gradually the time they spent together and how to develop their mutual interests when they were together. Her husband encouraged and helped her with her social work (he was a voluntary social worker), assisted her with her flat and generally reinforced her when he was with her. Thus, he started to become an encouraging stimulus for Jane rather than a threatening one. He began to be aware of her needs and aspirations and acted accordingly. He, in turn, became even more eager to help as he saw Jane's attitudes and goals develop into more realistic and productive aspects of her behaviour.

5 Eighteen months after admission

At this time Jane's work was progressing extemely well and she was enjoying her training as a social worker. Her marital relationship was good and growing stronger. She had been spending long periods at her husband's home and shortly would be moving back there. The ritualistic problems were minimal, and if exhibited at all were mainly in response to any sort of stress. The agoraphobia was non-existent and her depression had disappeared.

6 Present position

At two years after admission Jane is living at her family home and has adjusted well to her life as mother and wife. She has been working for a few weeks as voluntary aide on our research team with other obsessional patients. She has now recently started another job as social worker in her home area. She presents a much more confident picture and approaches life much more positively. Her present job in social work is somewhat boring. She is finding it difficult to express her abilities to get close to children in her work at an assessment centre. She is concentrating on administration as required by her director rather more than improving assessment procedures which should be her main work. Because of these frustrations she has lost some of her eagerness and faith in social work. But in other ways she remains much improved with her problems now at a manageable level.

Discussion

With such a complex case as Jane's it would have been very difficult and time-consuming to have made an attempt at a rigorous research design. Our main concern was our clinical responsibility towards Jane and our goal was to facilitate her functioning more adequately as quickly as possible in a way which followed the behaviour therapy approach which we discussed in the preamble. Thus, because of the lack of pure experimental rigour, it is impossible to say with certainty what was relevant in the patient's improvement and readjustment. However, we feel justified in our claim that the outcome of therapy was consistent with the original formulation. That is, when Jane overcame her fear of failure in the sense of achieving a career goal, her symptoms of agoraphobia, depression, low self-image and later her marital problems disappeared. Her response prevention treatment for obsessional ritualisation was successful and was maintained over an eighteen-month follow-up. We had predicted that any improvements would be maintained by treatment of the central problem of fear of failure and this prediction was not refuted.

Although it lacks rigour in a research sense, we hope that this case illustrates our use of an approach-oriented behaviour therapy programme. The treatment was extremely involved and complex and had to be planned in successive stages to be manageable. However, at all times the planning and execution of treatment was guided by learning principles and principles of experimental psychology. Unforeseen events, such as the difficult ward situation and the relationship with the male patient, had to be dealt with in the treatment approach in a flexible way within our guiding framework of experimental psychology.

We hope also that the case demonstrates how a treatment programme can follow with relative ease from a rigorous behavioural analysis and formulation of the problems. Having formulated that fear of failure was of primary importance, Jane's retraining along the lines of attempting progressively more difficult goals was clearly indicated.

It is worth noting that her previous behavioural technology

treatment, aimed at her agoraphobia symptom, had taken no account of the fear of failure. She had, as we noted earlier, relapsed after this treatment. We would have predicted that relapse might have occurred if symptoms were treated without treating the primary cause of those symptoms. We would argue that it is likely that the lasting results which were obtained with our approach were due to Jane's self-image becoming progressively more positive by our facilitating her successes in gradually more and more difficult areas concerned with her career.

In conclusion, it might be argued that the contrasts which are so often made between behaviour therapy and psychotherapy may not be the most appropriate areas in which behaviour therapists should expend their energies. Possibly a more profitable contrast and comparison appraisal could be made between the technological behaviour therapy schools and the flexible behaviour therapy approach used in this case. It is in this second approach to the use of learning principles and experimental psychology that the economical and effective treatment of complex cases be more easily found.

8   It's Never Too Late to Learn: An Application of Conditioned Inhibition to Obsessional Ruminations in an Elderly Patient

Anne Broadhurst

The patient

When first I met Mr Green, I realised at once that this was a patient with a difference. He appeared to be an educated and well-dressed man of about 60 years. In fact, as he later told me with great pride and with a twinkle in his eye, he had passed his 70th birthday and had just recently and voluntarily retired from the running of his own small manufacturing business. While he had handed over this work to his son, he still maintained an active interest in the business and in its workers. He related how, for over ten years, he and his wife had lived amicably with his son and family, consisting of wife and four children. He and his son and daughter-in-law attended to various aspects of the business while his wife had managed the house and the children, with the help of a nurse and a housekeeper. There was no shortage of money and the household entertained a constant stream of visitors of all ages. Gatherings at the house included meetings and outings concerned with the welfare of the factory workers as well as political social gatherings – the family were all active supporters of the local Liberal party – and many purely social occasions. In particular it appeared that Mr Green and his wife were confidants to the many and varied personal problems from divorce to the choice of clothes of their circle of friends. They were active, healthy and enjoyed company of all ages. Indeed they were the perfect grandparents and apparently without a serious care in the world.

The problem

This picture of life in the Green household was related clearly and with the occasional amusing anecdote, of doings of the grandchildren, for example, appropriately included. It was hard to determine why this charming, if rather old-world gentleman had been referred to a psychiatric clinic by his general practitioner. And indeed the fact that he could conceal his need for help was another source of pride for Mr Green. But problem there certainly was in his eyes and to tell of it he went back to events of forty-five years ago.

At the age of 25 he had been feeling the pangs of unrequited love when he was invited to stay with an understanding friend of the family and his young wife. This visit coincided with his own development of the family business (in which he spent his whole working life) and with the friend's gradual relapse into invalidism. More significantly still, Mr Green and the wife started an amorous relationship which brought intense pleasure to both but which they were careful to conceal because of the love they both still felt for the friend. In many respects, this was a triangle with harmony on all sides. Marriage between Mr Green and his lover was never anticipated and yet the couple were able to enjoy one another's company very freely. They had many mutual friends and mutual interests and, since they were confident that their affair could remain undetected, they were entirely free of thoughts of guilt or harm to others. Although in the blissful years that followed intercourse did not take place between them, there were many occasions of mutual masturbation with enjoyment for both.

This situation continued for seven years after which an incident occurred which affected the rest of Mr Green's days. His lover casually remarked: 'You know, after what we did yesterday', referring to a spill of semen and menstrual blood on her leg, 'you might easily have given me a baby.' Immediately, Mr Green was struck by fear of this possibility and the significance of this ill-informed remark grew out of all proportion in his thoughts. Gradually he found himself thinking of little else than blood and the disaster of pregnancy for his lover, whose husband was now increasingly ailing. Gradually also he found himself developing excessive washing rituals. Life and work continued for some years as before but the obtrusive thoughts and the washing rituals caused him great misery and fear for the safety of his lover. Though always one to conceal distress the problem was severe enough for him to confide in his lover and in his general practitioner at this time. Both were sympathetically alarmed on his behalf but the only treatments immediately suggested were hard work and distraction, of which there had never been any shortage. Washing rituals did in fact decrease over a period of about three years, only to be replaced more potently by the obsessive ruminations concerning the possibility that blood might be contaminating anything or any person that he or his lover encountered.

Then a change of events occurred in that his lover's husband finally died. After an appropriate interval, the general practitioner then recommended marriage between Mr Green and his lover, confidently predicting that this would effect a cure. They married and two years later they had their one child, the son already mentioned, and indeed spent a long and relatively happy life together but there was never any remission of the perpetual ruminations from which Mr Green suffered. In all the intervening years, no one, apart from his wife and his doctor, knew that he had any problem. He maintained that he could work and attend to other activities, such as conversation, without error and without others being aware of his constant ruminations on themes of menstrual blood.

The reason for his never having sought treatment previously was that his wife would have been embarrassed by his doing so. She was distressed at the thought that she had been the cause of his disorder and even more distressed that the marriage had been completely ineffective as a cure. Now he came for treatment as this hindrance was removed by his wife's death some months ago. 'I have had a good life and I'm still active and healthy and I would like to be *free* of this for my remaining years. I am seeking relief from this hell of thoughts that I don't want to have.'

The problem therefore was revealed as one of obsessional ruminations unaccompanied by actions or impulses. In this form it was a chronic condition of at least thirty-five years' duration.

Review of the problem

While many reviewers of obsessional disorders (for example, Mather, 1970; Carr, 1970) include reference to the ruminations which may accompany obsessional rituals, therapeutic endeavour (for example, Walton, 1960; Walton and Mather, 1964; Taylor, 1963; Meyer, 1966) and theoretical analyses (Metzner, 1963) have, not surprisingly, been concentrated on the most disruptive aspect of the disorder, namely the motor behaviours. Yet some describe the 'forced thinking' of the obsessional as his most 'truly characteristic' experience (Solyom, Garza-Perez, Ledwidge and Solyom, 1972). Prior to commencing investigation of this patient, the major reports of behaviour manipulation of the cognitive elements of obsessional behaviour had come from Wolpe (1958), who uses the technique of 'thought-stopping' (Wolpe and Lazarus, 1966), and from Bevan (1960) who describes a patient whose multiple, unwelcome thoughts were treated by reciprocal inhibition – in this case, drug-induced sedation paired with the anxiety-provoking thoughts. Thought-stopping is attractively simple to apply and has had a number of reports of success (Yamagami, 1971). However, it has also been known to encounter resistance (Wolpe, 1971a) and has little in the way of psychological rationale to recommend it. Thorpe, Schmidt, Brown and Castell (1964) had reported on the method of aversion-relief therapy for cases of obsessional neuroses (among other disorders) and this initially held some attraction for the case of Mr Green despite the fact that there has been little research flowing from the first reports of the use of this technique (Solyom, Zahmanzadeh, Ledwidge and Kenny, 1969).

First approach to the problem: an assessment failure

While arranging the construction of an aversion-relief apparatus, preliminary investigations were undertaken. Mr Green was interviewed on the details of his ruminative symptoms and he completed the Eysenck Personality Inventory, Form A (E 10; N 8; L 4). The Lie score was rather high but there was otherwise no indication of personality disorder.

It appeared that, after years of obsessional ruminations on the thought of contamination with blood, especially menstrual blood, the problem at the time of investigation had crystallised to become a series of thought jingles of the form

Marion – Basingstoke – blood – that's wrong,
Barney's – that's wrong,
Singing Kettle Café – that's wrong [etc.],

the names and places referring to incidents in Mr Green's prolonged premarital affair. In an attempt to obtain a baseline measure of the extent of the problem we asked such simple questions as 'How long does the thought sequence last?' (stopwatch at the ready), 'How often does it occur in a five-minute period of conversation?', 'Without conversation?', and 'during presentation of white noise of moderate intensity?' We also attempted to discover whether the duration of the obtrusive thought was modified by white noise.

This crude base-line assessment resulted in complete failure. Not only was there continuous rumination reported and quite unaffected by distractions of activity, conversation or noise, but the length of the ruminative jingle, although it had some repetitive consistency, was infinitely variable, depending on how many incidents or people were included. We could not therefore determine that the series occurred once in a minute, or in five minutes or in half an hour. The only consistent finding of the first base-line investigation was the patient's report of continuous, unwanted, disbelieved, and irrelevant thoughts of menstrual blood. 'I am never free of these bad thoughts except in sleep.'

Second approach: conditioned inhibition therapy

The unending continuity of the ruminations complained of provided a rough base-line for the assessment of future behaviour change. The continuity, however, also led to the abandonment of any plans to use thought-stopping or aversion-relief as therapy in this case and the development instead of a plan to use conditioned inhibition therapy.

The background

Interest in conditioned inhibition as a therapeutic device (Broadhurst, 1973) had been stimulated by the comparative experimental work of Kendrick (1958, 1960) and by the clinical experiments of Yates (1958) and of Jones (1960) with a tiqueur. Kendrick had shown that the paradoxical prediction of Gleitman, Nachmias and Neisser (1954) from Hullian principles was supported – that repetitively reinforced behaviour should first increase and then decrease to nothing because of the build up of reactive inhibition and, more importantly, of conditioned or learned inhibition, which has the more persistent properties of a (negative) habit. Despite theoretical and methodological criticisms of Kendrick's work (Keehn and Sabbagh, 1958; Keehn, 1959; Prokasy, 1960) it holds a strong interest for clinicians. Not only does it revive the early work of Dunlap (1932), whose notion of negative practice encouraged therapeutic (Lehner, 1954; Case, 1960) and experimental endeavour, but, more recently, it has been shown to be applicable to other motor disorders such as Gilles de la Tourette's syndrome (Clark, 1966) as well as the tic disorders first reported on (Yates, 1958; Jones, 1960). This work suggested the effectiveness, whatever the explanation (see Jensen, 1961), of massed practice techniques for the elimination of motor habits. It remained to be seen whether the method had anything to offer in the case of Mr Green's private cognitive habits or ruminations.

Application of conditioned inhibition therapy to the case of Mr Green

Essentially the plan was to require the patient to verbalise aloud his ruminations and to do so repetitively in such a sequence of practice periods and rest periods that inhibition, first reactive inhibition (I_R) and later the more permanent conditioned inhibition ($_sI_R$), would build up to make the repetition impossible. Thoughts were to be concentrated on the words so that, ultimately, it was hoped to eliminate not only verbalisation but also the undesirable thoughts.

Therapy by conditioned inhibition (with its attendant discomforts) was explained in outline and the patient embarked on it in March with some understanding and with evident great enthusiasm.

In the first session, using the major series of six phrases, it became apparent that repetition of six jingles was too cumbersome, long and varied a task to allow any build up of reactive inhibition. Since conditioned inhibition is postulated as developing as a result of the reinforcement from dissipation of reactive inhibition during rest pauses, the absence of reactive inhibition was theoretically crucial and it was necessary to think of a more effective procedure.

Taylor (1963), basing his approach on the experimental work of Solomon and Wynne (1953, 1954), pointed out that the most successful disruption of an obsessional sequence of behaviours followed the elimination of the first behaviour. This suggested that we could both reduce the length of the practised verbalisation and increase the efficacy of treatment by limiting the patient's verbalisations to the first phrase of the ruminative series, namely, 'Marion – Basingstoke – blood – that's wrong'. In the second and every subsequent session, therefore, this was the phrase repeated aloud time and again.

Sessions 1-6 employed the practice and rest periods found suitable by Yates (1958) for the elimination of tics – five-minute work periods alternated with one-minute rest periods. However, little reactive inhibition yet appeared and, hence, the desired conditioned inhibition could not be expected. Therefore some experimental increase in the length of work and practice periods began with session 7. Ten-minute periods of work on repetition of the first ruminative phrase were alternated with rest periods of three minutes in which rest from ruminations was encouraged. (The

FIGURE 8·1   *The average number of repetitions per minute of disturbing ruminative phrases counted in five- or ten-minute practice periods during eighteen treatment sessions*

The patient's private practice sessions at home are indicated by diagonal shading. Note that the ruminative exercise practised in the first session (white bars) consisted of the six major phrases together, whereas all subsequent sessions counted only one (the first) phrase as one repetition. Thus there is some improvement observable between sessions 1 and 2. The development of conditioned inhibition is seen in the decrease in number of repetitions within a session (particularly sessions 5, 7, 9 and 17), and the permanence of this change is seen in the decrease in frequency of repetitions in the first practice of each session from sessions 2-18.

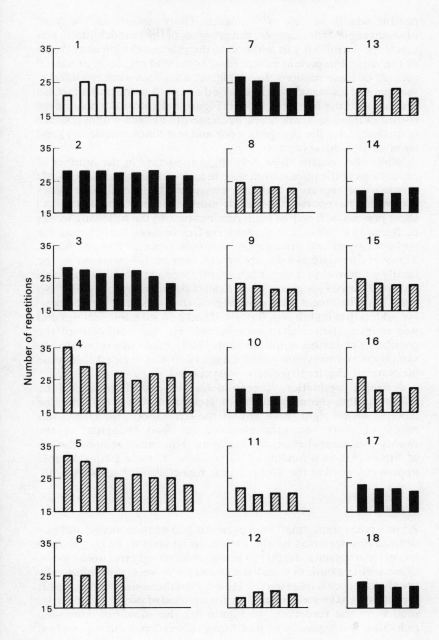

patient was ill at ease with silence. Conversation on the most pleasant topics, for example, the progress of the grandchildren, was therefore permitted.) In addition to the practice during attendance at the clinic the patient practised at home and regularly produced records of these sessions. In all, eighteen sessions were recorded in the space of six weeks which included a gap when the patient took a holiday with the family at Easter. Figure 8·1 shows the condensed record of these sessions. Some decrease can be seen within sessions (especially after the change in work and rest times at session 7) and from session to session.

While the records show only slight reduction in the number of repetitions of the phrase from session to session up to session 14, Mr Green's own reports at that date were remarkably optimistic. After four weeks he reported that he felt 'more composed' and that he had short periods of freedom from ruminations. In the following weeks he found that minutes at a time were free of thoughts of blood. He was overjoyed and arranged to continue practice daily at home. This was fortunate as a disruption in treatment followed during the family's removal to a larger house. Mr Green returned in June and reported further progress. 'Now, I can cope. I can say to myself, "No good" and believe it. I have more good thoughts than ever before.' He added that he felt less flustered, had now no panic feelings and was sleeping better than ever before. He was confident of the possibility of further improvement. While much of this related to symptoms not previously complained of, it was decided that some measure of the improvement was needed.

A simple ruminations 'thermometer' was used first in the June following the commencement of treatment. On a 25 cm. line labelled at the right 'Bad' and at the left 'Good', Mr Green was asked to mark the proportion of his 'bad thoughts' in the twenty-four hours before the recording. This can be seen on the left of Figure 8·2 as a reading of 78 per cent, already a considerable improvement over the 100 per cent reported prior to treatment.

Outcome

At this point some small improvement had been recorded and was subjectively reported by the patient to be such as to give him an incentive to practise further at home. Accordingly treatment in the clinic was discontinued and the patient was seen thereafter only briefly for reports on progress. He enjoyed these visits and made his reports approximately fortnightly for a period of two years. It can be seen from the recordings of Figure 8·2 that slow but continued reduction in frequency of bad thoughts occurred during the first

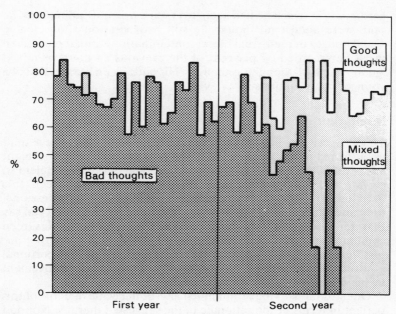

FIGURE 8·2 *The patient's report of proportion of 'bad thoughts' in the previous twenty-four hours recorded on clinic attendance days through a two-year follow-up period*

post-treatment year. Then in the second year there came a period of rapid improvement in the records and a day when he declared that there were no longer solely bad thoughts but that mixtures of good and bad thoughts remained for a part of the day. The two-year follow-up therefore shows no loss in the proportion of good thoughts achieved after the short treatment period and suggests even some further improvement in that the bad thoughts were now mixed good and bad. Mr Green remained convinced that a great change had occurred. He would admit, 'I'm not quite right yet. I'm not entirely *free*', but he showed relief over the change and he would resolve to practise harder and so continue the improvement. He commenced a new hobby, gardening, and was so successful in this that he won several prizes at his local club.

When seen again two years later after the last record shown in Figure 8·2, the report was even more encouraging. Now at age 74 he had had an eight-week period of hospitalised illness following a stroke. He had amazed his doctors by recovering from the initial paralysis and was now back to his previous activities including gardening, in which he had again won some prizes. Ruminations, he said, were almost nil though he still had occasional unwelcome visual images of menstrual blood contaminating familiar places. All in all he recorded 67 per cent of the previous 24 hours as mixed 'good' and 'bad' thoughts or images. His outlook on life was that of a younger man, optimistic as ever.

Discussion

This case, with its limited success although perceived by the patient as far from limited, raises several points of interest. First, one might ask what is the benefit of therapeutic endeavour for a problem so private and so non-disabling as that presented by Mr Green. It is hard indeed to ascertain how best we should share our professional time and skills among the population in need. In this case I can say that, far more than it has been possible to convey here, Mr Green communicated real distress at the initial interview. In *post hoc* justification of the decision to treat comes the proportional gratitude which he displayed for the apparently small improvement in his condition.

One hesitates to make too much also of the achievements of this patient in terms of the rationale of the suggested therapy. Nor do I wish to suggest that the progress was completely straightforward. (Mr Green later reported that he was plagued subsidiarily by visual images of menstrual blood – 'my blood pictures' – in all sorts of everyday and therefore unlikely situations. He was encouraged to deal with these also by practice in calling them up and practice in substituting pleasanter images and this achieved some success.) However, this treatment case and other successes previously reported must be included in the reflections of those who emphasise theoretical (Prokasy, 1960; Jensen, 1961) and methodological weaknesses (Fuchs, 1960; Mountjoy, Edwin and Rogers, 1960) of Kendrick's developments from Hull. From the clinical point of view, it may be that, with more sophisticated explanations awaited, there remain further applications of conditioned inhibition therapy to be explored. The present extension of the method to private ruminations requires to be replicated although a 50 per cent improvement in obsessive thoughts is claimed for a related new technique termed 'paradoxical intention' (Solyom, Garza-Perez, Ledwidge and Solyom, 1972). In this method the patients are trained to dwell on their obsessive thoughts until (hopefully) they disappear. No records are kept and practice is carried out by the patient during his daily life. Nevertheless, the authors relate their technique to the early work of Dunlap, as Yates and Kendrick did.

Their success, although reported after the completion of this case, gives us additional grounds for believing that conditioned inhibition may prove to be a valuable addition to our techniques against a most difficult symptom.

Finally one might ask the dual question of what is the value of therapeutic work with the elderly who may die at any moment and whose capacity for new learning is likely to be reduced. On the first point here, the answer must surely be that in this age of sudden death the old age of the patient can be little matter for consideration in deciding whether to treat or not to treat. Equally, one might argue that the old have contributed much and suffered much and are therefore more worthy of such help as we can offer. Hoyer (1973) argues convincingly that our current psychological techniques are already applicable and with increasing longevity and an ageing population we must adapt our techniques further to suit the population.

As to whether the patient is capable of rehabilitative learning, perhaps the clinician can make a judgment on occasions. However, we know that learning can occur, given the correct conditions, in organisms with very limited neural capacity so that it would seem very hard and a counsel of despair to deny any person the opportunity of help on the grounds of reduced learning capacity. While deprecating any attempt to reduce intellectual deficits of the aged by training, Looft (1973) makes a plea for intervention aimed at producing 'a happier kind of people'. It is my contention that this was achieved in the present case. And on the basis of this case in which symptom reduction was reported soon after the appropriate conditions of practice and rest had been instituted it may be said that 'it's never too late to learn'.

9 Outflanking 'Resistance' in a Severe Obsessional Neurosis

Joseph Wolpe and L. Michael Ascher

The therapeutic transactions presented here that were applied to an obsessive-compulsive case call attention to some aspects of psychotherapy that behavior therapy literature has largely neglected – the classes of behavior that in 'dynamically' (that is, psychoanalytically) oriented therapy are referred to as defense mechanisms, transference, and resistance. An important reason for this neglect is probably the idea that if a behavior therapist uses dynamic terms he is contaminated by the psychoanalytic theories associated with them. Locke (1971) went as far as to suggest that the use by behavior therapists of mentalistic sounding terms in the description of their patients' behavior is evidence that behavioral principles are not sufficient for the modification of certain types of maladaptive behavior. Actually, as Waters and McCallum (1973) point out, the mentalistic-sounding terms used by behavior therapists are shorthand for behavioral operations and devoid of 'dynamic' referents. When the behavior therapist uses the term 'anxiety' the referents are objective (Wolpe, 1958). The patient's reported perceptions and feelings are also behavioral data which it would be foolish to ignore.

'Resistance' was originally a term applied to behavior on the part of the analysand which the analyst perceived to be in opposition to therapeutic progress (for example, Fenichel, 1945). A great number of different behaviors can suggest resistance, for example, arriving late for an appointment, failing to keep an appointment, failing to pay the therapist's fee promptly, general uncooperativeness in response to the directions and suggestions of the therapist, and premature termination of therapy. By classifying these different responses under the same rubric, it is implied that all have similar 'causes' and treatments. However, it is more likely that each represents an independent class of behaviors with antecedent stimuli that vary from case to case. These classes of behavior are also observed in behavior therapy, but each instance of 'resistance' calls for a behavioral analysis. For example, if the behavior therapist assigns to the patient some task to perform during the interval between sessions, and he neglects to perform it, this is, by definition, an example of resistance; but its origin may or may not lie with the patient. Behavioral analysis may, for example, trace it to the therapist not having taken into account that the patient had too high a level of anxiety to be able to carry out the task, or not having defined the task clearly enough. Some patients react to their own non-performance by missing appointments because they are afraid to confess their failures. The practical point is that the solution to 'resistance' requires not psychoanalysis, but behavioral analysis.

Our obsessive-compulsive patient was consistently non-compliant and uncooperative to a succession of behavioral techniques. We have included a good deal of verbatim material to illustrate this. It should be noted that the therapist invariably responded in a non-judgmental way, in keeping with customary behavior therapy practice. Instead of efforts to 'break down' the 'resistance,' the therapist each time shifted to another technique, until he found one that was of significant benefit to the patient.

The 'resistance' was due to several factors. First, the case was of a kind that is characteristically refractory to treatment. Second was the pervasiveness of the complaint. This particular contamination phobia involved so many environmental stimuli that the patient found it anxiety-provoking to leave her home at any time; but she was also severely restricted within its confines. In addition, she had an intolerance of orders and instructions which made her oppose them automatically.

The presenting problem

Celia was a single girl of twenty when she came to us for help for obsessions and compulsions which markedly restricted her life. She was very much concerned with contamination by people who had in any way been associated with either xy University (the school she had attended after graduating from high school), the adjacent town, or za Hospital where she had more recently received extensive day care. She avoided touching objects which these people could possibly have touched. This eventually included almost everything inside her home, and a great deal outside. She markedly restricted her activities in order to be, as far as possible, 'uncontaminated.' However, occasionally circumstances would preclude avoidance of contaminants, leading her to engage in a ritualistic cleansing to overcome the effects of contact. For example, in preparing for the day she would be besieged with contaminated objects. She would begin the morning by washing her face, hands, arms, and as much of her body as was necessary (according to the degree to which she felt contaminated). She would then return to the bedroom to dress. After each thing that she touched (for example, drawer, article of clothing, closet door) she would wash her hands, in an effort to limit the spread of contamination. On the average morning Celia would wash her hands 20-30 times.

During the day she did many things to minimize the amount of contamination to which she might be exposed. She refused to touch anyone or allow anyone to touch her. She carried a sheet with her to cover every chair on which she would sit. She took precautions never to leave personal articles (for example, books, clothing, toiletries) in contaminated places (for example, shelves, dressers, tables), or where others might touch them. Her concern about contamination kept her anxiety level fairly high most of the day. Her waking level of 60 *suds* reduced to 35 after her morning cleansing ritual. During the day her *sud* level would gradually build up to 70, only coming down to 35 after showering before bed. The chronic constraint of these behaviors on her day-to-day existence led to the sporadic appearance of an agitated depression.

When we first saw her, Celia was rather plain and somewhat masculine looking. The latter could be attributed to an apparant disregard for her physical appearance. She kept her hair very short and uncombed, and wore a military style jacket with loose fitting jeans. Some of her behavior suggested extreme shyness. For example, she often arrived early for her appointment and, instead of entering the waiting-room where other people were engaged in conversation, she would stand in the adjacent passage where people were constantly walking back and forth. She avoided any interaction with passers-by, by poring over a book at all times. Yet, the most cursory conversation revealed her to be a very bright and interesting young woman, with a tendency to be self-deprecating in a sarcastic way.

Before her disorder began two years previously, Celia had always been precise and orderly. For example, she had insisted on handing in very neat papers throughout high school, going to such extremes as making sure that all four margins were identical on each page of any paper she submitted. At times this orderliness shaded into ritual, for example, each paper submitted had to be headed in just the format she had used since elementary school. Sometimes the behavior appeared to be superstitious. Her grandmother had not worn green after wearing that color on the day a brother had died. Although Celia occasionally wore green, it would never be on days in which she had something significant to do. In spite of this, she performed well above average at school, and was generally pleased with her way of life. She belonged to a small clique of intellectual snobs, who felt that others had less intelligence, and ridiculed them for this. At the appropriate time in the senior year, Celia's friends made application to, and were duly accepted by, the universities of their choice. Celia, however, was slow in getting started and by the time she applied, the institutions acceptable to her (and to her friends) were filled. To her great shame and chagrin she had to settle for XY University, an 'inferior' university. This led her to avoid her friends toward the end of her high school career; and subsequently, soon after starting at XY University, she found that she disliked most aspects of it and avoided associations with her fellow students, whom she characterized as mindless individuals interested only in fun and pleasure. She immersed herself in work and interacted almost exclusively with some of her professors. Becoming gradually more unhappy she withdrew increasingly into her studies.

Despite all her unhappiness, Celia showed no sign of obsessional behavior until the occurrence of an excruciating experience. Celia's room-mate had a friend, Grace, who, to Celia, was the epitome of everything despicable about the girls at XY University. Grace had the reputation of being filthy (admitting that she rarely washed herself or her clothes) and sexually permissive. Celia was uncomfortable in Grace's presence and made every effort to avoid her. One evening, Celia returned to her room and was disturbed to find Grace sprawled over her bed, describing her initial exposure to intercourse in graphic detail. Celia was always quite uncomfortable about sexual relations, especially pre-marital, but Grace's defloration was particularly distasteful – by a student whom she barely knew, who had done it after getting her drunk. To cap everything, while Grace was talking, Celia noticed lice crawling in her hair. The whole thing was a nightmare that had a profound effect on Celia. It seemed to verify her worst suspicions about the school and its students. Whereas previously Celia had avoided the company of the other students, now she began to avoid touching them or any object that they might have touched. She refused to allow anyone in her room. If, perchance, someone did enter, she would throw out anything they had handled (such as pencils, paper), unless it was a fixture. She usually scrubbed the floor, the furniture, and any clothing that the visitor may have touched.

Because of her great misery at XY University, Celia tried to transfer to AB College, a small, prestigious college, for the following academic year. She made several trips to that school for interviews and was finally accepted. This did not have the uplifting effect she had expected. Toward the end of her freshman year at XY University, she sought help at the counseling center, and was referred to a counselor. But soon after this the semester ended and Celia went home. Surprisingly her scholastic performance had remained well above average throughout the year.

During the summer Celia's behavioral difficulties abated somewhat. She was quite pleased about her impending move to AB College and did not avoid her friends and acquaintances as she had done during the previous summer. She arrived at college on schedule in the fall and her difficulties returned almost immediately. The trouble was that her avoidance of things associated with XY University had continued to spread. Since she had gone to and from XY University in her family's automobile on several occasions, she would no longer ride in it. She would not use any of the clothes, books, or other personal articles that she had used at XY University. Worst of all, because she had visited AB College while still a student at XY University, the whole vicinity of the college had become contaminated. Celia began to realize that something was really wrong and went to the college counseling clinic which referred her to a psychiatrist in the town. Her withdrawal now became more extreme; and she had what she called a 'nervous breakdown.' Among other things, she tried to hurt herself by banging her head against a wall, at first lightly and then gradually harder until it became mildly painful. After an occasion when she hit her head a bit too hard and became dizzy momentarily, she stopped the head banging behaviour, explaining that she wanted to hurt herself but not do permanent damage. In any case, since she felt uncomfortable touching the contaminated walls with her hands, she certainly did not want to touch them with her head. She was not clear why she wanted to hurt herself and no pattern emerged. She simply wanted to cause herself discomfort. After the head banging ceased, she sought other self-punitive behaviors, but found no satisfactory substitute and shortly gave up the search.

Within a few weeks, Celia, and also her parents, became dissatisfied with the treatment she was receiving. Instead of the improvement they had hoped for, her behavior and her academic performance were deteriorating. She therefore sought help at a hospital close to her home, leaving school in mid-semester. She refused to live in her parents' apartment because of its association with XY University, preferring to stay with her grandparents while attending the intensive day program that the hospital offered. This program consisted of a number of activities (for example, group therapy, individual psychotherapy, milieu therapy, various workshops, and planned social interactions) all guided by a general psychoanalytic orientation. At the end of six months, neither Celia nor her parents could perceive any improvement, but by this time, her fear of contamination had generalized to the hospital and its personnel. She then withdrew from the program, and after unsuccessful approaches to various mental health workers, as a last resort, came to us.

Early background

When Celia was 2 years old, her father suffered a 'nervous breakdown' and had to be hospitalized. The behavior she described that led to this hospitalization included withdrawal and delusions of persecution. Her father was always considered to be extremely intelligent and Celia was thought to resemble him in this respect. In her early years they were very close, but later, although they got along quite well, she felt that he became more remote. As Celia grew older, their relationship deteriorated further, most noticeably after her twelfth birthday, when several aspects of her behavior changed. She became less of a tomboy and behaved more like her mother; and the strong interest in the social sciences she began to develop upset her father, a brilliant physical scientist who ridiculed other academic pursuits. He became increasingly critical of her accomplishments. His constant sarcastically-toned criticisms were extremely upsetting to her until she was about 15 – by which time she learned how to avoid his hostility by withholding schoolwork and not speaking to him of her thoughts. Also, because she knew that other people approved of her, she became less concerned with her father's good opinion. When Celia came for treatment, they were getting along quite poorly and were constantly irritating each other. Part of the reason for this, she felt, was that he was somewhat domineering, and while others in the family offered little resistance to him, she refused to submit and thereby became the target of his hostility. She also thought that he looked upon her as a competitor. She was the only other member of the family who was a match for him intellectually, and this may have served to make him unfriendly toward her. Her behavioral disorder made relations with him even worse, for it did not facilitate smooth interaction between even the closest of friends.

Until the age of thirteen, Celia got along quite well with her mother, who reinforced her for behavior that was similar to that of her father – praising her for good scholastic performance and for other evidence of intelligence. But Celia felt that her relationship with her mother was eclipsed by that with her father. Apparently, her mother mainly served as mediator between Celia and her father.

While she liked her mother, she would have had more respect for her if she had stood up more to her husband's verbal assaults.

Celia's only brother, a year younger, with whom she has always had a good relationship, was outgoing and friendly toward her, and supported her in her difficulty to the best of his ability.

Sexually, Celia was inexperienced; she had not masturbated and had not gone beyond the point of light petting with males. Nevertheless, she seemed to be relatively successful in attracting male companions. She had had her first sexual encounter (necking) at fifteen, but without arousal. Since that time she had had a number of relationships with men whom she described as quite desirable (in that they were attractive, well mannered, and intelligent). Her relationship with a current boy friend was in a state of flux. She appeared to be uncomfortable when talking about sexual matters, and was particularly anxious on the topic of what she called 'illicit sex,' meaning, particularly, pre-marital relations. During the course of the initial interview she mentioned several relevant anxiety-related incidents. For example, she had separated from a very good friend when she found out that she was living with a man to whom she was not married.

Treatment

For reasons of expediency, Celia was treated by two therapists working successively. The initial therapist (JW) devoted the first few sessions to a behavioral analysis.

The first treatment plan centered on systematic desensitization to individuals and objects associated with XY University and ZA Hospital, where she had received treatment; because it was these individuals and objects that caused her the greatest discomfort. Since relaxation is the usual source of inhibition of anxiety used in desensitization, an attempt was made to instruct her in deep muscle relaxation (Wolpe, 1973). She was very uncooperative. Throughout the training, she made facial gestures indicating her repugnance to the procedure, followed instructions reluctantly, and was uncommunicative regarding the effects of the training – as the following transcribed passages indicate. Nevertheless, she was told to practice the technique several times each day.

T: Have there been any extra attempts to relax?
P: You mean those things that you said with my arms: I've been doing that twice a day.
T: Do you think you're getting any more control over it?
P: No, not really. I have no idea when it's working. I'm actually more comfortable when I'm not relaxing. I have no way of

gauging whether I'm doing it right.

T: Well, there is only one criterion for doing it right and that's if it makes you calmer.

P: Actually it doesn't. I mean, I might be relaxing the muscles but mentally I don't feel calm. It's boring and I get kind of itchy and the sensation isn't particularly pleasant either.

At the next session she was scarcely more encouraging:

T: Tell me, have you made any efforts to relax?

P: The past couple of days I've been too nervous to relax. I do those things with the forearms that you told me to do. Maybe not as often as I should, but I do it.

T: Does it help you in any way?

P: No.

T: Does it make you any calmer? What about your face?

P: Well the couple times I've done it, it kind of helps me fall asleep. I do it right before I've gone to sleep and that's kind of helped me. So sometimes it has been helpful and sometimes it's just been nerve-racking.

T: I see you haven't found it significantly calming?

P: No.

The therapist next instructed Celia in the *sud* (subjective units of disturbance) scale (Wolpe, 1973):

T: It's very important to be able to communicate how much tension or anxiety you feel. It's rather unsatisfactory to depend on language. If I ask you 'How do you feel?' and you say 'Pretty bad' that doesn't tell me much. So, we use a scale which you construct, in this way. Think of the worst anxiety you have ever had and call that '100' – one hundred degrees of tension. It would be something like panic. Then think of being absolutely calm, and that is zero. At any moment you can say where you are on your own scale.

P: Yeah. [Facial gestures of disbelief and shoulder shrugs.]

T: Why are you dubious about it?

P: I guess it's difficult to evaluate quantitatively. I've never thought of anxiety in those terms.

In spite of the difficulty indicated, Celia managed to communicate her anxiety in terms of *suds* after a great deal of pressure from the therapist. Her continuing resistance to the scale is brought out in the following exchange relating to the use of pleasant imagery to facilitate relaxation:

T: Well, how do you feel now?

P: What do you mean? [Gestures.]
T: How comfortable do you feel?
P: Oh, all right, I guess.
T: Well, in terms of our scale?
P: I don't know.
T: You reported 40 units before, what would you report now?
P: It's hard to say. I suppose 50 or so. More than before, but I'm not sure.

It became clear from Celia's responses and general attitude that relaxation would not procure significant anxiety reduction. During the next few sessions, other anxiety-inhibiting agents were tried. The pleasant scenes incorporated into the relaxation procedure seemed to enhance its calming effects initially; but this soon wore off. Relaxation under hypnosis during the greater portion of a session had no more effect on her level of discomfort. The following discussion of the use of hypnosis provides a good illustration of her attitude toward any technique:

T: Remember a few days ago we started training in relaxation and then you said that you didn't particularly like that. You felt it was a vacuum activity. Let me see if we can do something rather different. Uncross your legs. What I want to do is to see whether we can make use of hypnosis. Do you have any objection to that?
P: Hmm.
T: It might be interesting.
P: It might be a long laugh.
T: It might be.
P: I don't think it will work with me.

Carbon dioxide is sometimes indicated where a high level of pervasive anxiety seems to resist the effects of deep muscle relaxation (Wolpe, 1973). The typical procedure involves the inhalation of a mixture of 35 per cent oxygen and 65 per cent carbon dioxide. After the patient familiarizes himself with the apparatus, three or four inhalations are given to test out his reactions. Here, again, there was opposition:

T: Do I correctly understand from you that you practically never go below 60 *suds* ?
P: Yes.
T: That's the reason for this equipment behind you. I'll tell you what we're going to do. First, we're going to find out something about the nature of your anxiety. You see what there is: a mask and a couple of cylinders containing carbon

dioxide and oxygen, gases that, as you know, are in your respiratory system all the time. What I would like to do is give you a much stronger concentration of carbon dioxide than you are accustomed to having within you. Actually, this gas is used to revive people under anesthetics. It makes them breathe more strongly. When you inhale the gas mixture you will breathe very deeply and will also experience some other sensation like flushing of your face, and rapid pulse. You take just one breath, fill your lungs once, and that's it. Usually the patient holds the mask in his hand and applies it to his face. You may not want to do that. I will only allow you to do it if you feel it will only give you a minimal amount of anxiety.

P: No, I can do that all right.
T: I will tell you what to do now.

The therapist fully instructs Celia on the proper use of the apparatus and she inhales the gas mixture with the expected results.

T: It is quite a strong experience, isn't it? Will you describe what you felt?
P: I didn't like the way it smelled.
T: Well, it smells like soda water.
P: Right. It felt like a weaker version of the gas that the dentist uses. Well I don't know; it just made me cough and I couldn't see too well.
T: How do you feel now?
P: A little shaky.
T: Okay, now that you know what it is like, let's do it again.
P: Swell. [Sarcastically]

She shrugs and shows other signs of impatience. After further talk she receives a second inhalation; and when she has recovered her equilibrium the following ensues:

T: How do you feel now?
P: I feel the same. It passes, but I still have a rotten feeling in my stomach. It wasn't quite nausea but it was something.
T: That'll pass very quickly. What's your anxiety level?
P: Same as it was. About 55.
T: Okay, now let's do it again. This time I want you to take bigger breaths. The effect will be stronger.

After a third inhalation:

P: It was like you said, flushing of the face and breathing faster.
T: What's your anxiety level?

P: The same.
T: Did your anxiety level change when you were breathing?
P: Yeah, it went up.
T: Do you feel more anxious than when we began this?
P: Yeah.
T: We're going to do this slightly more strongly this time. I'd like you to hold your breath after you have taken in one breath. Hold your breath as long as you can.

After a fourth inhalation:

T: How do you feel now? Any change in anxiety in either direction?
P: I think it's higher. This produces an effect similar to nervousness.
T: So you really feel slightly more anxious. Do you have a strong feeling of wanting to breathe when you have this gas?
P: Yes.
T: You see, there seems to me to be a sort of constricted breathing. You don't seem to let yourself go. You seem to be holding back when you are breathing.
P: Yeah, because the more I take the worse I feel and I guess . . .
T: It makes you want to breathe. You seem to be fighting it. Am I right? Well I want to give you one more. Just let yourself go, and breathe as freely as possible.

After fifth inhalation:

T: How do you feel now?
P: Lousy.

The attempt to find a suitable anxiety-inhibitor was so far fruitless. Hierarchy construction was disconcerting to the therapist and generally annoying to Celia. Notwithstanding the lack of an effective anxiety-reducing procedure and a formally constituted hierarchy, desensitization procedure was tried experimentally. (This was done mainly for the sake of a professional group observing the treatment on closed circuit television.) Celia was instructed to relax to the best of her ability, and scenes were presented for her to imagine. Two main themes were used: dirt, and the people associated with XY University and ZA Hospital. After she reported that dirt and germs really did not bother her, work in this area was discontinued. In the case of the anxiety-inducing individuals, Celia was asked to imagine herself coming progressively closer to those low in the hierarchy. As might have been expected, the desensitization experiment was quite unsuccessful.

One variant of desensitization involves having the patient make an imaginal aggressive response to the phobic stimulus (Goldstein, Serber and Piaget, 1970). The hypothesis is that the hostile, aggressive feelings will be incompatible with, and consequently counter-condition, the anxiety evoked by the phobic stimuli. This was tried next:

T: Well, you have said that you are angry at your friend Sidney – how would you like to express this anger?

P: I wouldn't. There's no point to it.

T: There might be. Just let fantasy have reign. Supposing you decided to express this anger; how would you do it?

P: I'd probably tell him that he was a sniveling, self-indulgent pain-in-the-neck. But I'd never do it.

T: Why not?

P: Because besides being sniveling and self-indulgent, he's also quite pitiful and I wouldn't want to do anything that would . . .

T: You wouldn't want to do anything against him because of, shall we say, social conscience?

P: I mean I care a little bit about him. I would not want gratuitously to hurt him.

T: In fact, of course, you're not going to hurt him; but in fantasy you could, couldn't you?

P: I suppose.

T: Let's do that in fantasy. Imagine yourself saying these things to him that you just mentioned. Can you do that? Can you do that with spirit in fantasy?

P: I suppose.

T: Well then, give your fantasied statement lots of spirit.

P: Okay.

She closes her eyes, and presumably fantasizes castigating Sidney as a sniveling, self-indulgent pain-in-the-neck.

T: How did that feel?

P: It didn't feel like anything – I didn't feel purged.

T: You're not supposed to feel purged. I want to know how you felt.

P: I didn't feel anything.

T: But you said you would infuse it with spirit.

P: Yeah, well, I guess I take some tremendous pleasure in telling him that. It's kind of far-fetched, something I'd never do.

T: That doesn't matter. It produced two useful emotions – the anger and the subsequent pleasure. I want you to do it again and tell me when you've done it.

She signals.

T: How do you feel?
P: I don't know, I didn't really like it. I had the feeling that it was pointless.
T: It isn't pointless if it's an expression of real feeling.
P: So are lots of things, but that doesn't justify them.
T: When you speak of a thing being justified you're weighing a negative against a positive. Since you're not actually doing any harm to Sidney, it's hard to see what negatives there are.
P: It is also hard to see what positives there are.
T: Repeat the verbal fantasy, letting yourself go as much as possible, and indicate when you have done it.

She signals.

T: Did you do it with more feeling this time?
P: No, I did it with less feeling. I had a sinking in my stomach, and not much conviction.
T: But those are the words you have an impulse to use toward him. I'm asking you to follow your impulse through in fantasy.

After another attempt:

T: How was it that time?
P: It was hazy.
T: Let's see if we can unharness it in another way. I want you to verbalize that statement aloud. Now here Sidney is in front of you. Say the words. Start with 'Sidney.'
P: It is much easier to tell you what I think of him than to tell him what I think of him.

A lot of shrugging and signs of disgust.

T: This is a kind of play-acting. Nobody can be harmed.
P: I feel as though it's pointless.
T: Let me see how you would say it.
P: I would never say anything like that. I couldn't, to anybody. I would just calmly say, 'Sidney, you're a self-indulgent pain-in-the-neck.' But in a real situation, I can't act it out. I would never, unless he had provoked me and I were angry; then I would scream at him. But, that would be a spontaneous thing. I couldn't contrive it.
T: If you say to me, as you have, that the image of Sidney evokes

anger in you, then there is a real feeling.

P: Hmm.

T: What I am asking you is to express that real feeling in the mode that you, yourself, feel natural.

P: I don't know. It might be more natural to just throttle him.

T: Okay, then do that. Imagine yourself throttling him.

P: That would presuppose I'd be touching him. I forgot all about that.

T: But you can do it in fantasy.

She signals.

T: Now what happened to your anxiety when you did that?

P: Nothing. It was undercut by the feeling that it would never happen and by the awareness of how silly it would be if I ever did. Nothing happened. It was remote.

The therapist discusses the reasons why he wants Celia to fantasize aggressive acts toward Sidney and other people. She argues that it is not a humanitarian thing to do, and antisocial. He answers that nobody is harmed by her fantasy; but she has fear reactions to people, and if she can elicit other emotional reactions toward them in fantasy, this might inhibit her fear, and so decondition it. He also suggests the possibility of using weapons because she would then not be required to touch people; but Celia says she just could not consider that.

T: Let me permit you to throttle Sidney.

P: I don't think I'd even want to do it. I have no conviction.

T: But you're not being asked actually to do it.

P: Yeah, but he's just a total nothing. There wouldn't be any point in it.

T: Nevertheless, he is capable of upsetting you and that's the point. What we want is to substitute for this anxiety a strong feeling like anger, and this can be done by repeatedly fantasizing the expression of the anger which you genuinely feel. I now want you to do it four times. Imagine, in detail, how you go up to him, how you seize him by the throat, and what happens to him. Maybe he falls down a limp carcass.

P: I don't want to kill the poor fellow.

T: Well you can take it as far as you like.

P: I think I misunderstood the word throttling. I thought throttling was just faking a person out.

T: You do it to the extent that satisfies your feeling: four times in detail and tell me when you've finished.

After a while she signals.

T: How did you feel while you were doing it?
P: It was more exasperating than anything else.
T: As you repeated it, did you become more angry?
P: Yeah, angry and fed up mostly with having to do it.
T: Now you can open your eyes. What's the score?
P: I don't know?
T: I want you to practice that image 100 times in the next twenty-four hours.

She looks disgusted, and rolls her eyes.

P: Oh God. [Sighs] I should have opted for a more palatable image.
T: Well that wouldn't do, because you wouldn't have the anger then.
P: I don't even know if I have the anger now.

From the next session:

T: Did you practice that image?
P: Yeah, I suppose I did. I wasn't very convinced of it but I did what I could. I changed it around a lot to try to make it more convincing but I failed.
T: How did you change it around?
P: Well, I thought of all the various situations in which I might have been provoked with Sidney. I added some variety but it still wasn't very convincing.
T: You did it 100 times?
P: Yes.
T: Did you feel angry?
P: Well I didn't feel angry with him, I felt angry at having to do it.
T: Well then, you felt angry at me?
P: Yeah, I guess so.

The therapist goes into a renewed lengthy explanation of the procedure.

P: Well it wouldn't have mattered much. Now I understand it; but I don't think I would have acted any differently. I mean I can't contrive rage. I'm sure that somewhere I feel anger but I don't think that for me this is a viable way to release it. It was also unrealistic. I mean I just felt like an idiot; I would never do anything like that. It just totally isn't my style; and, I don't even see any reason to develop the style. I could even see it if in this fantasy I was experimenting with something that might be good to do; but I didn't see the value in doing it, so the whole thing was quite negated, I guess.

Since the therapeutic impact of all this effort was negligible, the therapist embarked on a long session of imaginal flooding, in which Celia was asked to imagine that Grace was sitting on Celia's bed with one arm around Celia's shoulder and the other hand on Celia's lap. Celia repeatedly writhed and grimaced, from which it was inferred that the procedure was succeeding in evoking anxiety; but Celia was annoyed:

T: How do you feel? What is your anxiety level?
P: As anxious as I can feel.
T: Well what do you want to say to me?
P: I don't want to say anything.
T: Are you mad? Tell me.
P: You've just destroyed all my plans. Now I've got to go back and wash before I do anything else.
T: But you're not to wash.
P: Yeah, are you going to stop me?
T: No, I'm asking you not to.
P: Till when?
T: Till tonight.
P: No way.

Because flooding had effectively increased Celia's level of anxiety, the following session involved more flooding. First, however, the therapist went into a detailed explanation of its purpose. Then:

T: Let's repeat the procedure. If you go along with it, change will follow.
P: I have to take it on faith. In the past people have said to me, 'What would happen if you didn't wash?' They would try to make me not wash, and I would see that when I walked outside I wouldn't get struck down dead and I would be fine. But that doesn't work. I can see the logic in that, but I have no reason to believe or disbelieve what you told me. I know nothing about it.

After a long flooding session featuring imaginary contact with Grace, with many failures:

T: What is your score?
P: It's really no different. I can't do it. I'm not at all convinced, so I don't have to be anxious.
T: You felt it yesterday?
P: I was more cooperative yesterday and that's why.

T: Why do you think you're less cooperative today?

P: I don't know, maybe it was the novelty yesterday, and maybe now that I know what's coming I don't believe it. I don't know.

T: It's not a matter of believing anything. It's just a matter of doing something.

P: I don't know.

T: Well, you do feel that Grace touched you, don't you?

P: Yeah, but I don't feel that it bothered me as much as it could.

T: Well, what's the highest your score went up to, doing that?

P: It was actually higher before you came here.

T: Why?

P: I don't know. I guess I insulated myself.

T: What do you mean, before I came here? You mean while you were here sitting by yourself? Well, what was your level then?

P: Oh, 80.

T: Was that in any way an anticipation of what you thought we were going to do?

P: Yeah.

T: Well, let us say that the realization was less than the expectation.

P: It may mean that, but probably only because I don't want to be masochistic and I'm basically obstinate.

T: Well, it's not a matter of being masochistic.

P: No, in the long run it's not, but I'm not into long runs nowadays.

T: It's like having an operation. It may be painful, but you say, 'I'll have the pain for the greater good.'

P: That's right, but when you're under anesthetics you can't do anything about it. I don't think there is anybody who would subject themselves to pain on the faith that worse pain would go away.

T: You might have a chronic sprain, perhaps, and you would submit to massage which would be quite painful, because of the understanding that through that submission you would be able to walk much better afterwards.

P: But here cognizance and belief have to enter into it, and if you lack it . . .

T: If you had an assurance, then you would submit to it, wouldn't you? And you might make the effort. Perhaps we have to find a way that does not call for effort from you.

P: It would seem that way, judging from all the things that I've done that required my effort.

T: Well, that's quite all right. Don't think that there is any kind of moral umbrage attached to this. It's just a fact of the situation.

It became clear early in the course of therapy that Celia was jealous of her reputation as an intellectual. There were people about whose opinion of her abilities she was quite concerned. Therefore, concurrently with the above techniques, and more intensively later, assertive training was applied to Celia's interactions with people, but without any satisfactory transfer to real-life interactions. There was in fact no serious acceptance of the appropriateness of the strategy, as exemplified in the following. After introducing assertive training, the therapist set up a 'behavior rehearsal' with Celia, himself taking the part of a person whose good opinion is important to Celia. Celia is supposedly observed by this intellectually snobbish person to be reading a mystery book.

T: Oh, Celia, I see that you are reading a new kind of literature.
P: Uh, yeah that's right, yeah. What are you reading? [Defensive tone.]
T: Don't say it like that. Don't say it in that hangdog way.
P: Well I – all right.
T: The important part about this is that when she says Celia, etc. you interpret it, perhaps correctly, as a kind of attack, don't you?
P: Yes.
T: Then you are only allowed to counterattack.
P: I counterattack? I would walk away . . .
T: You have to counterattack – because walking away is defensive; it is a retreat. Whether you make a defensive remark or you run away, you are behaving weakly. Now let's do it again. Take preliminary pleasantries as read. Now, 'Oh, I see you are reading a new kind of literature.'
P: Umhm, what are you reading lately – that's all. I would never say that. I might want to say, 'Oh, yeah, what are you reading – knock it off.'
T: That's beautiful.
P: I would never say that. That's a horrible thing to say.
T: You could leave out the 'knock it off,' because it's rude.
P: But that's essentially what I'm saying, 'Oh, yeah, well you're reading anything better.' I wouldn't say that to anybody. That's a terrible thing to say.
T: Why?
P: It's offensive and rude.
T: She can say it to you?

P: Oh sure. I mean I'm walking out in plain sight reading this, I'm asking for it.

T: But this is absurd. You are doing a perfectly normal, reasonable thing, and you think that people are entitled to knock you for it?

P: Oh, I don't know. There was nothing terribly critical in her remark – implicitly maybe, but that's my problem not hers. I have no business getting defensive and offending her.

T: There's nothing offensive in asking a person what she is reading. Let's try to break this down. When she says, 'Oh, I see you are reading a new kind of literature,' you are taking it as if she were saying, 'How lowbrow can you get?'

P: Maybe, okay.

T: Well now, if a person is saying that, and if you are correctly interpreting it, then you are entitled to counterattack.

P: I don't think she would really be saying that.

After 17 sessions, very little behavioral change had occurred. With the exception of a possible slight reduction of her mean anxiety level, Celia complained that she felt that she had the same difficulties as when she had started treatment with us. She was also now unable to live in her parents' and grandparents' apartments because they were 'contaminated' by objects associated with XY University and ZA Hospital. Worst of all, she felt that she was still in a state of 'limbo.' She had promised herself not to return home while she was still in this condition, because of the tension it was causing between her and her parents. In addition, she was very distressed at the likelihood that she would not be able to return to school in the fall.

The techniques that were thus far tried are commonly used behavior therapy methods that have frequently succeeded with behavior disorders similar to those of Celia. Since they had failed, it was now necessary to attempt more experimental procedures. Various possibilities were considered, including the option of cingulotomy as a last resort (Hunter-Brown and Lighthill, 1968; Kelly, 1972). The most attractive possibility seemed to be some form of *in vivo* flooding, such as originally advocated by Meyer (1967). We were particularly intrigued by the flooding with modeling program described by Rachman and his co-workers (Rachman, Hodgson and Marzillier, 1970; Rachman, Hodgson and Marks, 1971; Hodgson, Rachman and Marks, 1972). With patients with behavior difficulties similar to Celia's, Rachman makes a hierarchy of the actual objects that they anxiously avoid. He then models approach behavior to each object and requires the patients to copy his behavior. Since they are inpatients, he can restrict their post-exposure washing. In five severely disturbed patients of his, the modeling-flooding technique was quite rapidly effective.

We requested Celia's parents to send us various articles which she had used while attending XY University. Very shortly we received a package containing various pieces of clothing, pens and pencils, and several books. Since the technique required the therapist to handle the contaminated objects, it was decided that JW should not participate in it, because if it were to fail and Celia perceived him as contaminated, he would be excluded from any future therapeutic role. LMA therefore took over this phase of treatment.

After an appropriate introduction to LMA and a careful description of the new projected technique, Celia was escorted into an office containing a desk on which were arranged the XY University articles. After being assured that they would not be 'thrown' at her, a fear which she expressed only half jokingly, she was asked to list the articles in increasing order of discomfort. She balked somewhat at this because she said that they all made her very uncomfortable. However, after some additional explanation, she listed them in the required manner. Modeling was initiated during the next session. LMA first approached the objects that Celia reported as least anxiety-provoking (various pens and pencils). He picked one up and tried to get Celia to do the same thing, but she adamantly refused. The objects were then arranged on a table between him and Celia, and he proceeded in a gradual manner to place his hand on the table and move it closer to the writing implements, finally touching one, then another, with the tips of his fingers. Next he gingerly lifted a pencil off the table, held it more firmly, and, at last, wrote with it. Having completed this series of operations, he asked Celia if she would mind copying his responses while he repeated what he had just done. During most of the next two sessions Celia was unable to comply. It then occurred to LMA that even being in the same room with the contaminants might make Celia anxious, and he decided to treat this by desensitization. Having been instructed to relax, Celia was presented with a hierarchy starting with her entering the room, and going on to seeing the objects, learning of her task, watching the therapist modeling the task, and herself performing each step of the approach to the pens and pencils. Following the completion of this sequence, Celia was able, albeit with some difficulty, to write with each of the pens and pencils that she had used at XY University. The next few sessions progressed quite smoothly, culminating in Celia being able to use all the objects, and wear all the clothing, for the duration of an entire afternoon.

It should be noted that after each contamination session, Celia was asked to refrain from washing for progressively longer periods. Because she was not hospitalized it was necessary to rely on her voluntary cooperation. Her reports indicated that she was following the instructions.

An assortment of articles was now requested of her parents that Celia had used while an outpatient at ZA Hospital. Desensitization in imagination was again required initially, but after that there was little difficulty in getting her to touch and use these articles.

After previously consistent refractoriness, the success of this treatment was exhilarating, and lifted Celia and her therapists from gloom to optimism. Under further guidance, Celia exposed herself to many things she had feared for some time. She touched people, walls, door knobs and books. After several weeks she returned to her parental home and, although there was still tension between her and her parents, they applauded the improvement in her behavior. Soon Celia began giving serious thought to returning to school in the fall. Her greatest apprehension was that the behavior disorder might return and interrupt her education again; she felt very regretful about the large sum of money her parents had wasted in fees the previous year. She knew that this would be her last chance of a college education. A final series of therapeutic sessions was therefore directed at overcoming the anxiety related to the decision to return to college, and to the behaviors involved in returning. Systematic desensitization and several covert conditioning procedures (Cautela, 1970a, 1970b, 1971) were employed toward this end. Therapy concluded one week before Celia's return to college, and three months after her first session with us.

We have now kept in touch with Celia for a further 18 months. Her concerns about contamination and the related handwashing had not completely disappeared at the end of therapy, but were quite mild in contrast to its beginning. There has been an occasional recurrence of handwashing to a minor extent during the past 18 months, but these 'idiosyncrasies,' as she calls them, have had little effect in restricting her from a normal existence. She has completed a full year and a half of study at a prestigious college with a B+ average. Her parents report continued improvement in her behavior at home. They are getting along with her much better and now look forward to the holidays when she can be with them. She spent six weeks during the summer in Europe and reported that she had a wonderful time. Recently, when her beloved grandfather died, she was appropriately upset, but did not have any consequent behavioral problems. In fact, she was able to congregate with, and kiss, her relatives at the funeral. Thus, at the end of more than one and one-half years, Celia has improved in many areas of her life, and while she says she is happy, we realize that additional improvements might be undertaken. Certainly no new behavioral problems seem to have replaced those we overcame.

Discussion

The feature of this case to which we have mainly tried to draw attention is the characteristic behavioristic mode of dealing with a patient's 'resistance' to treatment. Rather than attempting to 'analyze' the reasons for the 'resistance' on the dubious theory that insight would put an end to it, the strategy was to switch techniques in a systematic and progressive manner. The supposition was that one technique or another that would bypass the patient's opposition would sooner or later be found – since this has frequently been observed in other cases. To be able to offer a logical succession of treatments is something unique to behavior therapy.

A couple of technical points are worth noting. First, that the change of therapists created no difficulties for the therapy as shown by the fact that most of the substantive success was achieved by the second therapist. This is in keeping with previous experience (for example, Wolpe, 1962). Second, although the successful therapy was flooding following modeling, it appeared to be a necessary prerequisite for it to desensitize the patient by the standard imaginal techniques to the general outlines of what was involved in the flooding. The need for such desensitization supports the impression elsewhere noted (Wolpe, 1973, pp. 199-200) that flooding is more likely to succeed with sub-maximal than with maximal stimulation.

Clearly, Celia's problems were not all done away with by this treatment; but she was transformed from a state of functional incapacity to being able to lead an effective and reasonably contented life. The remaining problems could now, if necessary, be optimistically attacked by behavior therapy techniques; but it is quite evident that major 'life-style' changes followed once we had overcome the specific anxiety responses on which the obsessional behavior depended.

10 Contingency Management of Neurotic Depression and Marital Disharmony[1]

Robert Paul Liberman and Johnie Roberts[2]

Sarah Jane F,[3] a 30-year-old married ex-secretary with three children, walked into the mental health center three days after moving to Oxnard, a small city fifty miles north-west of Los Angeles. She was a tall woman who looked at least ten years older than her years because of grey hair, frailty, pallid complexion and an immobile facial expression. She asked for an application form for treatment services in a monotone voice that trailed off inaudibly at the end of each phrase. On the information sheet she wrote her presenting problem:

> I've been depressed for one year and while living in San Francisco was hospitalized twice, once for five weeks and again for two weeks. Medication has helped, but I still feel no interest in living. I feel so immobile, like a nothing. I can't function properly at home in my responsibilities. My husband and I hope my coming to the clinic will help the situation.

Sarah Jane was indeed depressed. Under the influence of a heavy regimen of psychotropic medication — Doxepin and Chlorpromazine — she appeared haggard and sallow. She walked slowly and averted eye contact with the psychiatric social worker and psychiatrist who interviewed her that day. Mrs S, the social worker, noted that Sarah Jane's depression

[1] This case study, with a three-year follow-up, was supported in part by the Behavior Analysis and Modification (BAM) Project, grant no. 1RO1MH19880-0181 from the Mental Health Services Development Branch of the National Institute of Mental Health, Bethesda, Maryland.

[2] The authors appreciate the consistent encouragement of Dr Rafael Canton and Dr Sarah Miller, past and present directors of the Ventura County Mental Health Department, California; Dr Stephen Coray, director of the Ventura County Health Services Agency, and the active participation by the entire staff of the Oxnard Mental Health Center, California.

[3] The names and identifying characteristics of the patients in this study have been carefully altered to protect their anonymity.

takes the form of losing interest in everything, staying in bed, and being unable to cope with housework and child care. The patient feels that she is a 'nothing' and from this one contact, I feel that the husband plays into this by showing *no* emotion or affect with her.

Sarah Jane was referred to the Oxnard Day Treatment Center where she met Ms Johnie Roberts, the supervising mental health nurse.

Johnie oriented Sarah Jane to the activities of the Day Treatment Center and asked her to sign an agreement to participate in the center's Coupon Incentive System. Based on the concept of the token economy, the Coupon Incentive System (Liberman, 1973) was adapted for the more open setting of a community mental health center. The following agreement was signed by Sarah Jane.

Agreement to participate in the Day Treatment Program

Welcome to the Oxnard Day Treatment Center! We know that full and active participation in our program is the best therapy, and we want to encourage you to be involved in our activities.

The Day Treatment Center provides food for making lunches, coffee, and a weekly bowling trip. You can have whatever you want for lunch, but since we have no kitchen staff, each person must take part in the planning and preparing of meals. We have frequent outings for recreation, but, again, we expect everyone to participate in the planning of these outings. We also expect full participation in keeping the Day Treatment area neat and clean.

To assure maximum participation in the Day Treatment Program, we have adopted a coupon-incentive system. Here is the way it works:

Each day you will have a chance to earn coupons by carrying out various responsibilities in the Day Treatment Center. For example, you can earn five coupons for making coffee. You can earn two coupons by cleaning out the ashtrays. The full list of jobs and their pay in coupons is listed on the poster in the kitchen.

You are probably curious about what you do with the coupons. The coupons can be exchanged for coffee, lunch, and bowling. Those who do the work get to enjoy the fruits of their labor. There are enough jobs so that everyone can easily earn enough coupons to have lunch, coffee and go bowling. To eat lunch each day, drink two cups of coffee each day, and go bowling each week costs a total of forty coupons per week.

On the first Wednesday of each month the old coupons are destroyed. New coupons for the next month are printed and handed out starting on the last Tuesday of each month.

The patients manage the coupon-incentive system. Two patients are chosen each Tuesday at the planning conference to be the monitors for the week. The week starts on Wednesday. The monitors give out and collect the coupons for lunch and bowling and ensure that the jobs are done properly. Coupons for coffee are put in a jar next to the coffee urn. Staff members will be available to support the efforts of the monitors.

If you wish to participate in the Day Treatment Program, please sign below.

The Day Treatment Center functions on a behavioral educational model. Each patient is assigned to a therapist from among ten nurses, technicians or rehabilitation workers who staff the center under the supervision of a psychiatrist (the first author). Activities include workshops which aim to impart skills in community living such as personal finance and consumerism, grooming, conversational skills, recreational-social-educational activities (Liberman, King, DeRisi, Eckman and Wood, 1974) and use of public agencies. Twice weekly, the patients participate in personal effectiveness training (Liberman, King, DeRisi and McCann, 1975), a form of assertion training, where a wide variety of interpersonal, emotional expressiveness is taught using behavioral rehearsal, coaching, modeling, homework assignments and social feedback. Johnie decided to take Sarah Jane into her own case-load, thinking that having a nurse for a therapist would provide a good model and source of rapport for Sarah Jane, who had always wanted to be a nurse.

The next two weeks were spent gathering information from Sarah Jane and her husband for an evaluation of the problem. The format for evaluating patients at the Oxnard Mental Health Center follows the model suggested by Kanfer and Saslow (1969) and encompasses a biological-medical and a socio-cultural as well as a behavioral-environmental analysis of an individual's functioning. An abbreviated sample of the assessment format is shown in Table 10·1.

TABLE 10·1   *Behavioral analysis of clinical problems. Abbreviated format of assessment scheme used at Oxnard (California) Mental Health Center*

I   Background data
   Who lives with patient?
   Previous psychiatric treatment (including hospitalizations) and results.
   Age, marital status, family status, social class

II   Problems (frequency, intensity, inappropriate form, duration, inappropriate occasions)
    A   Behavioral excesses
    B   Behavioral deficits
III   Assets and strengths
    A   Grooming
    B   Self-help skills
    C   Social (including conversation, recreation and friendships)
    D   Work
    E   Education and vocational training
IV   Functional analysis of problems
    A   What are the consequences of current problems?
        Who persuaded or coerced patient into treatment?
        Who reinforces problems with sympathy, help, attention or emotional reactions?
        What would happen if the problems were ignored? Or reduced in frequency?
        What reinforcers would the patient gain or lose if problems were removed?
    B   What are the S^D's or conditions and settings which serve as occasions for the occurrence of the problems? Where? When? With whom?
    C   Does patient acknowledge problems and desire treatment? (Self-motivation). Is patient comfortable with problems or troubled by them?
V   Reinforcement survey (be sure to assess correspondence between *verbal* self-report by patient and *actions* observed by you and significant others)
    People — places — things — foods — activities — aversive stimuli
    Natural reinforcers which could be used in patient's program
VI   Biological analysis
    A   Medical and surgical problems and limitations to activity
    B   Date of last physical exam
        Date of last pelvic exam and pap smear
    C   Name and address of family physician
    D   Current medical treatment and drugs (including psycho-tropic drugs)
    E   Family history — other family members with significant psychiatric-behavioral disturbance?
VII   Socio-cultural analysis
    A   Recent changes in milieu (migration, inter-generational conflicts in family, changes in work)
    B   Recent changes in social relationships (separation, divorce, deaths)
    C   Language and values (conflicts between minority sub-groups and majority culture)
    D   Other recent traumas or stresses
VIII Formulation of behavioral goals — be specific
    A   Increase desirable behaviors (include strengthening assets)
        Short term (1 month)   Long term (3 months)
    B   Decrease or extinguish undesirable behaviors
        Short term   Long term

C   Treatment techniques and interventions
D   Recording and measurement systems
    Time-sampling   Direct observation
    Duration recording   Self-recording by patient
    Interval recording   Permanent products
    Event recording

The hospital record from Sarah Jane's previous admissions in San Francisco was received. She had been admitted with the chief complaint of 'I'm depressed and can't stand it at home. I am just falling apart.' She was observed to be agitated, tremulous and apathetic. Psychotherapy was not effective and she was placed on psychotropic drugs and discharged with the diagnosis of neurotic depression.

TABLE 10·2   *Problems and goals for Sarah Jane*

	Problems	Goals
	Deficits	*Behavior to strengthen*
1	Fails to perform housework and child care	Cleaning, clothes washing, making beds, going shopping, cooking meals, making snacks for children
2	Poor grooming	Fix hair more stylishly, wear more colorful clothes, iron clothes so they are not baggy or wrinkled
3	Infrequent conversation with husband and children	At least fifteen minutes of conversing with husband each day, reading to children in evening
	Excesses	*Behavior to decrease*
1	Complains about helplessness and worthlessness	Verbalizations about feeling sick, helpless, worthless, 'like a nothing'
2	Retreating to bed	Time spent in bed during daytime and before 11 p.m. each evening

Johnie and the day treatment staff, in consultation with Dr Liberman, pinpointed Sarah Jane's problems and formulated some intital treatment goals. The assessment is shown in Table 10·2. One clear finding was the excessive amount of time that Sarah Jane was spending in bed. She was lying down for 'naps,' retreating from her family and home responsibilities, several times a day and regularly from 4-6.30 p.m. She was retiring for the night at 8 p.m. instead of her usual bedtime of 11 p.m. The staff estimated that Sarah Jane was spending an excess of five hours per day in bed. The behavioral analysis which was carried out during the first two weeks of her participation in the Day Treatment Center targeted several possible explanations for the precipitation and maintenance of Sarah Jane's depression. While her marriage had been unsatisfactory from almost the beginning, Sarah Jane's husband Jack had taken a new job in a distant city shortly before she plunged into the depression. He was able to visit the family only on weekends and Sarah Jane felt alone, deserted physically as well as emotionally, and burdened with all of the family responsibilities. When she became depressed, Jack showed more solicitude and spent more time in her presence. To compound the problem, she decided to leave her job as a secretary as she began feeling unhappy, and lacking in self-confidence.

Treatment of depression

A treatment plan was developed which included ignoring the patient's negative self-references while she was at the center, giving social approval for improved grooming, a contingency management program which the patient herself would control at home, and future marital therapy once the patient moved out of the slough of her depression. As the scientific literature reveals no clear benefit of medication in neurotic depression, Sarah Jane was taken off her drug regimen. Johnie met with Sarah Jane and helped her prepare a small notebook which was to be used as a behavioral diary. Each page was divided into two columns which were headed 'Constructive Activities' and 'Nap Time.' Using the Premack Principle (Liberman, 1972, p. 207), Sarah Jane was instructed on how to use a high frequency behavior (nap time in bed) to reinforce desirable but lower frequency behaviors (performing adaptive, constructive activities at home). Sarah Jane was urged to use time in bed only *after* she first completed a designated amount of housework, shopping, or interactions with her children. The patient put together a long list of household activities which were classed as 'constructive.' Sarah Jane was intrigued by the idea of a diary and kept track of the time spent in constructive activities and the time spent in bed in a conscientious manner. In response to a suggestion from Johnie, she went to the beauty parlor and had her hair styled more modishly. Johnie noted in the chart, 'Sarah Jane seemed pleased when comments were made about her new hairstyle and lipstick.'

Johnie and Sarah Jane met daily to review the contents of her notebook and the graph illustrating the cumulative number of hours spent constructively v. in bed. During these sessions, Sarah Jane repeatedly tried to provoke a response in Johnie by complaining about how difficult it was for her to complete housework duties, how inadequate she felt as a mother and wife, and how she felt like a 'blob.' These remarks were ignored and instead Johnie inquired further about the details of Sarah Jane's adaptive strivings and small accomplishments. After the first week of the self-control, contingency management program, constructive activities increased and time in bed decreased. In Figure 10·1 is shown the results of this program.

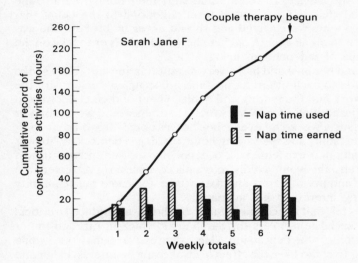

FIGURE 10·1   *Contingency self-management plan for Sarah Jane where a high frequency, depressive behavior (time in bed) was used to reinforce low frequency, adaptive behaviors (housework, childcare, socializing)*

After one month in the Day Treatment Center, Sarah Jane was showing visible evidence of brightening. Her appearance improved with the use of cosmetics and more stylish clothes. She initiated conversations with other patients as well as with staff and took on the job as menu planner and food supervisor for the daily luncheons held at the center. She smiled occasionally and even volunteered that she was 'feeling better.' At this point, the staff decided to begin marital therapy with the belief that unless the marital interactions changed for the better, Sarah Jane would continue to be susceptible to depression.

Marital therapy

Periodically Sarah Jane had mentioned to Johnie, her therapist, that she did not respect nor love Jack, her husband of eight years. In fact, they had separated for several months during the second year of their marriage. Seeking marriage counseling at that time, they were advised by a minister who carried out pastoral counseling that they were incompatible and should separate permanently. They decided, against this advice, to reunite and start their family. Sarah Jane indicated that she was raised from childhood in the belief that marriage vows were sacred and should never be broken. She was reluctant to break away from her cherished beliefs or to take on the challenge of independent living.

She and her husband had a very distant relationship. They spoke very little to each other. Sarah Jane preoccupied herself with the housework and the rearing and management of their children, and Jack poured himself into his work. He often would work three or four nights a week and even when he was home, he would sit apart from the family and spend long hours reading. Their sexual life was practically non-existent. Jack occasionally showed interest in sex, but Sarah Jane would coldly reject his advances. He retreated into fantasy and pornography and Sarah Jane abdicated her femininity by losing interest in her appearance.

It was felt that the couple's mutual withdrawal produced a critical loss of social reinforcers for Sarah Jane which in turn led to her susceptibility to depression. Her depressive behaviors, while maladaptive, did have the effect of awakening his interest in her and generating social attention and concern from him. Thus, marital therapy would be aimed at restoring a reciprocal exchange of social reinforcers between Sarah Jane and Jack with the contingencies focusing on positive and adaptive behaviors. Jack repeatedly expressed an interest to Johnie to come in to the clinic for conjoint sessions and Sarah Jane somewhat reluctantly and pessimistically agreed to the couple therapy.

The marital therapy was conducted by Johnie and Dr Liberman for 60 minutes once weekly. The first session was used for mutual elaboration of the problems as each saw them. They both acknowledged being on the brink of separation and were in despair and resignation about what they could do to remedy the situation. Before anything could be instigated of a positive nature between the pair, it was going to be necessary to have them learn to orient to each other, to talk plainly and honestly with each other, and to express feelings that they had been withholding and suppressing for so long. Both were encouraged to look at each other, express their positive and negative feelings directly to each other, and to give positive feedback when something pleasant was said. This instruction in basic communication skills was extended by guided practice at home with the programmed manual, *Improving Communication in Marriage* (Human Development Institute, 1969). Homework assignments were given from this manual for the couple to carry out in the privacy of their home between clinic sessions. During the first session, the therapists suggested that they make a verbal agreement or contract to exchange some desired behaviors with each other. Each night that Sarah Jane spent conversing with Jack for 15 minutes or more on a topic of interest to him (for example, current events), he would come to bed with her instead of staying up until his customary 1 a.m. hour of retiring.

When the couple returned the next week expressing satisfaction with the exchange they had agreed to, it was decided to negotiate a contingency contract. A contingency contract is an agreement between two or more individuals — usually in a family — which specifies the exchange of positively reinforcing behaviors that each wants from the other. Instead of 'reinforcing' unwanted behaviors with emotional reactions (anger, irritation, sympathy and concern are frequently paradoxical reinforcers for maladaptive behaviors) the couple negotiates a bargain which structures expectations and rewards for desired behaviors. A monitoring or record-keeping system is set up which enables the contractors and the therapist to assess their reciprocal fulfillment of the terms of the contract.

Sarah Jane wanted Jack to show greater commitment to the family and less to his job and private reading. Jack, on his side, wanted her to dress more modishly and to initiate affection toward him. The couple was assisted by Dr Liberman and Johnie to negotiate two contracts over a period of six weeks. The two contracts are delineated in Table 10·3 with the second contract building upon four weeks of progress produced by the first one. The couple's compliance with the terms of the contract was reviewed at each marital therapy session. Behavioral rehearsal with coaching was carried out to give both spouses experience in talking directly and emotionally with each other. Johnie and Dr Liberman modeled appropriate conversational skills with an emphasis on the nonverbal elements of eye contact, use of hands, posture, facial expression, vocal tone and fluency. Sarah Jane had opportunities in the couple sessions to practice, under supervision, the kinds of behaviors which her husband considered to be affectionate.

TABLE 10·3   *Contingency contracts negotiated by Sarah Jane and Jack during marital therapy*

Sarah Jane's responsibilities	Jack's responsibilities
Contract I	
Sit and talk with husband during breakfast, Monday to Friday	Arise from bed by 10 a.m. on Saturday and Sunday
Clean the living room for two hours each week	Engage in some mutual activity with wife between 10-11 p.m. on Tuesday, Thursday, Saturday and Sunday
Contract II Same as above plus the following:	
Dress in clothes that appeal to husband	Arrive at home by 5.30 p.m. each day
Initiate affection (kisses, hugs, hand holding, caresses) toward husband	Avoid expressing hostility or 'up-tightness' (coldness, rejection, annoyance, silence, withdrawal) when wife asks not to pursue sexual relations

This contract shall be monitored by a medium of exchange. Sarah Jane shall give Jack a receipt for each successful completion of his terms of the contract. Jack shall give a receipt to Sarah Jane for her successful completion of each term of her part of the contract. Each receipt will have the recipient's name, the date, and what was done to earn it. The receipts earned by each shall be brought to the therapy session each week.

The contract was monitored by a receipt system. Each partner wrote out and handed a receipt to the other for fulfilling a term of the contract. For instance, Jack gave his wife a receipt for initiating affection and she gave him a receipt for coming home on time. It was explained to them that the exchange of receipts might seem artificial and mechanical at first, but that it was a way to keep them both aware of the new reinforcement contingencies operating in their relationship. It also marked the occasion for each of them to provide 'social reinforcement' (compliments, praise, recognition) to the other for moving toward more desirable and pleasing behavioral goals. They were assured that the receipts would be phased out as soon as they found themselves settled in new interactional patterns. Figure 10·2 shows the receipts used in this therapy.

The results of the contract are shown in the cumulative record of receipts exchanged in Figure 10·3. Both spouses issued and

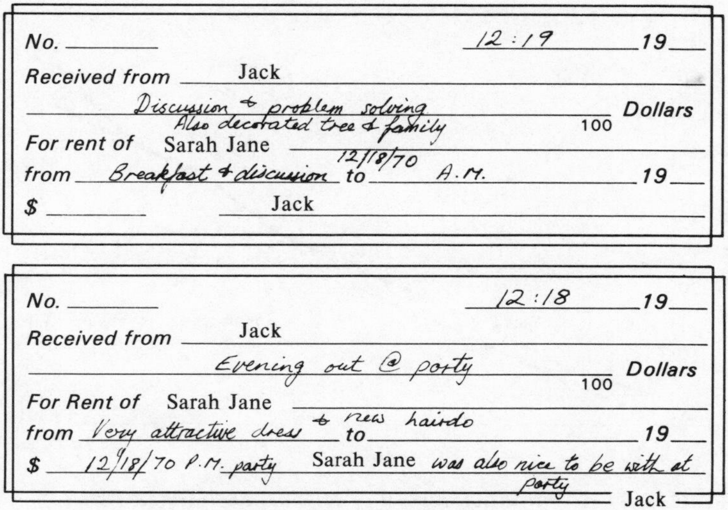

No. ______ 12:19 19__
Received from Jack
Discussion & problem solving
Also decorated tree & family Dollars
100
For rent of Sarah Jane
from Breakfast & discussion to 12/18/70 A.M. 19__
$ ______ Jack

No. ______ 12:18 19__
Received from Jack
Evening out @ party Dollars
100
For Rent of Sarah Jane
from Very attractive dress & new hairdo to ______ 19__
$ 12/18/70 P.M. party Sarah Jane was also nice to be with at party
Jack

FIGURE 10·2 *Receipts used by Sarah Jane and Jack to cue and monitor their exchanging social acknowledgment for accelerating desired behaviors agreed upon in their contingency contract*
Each single receipt was used by both spouses to acknowledge compliance by both to the terms of the contract.

received about the same number of receipts, indicating that the contract was promoting mutual, reciprocal behaviors. After ten sessions of marital therapy, Mr and Mrs F indicated a renewed willingness to continue their marriage and to work on further improvements. They had resumed sexual intercourse on a regular basis and reported satisfaction with their sexual experiences for the first time in five years. Their relationship was not yet mutually satisfying and both continued to report skepticism about the outcome, but the marital therapy had promoted efforts by both partners to do as much as possible to strengthen the union.

One month after marital therapy began, Sarah Jane and Johnie discontinued the initial self-control contingency with nap time because the patient had shown such steady improvement in her housekeeping and child-care functions. Instead, new goals were established with the focus being on Sarah Jane exploring opportunities for volunteer work outside the home. It was hoped that working on a part-time, volunteer basis would eventually lead to gainful employment with the natural reinforcers of a job further strengthening Sarah Jane's resistance to depression. The weekly marital therapy sessions were made contingent upon Sarah Jane

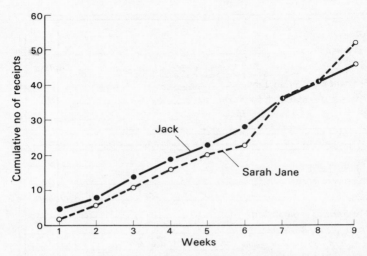

FIGURE 10·3 *Cumulative record of receipts exchanged between Jack and Sarah Jane under the terms of their contingency contract*
The close similarity in the number of receipts exchanged reflects the mutuality in their compliance with the terms of the contract.

documenting to Johnie that she had checked out at least five volunteer opportunities each week. This goal was reached each week and by the third week Sarah Jane had begun a three day per week stint as a volunteer at St Jude's Hospital. Less than four months after her admission to the Day Treatment Center, Sarah Jane told Johnie that she was too busy and involved with her home and volunteer job to continue coming to the Mental Health Center. Johnie and the patient jointly agreed to terminate treatment. The marital therapy sessions were also terminated with the couple being given instructions to gradually fade out their contract and their use of receipts. The future availability of the Mental Health Center, should they require assistance, was extended to them.

Generalization of treatment over time

Three years after Sarah Jane and her husband terminated treatment a follow-up was conducted by phone. The first author initiated the phone call to the F's home and the transcript of this conversation with Sarah Jane follows:

Dr L: It's been quite some time since we had contact
      with you and I've been curious to know how you

	have been doing since you left the clinic. How are things going?
Sarah Jane:	I've been really happy. My life has changed a lot, but for the better. It seems like such a long time ago that I was depressed and sick.
Dr L:	Tell me what has happened during the past two and a half years.
Sarah Jane:	Well, when I left the clinic I was working three days a week as a volunteer at St Jude's Hospital. I continued to work there, four hours each day, for over a year. I worked around medical patients, but did not do any clinical work. I did almost every kind of thing imaginable — read to patients, gave tours of the hospital, served in the gift shop, and helped with office work. The clinic helped to get me out into the community and I felt like I was beginning a new life — like I was doing something useful. Working as a volunteer kept me feeling good about myself.
Dr L:	How about your marriage?
Sarah Jane:	Jack and I split up in December 1971, just about a year after I left the mental health center. I knew that he wouldn't start divorce proceedings despite the fact that we talked about it so often and agreed that separation would be best. So I started divorce action and it was finalized in August 1972.
Dr L:	Then your divorce was a mutual decision?
Sarah Jane:	Yes. You know we had separated briefly about a year or so after we were first married. We should've known then that it wouldn't work out. We saw a marriage counselor back then — a minister who had a lot of counseling experience — and he recommended that we not continue the marriage. But I was so conditioned to think of marriage vows as permanent that I couldn't help going on even though Jack and I are so different. I don't think I felt any love for him for the last ten years of our marriage. I don't think he loved me, unless it was in some inner way that he couldn't show.
Dr L:	How has Jack reacted to the split-up?
Sarah Jane:	Jack is much happier now. He lives in a modern apartment house in the city and has friends. He

	still has his supervisory job at the office and is able to spend all the time he wants on the job without feeling guilty about not satisfying me and the kids.
Dr L:	Does he visit the children?
Sarah Jane:	Yes, but mostly with reminders from me. I have to push his interest in the kids. But we are on good terms with each other. We're friendly when we meet and both feel that our decision to separate was a good one.
Dr L:	Have you worked at all?
Sarah Jane:	Oh yes. When the divorce was finalized I immediately got a job as a secretary in a physician's office. Before that I went back to college and took a refresher course in shorthand. I worked in the doctor's office for three months and was suddenly let go with one day's notice! Imagine that — such unprofessional behavior from a doctor!
Dr L:	Did that setback get you feeling depressed again?
Sarah Jane:	Not really. I did feel angry and hurt, but I had faith in God and felt that His Spirit was with me. I was singing in the church choir and was attending a weekly adult discussion group at the church led by my pastor. That group, which met for about a year, was very helpful for my making decisions for myself. The pastor had some training in transactional analysis and we each had to make a 'pact' with the group to solve our problems, not simply complain about them. No one in the group actually told me what to do, but I knew that they were interested in how I was managing. It was a warm and supportive place.
Dr L:	I can see how the church group could be helpful. It sounds like an important experience in learning from each other. Were you able to get another job?
Sarah Jane:	Yes, I had to. Jack was giving child support, but that wasn't enough to keep us going and keep up the house payments. After I lost the first job, I spent a lot of time making Christmas presents — sewing and making decoupage things. I didn't have any money to buy presents that year. My father helped me paint the whole

house, so I kept myself very busy. Then I got a job working as a night secretary at St Jude's Hospital. I've been working there ever since, almost one year now. I enjoy the work, the pay is good and I'm still able to look after the kids when they come home from school. The kids are doing just fine, too.

Dr L: How about your social life? Have you gone out with men on dates?

Sarah Jane: No. I'm not ready for that yet. Sometimes I feel lonely, but so do many other people. But I have lots of friends from church and I do go to parties and dinners. You know, for the first time in my life I find that I can let my hair down and have fun. I can joke and be playful with friends. I used to be so serious. I feel normal like other people. It seems like a different lifetime that I was so depressed and sick.

Dr L: What would you say helped you out of your depression, looking back on it now?

Sarah Jane: The clinic was the push I needed to get out of bed and into the world. I didn't like coming to the Day Treatment Center at the time, but I knew that I had to. I didn't enjoy coming, and I let you and Johnie know that, but it was the kind of stimulation I needed to get out of my sickness. Keeping my daily activities in the diary and reporting each day to Johnie gave me some goal to reach that wasn't so far away.

Dr L: Thank you for sharing all this news about yourself and your life. I've noticed a tremendous difference in the quality of your voice — you sound much different with much more oomph and vitality in your voice. In fact, I hardly recognize your voice from before, it's so improved in tone. I also want to send regards from Johnie and the rest of the clinic staff. We do occasionally think about you and it's reassuring to know how well you are doing for yourself.

Sarah Jane: Thank you for calling. Please send my best regards to Johnie and the others.

A follow-up phone call was made independently to Jack who spoke to Dr Liberman from his business office. Looking back on the dissolution of the marriage he said, 'We both decided that the marriage wasn't working and handled the divorce ourselves without an attorney and without any hassles. We still have a hell of a lot of respect for each other but we realize that we have different value systems that just don't mesh.' Jack indicated that his wife's more spiritual and religious outlook on life had not changed since they met each other twenty years before, while he had become more worldly and materialistic. He spoke of a 'sense of release' from the pressures of being married, stating that he had an active social life in the large apartment development in which he lived. He occasionally dated women but mainly socialized informally with neighbors and friends around the apartments. In retrospect, Jack felt that the marital therapy was helpful in providing 'a necessary catharsis.' He said that the couple therapy gave them both a chance to seriously examine and repair their marriage. 'You don't know if a marriage will work unless you really try,' he said. Like his ex-wife, Jack reported that both he and she were reasonably happy and content with their new living situation and that no further episodes of depression had occurred.

Discussion

This case study illustrates the application of behavioral principles to the assessment and treatment of a woman with a chronic depressive disorder. The study reflects the complexity of the behavioral and environmental interactions which must be teased apart for a thorough understanding of a patient's clinical status. Behavior analysis and therapy are not simplistic or reductionistic, when carefully applied. Further advances in the field of behavior analysis will undoubtedly reveal great complexities and subtleties which will make the current state of the art, and even psychoanalytic approaches, seem like child's play.

The contingency self-management program established for the treatment of Sarah Jane's depression contained several behavioral components which were responsible for its success. Any instigative therapy involves a heavy reliance on the effects of *instructions* or prompts from the therapist to the patient. The therapists, Dr Liberman and Johnie, gave clear and explicit instructions to Sarah Jane on how she was to use her nap time to contingently reinforce her coping activities. Each time that Johnie met with her patient, these instructions were explicitly delivered. Another component of the program was the frequent dispensing of approval or social *feedback* to the patient for her progress shown in the public record-keeping of her behavioral diary. It was necessary to review

Sarah Jane's behavioral diary every day and to give praise and acknowledgment freely for her compliance with the contingency plan. When the review and feedback was conducted only twice weekly, the patient's progress noticeably slowed.

A third component in the self-management program was the patient's monitoring of her own behavior on a daily basis. Self-monitoring is an intervention by itself (Kanfer and Karoly, 1972; Watson and Tharp, 1972) and can be used to accelerate desirable behaviors or decelerate undesirable behaviors. Other behavioral problems which have been shown to change as a function of self-monitoring are overeating, smoking, nail-biting, and classroom disruptiveness (Mahoney, 1972).

The Premack principle itself was probably a minor contribution to the total therapeutic effect; however, it may have served as an anchoring point for the patient who at the start of treatment was spending a considerable amount of her time in bed. The use of the Premack principle has been described for treatment of depression (Todd, 1972), marital distress, and obesity (Goldiamond, 1965; Stuart, 1972).

Given the powerful technology of the behavioral clinician, based upon empirical laws of learning, his relationship with the patient also contributes to the therapeutic outcome. A therapist who does not have a positive alliance with his patients does not possess instructional control and will discover that his thoughtful instigations are not complied with when the treatment sessions end. Without a solid and respectful relationship, the therapist does not possess reinforcing or modeling properties for his patients. His role as an educator and lever for initiating changes in the behavior of an individual depends partly on his capacity to show empathy, warmth, and concern for those with whom he is working. Behavioral technology will be of little effectiveness when wielded by a therapist who lacks clinical and interpersonal skills.

That behavioral point of view leads to a total systems view of the problems of individuals. A key element in the successful treatment of Sarah Jane's depression was the recognition of the importance of natural, community-based reinforcers and the role of her husband in maintaining her freedom from depression (Liberman and Raskin, 1971). Thus, Johnie pinpointed volunteer activity for Sarah Jane as a means of establishing new social reinforcers which would be focused on the patient's adaptive behaviors. People with whom Sarah Jane interacted in the volunteer group became the natural reinforcers for healthy behavior, permitting Johnie to phase out her own, more artificial source of reinforcement in the mental health center. Involving the husband in the treatment plan was necessary since their coercive and distant relationship had reached a stalemate of uncertainty.

The marital treatment did not produce a long-lasting rejuvenation of the relationship between Sarah Jane and Jack. In fact, one might perceive the marital therapy as precipitating a rupture in their relationship. The important point to note, however, is that the marital therapy promoted a change in their relationship from the torpid *status quo* which prevented both spouses from gaining necessary reinforcers. Initially, under the impetus of instructions, behavioral rehearsal, and social feedback from themselves and the therapists, the couple experienced a positive change in their relationship. They talked and communicated more often and more effectively. Their sexual and affectional interchanges improved. They were getting more and giving more in the marriage. But as indicated from the follow-ups, they both realized that this decided improvement was not enough for their needs and desires. Given the benefit of trying to make the marriage work, both spouses were able to separate without animosity or guilt. They both felt that the investment of time and effort in improving their marriage was extremely useful in helping them see more clearly what the pros and cons of their relationship were and in unburdening their feelings of remorse and regret over the decision to separate. Eighteen months after separation, both expressed feelings of satisfaction with their separated status, indicating that they were enjoying active and happy social and vocational endeavors.

Summary

This case study reveals the process of behaviorally assessing and treating a woman suffering from depression. History-taking and clinical interviews as well as direct observation served as data sources for arriving at a behavioral diagnosis. The implementation of a contingency, self-management program required a therapeutic alliance between the patient and her therapists. This alliance was the foundation in which was imbedded the successful use of instructions, self-monitoring, and social feedback. Functional goals were chosen so that the patient would encounter natural reinforcers in the community and would not become dependent upon the support she received from her nurse-therapist at the mental health center. Marital therapy, using behavioral rehearsal and contingency contracting, was initiated as the terminal intervention for the patient. While the marriage did not survive more than a year after treatment, a three-year follow-up indicated that both spouses were happily involved in jobs and social relationships.

Clinical and research progress made by behavior therapists hopefully will challenge all therapists, regardless of their theoretical leanings, to specify more clearly their interventions, their goals, and their empirical results. Only when this happens can we develop a compendium of techniques with known and predictable effects on a wide variety of clinical problems.

11 A Case Study in Bereavement Therapy

R. W. Ramsay

Case description

A 34-year-old woman was referred to the outpatient clinic of a large hospital with presenting symptoms of agitation, sleeplessness, loss of appetite, inability to cope with everyday tasks, and aggressive impulses towards her 8-month-old daughter.

The psychiatric history revealed that Mrs S was married in 1961 to a school teacher, and became pregnant in 1963. Neither husband nor wife wanted children and at three months' pregnancy a miscarriage occurred. At the end of 1969 the wife again became pregnant, and this time the wife wanted a child but the husband was still very much against having children as he was asthmatic and was afraid that any offspring would be the same. There were fights between husband and wife in which the wife was physically abused and locked in the flat for days on end, and medication received from the gynaecologist was thrown away. At seven months' pregnancy she began to bleed and was admitted to hospital. The husband created such a stir in the hospital with his abuse of her and his attempts to throw away her medication that the staff barred him from further entry. The child was born dead in the hospital.

Ten days after she left the hospital Mrs S was informed that her mother had cancer, and a month later the mother died. At about the same time two riding horses that the couple owned and prized greatly had to be destroyed, one due to illness and the other because of an accident.

At the beginning of 1971 Mrs S again became pregnant, and there ensued more violent scenes between husband and wife, with Mr S doing everything he could to bring on a miscarriage and Mrs S protecting herself and the baby as best she could. In August 1971 after a violent fight Mr S suffered a severe asthma attack, was admitted to hospital and died there a few days later. Ten days after his death Mrs S gave birth to a daughter. She reported that she was so preoccupied with the pregnancy and the imminent birth that she had not cried either at the news of her husband's death or at his funeral.

After the birth of the daughter Mrs S became increasingly agitated, afraid of the baby, unable to cope with the demands that the baby made on her, became afraid that she would harm the child, began to suffer from insomnia and loss of appetite, and could not cope with everyday affairs because the events of the past year kept going through her head like a film which she could not turn off.

Her GP referred her to a psychiatrist, but on the day of the appointment the psychiatrist was killed in a traffic accident. She was immediately referred to the psychiatric outpatient clinic.

What to do?

Here we were confronted with a classical case of reactive depression in an acute form, with a high risk of infanticide and suicide. The psychiatric textbooks suggest hospitalization to take care of the risks involved, and then psychotherapy of an empathic, understanding, and non-exhortatory nature, with sedative drugs when considered necessary (for example, Mendelson, 1967). Gutheil (1959) suggests that movies, TV and sleep can be a great help in filling in time and providing diversion from worries. Most writers agree that spontaneous remission often occurs, and our impression is that most therapists will provide understanding support while waiting for the crisis to pass.

We felt that in this case just hospitalization and support while waiting for the mourning process to proceed by itself might have taken a year or more, and that Mrs S would deteriorate during such prolonged hospitalization. A more active therapy therefore seemed indicated.

Characteristics of mourning

All writers on this subject agree that mourning is a common human experience which is extremely painful. Freud (1917) gives as the characteristics of mourning a profoundly painful dejection, loss of the capacity to love, inhibition of all activity, and a loss of interest in the outside world in so far as it does not recall the dead one. Bowlby (1961, 1963) uses the word 'mourning' to denote the psychological processes that are set in train by the loss of a loved object and which commonly lead to the relinquishing of the object. The word 'grief' Bowlby uses to denote the subjective states that follow loss and accompany mourning. Averill (1968) described bereavement behaviour from cultural, biological and psychological perspectives.

He sees in bereavement behaviour two components: mourning and grief. The former, according to him, is of cultural origin, while grief is the product of biological evolution. He summarizes the major features of grief as follows (p. 744):

(a) grief is a complex but stereotyped response pattern which includes such psychological and physiological symptoms as withdrawal, fatigue, sleep disturbances, and loss of appetite;
(b) it is elicited by a rather well-defined stimulus situation, namely, the real or imagined loss of a significant object (or role), and it is resolved when new object relations are established;
(c) it is a ubiquitous phenomenon among human beings and appears in other social species as well, especially in higher primates;
(d) it is an extremely stressful emotion, both psychologically and physiologically, and yet behavior during grief is often antithetical to the establishment of new relations, and hence the alleviation of the stress.

No attempt will be made here to differentiate between normal and pathological mourning; it will be normal unless it is so severe or prolonged as to need clinical intervention — then it will be pathological. Siggins (1967) in her review states:

I myself regard mourning as pathological if any of the reactions are excessively intense or violent, or if the process of mourning is unduly prolonged. Such a prolongation of mourning may be due to a delay in beginning the process, or to a retarding of the process once it has begun, or both.

Behaviour therapists do not seem to have come to grips yet with the problems of depression and grief as there are only a handful of articles in this area (Burgess, 1968; Lazarus, 1968b; Lewinsohn *et al.,* 1968; Liberman and Raskin, 1971; McAuley and Quinn, 1971; Wolpe, 1971b).

Phases or components of mourning

There seem to be certain phases in a mourning process which can be distinguished from each other and which are necessary for proceeding further in the resolution of the problem:

1   *Denial* — the person denies that there has been any loss and lives as if the loved object still exists, which often necessitates dissociation from the real world in order to preserve this as a fantasy.

2   *Depression* — as denial starts breaking down the person begins to experience the full force of the loss and the painfulness and emptiness of life without the loved one.

3   *Guilt* — the person begins to blame himself for the loss, or for not having made things easier for the loved one before the parting.

4   *Aggression* — the person is aggressive towards others for their not being able to ease the pain, for not having done enough to prevent the loss. There is also sometimes aggression against the loved object itself for having caused the pain.

5   *Anxiety* — the guilt and aggression always contain elements of anxiety, and there is also possibly anxiety about the uncertainties of a different life in the future.

6   *Re-integration* — the person organizes a way of life in which the lost object has no place.

There is no agreement on this classification in the literature. However, it does seem to be of value to try and identify what takes place and to know what to expect. It might be better to view this sequence as being made up of reactions that occur in any order, rather than phases which follow in systematic order.

Behaviour therapy approach to a mourning reaction

The suggestions of empathic support, talking it through and sedation while waiting for spontaneous remission seem to us rather weak and time-consuming, and we started a number of years ago trying out some more active approach to mourning processes. The results appeared to be promising as changes occurred quickly, usually within a few sittings.

From our experience with phobic reactions of various kinds, it would seem that the best results with severe and complex cases are achieved by a confrontation with the anxiety-provoking stimuli — a prolonged-exposure flooding either *in vitro* or *in vivo*. (For a review of the literature on this see Marks, 1972.) From there, we argued that a pathological mourning process could best be 'worked through' by confronting the client with the problems, to break down the denial, to have the client experience the depression, anxiety, aggression and guilt with no escape possibilities, and to allow time for the intense emotional reactions to extinguish. A grief reaction will only become pathological if no confrontation takes place and the emotional reactions have no chance to extinguish. This exposure in phobic patients is usually fairly straightforward, but can tax the therapist's ingenuity in the case of grief reactions.

The principles involved, however, are essentially similar, and they will be described in detail as with this particular case.

Treatment

Arrangements were made to have friends look after the child, and Mrs S was admitted as an inpatient to the psychiatric ward of a general hospital. The therapy strategy was explained to her by the psychiatrist who had taken the case history; she agreed to take part in an intensive programme which would be carried out daily by the author and the intake psychiatrist, and a nurse was assigned to be with her when necessary. (Many of the sittings were recorded on video-tape, with her consent.) In her room in the ward the client was asked to sit in a comfortable chair, close her eyes, and to imagine her husband, to describe him, and then to say to herself such phrases as 'but now he's dead', 'I'll never see him again'. This did not work, as she reported that he was constantly present, they conversed with each other, and even went to bed together. She even smiled when the therapist said that the husband was dead, as she knew in her own mind that Wim was sitting right beside her. She was then instructed that if he did not go away she was to try and send him away, to tell him that he was dead and must go. This also did not work, as he refused to leave. She appeared to have imaginary discussions with Wim, periods where it was obvious to the therapist that she was busy with something, but the therapist could only find out afterwards what it was all about by asking her what had happened. She was then instructed to forcibly send him away, to fight with him if necessary. This didn't work either, even though the emotional reactions were intense. She lost every fight with him. She was then instructed to fight with him, and the therapist would help her to win. The first time she tried this there was a strong reaction for about ten minutes, and then she reported that after the struggle involving the three of them, the scene ended with the therapist lying in the coffin. After reassurance that the therapist felt fine, the scene was repeated a number of times. All this took about two weeks, in sessions of $1\frac{1}{2}$ hours daily, and she became obviously extremely agitated in every session. During the third week of treatment she finally succeeded in sending the husband away temporarily, but then became severely depressed, aggressive towards the therapist, wanted to stop the therapy, to leave the hospital and to do away with the child and herself. The hospital staff were prepared to hold her against her will, but this proved not to be necessary. Within a few days she was again prepared to continue the therapy, although she was still very depressed. At this stage she stated that she had come to realize that it was not that he refused to leave, but that she did not want to let him go.

This phase of breaking down the denial took weeks, with constant shifting into aggression, guilt and anxiety. The aggression was directed against the doctors who had treated the husband, against the therapist, the child, and against the husband himself. During this time, the 'film' that had been playing through her mind gradually became fragmented and fainter, but one scene remained strong: a fight that she and the husband had had just before his death. She was asked to remember this, to go through it in her mind, and it took five long and violent sessions to extinguish the anxiety that was coupled with these memories. Each session produced more and more details of the fight, with the last detail being that the husband had almost murdered her by holding a pillow over her face. At times the content of the imagined scenes changed, sometimes to the baby that had been stillborn, sometimes to the mother, and sometimes to the horses that had had to be destroyed. Where she spontaneously came up with these shifts, the therapist followed and tried to work through the grief concerned with these events. The husband, though, took the central role.

After six weeks of treatment she wanted to see the child again, but was still afraid, and could not hold the child close to her. At the same time she started going home again for short periods, but suffered severe anxiety attacks in the home. The therapist made the mistake of allowing her to go home alone the first time and she returned to the ward within two hours in a state of complete panic. This was treated by forced prolonged exposure with the therapist present, during which she had to clean up the house and put away all the husband's belongings. They owned two cats which the husband had liked very much, and it took 2 sessions for her to bring herself to tell the cats that the husband was dead. It took another 3 sessions to be able to tell the child that the father was dead, and still 3 more sessions to tell herself that he was dead. Each session was a highly emotional experience.

After two months the client was discharged from the hospital and therapy was continued on a less intensive basis. The 'film' had ceased to exist, the anxieties connected with the child had not completely disappeared but had been considerably reduced, and the panic attacks at home had ceased. She reported that for the first time in a year she occasionally felt lonely and sought contact with other people.

Intensive therapy time in the two months totalled 60 sittings of $1^1/_2$ hours average duration, plus a full-time nurse for four weeks.

The further treatment was carried out by the psychiatrist who had done the intake and who had acted as co-therapist during the flooding sessions. As an illustration of the application of behaviour therapy to the treatment of a pathological mourning process, the account could be ended here, but it may be of interest to give a résumé of how the case developed further. A few months after discharge from the hospital the client suffered a bout of influenza which was followed by a depressive phase lasting for a week or two. Another relapse occurred when the two cats died.

The client intimated that at that stage she was having great difficulty with her feelings towards the co-therapist. The psychiatrist was in psycho-analytic training, and during the reintegrative phase wanted to 'work through' the transference in the usual analytic way, to discuss the transference in therapy and give the patient insight in the mechanisms involved. The co-therapist was, however, persuaded to tackle the problem of transference not by discussing it, but by giving the client tasks to do which brought her into contact with other people. This seemed to work, as the 'difficult' feelings towards the therapist diminished. A year after therapy had started, however, she once again became suicidal and had to be readmitted to hospital for a few weeks. She had fallen in love with a minister who ran a community contact centre, and she thought that he was also in love with her, but she subsequently found out that he had a regular 'harem' of girl friends. Supportive therapy at a rate of once every five weeks will continue until she can make a more suitable partner choice.

Personality of the client

It is very difficult to assess the premorbid personality in such a case, but we can make some guesses. When first seen in the clinic she did not appear to be depressed, she could talk to everyone and was often smiling. When asked about this difference between what she reported about her feelings and difficulties, and what was observable, she stated that she had always been able to hide and suppress her feelings, and could not let others see how she felt. Emotions of great happiness, sadness, or anger she found impossible to either feel or express. This suppression of feelings probably was causal in the bereavement process becoming pathological, and certainly made the therapy extremely difficult and prolonged. After the intensive therapy she was still emotionally inhibited, but was beginning to feel and express more than she had ever done before.

The Dutch version of the MPI taken before therapy started produced scores of: neuroticism, 98th percentile, psychosomatic tendencies, 96th percentile, extraversion, 9th percentile, and Lie scale 32nd percentile. The MMPI was also taken both before therapy and after one year, but the scores on both these administrations were probably unreliable. She answered all 566 questions in less than an hour, and told the nurse that she thought the tests were a lot of nonsense. Table 11·1 gives the *t* scores.

TABLE 11·1 *MMPI* t *scores before therapy and one year later*

L	F	K	Hs	D	Hv	Pd	Mf	Pa	Sc	Ma	Si
62	63	61	82	90	82	69	52	48	81	75	37	69
62	70	66	73	73	78	82	45	51	71	71	39	63

In the second administration there is a definite lowering of the scales measuring neurotic reactions, but an increase in Pd which is probably due to the careless way in which the test was done. However, in spite of the lower scores on the second administration, the profile is far from that of a healthy personality.

Discussion

Most therapists would maintain that the aims of therapy for reactive depressions are support during the acute phase and then treatment designed to strengthen the personality so that further losses can be more easily dealt with. The treatment described above has little to do with the second part of that goal, but only deals with the acute phase. We would only claim that the time necessary to pass through the acute phase is probably shortened. In other cases where we felt that a chronic pathological mourning process was contributing to personality problems, and the diagnosis was not reactive depression, we have been surprised at the changes a few flooding sessions can bring about.

In carrying out therapy such as this, we have been impressed by the violence of the emotional outbursts, and in some cases the therapist has needed support in going on with the presenting of the stimuli until the response extinguishes. The therapist must expect strong reactions: crying fits, angry outbursts, panic reactions, and threats of suicide, and the therapist *must* in any one sitting continue to present the stimuli which elicit an outburst until the reaction subsides. This may take a number of hours, but it is considered essential that the reactions subside before a sitting is ended.

A further problem which has arisen is that the therapist is often frightened or reluctant to deal with the concept of death. The therapist is quite liable to find that his own bereavement experiences hinder him in the therapy, and that he has to face his own fears of breaking the taboo of dealing openly with death.

Until now, no experimental work has been done in the area under discussion. The technique of treatment has been borrowed from other areas of behaviour therapy, the indications for when to use this technique are no more than clinical hunches, and the assessment of results is completely subjective. However, in spite of these criticisms, it is felt that it will be worthwhile going further into these problems. The theoretical behaviour therapy articles on depression barely touch on the effects of bereavement, and much serious work will have to be done in order to understand depression and mourning, and the differences and similarities between them.

Diagnosis and indications for treatment are another field sorely in need of careful work. A behaviour analysis of a client will indicate many problem areas, but to relate these problems to each other, and to show that they form a syndrome which we may call pathological mourning, is not easy. Even assuming that we can show that such a syndrome exists, we are still faced with the choice of treatment focused on the precipitating event or an ahistorical treatment of the here-and-now lack of positive reinforcement, anxiety, aggression, and conditioned helplessness that Wolpe (1971b) advocates.

It will be necessary to show experimentally if this method has more to offer in terms of efficiency than other more conventional forms of therapy and to find out in more detail what these other therapies consist of so that comparisons can be made. Controlled studies will have to be carried out using different approaches in order to evaluate this behaviour therapy attack.

Summary

A case study of an implosive therapy approach to the problems of pathological mourning is described. A form of flooding is used whereby the patient is confronted with the stimuli which elicit the painful emotions associated with bereavement, and this confrontation is repeated again and again in the form of prolonged exposure until extinction of the emotional responses occurs. Some suggestions for further exploration of this technique are discussed.

12   A Closer Look at 'Simplistic' Behavior Therapy for Sexual Dysfunction: Two Case Studies[1]

W. Charles Lobitz, Joseph LoPiccolo, Gretchen K. Lobitz and Jacqueline Brockway

When people first began to turn to psychotherapists for help with their sexual inadequacies, their dysfunction was usually considered to reflect a deep-seated personality disorder. As a result, the therapy, generally psychoanalytic in approach, did not focus on their current behavioral deficits but on the presumed dynamics and historical roots of the current symptoms. Such psychoanalytic treatment has not been successful for sexual dysfunction (Lorand, 1939; Moore, 1961) and is both lengthy and expensive. For example, Bergler (1947, 1951) has stated, 'an appointment several times a week for a minimum of eight months' is necessary for treatment of orgasmic dysfunction, and therefore, 'as a mass problem, the question of frigidity is unfortunately not to be solved.'

Over the last few years, an emphasis on learning theory determinants of human behavior has led to new direct treatments for sexual dysfunctions (Wolpe and Lazarus, 1966; Masters and Johnson, 1970). In this behavioral approach, the specific dysfunction is seen as a behavioral deficit, caused by lack of skills, anxiety about performance, and guilt induced by societal conditioning. Treatment does not focus on uncovering childhood events, lifting repressions, and working through the transference, but on providing information, changing attitudes, and teaching new and adaptive sexual behaviors and skills. Unlike the psychoanalytic treatment, behavior therapy of sexual dysfunction has been found effective (Lobitz and LoPiccolo, 1972; Masters and Johnson, 1970; Obler, 1973) and can be completed in as little as two weeks (Masters and Johnson, 1970).

Unfortunately, a current problem in the application of behavioral techniques to sexual dysfunction has been the lack of training

[1] This paper was co-authored equally by Joseph LoPiccolo and W. Charles Lobitz. Authorship order was determined arbitrarily. Gretchen K. Lobitz and Jacqueline Brockway were the co-therapists in the cases presented.

opportunities for therapists. Even those graduate training programs in psychology and psychiatry which are behaviorally oriented often do not include treatment of sexual dysfunction as part of their curriculum. Therefore, clinicians who want to use the newer behavioral techniques for treating sexual dysfunction are often 'trained' only by reading professional books and journal articles on the subject. Although such literature is not voluminous by any means, a number of publications clearly specify the major *strategies* of behavioral treatment for sexual dysfunction (for example, Hastings, 1963; Wolpe, 1969; Masters and Johnson, 1970; LoPiccolo and Lobitz, 1972, 1973; Lobitz and LoPiccolo, 1972; LoPiccolo, Stewart and Watkins, 1972). Unfortunately, these sources lack information on the specific *tactics* of therapy, although the strategic elements of therapy are delineated in a simple, straightforward and step-wise manner in much of the above cited literature (for example, LoPiccolo and Lobitz, 1972). The reader may get the impression that the behavioral program is rather invariant for all clients: the client presents the problem, the therapist gives a standardized set of instructions for new behaviors to be instituted, the client cheerfully follows these instructions, and the case is cured. The literature neglects such issues as how to modify the program to fit the idiosyncratic personality structure of a particular client, what to do when the client resists or refuses treatment interventions, what to do when the program is not producing results, and how to deal with attitudes, personality traits, or interpersonal problems which prevent the basic treatment strategies from being effective.

The authors have been approached more than once by a professional colleague who states something like 'I read your article on treating orgasmic dysfunction. I followed the procedures with a client of mine, but it didn't work.' Usually, inquiry reveals that while the therapist followed the general treatment strategy, he made a number of specific *tactical* errors in dealing with his particular client which defeated the overall treatment strategy. Obviously, the root of this problem lies in the failure of previous literature to include this type of information.

The purpose of this paper is to present two case studies in the treatment of sexual dysfunction, focusing not on generalized treatment strategies, but on how these strategies were modified and adapted to fit the needs of particular clients. While the overall treatment strategy is uncomplicated (perhaps even simplistic), and seemingly could be implemented by anyone who has read the available literature, the therapy process is complex and involves clinical and interpersonal skill. In order to cover the major areas of sexual dysfunction, a case of erectile failure (impotence) and a case of orgasmic dysfunction (frigidity) are presented.

Case I: Erectile failure

Introduction

The basic treatment strategy for erectile failure is well established in the literature and is basically an anxiety reduction procedure. Erectile failure is conceptualized as resulting from anxiety about performance or fear of failure. Masters and Johnson (1970, p. 196) state: 'the prevalent roadblock [to erection] is one of fear. Fear can prevent erection just as fear can lead to diarrhea or vomiting.' If a man is frightened or anxious about achieving an erection, he is not likely to become sexually aroused. Obviously, if a man is not aroused, he will not have an erection. Thus a self-maintaining vicious cycle is established: anxiety about erection *actually prevents* an erection. Each successive failure of erection leads to greater anxiety on the next attempt at intercourse, which insures maintenance of erectile failure.

This anxiety produces a number of side effects. The man may closely monitor his state of penile erection, leading him to take a 'spectator role' (Masters and Johnson, 1970, p. 196) in sexual activity. Being a 'spectator' interferes with becoming an aroused participant. Similarly, he may become quite depressed about his lack of 'manliness' and his inability to satisfy his wife. His wife may become hostile, derogatory and demanding towards him. All of these factors invariably serve to further elevate the client's anxiety about erection and to exacerbate the pattern of erectile failure.

The treatment paradigm for this syndrome has been perhaps most elegantly described by Masters and Johnson (1970). However, the paradigm is not new, having been similarly described (ignoring differences in terminology) by many others, including Wolpe (1958, p. 131), Lazarus (1965), and even by an eighteenth-century British physician, Sir John Hunt.

Basically, the treatment strategy involves eliminating fear of failure by making failure impossible and eliminating performance demands by forbidding the client to perform. Initially, all sexual activity, except some kissing, embracing, and body massage (not including genitals), is proscribed. The male is specifically forbidden to have an erection. Even if he should have an erection, the couple are jointly forbidden from intercourse. Once the man has learned to relax and enjoy this low level of sexual activity, with all performance fears and demands eliminated, erection will occur even in the absence of direct physical stimulation. Treatment then consists of rebuilding the couple's sexual behavior, step by step.

This treatment sounds simple, as if it could be applied to any couple merely by giving them some simple instructions in one session. While this is occasionally the case, far more often the basic program must be extensively modified and elaborated to produce a successful outcome. In this particular case, such modifications and elaborations focused on four factors:

1 These clients were an older (late fifties) couple, with certain physiological changes in sexual functioning.
2 The wife was dominant in the relationship and was quite resistant to treatment.
3 Both husband and wife had a number of unrealistic expectations regarding sex.
4 They manifested a number of fairly serious, non-sexual marital problems with potential for disrupting therapy.

Case History: Mr and Mrs T

The clients were a married couple in their late fifties who were seeking treatment for the husband's erectile failure. They had been married approximately two years. This was their second marriage, both having been divorced. Both clients were college graduates, and Mr T held a master's degree in his professional speciality. They were referred to the clinic by a local psychiatrist, whom the husband had seen briefly for his erectile problem. A complete urological evaluation had revealed no physical basis for his difficulty.

The clients reported that during the two years of their marriage they had been able to have intercourse successfully four or five times. Currently they were not attempting to have intercourse more often than once every month or two. In the early part of their relationship they had initiated intercourse more frequently, but because of the erectile problem they had almost discontinued sexual relations. The husband reported that he was sexually aroused by and attracted to his wife. However, to his great frustration, when they would attempt to have intercourse, he was almost invariably unable to achieve an erection. On those occasions when he did achieve an erection, he would lose it almost immediately; thus, intromission was rarely possible. The wife reported being extremely frustrated by this pattern and, at the time they began treatment, was considering discontinuing sexual activities entirely. The husband did not like her suggestion and was extremely motivated to find another solution.

Sexual history: Mr T

The husband had been married previously for some twenty-five years and had never experienced erectile problems in this marriage. His marriage ended traumatically when his wife informed him that she was having an affair with another man and wanted a divorce.

After obtaining his divorce, the client remained celibate until he met his second wife and began dating her. As their relationship progressed, she initiated sexual activity, which pleased and surprised him. However, to his great dismay, in their first attempt to have intercourse, he did not have an erection. As he said, 'I couldn't believe I didn't have an erection. I had never had this problem in my life before.' To his bewilderment the problem continued during their courtship. Both believed his failure was due to his feelings that pre-marital and extra-marital sex were immoral. However, when his erectile problems continued after they were married, Mrs T became upset and began to pressure Mr T for sexual gratification.

Around this time, Mr T tried masturbating, which he had not done in many years, to see if he could obtain an erection. To his chagrin, he experienced absolutely no erectile difficulties in masturbation. He continued to masturbate two to three times weekly over the next two years, until entering treatment.

Sexual history: Mrs T

Mrs T's first marriage, of some twenty-five years' duration, had also ended in divorce. She reported that her husband had been an alcoholic, who had beaten her severely on several occasions in their last year of marriage. Her first husband had been an unskilled, violent and inconsiderate sexual partner, who had frequently forced her to have intercourse against her will. Consequently, although she had been raised in a family that was relatively relaxed and accepting regarding sexuality, Mrs T had come to dislike sex. Most relevant to Mr and Mrs T's current sexual problem was the fact that Mrs T's previous husband usually had an erection *before* beginning any overt sexual activity and never allowed Mrs T to touch or manipulate his penis in any way.

During the three years between her divorce and her marriage to Mr T, Mrs T had sexual relations with two or three other men. She enjoyed these sexual encounters but did not reach orgasm in intercourse, as had been the case all her life. She did attain orgasm in both oral and manual clitoral manipulation during these encounters, as she had during her first marriage.

Mr and Mrs T's current sexual behavior

At the time the clients entered treatment, Mrs T was clinically depressed, with symptoms of weight loss, insomnia, low energy level, and pervasive sadness. She reported feeling suicidal at times and was receiving antidepressant medication from a local physician. This depression was partially related to her husband's erectile problems but was more centrally related to Mr T's impending unemployment due to a reorganization of his company. Mrs T feared that they might have to move to another city for a new job and that their economic status would suffer.

Because of Mrs T's depression and Mr T's erectile failure, sexual activity between them had become quite infrequent by the time they entered therapy. They estimated that they would have sex about once every six weeks, at Mr T's initiation. Mr T attempted to initiate sex two or three times per week, but Mrs T usually refused. In their sexual sessions, Mr T would use a variety of sexual techniques to bring Mrs T to orgasm, including manual and oral manipulation. In contrast, Mrs T was quite unwilling to manually or orally manipulate Mr T's genitals, as she found those activities mildly repugnant. Mrs T had not masturbated since adolescence. Mr T masturbated two to three times weekly, with no erectile difficulties.

Course in treatment
Mr and Mrs T were seen daily by a male-female co-therapy team (JL and JB), one hour per day, for a total of fifteen therapy hours. On each day of treatment they were given a 'homework' assignment of sexual activities to be carried out in the privacy of their own home. Mr and Mrs T each separately filled out a daily record form in which they described the activities performed, rated them for arousal and pleasure experienced, and made comments. These forms were returned to the therapists before the next appointment. After a brief initial intake session, separate histories were taken from the husband and wife. Actual treatment interventions began with session 3.

Session 3
In this session, the therapists explained the general dynamics of erectile failure to the clients and personalized this formulation in terms of Mr and Mrs T. It was pointed out that both of them had some rather unrealistic expectations regarding sexual functioning. On the basis of her experience in her first marriage, Mrs T expected her husband to have erections before beginning sexual activity and in the absence of any direct penile stimulation. The therapists remarked that very few men functioned this way and that it was an undesirable behavior pattern in any case. The female co-therapist emphasized the pleasure *she* obtained from caressing her husband and arousing him to the point of erection. The male co-therapist

revealed that he did not have erections before beginning sexual activity and also very much enjoyed his wife's caressing his genitals. Both therapists emphasized the research findings (Rubin, 1968) that older men become erect more slowly and require more stimulation; thus Mr T was unrealistic in expecting himself to perform sexually as he had in the distant past.

Although Mr T seemed relieved by this discussion, his wife was negativistic and at times argued and disagreed with the therapists. Her negativism became more marked when the therapists discussed how Mrs T contributed to her husband's erectile problem by making hostile and derogatory remarks regarding his sexual functioning. The female co-therapist tried to be supportive and non-threatening in this discussion, saying that she understood how Mrs T's sexual frustration precipitated these remarks without her realizing their impact on Mr T. At this point, Mrs T became quite upset and began to cry. She denied making such remarks and insisted that she had always been supportive of her husband. When the male therapist asked Mr T to repeat what he had reported in the history interview about his wife's remarks and pressure to perform, he instead made several conciliatory statements to his wife. The therapists thus found themselves in a seemingly untenable position: for treatment to succeed, Mrs T must realize and accept her role in Mr T's problem. However, she refused to do so, and Mr T was unwilling or unable to confront her.

The therapists first tried reminding Mrs T of several derogatory remarks that she had made during the history interview. Mrs T steadfastly insisted that such statements as 'My first husband was much more masculine' and 'Even when he gets an erection, it's not very big' were not threatening or hostile to Mr T. She continued to cry, while Mr T continued to comfort her and undercut the therapists by saying that such statements really did not bother him.

The therapists escaped from this impasse via a two-pronged approach. The female therapist supported Mrs T by agreeing that, indeed, she had never meant to be hostile or derogatory to Mr T, but that many of her statements had inadvertently negative overtones or connotations in spite of their positive intent. Mrs T was able to accept a partial role in Mr T's difficulty through this 'face saving' maneuver, and a larger confrontation was avoided. At the same time, the male therapist capitalized on the female therapist's supportiveness and insisted that, whatever her intentions, her actual statements were quite harmful to Mr T's sexual functioning. As Mr T would not speak for himself (in the presence of Mrs T), the male therapist spoke for him at some length. The male therapist reflected how he would feel if he were Mr T, and capped his remarks by saying, 'I don't have any erectile problems at all, and I never have had, but I'm sure I would if I were married to you.' This statement essentially forced Mrs T to rethink her role in their sexual problem.

At this point, the overall treatment strategy was briefly outlined to the clients. Mr T was eager to begin; Mrs T expressed reservations, citing her depression and busy social schedule as reasons for her reluctance. The therapists had anticipated this reluctance and previously had discussed a number of possible tactics for dealing with it. The male therapist simply agreed with Mrs T, saying that the demands of treatment were probably beyond her present capabilities. At this, Mrs T visibly bristled and insisted that she could carry out treatment successfully. The female co-therapist agreed with Mrs T, and the male therapist then 'reluctantly' allowed himself to be argued into commencing treatment.

For their first assignment, Mr and Mrs T were told to go home, bathe together, and give each other a complete body massage while nude, excluding the breasts and genitals. All other sexual activity was forbidden, except masturbation if desired.

Session 4

The clients reported pleasure, but little arousal during their assignment. The next assignment was increased to include some hugging and kissing and a complete 'visual examination.' Each of them was to examine the other's nude body while massaging it (again not including breasts and genitals) and to talk more or less continually about what they saw and how they felt about the various parts of the body. This exercise was included to break down the embarrassment that each of them felt about their bodies.

Session 5

The clients reported considerable pleasure in their 'homework' activity. To their great surprise, Mr T had experienced a partial erection. The therapists repeated that erection would naturally occur, provided Mr T was not pressured to perform. Forbidding them to do anything but their assigned activities was re-emphasized as a way of removing the performance pressure.

Mr T had reported that Mrs T had been quite aroused during their activities. Specifically, he had observed heavy breathing and nipple erection. Mrs T had not reported arousal and suggested that she had probably been cold. As it was approximately 32°C in their bedroom, this explanation seemed unlikely. The therapists suggested to Mrs T that people frequently mislabel their emotional states and that she should allow herself to *psychologically* experience her obvious physiological arousal. The female therapist added that Mrs T had learned to 'turn herself off' in the past to avoid disappointment and that she now must allow herself to 'let go' and become aroused. The male therapist here suggested that treatment might also focus on enhancing Mrs T's sexuality, since she had never been able to experience orgasm in coitus. Mrs T did not like this suggestion, saying she was happy with her present mode of reaching orgasm. After much discussion, the therapists reluctantly agreed that therapy would not focus on Mrs T's ability to reach orgasm. To insist on this seemed too threatening to Mrs T, and in any case the clients had not sought treatment for her.

The clients' new assignment repeated the previous day's, but included genital caressing for both of them. It was emphasized that Mr T should not try to have an erection, should not expect one, and should not 'watch' for one to occur. He was simply to enjoy her caressing of his *flaccid* penis.

Session 6

The clients did not appear for session 6. Mr T called and explained that Mrs T had been hospitalized, following what appeared to be a stroke or epileptiform seizure. For the next two days, Mrs T had an extensive series of medical and neurological tests, which revealed no physical basis for the seizure. Mr and Mrs T then called and made an appointment with the therapists, three days after session 6 had been originally scheduled.

In this session Mr and Mrs T emphasized their belief that there was some organic cause for her seizure. They had rejected the neurologist's suggestion that Mrs T was having psychogenic seizures to escape from some life stress. The therapists did not become involved in this issue, and treatment was resumed. Their records indicated that the last assignment had been a success. Mr T had orally manipulated Mrs T to orgasm. In response to his wife's genital caressing, Mr T had had two brief erections. While he had been quite elated, Mrs T reported feeling resentful, since now that intercourse was forbidden, he was having erections, while he had not been able to for the last two years. The therapists pointed out that this was a rather hostile remark, typical of her earlier statements. Eventually Mrs T admitted this and was able to verbalize pleasure that progress was being made.

Their next assignment was for the 'teasing technique' described by Masters and Johnson (1970), an exercise which demonstrates to the couple that if an erection is lost, it can be re-established. The female caresses the male's penis, but stops periodically, lets the erection subside, and then resumes. To reduce performance pressure, the clients were actually told to 'caress his flaccid penis, manually or orally, as you prefer. If he should get an erection, stop caressing at once and let the erection subside. Then resume caressing his flaccid penis. Repeat this as often as necessary for twenty minutes.'

Session 7

The assignment was again successful. Mr T had seven erections in the twenty minutes. Both clients were amazed at how quickly his penis became erect as she caressed him. Mrs T reported feeling no arousal, but also no repugnance, while touching Mr T's penis; this was a positive change. Mr T also caressed Mrs T's genitals, but she had not reached orgasm until she masturbated somewhat later in the day. Accordingly, their next assignment included Mrs T teaching her husband how to manipulate her genitals as she did during masturbation. The therapists recommended that Mr T teach his wife how to caress his genitals and discussed some genital caressing techniques. Mr T's assignment was to have Mrs T caress his genitals and to 'try to maintain an erection for five to ten minutes, since you had erections constantly during yesterday's assignment.' The perceptive reader will realize that this was a tactical blunder; the therapists had put a specific performance demand on Mr T, ensuring that he would assume the role of anxious spectator instead of aroused participant.

Session 8

As a consequence, the activity session did not go well. Mrs T had used both manual and oral manipulation, but Mr T experienced only three brief partial erections, each of which lasted about thirty seconds. Mr T reported feeling anxious, very conscious of having to live up to a ten-minute expectation and fearful that his erection would not last. The therapists reassured Mr T by taking all the blame (which they deserved) for his difficulties. However, the episode did lead to a productive discussion of performance demands and their role in erectile failure. The therapists felt that, for the first time, Mrs T really accepted this formulation. The rest of the assignment had been successful. Mrs T had demonstrated her masturbation techniques for Mr T, and he had quickly manipulated her to orgasm.

The next assignment was to caress each other's genitals while assuming the body positions recommended by Masters and Johnson (1970). In one position the male sits behind the female and reaches around her to manipulate her genitals. In the other position, the male lies on his back while the female sits between his legs and caresses his genitals. These particular positions help the client to learn to relax and simply receive pleasure 'selfishly,' with no obligation to give pleasure at the same time.

Session 9

The negative effects of the therapists' tactical mistake were still apparent in the previous day's assignment. Mr T had had considerable difficulty in relaxing and focusing on his arousal. He reported being unable to avoid, the spectator role, was very conscious of his wife watching his penis, and had only partial erections which he rapidly lost. At this point, he had suggested switching positions and his caressing her genitals. To his surprise, once he was sitting behind her, where she could not see him, he had a full erection during the entire ten to fifteen minutes he was caressing her genitals. During this time he was not receiving any direct genital stimulation. Mr T then told Mrs T of his erection, and she turned around and resumed stimulation of him. This time he was able to focus on his pleasure and maintained a full erection until ejaculation. Mrs T was unable to reach orgasm during this session. However, given their progress, their next assignment was to assume the female superior sitting position and place his penis at the entrance to her vagina, but not to insert it. Instead, it was stressed that this was an exercise that could be done quite well with a flaccid penis, thus they need not worry about erection.

Session 10

The clients reported that yesterday's assignment had brought mixed results. Since they were both experiencing some genital soreness after several days of genital caressing, arousal had been painful. Mr T had experienced some difficulty maintaining his erection. However, when he had caressed her genitals with his penis, he had obtained a strong erection. Unable to restrain themselves, they had inserted his penis and engaged in several minutes of vigorous intercourse. Both of them reported being concerned about breaking the ban on intercourse, which led them to stop before either of them climaxed.

The therapists responded to their violation of the ban on intercourse in two ways. On the one hand, they stressed that moving ahead too quickly usually brought disastrous results and that breaking the ban on intercourse rarely turned out to be a positive experience. On the other hand, the therapists re-emphasized the positive aspect: as long as Mr T did not have a performance demand to meet, he had no problems in achieving or maintaining an erection. Since both clients were reporting genital soreness, they were given a one day 'holiday' from sexual activity.

At this point in treatment, the therapists were becoming concerned about Mrs T. Since Mr T had been given notice that his job would cease to exist in about one month, Mrs T's depression had deepened significantly. She reported that she was having difficulty in becoming sexually aroused, due to her pervasive depression. She was also concerned because she had not experienced orgasm in their last few activity sessions.

Accordingly, following the 'holiday' their assignment included Mr T caressing Mrs T's genitals with the aid of an electric vibrator. In addition, Mr T was to lie on his back with Mrs T kneeling over him. Mrs T was to 'stuff' Mr T's penis into her vagina. They were to experience penile containment but not to engage in pelvic thrusting. The therapists again stressed that this activity could be carried out with either an erect or a flaccid penis; therefore, Mr T was free of performance demands.

Session 11
The clients reported that all had gone well for Mr T. He had maintained a strong erection during their entire session, and the insertion had been done with his penis erect. They had enjoyed the penile containment and had found it difficult to restrain themselves from pelvic thrusting. Mr T had stimulated Mrs T with the electric vibrator. She had been very aroused by his manual, oral, and vibrator stimulation of her genitals but again had not been able to reach orgasm. She insisted that she had never had such difficulty before and blamed her depression. The therapists tentatively accepted this explanation and told her not to *try* to reach orgasm, since this performance demand would interfere with her arousal. She was also placed on a program of Kegel's exercises (1952) to enhance her orgasmic potential by strengthening her pelvic musculature.

Their next assignment added slow pelvic thrusting to their activity. To avoid placing another type of performance demand on Mr T, intravaginal ejaculation was forbidden.

Session 12
Results continued to be positive for Mr T and mixed for his wife. They had had two sessions of intercourse with slow thrusting. Mr T's only problem had been in keeping himself from ejaculating. Mrs T reported arousal and pleasure, but no orgasm, despite oral, manual, and vibrator stimulation by her husband.

Their next assignment was simply to resume a normal sex life with no restrictions whatsoever. Previous experience indicated that clients sometimes suffer a relapse at this point, since they perceive an implicit demand to function normally. The possibility of relapse was explained to the clients. The therapists predicted that with all restrictions removed Mr T would experience some erectile difficulty at first but that experience indicated this difficulty was always short-lived. The logic of predicting failure to the client is as follows: by telling him he will likely fail to have an erection, the demand on him for performance is virtually eliminated. If the prediction is correct and the client fails to have an erection, he is reassured by the therapist's statement that this is typical at this point in treatment and is always short-lived. If he does not fail, he is too elated by his success to be concerned about his therapist's mistaken prediction. Thus, the therapist cannot lose by predicting failure.

Session 13

The clients reported that Mr T had been somewhat slow to obtain an erection because he was *trying* to get one preparatory to intercourse. However, once they discussed this, he had had no further difficulties. They had engaged in several minutes of vigorous intercourse, until Mrs T insisted they stop (just as Mr T was approaching ejaculation), since she was 'hot and tired.'

After a brief private consultation, the therapists directly confronted Mrs T. As in the past the female therapist was deliberately supportive, whereas the male therapist was more confronting. The male therapist told Mrs T that he was convinced she was deliberately sabotaging the treatment program and at some level did not want to resume a full sex life with her husband. The female co-therapist 'disagreed' and suggested Mrs T was just too depressed and physically frail to cope with a full sex life. Mrs T vehemently argued that neither of these explanations was correct but that she had been hot and tired, since it was summer and their home was not air-conditioned. The male therapist indicated that he felt this was merely an excuse. He offered to prove it to Mrs T by refunding a portion of their treatment fee so that they could spend the last two days of treatment (a weekend) relaxing at a luxurious air-conditioned motel. Mr and Mrs T accepted this offer and challenge.

Sessions 14 and 15

Whether the challenge worked because Mrs T was right or because the therapists had finally succeeded in getting her interested in treatment will never be known. In any case, on both days they had successful intercourse, with Mr T ejaculating and Mrs T greatly enjoying it. He also manipulated her to orgasm several times during the two days.

The final treatment step was developing a maintenance plan to ensure the clients' continued success after termination. To this end, Mr and Mrs T were each asked to develop two lists: one specifying what they had been doing that contributed to their difficulties and one specifying ways they had learned to correct these problems. These lists are shown in Tables 12·1 and 12·2.

TABLE 12·1 *Mr T's list*

Errors	Corrections
1 'Sex' was kind of a dirty word	1 Realization that sex and sexual activities are natural, essential and a wonderful part of living
2 That a woman, particularly a 'good' woman, either didn't want sexual intercourse or only wanted it in order to have children	2 Realization that a healthy woman has just as strong a need and (though latent) drive for intercourse as a healthy man
3 That masturbation is a type of self-abuse and could or would result in physical or mental damage	3 Realization that masturbation in moderation is a healthy method to achieve a degree of sexual satisfaction, particularly when heterosexual intercourse is available
4 That normal sexual intercourse is a manifestation of a male physically dominating a female solely for the male's satisfaction	4 Comprehension (and this was difficult to accept) that a woman intensely wants and needs penetration to feel fulfilled (completely apart from the needs for procreation)
5 That taking visual delight in the nude figure (or partially clothed figure) of my wife was sinful	5 Acceptance of the fact that a wife wishes her husband to enjoy the sight of her body
6 That an erection should 'just come naturally' when circumstances indicate that intercourse may be consummated or that I can 'will' an erection	6 Except for teenagers and those in their twenties, some type of overt stimulation is needed to produce an erection; that willing 'an erection is impossible'
7 That personal gratification in and from intercourse was selfishly wrong	7 Acceptance that the only way for my wife to be completely satisfied sexually was for me to concentrate on my 'selfish' desires

TABLE 12·2 *Mrs T's list*

	Errors		Corrections
1	Hadn't been stimulating Mr T by caressing his genitals manually or orally	1	Learned to do this and the places that it felt best
2	Unmeaningly (*sic*) undercutting Mr T on occasion by unthinking remarks	2	Will be more careful of his ego
3	Trying too hard for climax	3	Will try to relax and just enjoy feeling
4	Start thinking of many things when Mr T is caressing my genitals to produce climax	4	Will try to turn mind off and just participate

As a couple, they were also asked to develop a plan for their sexual activities over the next three months, after which a follow-up interview was scheduled. This plan is shown in Table 12·3. The therapists suggested only one addition to this plan. Since Mrs T was now having orgasm during Mr T's manipulation of her genitals, they recommended that the clients continue this manipulation during intercourse. In this way Mrs T could experience coital orgasm.

TABLE 12·3 *Maintenance plan*

1 *Frequency of love making:* At this time we don't know how often, on the average we will make love. Initially, though, we intend to enjoy each other about two to three times per week assuming near optimum conditions. If this pace is not adequate, or is agreed to be excessive, we will modify it.

2 *Conditions:* We will endeavor to make love under the most favorable conditions such as:
  A when there is no sense of time pressure and when we have no house guests (may have an exception to the latter if we are reasonably assured of privacy).
  B both will, as time and finances permit, read sexy books and see sexy movies together.
  C 'set the stage' by taking phone off the hook, ignoring the doorbell, turn lights on dimly (or use candles).

3 *Signals:*
  A To indicate a desire, either may initiate by the oral invitation, 'Let's make love.' (We have agreed that the request 'Let's go to bed' will not mean a desire to make love.) The invitation to make love will be made only when the inviter really desires to carry through. The responding partner will be frank and candid in his or her oral response and will *not* deny the request to 'get back at' the inviter for

some unconnected 'reason' *nor* for flippant reasons. A full and clear statement of the actual reason for denial will be given.

B   When or if either partner feels dissatisfied in any way with the other partner's sexual behavior, he or she will not 'bottle it up' but will present a fair statement of the problem for candid and full discussion with his or her partner.

4   *Positions:* We have agreed we will experiment from time to time with a wide variety of positions and freely discuss our reactions and responses to each new position tried.

5   *Loss of erection:* We both realize this will happen occasionally. Upon occurrence, we will stop whatever particular activity was in process and go to a new activity, frequently shifting roles. (For example, if the penis is in the vagina, it will be removed and Mrs T may begin general, non-genital stimulation.)

6   *Slow orgasm for Mrs T:* Normally, Mr T will continue to caress Mrs T for up to twenty minutes, alternately using manual, oral or vibrator method. At the end of the period, unless Mrs T wishes him to continue, Mr T will desist. If Mrs T becomes tired or tender at any time, she will tell him so and Mr T will desist. Mrs T will not feign tiredness or soreness.

7   *Spectator role:* If either finds him or herself in the spectator role, he (she) will try to relax and experience the sensations. If unsuccessful in this he (she) will assume a new and positive role.

8   *Mind wandering:* Each will always try to concentrate his (her) attention on the sensations being experienced but may consciously use fantasies and mental images.

9   *Performing role:* Neither of us is to consider him (her) self as a performer for the other nor consider the partner as a performer as such. Sexual play and activities are mutual efforts.

Assessment of treatment results

The clients filled out an assessment battery at the start of treatment, the end of treatment, and three months after the end of treatment. This battery included a self-report questionnaire, the Oregon Sex Inventory (LoPiccolo and Steger, 1973), and the Locke-Wallace Marital Happiness Scale (Locke and Wallace, 1959). Scores from the self-report questionnaire and Locke-Wallace are shown in Table 12·4. These scores all indicate that treatment was successful. Mr T continued to be somewhat slower in attaining an erection than he would have liked, as reflected in his report that he had difficulty in achieving an erection on 25 per cent of coital occasions. However, he had little or no trouble in maintaining an erection and rated his sex life as extremely satisfactory. Mrs T, while less satisfied at follow-up, was now reaching orgasm in coitus 75 per cent of the time, provided clitoral stimulation was continued. Verbally, both of them reported being very happy now. Mrs T reported that her depression had lifted once Mr T had obtained new employment.

TABLE 12·4 *Written self-report measures: Case I*

Item Time of assessment

	Pre-therapy	Post-therapy	Follow-up
1 Frequency of intercourse	once/6 weeks	daily (4 days)	twice weekly
2 Duration of foreplay (minutes)	1-3	7-10	16-30
3 Duration of inter-course (minutes)	1-3	7-10	4-6
4 Orgasm in coitus, % of occasions			
male	25	50	90+
female	0	25	75
5 Problem in getting an erection, % of occasions	100	50	25
6 Problem in maintaining an erection, % of coital occasions	100	10	10
7 Rating of sexual satisfaction (scale of 1-6)			
male	1	6	6
female	1	5	5
8 Locke-Wallace marital happiness score			
male	104	129	109
female	78	112	104

The Oregon Sex Inventory profiles for Mr and Mrs T are shown in Figure 12·1. Before treatment, Mrs T was dissatisfied with their frequency of sexual activities (scale 2). Mr T was dissatisfied with Mrs T as a sexual partner (scale 9), and Mrs T was also unhappy with her sexual responsiveness (scale 4). With the exception of scale 4, these scores were all in the normal, satisfied range after therapy. The fact that Mrs T continued to be unhappy with her own sexual responsiveness following treatment suggests that the therapists should have tried harder to convince the clients to include a treatment program for her in the course of therapy.

Long-term follow-up

One year after the end of treatment, the clients were contacted for follow-up. Mr T reported that their sex life had been extremely gratifying to them both until Mrs T's sudden death from a stroke some two months earlier. The therapists were shocked and saddened at this news. Mr T thanked them for their help and accepted their condolences on his wife's death.

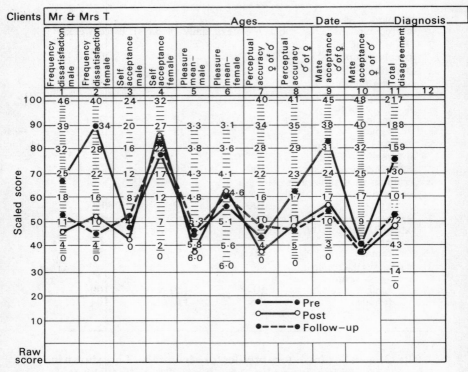

FIGURE 12·1 *Oregon sex inventory (Mr and Mrs T)*

Case II: Primary orgasmic dysfunction

Introduction

As described by Masters and Johnson (1970), a primary inorgasmic woman has never experienced an orgasm by any means of physical stimulation. In the present era of sexual liberation, a woman who complains of never having had an orgasm is likely to be experiencing considerable performance demands, if not from her partner, then from herself. The basic treatment strategy for this dysfunction combines anxiety-reduction procedures with skill-training in sexual arousal. As with erectile failure in males, the woman's failure to reach orgasm is maintained by an ever-tightening cycle of performance demands and anxiety followed by failure to climax followed by increased demands and anxiety. Thus, each new sexual contact becomes a source of heightened anxiety, which further inhibits sexual response, until sexual contact becomes a conditioned aversive stimulus. Moreover, the woman may be so unfamiliar with her own sexual response as to be ignorant of the skills necessary to enhance her arousal. Her increasing aversion to sexual contact makes it even more likely that she will remain ignorant.

Performance anxiety is treated through *in vivo* graded exposure tasks following the systematic desensitization format developed by Wolpe (1969) and refined by Masters and Johnson (1970). In this sense, the strategy resembles that for cases of erectile failure in which intercourse is temporarily prohibited while the couple's repertoire of sexual behavior is rebuilt.

The woman's skills for enhancing her own sexual arousal are increased through a nine-step masturbation program. This program is based on evidence that more women can reach orgasm through masturbation than through any other means (Kinsey, Pomeroy, Martin and Gebhard, 1953) and that masturbation produces the most intense orgasms (Masters and Johnson, 1970). The nine steps follow a graduated approach model to desensitize the client to masturbation. The details of the program have been described elsewhere (LoPiccolo and Lobitz, 1972) but can be summarized as follows:

Step 1: The client is given the assignment to increase her self-awareness by examining her nude body and appreciating its beauty. She uses a hand mirror to examine her genitals and identify various parts with the aid of diagrams.

Step 2: The client is instructed to explore her genitals tactually as well as visually. To avoid performance anxiety, she is not given any expectation to become aroused at this point.

Step 3: Tactual and visual exploration are focused on locating sensitive areas that produce feelings of pleasure when stimulated.

Step 4: The client is told to concentrate on manual stimulation of identified pleasurable areas. At this point the female therapist discusses techniques of masturbation, including the use of a lubricant.

Step 5: If orgasm does not occur during Step 4, the client is told to increase the intensity and duration of masturbation. She is told to masturbate until 'something happens' or until she becomes tired or sore.

Step 6: If orgasm is not reached during Step 5, the client is instructed to purchase a vibrator of the type sold in pharmacies for facial or body massage. She is to repeat Step 5 using the vibrator.

Step 7: Once the client has achieved orgasm through masturbation, the husband is introduced to the procedure by his observing her. This desensitizes her to displaying arousal and orgasm in his presence and also functions as a learning experience for him.

Step 8: The husband manipulates his wife in the manner she has demonstrated in Step 7.

Step 9: Once orgasm has occurred in Step 8, the couple is instructed to engage in intercourse while the husband stimulates his wife's genitals, either manually or with a vibrator.

In the best of all possible worlds it would be possible to present the clients with a description of this program outlining the nine steps, and they would be able to cure themselves. However, within this general outline, the program needs to be modified to accommodate the idiosyncratic needs of the clients, their particular personality traits, and their attitudes toward various sexual behaviors.

In this particular case, the program was modified in keeping with the following factors:

1 Both partners had had considerable sexual experience, had read on the subject of sexual dysfunction, and had previously attempted their own treatment.
2 Unlike many primary inorgasmic women, initially the female partner did not report aversion in love making, reported high levels of pleasure during love making, and was accepting of her own level of sexual response. She was, however, highly anxious in regard to her inability to reach orgasm.
3 The male partner's self-esteem and pleasure level during love making were low.

Case history: Mr and Mrs R

Mr and Mrs R were university juniors in their twenties who had been married for three weeks, but who had been cohabiting and having sexual relations together for two years. They complained that Mrs R had never been able to achieve orgasm through any means. Paradoxically, Mr R's concern with this dysfunction appeared more intense than his wife's.

Sexual history: Mr R

Prior to meeting his wife, Mr R had experienced sexual intercourse with more than a dozen different partners. He had engaged in prolonged sexual relationships with three of these women. His childhood history revealed no unusual or traumatic sexual experiences. Although his parents had had an open attitude about nudity and masturbation, Mr R expressed some guilt about masturbation and reported that he did not enjoy being brought to orgasm either manually or orally. These attitudes were reflected in an unusually high (pathological) pre-treatment self-acceptance score (scale 3, $t = 85$) on the Oregon Sex Inventory (Figure 12·2). In addition, his pre-treatment Minnesota Multiphasic Personality Inventory profile ($5'86403$-217/9) suggested a sensitive personality with aesthetic interests and a possibility of homosexuality or sexual deviation. Mr R reported four incidents of mutual genital exposure with strange men during high school but no sexual contact. Taken together, these data suggested that Mr R may have been experiencing some conflict over his sexuality, possibly over homosexual impulses or past experiences. In light of these data, his insistence that his wife be able to reach orgasm was viewed as an attempt to confirm his masculinity.

Sexual history: Mrs R

The eldest of three daughters, Mrs R was reared by parents who were 'very closed mouthed' about sex and were not openly affectionate. Her mother answered Mrs R's sexual queries, but always by reading the answers from a book. However, her parents did not moralize nor establish sexual prohibitions.

Mrs R did not date during junior high or high school. She reported masturbating a few times during her junior year in high school; however, only for about 10-15 minutes at a time. She did not feel guilty but stopped 'because nothing was happening.' Her first experience with intercourse was motivated by curiosity. Although she did not experience climax, she found it both arousing and pleasurable. Her second experience was a six-month affair with a man she met while living with a group of friends during her senior year in high school. He had become very concerned about her failure to experience orgasm, and consequently she had begun feigning it. When she finally told him she was simulating orgasms, he moved out. Since living with her present husband, she had engaged in one extra-relationship heterosexual affair.

Although Mrs R reported mild concern over not being able to achieve orgasm, in contrast to her husband she felt their sexual relationship was 'moderately satisfactory.' Unlike most women who seek treatment for primary orgasmic dysfunction, Mrs R had an unelevated self-acceptance score (scale 4, $t = 45$) on the Oregon Sex Inventory (see Figure 12·2). In addition, she found most sexual activities to be extremely pleasurable (OSI, scale 6, $t = 40$) whereas her husband did not (OSI, scale 5, $t = 63$). Her unelevated MMPI profile (0-42/87 963:15) indicated a passive, accepting personality who tended to present herself as withdrawn and unconflicted. This profile was consistent with her initial lack of concern about her sexual dysfunction.

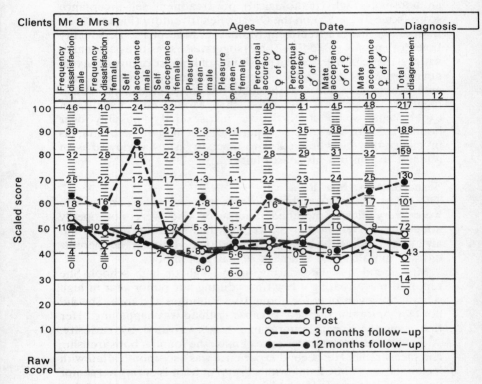

FIGURE 12·2　*Oregon sex inventory (Mr and Mrs R)*

Mr and Mrs R's current sexual behavior

On entering treatment the Rs were having sexual intercourse once a day. As a result of their past reading about sexual behavior, they were both 'working on' an orgasm for Mrs R. Despite a variety of foreplay techniques and intercourse positions, their active quest for female orgasm was proving futile. Moreover, the performance demands accompanying intercourse made it an increasingly anxiety-provoking situation. Mrs R's failure to reach orgasm left them frustrated yet determined to try even harder the next time. Although their relationship appeared solid, they reported an increasing level of conflict as a result of their frustration and anger over their sexual problem.

Course in treatment
Mr and Mrs R were seen daily by a male-female co-therapy team (WCL and GKL), one hour per day for a total of fifteen therapy hours. As with Case I, the Rs were given daily 'homework' assignments and kept records reporting their sexual behaviors and feelings of arousal and pleasure. Following the history taking sessions, treatment commenced with session 3. The general strategy was to allay Mrs R's performance anxiety directly and increase Mr R's self-esteem.

Session 3
The therapists explained the anxiety loop the Rs had created for themselves and presented their general strategy for breaking that loop, including proscribing intercourse and attempts to reach orgasm and assigning sensate pleasure sessions in which the objective was to produce pleasure, not arousal. In most treatment cases, the clients' daily records include ratings of pleasure and arousal. In the present case, the therapists underscored the non-demanding focus on pleasure by deleting the arousal ratings from the record forms.

Mrs R appeared relieved at the therapists' explanation and assignments. Mr R, on the other hand, reinforced his wife's anxiety and demonstrated his own insecurity by demanding to know when they could resume intercourse and focus on his wife's orgasm: 'After all, isn't that why we came here?' The female therapist replied that if she were his wife, his remarks would make her feel under even more pressure and that what they *both* needed at the moment was relief from the pressure.

Mrs R was assigned a genital self-exploration session in accordance with the first step of the masturbation program (LoPiccolo and Lobitz, 1972). In addition, the couple was assigned a nude mutual pleasuring session in which they were to experiment with different types of relaxing non-genital caresses and give each other feedback on how pleasurable each type of caress was. Because psychological testing had indicated a high level of romantic and aesthetic interests in Mr R, his assignment was to set the mood for the mutual pleasuring session. This was designed to encourage his potential strengths as a lover, especially after he had been criticized by the female therapist.

Session 4
The clients reported having had an enjoyable mutual pleasuring session. The therapists reinforced the clients' carefully detailed records and remarked on how Mrs R seemed to appreciate Mr R's mood setting. However, Mrs R complained that she had had difficulty getting into her own self-exploration session. That is, her mind would wander to thoughts of schoolwork and housekeeping. The female therapist mentioned that this was a common complaint in the first few sessions since women are rarely encouraged to explore their own bodies. She suggested that Mrs R listen to music or read a romantic novel to remove herself from her everyday world. At the end of the session, the male therapist casually remarked that Mr R might masturbate if he wished. It was purposefully phrased as a permission rather than an assignment because of Mr R's negative feelings about masturbation.

Session 5
The clients reported increased pleasure during their mutual session. Mrs R remarked that the radio was effective in helping her to focus on the feelings in her genitals and also helped her to fantasize during her self-pleasuring session.

During the therapy session Mr R appeared withdrawn and less enthusiastic than before. When the therapists remarked on his behavior, he shrugged off their concern. At this point the males and females separated so that the male therapist could pursue Mr R's reticence. Mr R expressed his embarrassment about discussing masturbation in front of both his wife and the female therapist. He maintained that while masturbation was permissible for men without partners, it was a sign of weakness in a married man. The male therapist emphasized the research (Kinsey, Pomeroy and Martin, 1948) that masturbation is common even among married men. The male therapist self-disclosed about his own masturbation and added that experts in the field of human sexual behavior have advocated that couples masturbate together as part of their love making (Comfort, 1972). When Mr R appeared relieved by this 'man-to-man talk,' the male therapist suggested that they rejoin the women and tell them what they had discussed.

When Mr R described his fears of appearing unmasculine if he masturbated, his wife assured him that she thought he was a 'manly' person. She pointed out that since she was masturbating as part of her self-pleasuring, he might as well join the fun! This exchange was a surprising contrast to the typical interaction between an inorgasmic woman and her husband. Usually the husband needs to support his wife's masturbation; however, in this case Mr R's attitude was the one which needed to be changed.

The clients were assigned mutual pleasuring sessions including breast stimulation and self-pleasuring for Mrs R. Mr R could masturbate if he wished.

Session 6

Mr R reported that after their mutual pleasuring session, his wife began her genital self-pleasuring. He had become so aroused during their session that he asked her if he could remain with her and masturbate, and she had consented enthusiastically. During her self-pleasuring, Mrs R reported extreme pleasure, but had also become tense and said at one point, 'I felt like crying.' Since Mrs R indicated that she had not felt performance anxiety, the therapists labeled her tension feelings as sexual arousal.

Now that Mrs R had experienced feelings of sexual arousal, the Rs were asked to record ratings of both pleasure and arousal for the rest of the 'homework' session. In this way, the therapists minimized Mrs R's performance anxiety by asking her to monitor her arousal only *after* she had already been experiencing it. The assignment was for mutual and self-pleasuring sessions as before.

Session 7

Mrs R reported that she had become very aroused during her self-pleasuring and thought she might have an orgasm — but did not. The therapists continued to minimize the pressure to perform by stating that it would have been a mistake to have had an orgasm then. As explained to Mrs R, 'this part of the program is for you to experience arousal, not orgasm.' The assignment was the same as before except that genital stimulation was added to the mutual pleasuring sessions.

Session 8

Mr and Mrs R both appeared depressed when they arrived at the clinic. Mrs R tearfully explained that the genital stimulation during mutual pleasuring had started off well,

> but then my body was so tense and aroused that every muscle was quivering, even my teeth were chattering. At this point I felt I couldn't take any more — my same old excuse. We had a stupid fight. I thought he [Mr R] wanted me to have an orgasm, and I just couldn't let myself go. It's so frustrating!

Both partners felt that they were 'back in our same old pattern of doing things — with the same old expectations.' The therapists used this as an opportunity for discussing the possible danger of pushing sexual expectations either on oneself or one's partner. They reinforced the point by disclosing that for them the best way to have a miserable love-making session was to carry a load of expectations into the bedroom. As the male therapist said, 'It's hard to act sexy with all those "shoulds" hanging around my neck.' This discussion had two foci. First, it attempted to change the clients' attitudes about what constituted a healthy sexual relationship, viz., one without expectations. Second, it helped reduce their anxiety and disappointment by showing them that other people, sex therapists included, occasionally have unpleasant sexual encounters.

In giving the assignment, the female therapist told Mrs R that her response indicated she was clearly able to feel arousal and was capable of having an orgasm, but probably she was not ready for one yet. In order to interrupt the already developing anxiety pattern during self-stimulation, Mrs R was directed to purchase a hand-held vibrator (the kind used for facial and scalp massage) and to explore the sensations it produced in different parts of her body, including her genitals. Moreover, Mrs R was instructed not to try to have an orgasm. 'Your body will have one when it's ready. Just relax and let the vibrator do the work.' The clients left feeling relieved.

Session 9
The clients were excited about their mutual and self-pleasuring sessions. Mrs R reported that she was able to relax and concentrate much more on her feelings of arousal when the vibrator was doing the stimulating. She had used it in self-pleasuring, and Mr R had stimulated her with it during their mutual session. She had also brought Mr R to orgasm through manual stimulation, an activity which he now reported enjoying without embarrassment. The therapists instructed them to have mutual and self-pleasuring sessions as before.

Session 10
Mrs R reported that she had become extremely aroused in their sessions but 'could not let go.' Following their sessions she was in a state of sustained arousal. She said, 'Every time the car went over a bump, waves of excitment raced through my genitals.' It was clear that the pelvic vasocongestion and myotonia produced by the pleasuring sessions were so intense that Mrs R was on the verge of orgasm most of the day. However, after a while she had become irritated and had picked a fight with her husband over his behavior

in the mutual pleasuring session. The therapists ignored the content of the clients' argument and instead focused on the feelings Mrs R was experiencing. Since she seemed to need help in 'letting go,' they instructed her *not to have* an orgasm next time, but to 'role play' one, the wildest, most uncontrolled orgasm she could imagine. The purpose of this assignment was not to deceive her husband; he was present when the assignment was made. Rather, the purpose was to help her to learn to feel comfortable with behaving in an uncontrolled, unrestrained manner.

Session 11
Mrs R seemed happy but embarrassed when she reported her 'role playing.' Rather than role playing, she had experienced two real orgasms, one by Mr R's manual stimulation and one by masturbation with a vibrator. Her embarrassment came not from her orgasms, however, but from her urinating at the same time. The therapists empathized with her distress but reassured her that her experience was not unique. She was told that their consulting gynecologist reported that urination at orgasm occasionally occurred in women with poorly developed pelvic musculature. The therapists gave Mrs R the rationale that since she had been completely controlled for so long, it would take some time before she could let go of some bodily functions while controlling others. This discussion, combined with supportive comments from her husband, relieved Mrs R's concern.

At this point in treatment, the couple was asked what they thought their next assignment should be. They decided that in spite of Mrs R's bladder control problem, they were ready for intercourse. The therapists agreed and reinforced their decision, adding intercourse to the self and mutual pleasuring sessions. The couple was instructed to use manual and vibrator genital stimulation during intercourse so that Mrs R's orgasmic response would generalize to that situation. The therapists also put Mrs R on a program of Kegel's (1952) exercises to increase her pelvic muscle tone.

Session 12
The clients reported that Mrs R was not orgasmic in intercourse but had reached orgasm twice during vibrator stimulation. She had also urinated twice. The therapists reassured her that she could expect this for a while until her body got used to having orgasm. If the problem persisted for more than two weeks, they would arrange an examination with their gynecological consultant. The clients were assigned intercourse with concurrent vibrator stimulation. The

self-pleasuring sessions were continued as a way of giving Mrs R as many orgasm trials as possible.

Session 13

Mrs R reported having had two orgasms, one in masturbation during which she urinated and one in intercourse without urinating. The therapists and clients both viewed this as improvement. Mrs R seemed relieved to know that urination did not always have to accompany orgasm.

However, another problem had surfaced for the clients. While attempting intercourse, Mr R had lost his erection. Since this had never happened to him before, he had become anxious, thereby further inhibiting his erectile response. His repeated efforts to regain an erection had proven futile. However, after relaxing for a few minutes, his wife had restimulated him, and they were able to complete intercourse with both of them reaching orgasm. In reporting this incident to the therapists, Mr R appeared embarrassed and shaken. The therapists, on the other hand, viewed the incident as a blessing in disguise. It provided them with an opportunity to discuss the vagaries normally inherent in any sexual relationship. The therapists reminded the clients of their previous discussion about anxieties and expectations.

To capitalize on this learning experience, the therapists decided to turn more of the treatment planning over to the clients. They instructed them to prepare a program for maintaining their treatments gains. The clients listed the problems for which they had sought therapy, the treatment methods used to overcome them, the problems which might arise in the future, and their strategies for handling them. This maintenance program was similar in form to that in Case I. No other assignment was given.

Session 14

The therapists reviewed the clients' maintenance program and reinforced their joint effort. However, they did make one specific suggestion, viz. to include a shaping procedure whereby Mrs R could depend on the vibrator increasingly less over time. The procedure involved gradually withdrawing the vibrator from masturbation and then from intercourse until Mrs R could regularly experience orgasm without it. Once this point was reached, the vibrator could be used occasionally as desired for variety. Typically, this procedure would have been part of the treatment plan, but Mrs R's unexpected bladder control problems slowed down the regular 15 session program. Since the Rs had reached their treatment goals and since the shaping process usually took several weeks, the therapists agreed that Mr and Mrs R could manage it on their own, contacting the therapists if any problems arose. The clients were then asked what they thought their final assignment should be. They decided to engage in intercourse with concurrent vibrator stimulation and to masturbate as well.

Session 15
Mrs R reported having had orgasms in intercourse, after intercourse, and during masturbation, all through vibrator stimulation. She did not urinate during any of these sessions. The clients were pleased with their progress. They agreed that their three treatment goals had been reached: Mrs R was able to experience orgasm in and out of intercourse; Mr R was comfortable with masturbation and with mutual genital stimulation; and both partners felt able to communicate openly with each other about their sexual preferences.

Epilogue
Two weeks after termination, Mr R came into the clinic to talk with the male therapist. Mrs R had told her husband that for the past week she had been feigning orgasm during intercourse. The male therapist therefore scheduled another appointment for the couple. In their meeting, Mrs R explained that her husband had put increasing pressure on her to have orgasms without the vibrator. He had accused her of 'being wedded' to the vibrator and had threatened to lock it away. Rather than confront him with his unreasonable demands and expectations, she feigned orgasm for a week. Finally, she decided she could not continue her deceit and confessed to him.

This situation had arisen from two therapeutic errors. First, the therapists should have anticipated the threat the vibrator presented to Mr R, given his low self-esteem. Second, Mrs R had a history of feigning orgasm with a previous partner. The therapists could have anticipated a recurrence of this pattern if Mrs R were again put under pressure to perform. Just because Mrs R had had her first orgasm within days did not mean that she should learn a complete new repertoire in weeks.

Since both clients were feeling threatened, the therapists supported them at the same time. The female therapist reflected how pressured Mrs R must have felt, while the male therapist remarked on Mr R's reaction at having been deceived. He added that since Mrs R could not have a coital orgasm without the vibrator, Mr R must have felt less secure as a man, but that masculinity had nothing to do with how his wife was orgasmic: 'Her orgasm is for her to enjoy and yours is for you.' Mr R agreed that he felt threatened by the vibrator and apologized to Mrs R for turning his anxiety against her. Mrs R volunteered that her insistence on always using the vibrator derived from her fear that she would never be able to reach orgasm any other way. The therapists reflected that the crisis seemed to result from each of the clients' fears of not meeting his own and his partner's expectations. The clients agreed that it would have been better to express their fears directly and revised their maintenance program explicitly to allow for this.

Assessment of treatment results

The clients filled out an assessment battery pre-treatment, post-treatment, and three and twelve months after the end of treatment. The assessment battery included the same inventories as in Case I, plus an MMPI pre-, post-treatment, and at three-months follow-up. The results of the self-report and the Locke-Wallace questionnaire are shown in Table 12·5. These scores indicate that treatment was successful. Mrs R's post-treatment orgasmic response with the vibrator in masturbation had generalized to manual stimulation in both masturbation and intercourse over the twelve-month follow-up period. In addition, her percentage of orgasmic response had increased to near 100 per cent of the time for all forms of genital stimulation. Intercourse was lasting twice as long after follow-up, suggesting that Mr R's latency to ejaculation had increased. Both partners were extremely satisfied with their sexual relationship and both reported greater marital happiness post-treatment and after follow-up.

As can be seen from Figure 12·2, all elevated scores on the Oregon Sex Inventory had declined to within normal limits. Both partners had become more satisfied with their frequency of sexual behaviors (scales 1 and 2), more accurate in perceiving each other (scales 7 and 8) and more accepting of each other's sexual preferences (scales 9 and 10). However, after twelve-months' follow-up, scale 9 had returned to near its pre-treatment level. This change was primarily due to Mr R's wanting his wife to enjoy fellating him to orgasm more than she did. Mr R's own self-acceptance (scale 3) changed markedly, as did his pleasure in a variety of sexual behaviors (scale 5). Thus, his sexual self-concept, as measured by the OSI, improved considerably and was stable throughout follow-up.

With two notable exceptions, the clients' MMPI profiles remained unchanged across treatment and follow-up. Mr and Mrs R's scale 7 (psychasthenia) increased ten t scores from pre- to post-treatment,

TABLE 12·5 *Summary of client self-report data: Case II*

	Pre-treatment	Post-treatment	3 month follow-up	12 month follow-up
Frequency of intercourse (average times/week)	6	4	6	4
Duration of intercourse (average minutes)	5	5	5	13
Percentage of female orgasm through masturbation				
vibrator	0	100	100	100
manual	0	0	75	100
Percentage of female orgasm through genital stimulation by partner				
vibrator	0	25	25	100
manual	0	0	25	100
Percentage of female orgasm through intercourse with concurrent stimulation by partner				
vibrator	0	0	25	100
manual	0	0	25	100
Satisfaction with sexual relationship (1 = extremely dissatisfied, 6 = extremely satisfied)				
male	3	6	6	6
female	5	6	6	6
Marital adjustment score (Locke-Wallace)				
male	106	120	119	127
female	113	117	118	120

suggesting increased anxiety for both of them. This reflects their anxiety over termination as well as those mutual insecurities which the therapists addressed in the post-treatment meeting. At three-month follow-up, the clients' scale 7 scores had decreased equal to or below their pre-treatment level. The second notable change in the clients' MMPI profile was a 10 *t* score increase in scale 6 (paranoia) and 8 (schizophrenia) and a 10 *t* score increase in scale 9 (mania) for Mr R from pre- to post-treatment and through three month follow-up. This suggests that Mr R had become less guarded and more energetic over the course of therapy.

Twelve month follow-up interview

In addition to completing the assessment battery twelve months after treatment ended, the clients returned to the clinic for a follow-up interview. Mrs R reported that she was multiply-orgasmic on most sexual sessions. She added that even though she was not always orgasmic neither of them were concerned when she was not. Mr R confirmed her report, stating, 'I'm having too much fun myself to worry about her orgasms.' Mrs R said that she felt comfortable asserting her likes and dislikes, including her aversion to fellatio, even though her husband might not accept that. Mr R stated that he was comfortable masturbating and that they occasionally would masturbate in each other's presence as part of love making. Mr R added that at present she frequently used the vibrator during masturbation, but not during intercourse. The clients ended the interview by stating that they were pleased with how well they could communicate about sex. Mrs R added, 'We talk about it all the time. I just wish we were as open about everything else in our lives.'

Discussion

The focus of both case histories was a change in the sexual responses of the clients. The treatment strategy followed a general anxiety-reduction, skills-training model. However, both cases presented problems in the direct application of this model. In Case I the husband's erectile failure was deeply imbedded in the interpersonal dynamics of the marital relationship. In Case II the wife's orgasmic dysfunction masked and contributed to the husband's fears of sexual inadequacy. In both cases the general behavioral treatment strategy required moment-to-moment tactical modifications by the therapists. Some of these tactics were amplifications of the general anxiety-reduction model and are common to behavior therapy, whereas others derive from cognitive, personality and existential psychology. As presented in the case histories, the therapists' tactics speak for themselves. However, a few of these tactics deserve special comment.

The general strategy for reducing performance anxiety followed a step-wise, gradual approximation to the sexual response, including initial prohibitions on intercourse (Masters and Johnson, 1970; Wolpe, 1969). In addition, the therapists further minimized the pressure to perform by 'giving permission' to the client (Mr R, Case II), rather than directly instructing him to engage in masturbation, and by predicting failure to limit the client's expectations (Mr T, Case I). The latter tactic has been used by hypnotherapists and others (Haley, 1963) to present clients with a no-lose situation. The therapists in both cases further minimized performance anxiety by setting the clients' expectations for success no higher than their performance at any given point in treatment. For example, Mrs R was told that it would have been a mistake if she had experienced an orgasm in the early part of therapy. Bandura (1971) has suggested that the self-reinforcement process is partly a function of the individual's expectations. In that sense, lowered expectations enhanced the probability that the clients would self-reinforce their progress.

In addition to tactics designed to motivate the clients' behaviors and to reduce their anxiety, the therapists directed much of their intervention toward client attitude change. One way of changing client attitudes is to appeal to relevant literature. The therapists did this to support the universality of male masturbation (Case II: Kinsey et al., 1948) and the longer latency of erectile response in older men (Case I: Rubin, 1968). Another attitude change tactic reported in both case histories was the relabeling of certain physiological states. For example, in Case I when Mrs T had defined her nipple erection as a response to temperature change, the therapists relabeled it as sexual arousal. This tactic derives from the work of Schacter and Singer (1962) on the importance of cognitive labeling in interpreting physiological arousal.

Throughout both cases, therapist self-disclosure was used to change the clients' attitudes about their sexual behaviors. This tactic has been advocated by Jourard (1964) as a way of spontaneously reacting to the clients during the therapy hour. In the present cases, the therapists extended this tactic to include self-disclosure about the therapists' own sexual behaviors in the privacy of their homes.

As Bandura (1969) and others have shown, behavior change in non-threatening situations is a potent technique for changing client attitudes. In particular, behavioral rehearsal ('role playing') has enabled clients to perform behaviors previously inhibited by anxiety (Lazarus, 1966). In Case II the therapists used this tactic to disinhibit Mrs R about 'letting go' and losing control. This use of 'role playing' is analogous to Kelly's (1955) fixed-role therapy in which the client is instructed to enact the role of someone different from himself. In the present case the role was a different sexual response rather than a specific personality change.

The use of different tactics at different points in therapy depends on several factors: the progress of therapy, the therapists' familiarity with various methods, and the clients' personality traits. While the first two factors are generally recognized as important variables in behavior therapy, the client's personality traits deserve special comment. In describing several behavior therapy methods, Eysenck and Beech (1971) have argued that the appropriate behavioral stratagem depends on the client's personality type. In a similar vein, Kanfer and Saslow (1969) have advocated a pre-treatment assessment of the client's behavioral strengths and weaknesses to determine the appropriate treatment approach. In the present cases, the therapists used personality information, as well as pre-treatment behavioral data, to guide their therapy tactics. The therapists' challenge to Mrs T (Case I) that she was too depressed and frail to cope with a full sex life was based on their assessment of her personality pattern; that is, that her 'passive-aggressive' style would lead her to resist whatever directives the therapists gave. Similarly, the therapists non-directive approach with Mr R (Case II) was based on their clinical impressions and personality data that he was more easily threatened than his wife. In the one instance where the therapists did not tactically anticipate problems in therapy (that is, client's post-therapy conflict in Case II), the behavioral and personality data were available. Thus, the failure lay not with the data themselves but with the therapists' neglect of them. This example illustrates that while the behavior therapist may not attempt to change the client's 'personality traits,' he needs to be cognizant of them to best adapt the treatment to the client.

While elucidating the therapy used in the behavioral treatment of sexual dysfunction, the present cases do not establish the efficacy of the tactics employed. These case histories are presented as demonstrations for the practitioner of the moment-to-moment tactics which complement the general behavorial stratagems. The relationship between the successful therapy outcome and the tactics employed is correlational. A causational relationship between outcome variables and therapy tactics can only be established through experimental manipulation. The authors are engaged in research to determine those variables which are necessary and sufficient in the behavior therapy of sexual dysfunction.

13 Can (Alcoholic) Case Studies Demonstrate General (Behavioral) Principles?[1]

Robert S. Davidson

Ever since the potential contributions of the Pavlovian and Skinnerian conditioning paradigms to clinical psychology became apparent, the possibility of clinically treating single cases with scientifically rigorous methodologies has become more obvious. As the two historical conditioning traditions became the foundation upon which the behavior modification movement was elaborated, so the transition from the early animal laboratory to the modern clinic or human laboratory has built a number of methodological bridges and analogs.

This transition from laboratory to clinic, from animal to human, has taken many avenues, only a few of which will be dealt with in detail here. Behavior modification, which only began to identify itself as a separate discipline in the 1950s and which flourished in the 1960s, has sought to apply the conditioning and learning principles developed in Pavlovian and Skinnerian laboratories to the treatment and amelioration of human problems. Although many of the latest technical innovations within the behavior modification movement have required the study of groups of treated subjects within statistical-factorial designs, this was not the methodological choice of either Pavlov or Skinner. Both scientists, and, indeed, Freud before them, chose to work with one individual at a time. Pavlov introduced and Skinner elaborated methodologies with all the rigor, control and precision of methods previously available primarily in other sciences, such as physiology, chemistry and physics.

But let us see how their methods differed from the still popular method of clinical psychology, the case study. Clinical psychology

[1] Conduct of the reported program has been supported by VA Research Grant 1777-01, Modification of Alcoholic Behavior. Previous reprints may be obtained from: Robert S. Davidson, Ph.D., Clinical Research Psychologist, Veterans' Administration Hospital, 1201 N.W. 16th Street, Miami, Florida 33125.

borrowed from psychoanalysis and psychiatry the method which seemed most appropriate to the treatment of pathological behavior in a single individual at a time. The case study focuses upon the individual patient or client and attempts, through analysis of historical and current material, to learn everything which might be relevant to the etiology and treatment of the patient's problems, globally considered. In the hands of the analyst, it might take months or years to reconstruct all the pertinent material. In clinical psychology, the case study usually includes at least: information from interviews (self-reports of both historical and current material), behavioral observations, and perhaps standardized tests (probably some combination of objective and projective items). In actual practice, the case study is too often a hodge-podge of subjective, unverifiable impression, historical material with little relevance to the presenting problem and diagnostic test material similarly lacking focus on pertinent behaviors.

Since most of the material contributing to etiological formulations or hypotheses as to how the patient got that way are historical in such a model, only a retrospective analysis is often possible. To the extent that the clinician weighs heavily in his analysis unstandardized self-report and historical interview material which has high probability of being unreliable, he will be in error. To the extent that he relies more heavily upon standardized tests, he may be able to determine classes of response which deviate from expected norms, but not necessarily to infer any specific etiological antecedents. All things considered, the traditional case study may produce prognostic indicators and general antecedent conditions, when put to its best use by a well-trained clinician. At its worst, the case study provides an excess of information irrelevant to the analyses of etiology or treatment planning. Only rarely can the case study, as traditionally designed, reveal the specific antecedent or 'causal' conditions responsible for a particular class of pathological behavior.

Part of the difficulty with the case study may have been the attempt to use it as a panacea to fill the void formed by a real lack of information. When all the information relevant to all aspects of a personality is sought at once, the seeker may, like Don Quixote, be tilting at the windmills of an impossible dream. Perhaps it is time to put aside the armor of global personality assessment and treatment and strive to accomplish what is possible.

Granting that global assessment and broad spectrum treatment may work in some cases it would seem more efficient and more helpful to the patient, more heuristic and productive of new knowledge, to begin more modestly, in a word, univariate: to manipulate one thing at a time, as in the classical scientific experiment.

As handed down to us by generations of scientific past, the classical experiment seeks to control all conditions relevant to the problem in question and then to manipulate only one, presumably central variable. If this manipulation produces a consequent change in the measured (dependent) variable, then the first step in a complete experiment has been accomplished. If, in addition, the change is sufficiently large to generate a new set of quantitative values which does not overlap the old, then no statistics are needed to tell us that a change has indeed occurred. For example, if an alcoholic patient who previously would accept whatever liquor was offered to him is subsequently taught to reject each new offer of alcohol, then the same first step has been accomplished. This major first step, although satisfying to the clinician, is not sufficient to satisfy all the rigorous demands of the scientist, however. How does one know, in this case, that the change was not due to concomitant variation in some other factor? It is very difficult, but not impossible as some would maintain, to control all possibly relevant variables in research with humans. One must consider as possible alternatives which could have produced the change in our alcoholic patient his history, including prior conditioning and treatment for alcoholism, previously suffered aversive consequences (such as number and severity of hangovers, withdrawal symptoms and other physical symptoms resulting from drinking), as well as the stimuli currently maintaining his behavior (all the way from waiting wives and motherly nurses to legal constraints).

To prove in any ultimate way that treatment was responsible for the change in our hypothetical patient's behavior may be difficult, but there are several distinct possibilities. In the classical single subject design, as developed by Skinner (1938, 1953) and elaborated by Sidman (1960a, 1960b), a reversal of the two original (control and experimental) conditions may be conducted. To do this, treatment would be withdrawn and, if the person drinks again, reinstituted. If the patient again responds to treatment in the same fashion (that is, turns down available liquor), then a successful reversal design of type ABAB (A=control condition, B=treatment) has been completed. Further reversals may not be necessary to demonstrate that it was treatment, and nothing else, which produced the change in the patient's behavior.

Frequently, clinical research may not be cast within this paradigm, for what if the patient does not take liquor again, even though treatment is terminated? Again, the goals of the clinician have been attained, for a large and constructive change in the patient's behavior has been observed, but the scientist may again have justified doubts. Just as before, the change might conceivably have been due to a number of concomitants of treatment. To ascertain whether this is the case, one might employ the same treatment, but at a later time and to treat another behavior or class of response. This has been called the multiple base-line design by Baer, Wolf and Risley (1968). For example, one might use the same form of treatment, but this time with cigarette smoking. If at the end of treatment, the patient rejects cigarettes as well as liquor, the probability is increased that both changes were due to the specific form of treatment and nothing else. The same thing could conceivably be done with attitudes toward drinking or responses preceding drinking, instead of with smoking.

Lacking all else, it is still possible to replicate the simple ABA design first described across individual subjects. For example, if treatment is introduced and a substantial change observed which shows some irreversibility (the alcoholic patient does not begin to drink again in our hypothetical example), then the same procedure can be exactly replicated in the next patient at a later time. If the changes observed and the functional relationships (responses to treatment) are the same, the probability is increased that the change is due to treatment and no other concomitant extra-treatment variation. This has been the design of choice in most of the case studies in behavior modification to be reported here. The same procedure is usually replicated across 12-15 patients to determine its generalizability, at least within the sample of patients treated in the program.

Thus, it appears that there are a group of rigorous methodologies which seem ideally suited to the ⌐linician's goals of modifying in a more constructive direction the behavior of individual patients. These methodological advances have been largely the contribution of behavior modification, which has also influenced several other traditional areas. Before the individual case studies are presented, let us examine the related issues of assessment, control, variability, clinical follow-up and generalization.

In keeping with the general behavior modification movement, the focus of assessment programs has become less global and more specific with regard to target behaviors to be treated. As a result, behavioral assessment frequently may include behavioral observations, self-ratings of behaviors and their frequencies of occurrence, reinforcement surveys, and less of the indirect types of measurement, such as projective tests. The most rigorous strategies may include direct measurement of rates of the target behavior under specified circumstances. For example, rates of response to produce alcohol as reinforcement or kinds and amount of alcohol consumed by an alcoholic patient under controlled conditions could be good potential assessment devices.

Control and variability are usually the two opposing faces of the same coin. The traditional assumption that human behavior cannot be precisely controlled is now open to question, as laboratories find ever more precise ways of experimentally controlling human behavior with reduction in variability the result. The traditional alternative to experimental control usually requires the statistical control of groups of treated subjects, often to be compared with a group of 'untreated' subjects (who usually receive unspecified forms of different treatment or 'no treatment'). This design is frequently incompatible with the preferred strategy of the therapist to work with individuals and not to deny treatment to anyone who qualifies and needs it.

If, as suggested earlier, all pertinent extra-treatment variables can be controlled, variability may not be observed. If, on the other hand, several efforts such as time sampling, objective or machine definition of the response and control by reinforcement, do not restrict or eliminate variability, then a rigorous single subject design may not be accessible. One general principle here is that, the more 'noise' or variability in the data, the more powerful the behavior change technique which will be needed to demonstrate indisputable effects. The goal often is a criterion of stability which must be reached before treatment can be initiated. The more stable the measure, the less behavioral change treatment will have to produce in order to be detectable. Thus, stable dependent variables may be needed to show the effects of mild therapeutic techniques, while more variable measures may be clearly responsive only to major interventions.

When control adequate to produce stable dependent variables is available, the single subject method is the preferred clinical-research design for working with individual patients. When such control is not attainable, group designs may be preferable. Another situation which may not be appropriate for single subject design involves long-term clinical follow-up in uncontrolled environments. As long as each subject to be treated comes from a somewhat homogeneous subject sample (for example, similar reinforcement history), is exposed to identically replicated treatment, and goes thereafter to a homogeneous environment, subject generality should hold up from subject to subject. That is, all such treated subjects should demonstrate similar functional relationships. However, as the subject sample and follow-up environments become more heterogeneous, subject generality may be obscured.

Take, for example, a group of chronic, long-term Skid Row alcoholics who share similar histories and environments. Following any hypothetical form of treatment, the probability of successful rehabilitation would be much lower for subjects who returned to the same environment as before than for those who went to a half-way house, where drinking could be moderately controlled, for example.

To attempt to generalize from one group to the other, on the basis of a single treated subject, would probably be fallacious, even though the functional relationships within treatment might be identical. This is only one reason why group designs are so popularly used in studies of treatment outcome, although the possibility exists of controlling post-treatment environments. If all treated subjects went to a single half-way house, for example, a single subject design might still be preferred.

Stimulus and response generalization form a parallel or analog to the side effects of drug therapies, and have important implications for behavior therapy. Stimulus generalization forms a bridge with the last topic, since it concerns the maintenance of a response or set of behaviors by stimuli other than those involved in the original learning. For example, if an alcoholic learns not to drink in a hospital setting and this learning is 'transferred' to another environment following treatment, stimulus generalization may have taken place (assuming that current events are as important controllers of behavior as historical, treatment variables). Thus, whenever successful treatment is seen to be maintained through long-term follow-up, some generalization of this kind may have occurred. In order to study stimulus generalization more precisely, the similarities and differences between controlling stimulus variables during and after treatment should be specified, as well as their functional relationships to target behaviors.

Response generalization deals with new responses learned as an indirect, rather than a direct, effect of treatment. For example, if an alcoholic learned, not only to quit drinking, but also to quit smoking, as a result of treatment directed at drinking, response generalization has probably occurred. This kind of observation, in which many more constructive changes, rather than increases in other forms of pathological behavior ('symptom substitution'), has often occurred following behavior therapy, but it is sometimes mysterious. It is difficult, for example, at this point, to determine whether smoking and drinking, in our earlier hypothetical case, may have been correlated response variables, in which case treatment of one may have been functionally equivalent to treatment of both simultaneously. Other possibilities are that smoking may have been an early response in a chain of behaviors leading to alcohol reinforcement, or that drinking most frequently gave rise to smoking behavior. In any case, more responses than a single target behavior should be measured during treatment, in order to detect changes of this sort which might conceivably occur.

Let us now examine some specific clinical case studies to determine whether one might demonstrate general principles, as well as exemplify some of the issues just discussed. In each of the following six cases, the history of the case will be discussed first. This information is based on hospital records, clinical interview data and information from questionnaires. Treatment data is based primarily on direct behavioral observations, sometimes elaborated by interview or other verbal behavior. Follow-up data comes from direct behavioral observations, self-reports, questionnaire data, outside objective observers and hospital data.

The first case, S1, a 55-year-old white male veteran who was divorced with no children and who had worked on a newspaper most of his life, reported drinking 450-900 cc. Scotch per day, eleven months out of the year, for at least the previous 11 years. This patient had been hospitalized previously for alcoholism, had been convicted of driving while intoxicated, had attended 16 meetings of Alcoholics Anonymous and had not worked for three years, because of drinking. In treatment, he was allowed to pull a plunger (the one on the right depicted in Figure 13·1) thirty times to produce 2 cc. Scotch diluted 50 per cent with water. Each reinforcement was automatically dispensed into a shot glass in the magazine on the right in Figure 13·1. Once he stabilized in response rate (86 rpm, shown in Figure 13·2), electric shock was delivered through electrodes mounted on his left arm, 2·5 cm. below his elbow, beginning at an intensity he could subjectively just detect (0·05 mA). The current was delivered from a Grason-Stadler 6070B constant current shock generator. This patient, and all others, responded in a sound-attenuated isolation booth (IAC acoustical chamber 403A). Shock was delivered contingent on the thirtieth or reinforced response and increased in logarithmic steps to 6 mA, until he showed behavioral suppression (quit responding). Once he sat without responding through two consecutive half-hour sessions (conducted morning and afternoon each weekday), the shock electrodes were removed, allowing him to respond at will for two more sessions (labeled 'Generalization' in Figure 13·2). This patient pulled the plunger 125 times, producing four alcohol deliveries, in the first session, but did not drink the delivered alcohol, and did not respond thereafter, so that his discharge from the hospital was recommended, following

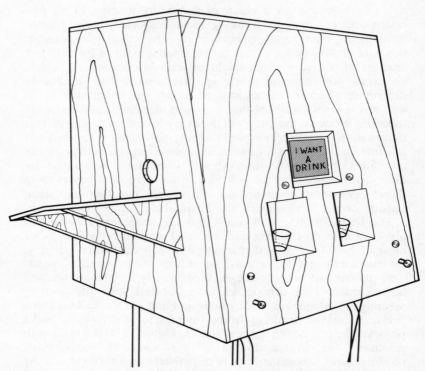

FIGURE 13·1 *Sketch of the operant conditioning console, with Lindsley manipulanda (lower left and right) stimulus lights (white above each plunger, red above each magazine) and rear projection screen on which slides could be projected*
Beverages were dispensed into a 0·28 cc. shot glass placed in either 15 cm. square cutout magazine.

placement in a half-way house and assignment to a job in one of the clinical laboratories in the hospital.

Follow-up revealed that this patient secured work in the hospital for six months, after which he was laid off. Approximately two weeks after treatment, this patient went to a bar and ordered one drink of everything he 'ever liked,' but reported that these drinks tasted 'like water, produced no bounce,' so he drank no more. He re-entered the hospital almost a year after treatment, at which time medical problems were detected, and he was hospitalized for most of the following year, during which time he underwent surgery four times and was almost totally incapacitated. He was confined to a wheelchair, but, despite these precipitating circumstances, he remained abstinent throughout. At three years post-treatment, the patient still entertained plans to return to school, apparently adapting well to his confinement to a wheel-chair. This case demonstrated, like twelve others treated in the same paradigm, that

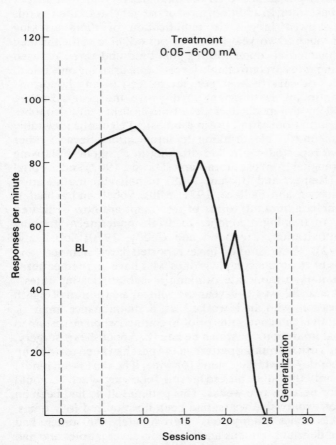

FIGURE 13·2 *Graph of response of S1 to treatment*
Each point represents mean rate of plunger pulling per session over 5 base-line (BL), 25 Treatment and 2 Generalization sessions. Reinforcement (2 cc. 100° proof Scotch diluted 50 per cent with water) was delivered on FR30 schedule. During treatment, each reinforced (30th) response produced 0·5 second shock of 0·05-6·00 mA intensity.

complete behavioral suppression of responding to produce the preferred alcoholic beverage consumed most frequently in the past was predictive of modification of the drinking response, particularly within the experimental treatment situation. Only one of the thirteen treated cases responded to produce alcohol in the Generalization phase, and then this patient responded at 25 per cent of his basic rate. In addition, most of the patients treated by this technique showed large-scale modification of their drinking behavior through a two-year follow-up period. Five of the thirteen patients remained abstinent during this time and three reduced their drinking rates to controllable levels, often drinking only one to three bottles or cans of beer per day instead of any liquor.

This last finding is sufficient to disprove the generalization, perpetuated by the medical model of alcoholism and Alcoholics Anonymous, that one drink by an established alcoholic inevitably launches uncontrollable drinking to intoxication. Several other studies have reported controlled drinking in alcoholics following treatment ranging from psychotherapy (Davies, 1962) and hospital treatment (Reinert and Bowen, 1968) to behavior modification (Cohen, Liebson and Faillace, 1971; Mills, Sobell and Schaefer, 1971). Some conditioning forms of treatment are now dedicated specifically to training alcoholics to drink moderately, stopping short of intoxication (Lovibond and Caddy, 1970; Sobell and Sobell, 1972). These studies have reported large numbers and proportions of treated alcoholic groups who have learned patterns of well-maintained moderate drinking at subintoxicating rates.

The next case, S2, was a 49-year-old white male veteran of eighth grade education who had worked as a maintenance man or mechanic until eighteen months prior to contact, when he sustained a myocardial infarction, for which he later had open-heart surgery. This patient's usual drinking pattern in the past had been to drink up to 900 cc. per day of whiskey blend (or wine, if he ran low on funds) for days or until the police picked him up, following which he would not drink for perhaps two weeks. This patient felt he had been an alcoholic for twenty-five years, had been hospitalized four times, attended Alcoholics Anonymous approximately 100 times, had experienced delirium tremens and blackouts several times and had lost a wife, mainly because of his drinking. Previous court convictions included one driving while intoxicated, 15 drunk and disorderly and 8 public intoxication.

Due to this patient's cardiac condition, he was treated, not with electric shock, but with a clinical technique called covert sensitization (Cautela, 1967). In this procedure, the patient is instructed by a therapist in muscular relaxation (Jacobson, 1938).

While in a relaxed state, the patient is then trained to visualize drinking scenes from his own history. Once he gives every indication of doing this properly, he is next instructed to imagine natural aversive consequences following the imagined drinking scenes. For example, he might be asked to imagine going into a bar, which is followed by a queasy feeling in the stomach. He imagines approaching the bar, at the same time feeling heart palpitations and stomach contractions. He imagines ordering a beer, feeling nauseous, drinking it, and vomiting it all over himself and neighboring drinkers. This is a typical covert sensitization sequence, in which several behavioral components ending (in imagination) in alcoholic reinforcement are immediately followed by aversive consequences. Cautela's technique usually includes negative reinforcement, in which the subject escapes the whole situation in imagination (for example, by leaving the drinking scene), and assignment to practice the technique at home to increase the number of trials, but it was felt more parsimonious in this study to examine the effects of one variable at a time. In addition, the simple pairing of aversive stimuli (in imagination) with imagined drinking scenes more closely paralleled shock aversive conditioning.

Unfortunately, this patient, perhaps due to his limited educational background and lack of verbal facility, failed to respond as expected to treatment. That is, he seemed to relax properly, but frequently corrected the therapist on the details of the instructed scenes, as if the assignment had been to remember past events. He also never did show the muscular tightness, apparent stomach contraction or peristaltic contractions of the throat that often accompany feelings of nausea and occasional vomiting observed in some covert sensitization patients. Even more surprising was his behavioral profile of response to treatment. Figure 13·3 reviews this profile. As in Figure 13·2, this is a plot of the rate at which the patient pulled a plunger to deliver alcohol to himself. Each point in this graph represents the mean rate at which the patient pulled the plunger to deliver 2 cc. whiskey blend following each thirtieth response. As the graph reveals, only increasing rates of response were observed, which were interpreted as a generally rising probability of drinking outside the experimental treatment situation. Because the covert sensitization was not effective in reducing these response rates and because the therapist-trainee left the hospital, two other manipulations were introduced. First, in sessions 22 and 23, coke was made concurrently available with alcohol. Because the patient reported eating very little (partly because he made only very little money on a part-time job as a cook's helper), the hypothesis was advanced that he might have

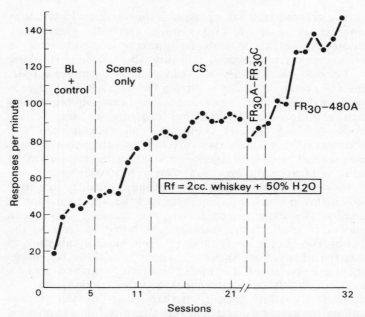

FIGURE 13·3 *Graph of mean rate of response by S2 for 2 cc. whiskey diluted 50 per cent by water (or Coke in sessions 22 and 23)*
Reinforcement schedule was FR30 (30 responses per reinforcement) in sessions 1-23, and increased (doubled) from FR30 to FR480 in sessions 24-32.

been relying on alcohol for its caloric (food) value. His continued preference for alcohol demonstrated that this was not the case. Next, in sessions 24 through 32, alcohol, the only available reinforcer, was made more difficult to obtain by doubling the number of responses required to deliver each reinforcement. Thus, as the graph indicates, the response requirement increased from 30 to 480, at which point (following session 32) the patient declined further treatment. He stated that he felt he had the situation under control and that the amount of alcohol he was getting in treatment wasn't worth the trip.

Unfortunately, as seen in Figure 13·3, this patient's response rate had shown only increasing trends throughout both these phases of treatment. Since he had never shown any evidence of decreasing or stopping his operant rates of responding to produce alcohol, the prediction was made that he would soon return to drinking outside the experimental treatment environment. It was suggested to the patient that if he did not stay in treatment until its completion, he could not expect as good results. Although the patient claimed he had not drunk for sixteen months, nine weeks later he was brought to the hospital for treatment of alcoholic withdrawal and badly cut and infected feet (he claimed he had dived into the river to save a fellow alcoholic!).

Thus, this case serves to illustrate the general principles that:

1 operant response rates are good predictors of drinking behavior in the natural environment; and

2 any treatment which does not effectively reduce or eliminate these operant rates may have no effect or may even exacerbate the pathological behavior outside of treatment.

Thus, unless the patient's response rates approximate zero at the end of treatment, effective modification of drinking probably cannot be predicted. Twenty other patients who began treatment but dropped out while their response rates were high, like those of S2, also returned to pathological rates of drinking within one to six months.

The next case study illustrates an ineffective treatment technique, followed ten weeks later by successful modification, both conducted with similar procedures, the same staff and in the same laboratory. The patient in this case (S3) was a 51-year-old Protestant divorcee with a college education who had worked as an accountant. He drank in excess of 840 cc. whiskey per day, which had led him to seek hospitalization five times in the past, to attend Alcoholics Anonymous, to lose control over his drinking and to suffer multiple withdrawal symptoms (shakes, behavioral anomalies and gastrointestinal upsets).

This patient was enrolled in an experimental treatment program, the goal of which was to modify the drinking preference of the subject from alcoholic to non-alcoholic beverages. In the first phase of treatment, S3 was exposed to the console (see Figure 13·1) and both manipulanda, which he was instructed he could pull at his own rate and, if a light flashed, he might receive coke or his favorite alcoholic beverage (whiskey) for his efforts. Actually, the discriminative stimuli (S^Ds which were the white lights above each manipulandum) were made available contingent upon pulls of one or the other plunger and then automatically exchanged every five minutes of the thirty-minute session. As soon as the patient could follow four of these changes with less than thirty responses in extinction (after the light had been removed), the light was again made available contingent on responses on either manipulandum.

At this point, then, the patient could choose whether he wanted to work for coke or alcohol.

The choice was perfectly predictable in all patients on this program but one, who denied he was an alcoholic. All the rest invariably responded to produce alcohol. Once they responded at stable rates, the number of responses required to produce alcohol was doubled every one to five sessions, until more responses were required than the patient could emit in one session. In animal laboratories, such rapid increase in ratio requirements has produced 'ratio strain,' or 'abulia,' as Skinner has redefined the latter older term to indicate the cessation of responding. It was hoped that, in this case, responding to produce alcohol would diminish or stop and the patient might show an increase in responding to produce coke.

As seen in Figure 13·4, this patient did not exhibit the classic features of gradually decreasing response rate in extinction, but

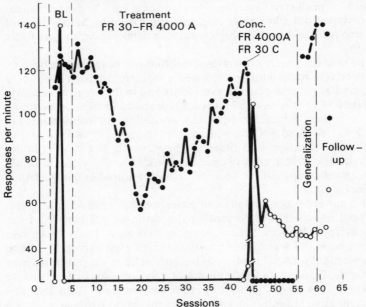

FIGURE 13·4 *First treatment profile of S3, in response per minute* Reinforcement was 2 cc. dilute whiskey delivered on FR30 in base-line (BL), increased FR30-FR4,000 in Treatment and FR30-extinction in Generalization. Coke was also available on FR30 in sessions 42-55 in Treatment and during the last 29 minutes of each Generalization session.

suddenly switched from a high rate of response on the formerly alcoholic bar to the coke bar, where he continued to respond (even with alcohol again available), but at vastly decreased response rate.

As a test to determine whether any treatment effects (change in probability of responding to produce alcohol) had occurred, the following were the defining features of the last sessions, marked 'Generalization' on the graph in Figure 13·4:

1   During the first one minute, neither the left white light (S^D for coke) nor coke were available, although both were available contingent on FR30 for the rest of the 30-minute session,

2   In the first ten minutes, alcohol was available contingent on pulls of the right plunger on FR30 for ten reinforcements, then the ratio requirement was doubled for each successive reinforcement,

3   During the second ten minutes, only the white light (S^D for alcohol) was available,

4   In the final ten minutes of the session, neither alcohol nor S^D lights were available on the right side.

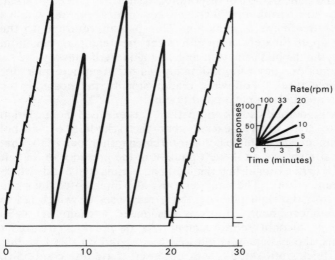

FIGURE 13·5 *Cumulative record of responding of S3 during Generalization for alcohol during the first 10 minutes, white light (S^D) alone for second 10 minutes, and Coke the last 10 minutes*

Responses moved the pen upwards; pen reset automatically at 550 responses or 10 minutes, hatch marks indicating reinforcement delivery.

Figure 13·5 illustrates the behavior of S3 in Generalization, a pattern also observed in every one of six patients who were exposed to this treatment and who remained to completion. This is a cumulative record which indicates responses and reinforcements in each condition. As the graph indicates, this patient responded at very high response rate (higher, in fact, than his original base rate) to produce all the alcohol reinforcements available, then continued responding through the S^D only condition, and switched to the 'coke' bar only when the 'booze' bar side fell dark (no S^D and no alcohol). Once he switched, he worked the last ten minutes at the lower response rates he had exhibited earlier while working to produce coke.

We could only conclude at this point that this sequence of increasing FR requirements had brought about little, if any, modification, and that patients continuing to respond as this one did would be at risk to drink soon after leaving the hospital. Again, this prediction was based on their continued high rate of responding to produce alcohol at the end of 'treatment.' As indicated by the follow-up rates on the graph in Figure 13·4, this patient continued to show the same pattern of responding as shown in Generalization, and returned to drinking 900 cc. whiskey or more per day within a month of treatment termination. This patient returned to the hospital approximately a month after treatment termination, reporting that he had been drinking over a quart of whiskey and six to ten beers per day (approximately his pre-treatment rate) for about three weeks. Following readmission to the hospital, the patient requested aversive conditioning.

Following detoxification, the patient was enrolled in a program similar to that of S1, except that the schedule of alcohol reinforcement was a simple behavioral chain rather than FR30. That is, the first response on the left plunger in the presence of the left white (S^D) light extinguished the light and illuminated a slide which read 'I want a drink.' The same response also illuminated the white S^D light over the right plunger, thirty responses on which led to alcohol reinforcement. This was designated a chain FR1 FR30 schedule of alcohol reinforcement. As in previous treatment paradigms, the patient was allowed to respond on this schedule without shock until stability was observed (base-line condition), after which shock of increasing intensity was programmed, this time contingent upon the first response in the chain (left plunger). This patient's response to treatment is plotted in Figure 13·6, which shows responding during 4 sessions of base-line, 55 sessions of treatment and 4 sessions of generalization (shock electrodes off).

This patient's response to aversive conditioning was unusual in

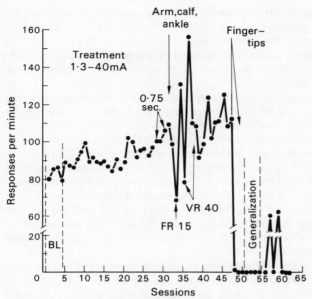

FIGURE 13·6 *Second treatment profile, in response per minute by S3 on Chain FR1 Fr30 with whiskey reinforcement*

Shock was contingent on the first response and was increased to 40 mA by session 27, then lengthened from 0·50 to 0·75 seconds in sessions 28, 29 and 30. Variations in reinforcement schedule and electrode site appear on the figure. Following 50 treatment sessions, no responses were observed in 4 Generalization sessions, and in all but one follow-up session, in which none of shock was delivered.

that he showed very high initial shock thresholds and showed little behavioral suppression during treatment, even at very high intensities, until the site of the electrodes was moved several times. Prior to treatment with each patient, subjective shock thresholds are measured by instructing the patient to emit a motor response (raise his arm) when he first feels a brief (0·50 sec.) shock, as well as when he can tolerate no more. These thresholds are measured as a function of an ascending series of increasingly intense shocks. In most patients, these thresholds range between 0·05 and 1·0 mA at the lower value and 1·0 mA and 3 mA at the higher, while this patient ranged between 1·3 and 2·5 mA at the lower and 8·0 and 10·0 mA at the higher threshold value. This perhaps indicated that he had suffered some peripheral neuropathy, which may have reduced his sensitivity to stimuli impinging upon his extremities (the electrodes were mounted just below the elbow of his left arm, until late in treatment). Possibly because of this reason, this patient (like 25-40 per cent of the patients treated in this program) did not show significant decrease in response rates up to the maximum shock intensity (40 mA).

In order to produce suppression in S3, the following experimental manipulations occurred in the sessions indicated: the shock duration was increased from 0·50 to 0·75 seconds in sessions 28, 29 and 30; shock electrodes were switched to the right arm in sessions 31 and 32; alcohol was delivered on FR15 in session 33 (the rate decreased, but the patient got tipsy); alcohol was delivered on VR40 in sessions 34, 35 and 36 (the rate shot up); alcohol was delivered again on chain FR1 FR30, but the electrodes were transferred from arm to arm and calf to calf in sessions 37 to 46; and, finally, the electrodes were put on the fingertips of the left hand in sessions 47 through 50, which did produce suppression in session 48 and cessation in sessions 49 and 50.

Following this treatment, the electrodes were removed for four consecutive generalization sessions, in which no responding or drinking occurred. Discharge from the hospital was recommended at this point, and the two-year follow-up period began. As indicated by Figure 13·6, S3 did not respond to produce alcohol in follow-up sessions, with one exception (the fifth follow-up session, which occurred three months after discharge). Consistent with observed operant rates and corroborated by reports from his landlady, S3 was abstinent from alcohol on the occasion of all follow-up visits but this one. Questionnaire, interview and objective report data all indicated that S3 drank ¼-1 litre alcohol per day for one week following the second follow-up visit, apparently precipitated by several job rejections. The second drinking binge followed on the tail of a job S3 held for three weeks, but quit when he felt he had too many bosses pulling in different directions. He began drinking soon afterwards and continued for three weeks, but at lower rates than before (about ¼ litre per day). Following this binge, the patient stopped drinking again, got himself a good job as accountant for a corporation and, at last report, had been abstinent from alcohol for over one year.

Of fourteen other patients treated by this technique, 40 per cent remained abstinent, 20 per cent drank at low, controlled rates and 20 per cent drank to intoxication in binges over one to two years, essentially replicating the outcome of the study in which S1 was treated (FR30).

This case was selected since it demonstrated very clearly that there was no magic in simply exposing patients to the experimental environment or to one of the treatment procedures (since the first one failed so miserably), and that, following the worst of failures, modification and treatment are still possible.

The next two cases demonstrate two treatment procedures, used for the first time with a retired couple who had been drinking together long enough to have sustained significant brain damage. This couple, aged 48 and 50, both appeared 60 or 65 at intake, and had been sending out to a package store which delivered 1 liter or 2 liter bottles of vodka, which they had divided every day for five to ten years. The husband had been hospitalized three times, the wife seven times, for alcoholism, and both had been treated by private doctors and attended fifteen meetings of Alcoholics Anonymous. Although both had worked in the past, neither had been employed in the previous year (the husband had been medically retired three years previously). Their typical drinking pattern was one of starting to drink sometimes in the morning, drinking uncontrollably, ending with the husband beating the wife almost every night. They reported that most of their good furniture was smashed or broken down, and, on the night before they were brought to the hospital by ambulance, the husband had wandered around the house, passing out in several rooms, but destroying their television and breaking a set of dishes before finally passing out in bed. The wife said she thought it was time to end it all, so she went to the kitchen and got a butcher knife, which she drove into his side, but, failing to kill him, cried, mopped up the blood and called the police, to whom she turned herself in. The police called an ambulance, which transported them both to the hospital.

Following detoxification and medical treatment, neuro-psychological examination revealed that both patients were anxious, depressed and significantly brain damaged. The husband showed severe memory losses (on the ward he was confused and forgetful, not able to find his room, remember his doctor's name or find his way to treatment), progressive and diffuse impairment consistent with mild to moderate Korsakoff's syndrome produced by alcohol.

Examination revealed the wife to be in reactive depression with mild to moderate scattered loss of nonverbal memory, psychomotor and motor skills, all consistent with alcoholic encephalopathy and possible closed head trauma. Interview supported the latter, since the wife said her husband had knocked her head into the wall several times, and she had passed out and struck her head on their concrete driveway once.

In alcoholic treatment, the wife was assigned to a free-operant avoidance conditioning program which delivered 2 cc. alcohol at the end of a twenty-second white light (S^D) in the absence of responding. Each response re-initiated the S^D for twenty seconds, postponing the deliveries of both alcohol and shock (later in treatment). When shock was delivered after a base-line period, it occurred contingent on the offset of the S^D. Subjective shock thresholds, taken at the outset of treatment, indicated an average lower threshold (range=$0\cdot20 - 0\cdot40$ mA), while the upper threshold was somewhat elevated ($2\cdot50 - 5\cdot00$ mA), perhaps consistent with peripheral neuropathy. In short, all the early predictors were consistent with a most dismal prognosis for this woman.

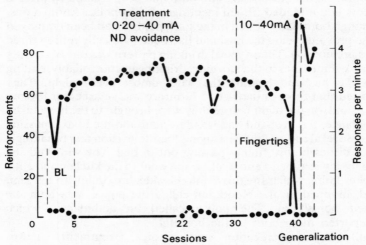

FIGURE 13·7 *Graph of number of alcohol deliveries and mean response rate during avoidance conditioning of S4*

Alcohol was dilute vodka. Shock was delivered contingent on 20-second light offset, just prior to alcohol delivery. Shock intensity was increased to 40 mA on the arm by session 31, then 10-40 mA on the fingertips in sessions 32-40. Responding remained high enough to avoid all alcohol deliveries in the Generalization sessions, with electrodes removed.

Observations during treatment did not reverse this impression. As indicated by Figure 13·7, this patient (S4) responded minimally during baseline, then stopped responding and drank every reinforcement available while receiving shocks up to 40 mA. Since no responses had occurred at this point, the electrode site was shifted to the fingertips of the left hand (in session 32, Figure 13·7).

The intensity was decreased to 10 mA, then increased again to 40 mA by session 38, where responding began and increased to a rate high enough to avoid all shock and alcohol deliveries by session 40. After two sessions with zero alcohol deliveries and no shock, the electrodes were removed during two generalization test sessions, in which responding remained high enough to avoid all alcohol deliveries. Discharge was recommended and took place three days after treatment termination and about five weeks before her husband's discharge, which was delayed until he could be assigned to a nursing home, since it was considered he might not be able to take care of himself.

The wife reported going home alone, feeling lonely and drinking one drink the first day, then about half a liter of vodka (her formerly preferred drink) daily for two days about two weeks later. She stopped drinking without further treatment, however, and improved while visiting her husband during the three months he was in the nursing home. Christmas occurred during this time and she drank about a quarter liter of vodka for two days, then no more until five months later, when she and her husband both witnessed a car hit their dog, an old family pet, which launched a four-day drinking binge for both of them. During this binge, they split a bottle of vodka daily, as was their previous pattern, but quit without treatment when they said they were getting too sick to continue. This was the only drinking on the part of the wife, which represents vast improvement over her previous pattern of daily drinking. In addition, she has reported that she feels she can now remain abstinent, which is her goal, and that she does not feel as depressed as before treatment, and that her life has improved in several respects, which she attributes to treatment.

Seventeen other patients were treated, like S4, with avoidance conditioning, of whom four have been abstinent, four more showed controlled drinking and seven drank in binges over a 3-16 month follow-up period. The initial impression is that this program was not as effective as those used with S1 and S3.

The husband was assigned to a treatment which required a variable number of responses on the plunger to produce alcohol reinforcement. The number of responses required ranged from 5-60 and averaged 30 (VR30 schedule of reinforcement). When shock was delivered later in treatment, it was contingent upon the same response which produced reinforcement. Thus, both shock and reinforcement occurred at times unpredictable to the patient. Two cc. 90° proof vodka mixed 50 per cent with water was reinforcement.

This patient (S5) showed very high subjective shock thresholds (the lower threshold ranged 0·13-1·30, the upper ranged 3·00-16·00 mA, among the highest recorded in the program). This finding alone might have supported the hypothesis that this patient had sustained significant peripheral neuropathy.

S5 stabilized rather quickly during the base-line condition, and at a basic rate somewhat lower than predicted. However, it was not inconsistent with his reported previous alcoholic intake of about a pint of vodka per day. His tolerance and, consequently, his rate of intake, may have decreased following his 25-year history of alcoholism.

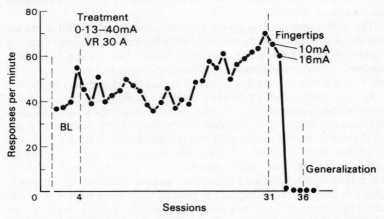

FIGURE 13·8 *Treatment profile of S5, who responded on VR30 to produce dilute vodka*
Shock was delivered contingent upon the alcohol-producing response at intensities from 0·13-40 mA on the arm, after which the site was moved to the fingertips. No responses occurred in Generalization.

As indicated in Figure 13·8, treatment began at 0·13 mA and continued through increasing intensities up to 40 mA in session 34, when the intensity was decreased and the electrode site changed to the fingertips. Three sessions later, at 20 mA, the patient stopped responding and did not respond again, even when the electrodes were removed in the Generalization test sessions.

S5 stayed in the hospital one month after treatment termination while an assignment to a convalescent home was being secured for him. The assignment was not his choice, but he submitted when he found the fees would be paid for his three-month stay there. It was the evaluation of the staff that S5 would need this care, since he appeared so confused and forgetful through treatment as to warrant it. From the outset, he did not appear to have very good prospects for rehabilitation.

Despite the gloomy outlook for this patient, he has done very well in the follow-up period, engaging in drinking only during the four-day binge previously reported for S4 after both together witnessed their dog run over. During the convalescent period at the nursing home, S5 seems to have worked hard to improve, resisting the tendency of most patients in such homes to drift into helpless dependence. This earned him the privilege of an increasing number of visits home to his wife, so that he was spending week-ends with her by the end of his stay there. During this time, his appearance, speech and memory all seemed to improve. In the six months since he has been home, he has continued to improve in many areas of his social and married life. According to both his and his wife's reports, he now helps around the house, is not abusive to his wife and looks for constructive things to do to improve their relationship and their house.

At latest word, just before going to press, the wife (S4) called to say that her husband had begun to drink heavily again, and that she had occasionally joined him, but never drank more than 85 cc. per day. Her husband had again become assaultive and abusive with her, according to her report, and she had called the police on one occasion, but no charges or action resulted. We are currently in process of corroborating these reports.

Nevertheless, it appears that this couple has benefited from two experimental forms of behavior therapy and they have shown progress in many areas, despite occasional set-backs. The reader should remember that these two patients were in bad enough shape and had sustained sufficient brain damage at the outset of therapy to have earned them rejection from most programs.

Thirteen other patients were exposed to the same (vr30) program as S6, with the following outcome, at 3-11 months: 4 have maintained abstinence, 2 have shown controlled drinking, 3 are still drinking heavily and 4 have been lost to contact. Thus, this program does not appear as effective as those used with S1 (fr30) or S3 and S6 (chain).

S6, the last patient to be reviewed in depth here, like S3, went through treatment more than once and showed benefit from the last more than earlier treatment courses. This patient had received aversive conditioning in an earlier experimental program six years previous to this contact, but was drinking at intoxicating rates again within six months. At intake, S6 was 48 years of age, a white divorced male veteran who received service-connected compensation for chronic anxiety in addition to his alcoholism. This patient had been drinking 1250-1500 cc. bourbon per day, 2-7 days per week or per month, for twenty-five years. He said he had an alcoholic uncle and a grandfather who died an alcoholic. The patient had worked sporadically on surveying jobs that lasted 1-10 months, but had lost an increasing number in recent years due to drinking. He said he usually drank in bars with others, soon reaching uncontrollable rates, which had produced blackouts, memory losses, shakes and delirium tremens. S6 had also received numerous court convictions, including 5 driving while intoxicated, 8 drunk and disorderly, 1 assault and battery and 3 public intoxication. He had been hospitalized for alcoholism fifteen times in the past, beginning twenty-five years previously, had been treated with antabuse (which produced 6-7 months sobriety), psychotherapy (little or no effect), electro-shock therapy (no apparent effect), Alcoholics Anonymous (temporary effects during regular attendance) and previous aversive conditioning (six months sobriety). He felt he drank to relax, to a point, and used drinking 'as a crutch.'

This patient was assigned to the same treatment modality as was finally successful with S3. That is, he also was exposed to chain FR1 FR30 which required one pull of the left plunger in the presence of the left S^D, then thirty more responses on the right manipulandum to deliver alcohol. Since this patient had been drinking primarily bourbon before treatment, he was allowed to respond to produce bourbon in treatment, which did not proceed without incident, as indicated in Figure 13·9. As the figure shows, S6 endured three weeks of treatment, which reduced his response rate to less than 15 per cent of his pre-treatment rates, but then left the hospital one day, got drunk and was not readmitted until two months later.

A closer look at the first treatment profile shows that electric shock contingent upon the first response in the chain had little effect upon the response rate until 13 mA, after which each higher intensity had suppressive effect. After approaching suppression and cessation of responding at maximum intensity (40 mA), the patient left the hospital, got drunk, was not readmitted and apparently was arrested. He later reported that he had been under pressure on the psychiatric ward and that a large sum in back pay from the VA had not arrived, which precipitated his drinking episode. Also according to his report, during this episode and the two months following, he drank no bourbon (which was used in treatment), but only beer, which he felt was potentiated by his medication (chlordiazepoxide, which does apparently have some cross-tolerance with alcohol). Thus, he felt his drinking during this period was vastly reduced over his former consumption, and under more control.

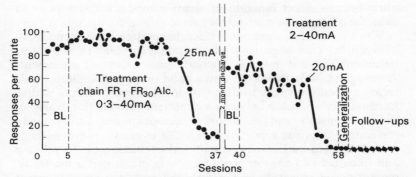

FIGURE 13·9 *Response to treatment of S6 with Chain FR1 FR30 schedule of bourbon reinforcement*

Shock was delivered contingent upon the first response in increasing intensities from 0·30-40 mA in the first treatment course, then 2-40 mA in the second. No responses were observed following completion of the second course.

The second course of therapy was much smoother, involving only 23 sessions, beginning at base rates slightly less than earlier and producing suppression at every intensity beyond 20 mA. The patient did not respond in generalization when the electrodes were removed, nor has he responded to produce bourbon in any session through eighteen months' follow-up. He has successfully kept seven follow-up visits, reporting abstinence each time (as well as during the entire intervening period), despite the fact that he was out of the country for several months and had been frustrated during some months by unemployment.

Thus, S6 is another patient, who, like S2 and S3, left the hospital before treatment was completed or before his response rates under alcohol reinforcement were reduced to zero, and who continued to drink until completing treatment in the second course. This again would seem to substantiate the utility of the current criteria of treatment completion (complete suppression of response rates).

In summary, several case studies have been presented and used to illustrate general behavioral principles. The overall thrust of these studies has been to suggest a more rigorous methodology and design than has been available to traditional case studies. The power and resolution of the replicated single subject design in which one principal variable is manipulated to produce treatment which is compared to control conditions before and after treatment has been amply demonstrated. In the cases reported here in which electric shock was used, the changes observed during treatment have so often been a direct function of changes in shock intensity as to demonstrate a functional relationship.

When successful, treatment effects have often been found to be irreversible. That is, patients who responded at high rates prior to treatment did not usually respond again following treatment. Although satisfying clinically and a good prognostic indicator, this raises a scientific spectre in evaluation. However, when a similar functional relationship between a treatment variable (for example, shock intensity) and behavior is demonstrated across many replicated cases (as reported here), the evidence is compelling.

As indicated earlier, assessment and evaluation of the process and outcome of behavior modification is oftentimes a matter of measuring, as precisely as possible, the response rates of target behaviors. Not since Lindsley used operant rates to assess psychotic behavior (1956, 1960) has there been much precise measurement of this kind. However, operant rates under schedules of alcohol reinforcement were found more predictive of future behavior and more closely correlated with previous behavior outside the laboratory than any other source of data. Thus, the operant rates during the pre-treatment control condition correlated best with the rates of drinking prior to treatment, while the rates after treatment were the best predictors of each patient's response to treatment. Several other behavioral measures (self-reports of attitudes toward drinking, levels of anxiety and self-control) are currently developed to correlate with operant rates and to help detect the occasional patient who does not respond well to aversive conditioning.

The cases reviewed here have supported several general behavioral principles, some in contradiction to traditional views regarding alcoholism. For example, S6 and several other patients treated in the same programs as S6 and S1 showed periods of controlled drinking at subintoxicating rates. This directly challenges the medical model of alcoholism, which strongly posits that alcoholism is a medical disease which cannot be treated and modified, only arrested, as well as that one drink always leads an alcoholic to intoxication. Outcome data from our studies as well as several others now suggest that it is perfectly feasible to teach alcoholics new patterns of controlled, subintoxicating rates of drinking.

By comparison with aversive conditioning using electric shock, a non-aversive technique which aimed to modify preferences of patients for alcohol v. coke and a more clinical technique (covert sensitization) were found much less effective as treatment. In both cases with whom the latter two techniques were used, operant rates under alcohol reinforcement remained high throughout treatment to its completion and were predictive of early drinking following treatment. To answer questions of scientific interest as well as clinical utility, several other non-aversive techniques are currently being developed and given clinical trial. Among these is an application of the DRL (differential reinforcement of low rate responding) schedule of reinforcement, which requires pausing of some duration between reinforced responses. Such methods have great potential for teaching the patient constructive new forms of behavior, as well as making treatment available to patients with cardiac or other conditions which militate against the use of electric shock.

In addition, four types of aversive conditioning were compared, with two types (those used with S1, S3 and S6) clearly superior to the others. This outcome was clear, not only in the case studies reviewed, all of whom reached abstinence after treatment, but in the data reported for the rest of the groups treated with the same techniques.

Thus, it appears that the wedding of laboratory procedures with clinical treatment represented by this program has produced a powerful means of assessment, as well as several very effective treatment modalities. A great advantage of the program, in addition, is its research base, which provides for replication of each technique with groups of patients sufficiently large to allow precise evaluation of each one. By comparison of treatment process and outcome data, those techniques which are not productive may be discarded in favor of the more effective ones. Thus, the program is self-corrective.

Once the basic research regarding the effectiveness of a group of univariate treatment techniques is completed, more complex sets of treatment paradigms may be included in the program. Proceeding conservatively in this fashion, it may be possible one day to extend the precision of this program to more complex treatment models, such as broad spectrum behavior therapy, token economies, vocational rehabilitation or other multi-modality therapeutic models. However, without specification and separate analysis of some of the many variables known to make up most such programs, precise analysis may be impossible at this time.

14 Automated Aversion Therapy and Assessment: Two Contrasting Case Studies

Jean E. Sambrooks and
Malcolm J. MacCulloch

Introduction

In this section we present two behaviour therapy case histories. The majority of papers on the application of learning theory to unwanted approach behaviour do not describe their cases in detail; they are not, therefore, able to demonstrate the tactics which the therapist employs in his initial assessment and planning, or the on-going tactical manoeuvres which become necessary in the light of progress and additional case material.

The first case is a complex one which involved psychotropic drugs, suicidal risk, the possibility of legal action against the patient, and a constant change of demands on the therapists. The second case is included as a simple, uncomplicated exercise in assessment and treatment using the Sexual Orientation Method scale, sexual interest latencies and avoidance latencies.

Case 1

The patient was a 34-year-old married man referred by his general practitioner complaining of strong anxiety and depression related to his homosexual feelings and behaviour. He presented with depression of mood and withdrawal existing over the previous ten months; on examination he showed early morning waking, thought retardation, impaired concentration, spontaneous weeping and marked agitation and tension; that is, his mood was both anxious and depressed. He related his depression to his sexual problem and his illness was formulated as 'endo-reactive'. He stated that he wished to change to a 'normal' way of life completely.

Sexual history

At 9 years old the patient noticed a strong sexual attraction to a boy of the same age and practised mutual masturbation for a period of one year; his auto-masturbatory fantasy was, at that time, partly homosexual. From 10 onwards he practised mutual masturbation with a series of boys of his own age and some boys younger than himself. At 16 he went to sea, where he had one or two homosexual affairs, for example, homosexual behaviour in the setting of an emotional attraction and relationship, although he never practised anything apart from mutual masturbation. Other homosexual activities were suggested to him in the Navy but he found these ideas frightening. He found that facial features were the most important arousing factor during mutual masturbatory activity. In the three years prior to presentation he had been having a homosexual affair with a boy who was 14 at the onset of the affair and who was, at the time, under a quasi probation order to the patient (the patient was set in a therapeutic role by the boy's probation officer). At the time of presentation the boy was attempting to avoid the patient's assignations and was also again becoming involved in criminal activity which the patient could not control.

The patient stated that his main interest was in men, although he was occasionally interested in boys between the ages of about 14-16. His heterosexual interest was also strong and he had been interested in girls from the age of 10, although he had never taken any out or made any overt sexual approach to females until he was in his early twenties when he married his present wife. In his marriage he had, at times, to practise homosexual fantasy in order to maintain an erection during intercourse, or to think of younger women, but on presentation he had just ended an extra-marital heterosexual association with a girl of 24 which had lasted two years. He was strongly interested in her and kissing and petting (short of sexual intercourse) had taken place, but the affair had been ended after his wife had attempted suicide on discovering the affair's existence. On presentation the content of his thinking related to his homosexual problems and guilt associated with both homosexual and heterosexual extra-marital affairs.

Family history

The patient's parents were never married, although they lived together as a family, but there was no evidence that this had particularly distressed him. There was no other relevant family history.

On presentation the patient was initially diagnosed as a self-insecure personality with both sensitive and obsessional personality features; he looked extremely depressed and tense and he also had a hand tremor. He did not appear to be suicidal but was clearly agitated and his concentration was markedly impaired. He had sensitive ideas of reference but no delusions or hallucinations. He was designated a secondary homosexual (Feldman and MacCulloch, 1971) and initially prescribed Trimipramine 25 mg. mane and 50 mg. nocte, and Diazepam 5 mg. t.d.s. in order to improve his mood.

Pre-treatment assessment

Previous work has suggested that it is possible to predict treatment outcome when aversion therapy is used. The first important predictor is categorisation in terms of primary versus secondary homosexuality. Feldman and MacCulloch (1971) have suggested that subjects who clinically report a total absence of prior heterosexual arousal, practice or interest, do very badly in treatment. They termed this group primary homosexuals; they supported this clinical finding by use of the Sexual Orientation Method (SOM) (Feldman *et al.*, 1966), by showing that patients with a pre-treatment heterosexual score of less than 20 almost invariably did badly in treatment, and, furthermore, this group coincided with the clinically described primary homosexual group. The Sexual Orientation Method has thus become a predictor for the pre-treatment assessment of homosexuals; however, its original form was susceptible to technical criticism (Phillips, 1968), and the present authors therefore modified the test to its present form which is administered by an automatic machine-subject interface and scored by a computer (Sambrooks and MacCulloch, 1973). This patient was repeatedly administered the automated form of the SOM before, during and after treatment. His pre-treatment scores were as follows:

Male = 48 (range 6-48) *Female* = 36 (range 6-48)

Forty-eight is the high end of the range in each case, that is, 6-48 would be a maximally heterosexual score. On this prognosticant this patient, a 'secondary' homosexual, was predicted to do well with aversion therapy.

Personality assessment

MacCulloch and Feldman (1967a) suggested that personality was also prognostic for patients undergoing aversion therapy; this general idea was supported in later work (Feldman and MacCulloch, 1971). Briefly, they assigned patients an 'O' scale score which relates to personality disorder (Schneiderian classification; Schneider, 1959) other than the self-insecure rated as follows:

5, severe   2, abnormality
4, disorder   1, mild abnormality
3, marked abnormality   0, normal

They demonstrated that the Cattel 16 PF 'C' scale sten score, minus the clinical 'O' scale score, could be used to predict male SOM scores during treatment. No patient with a combined personality scale score of 5 or more failed treatment. The present patient was administered the Cattel 16 PF and his 'C' scale score was 1. Before his first treatment the patient was thought to show a self-insecure personality abnormality, not amounting to a disorder. His 'O' scale score (see Feldman and MacCulloch, 1971, Table 7·10) was judged to be O. His combined score was therefore Cattel 'C' scale $1 - 0 = 1$ and he would therefore be predicted to have a poor chance of improvement on this measure.

Subsequent events and further history demonstrated that the patient was hypochondriacal, weak-willed and attention-seeking. Therefore, we would now, albeit *post hoc,* assign him an 'O' scale score of 5, that is, a severe attention-seeking and weak-willed disorder. The C — O formula would therefore have given a score of (—4), which suggests a much poorer chance of successful outcome. As MacCulloch and Feldman (1967a) and Feldman and MacCulloch (1971) have already pointed out, this clinical assessment of personality is very unsatisfactory for general use. In the three group trials reported in Feldman and MacCulloch (1971), personality descriptions were made by M. J. MacCulloch, and assigned scores blind by a psychologist (JFO), and not changed; however, it is within the experience of all clinical workers that patients' personalities unroll to reveal ever more interesting facets of their life styles which they had at first concealed from the therapist. So it was in this particular case, that the hysterical (attention-seeking) and irresolute facets of the patient's personality remained concealed for many months.

Summary

In the first instance we assessed the patient as bisexual, with a minimal interest in younger persons, and as having a self-insecure personality. It later transpired that his area of maximum sexual deviance was young boys of 15 years, and that he had massive unresolvable conflicts, including strong religious beliefs, barely disguised sexual disinterest in his wife and strong paedophilic interests. He tended repeatedly to ensnare himself in attention-getting situations, such as lay preaching and amateur dramatics.

Perhaps the major interest of this case has been the constant change in tactics which the therapists have had to employ in order to support and treat him.

Treatment method and in-treatment assessment

In 1964 Feldman and MacCulloch described anticipatory avoidance aversion therapy in the successful treatment of a single homosexual; a further report, MacCulloch and Feldman (1967b), showed that 60 per cent of 'unselected' patients could expect to be rated either Kinsey 'O' or '1' up to a year after completion of treatment. These findings have been confirmed in over seventy cases reported in detail by Feldman and MacCulloch (1971). One of the central features of the technique is the anticipatory avoidance paradigm with the possibility of response shaping, together with the facility for an instrumental method to encourage heterosexual approach behaviour.

MacCulloch and Sambrooks (1974) regarded the avoidance latencies in the original anticipatory avoidance paradigm as a crucial dependent variable; therefore, sexual interest latencies (SILS) were developed both as a measure of slide preference for treatment and as an indication of the course of treatment.

Sexual interest latencies were administered to this case as follows:

Two series of slides, male and female, were rated by the patient for sexual interest 1 through 10, 10 being very highly interesting. Slides were then selected over the interest range, randomised and presented sequentially to the patient. His instruction was as follows: 'Leave the slide on so long as it is sexually interesting to you, when/if it is no longer of interest switch it off.' No shock electrodes were connected.

The apparatus was a Lucas PACE[1] modified to switch the Kodak carousel slide projector forward on each trial. The patient's avoidance button also moved the magazine forward, the output of the PACE and the subject interface (Birtles *et al.,* 1971) were logged onto eight-channel computer tape. The programme on the PACE switched on the first slide, the subject then obeyed the instruction by pressing the avoid button which advanced the carousel to the next slide position which contained a blank. If the patient did not respond after two minutes the slide was removed by the therapist in order that the assessment session was kept to a manageable length.

[1] Obtainable from: G. & E. Bradley Ltd, Electrical House, Neasden Lane, London N.W.10.

The SIL trial is displayed diagrammatically in Figure 14·1.

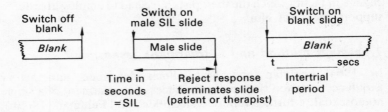

Machine (PACE) function

FIGURE 14·1   *Scheme of machine/subject interface function for taking sexual interest latencies*

This sequence was repeated for all slides and provided a set of sexual interest latencies for both the male and female series of slides. After the SIL session the patient was asked to re-rate the slides.

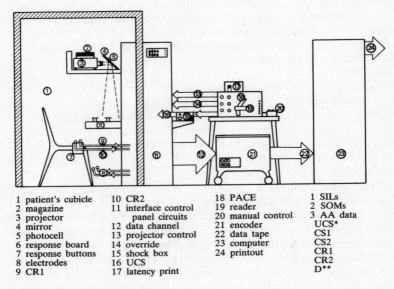

1 patient's cubicle	10 CR2	18 PACE
2 magazine	11 interface control	19 reader
3 projector	panel circuits	20 manual control
4 mirror	12 data channel	21 encoder
5 photocell	13 projector control	22 data tape
6 response board	14 override	23 computer
7 response buttons	15 shock box	24 printout
8 electrodes	16 UCS	
9 CR1	17 latency print	

1 SILs
2 SOMs
3 AA data
UCS*
CS1
CS2
CR1
CR2
D**

*UCS: unconditioned stimulus.

**D: trial where patient's avoidance response is delayed.

FIGURE 14·2   *Aversion therapy laboratory and data processing*

The patient was treated in a specially designed laboratory using an automatic machine for administering aversion therapy; the PACE coupled to one of our computer assisted psychometric system (CAPS) interfaces (see Figure 14·2).

TABLE 14·1   *Treatment programme as used to determine sequence of stimuli*

A	B	C	A	B	C
1	4¹/₂	2+	13	NR	—
2	R	2+	14	R	2+
3	6	2+	15	R	2+
4	R	2+	16	6	2+
5	NR	—	17	7¹/₂	2+
6	4¹/₂	2+	18	NR	—
7	7¹/₂	2+	19	4¹/₂	2+
8	NR	—	20	R	2+
9	NR	—	21	NR	—
10	R	2+	22	R	2+
11	NR	—	23	NR	—
12	R	2+	24	7¹/₂	2+

A: trial number.
B: trial type. 4¹/₂, 6, 7¹/₂ of override delay in seconds.
C: number of female requests granted.
NR: non-reinforced trial, where the patient is not allowed to make an avoidance response to shock, but only an escape response.
R: reinforced trial, where a female may be granted.

Table 14·1 shows the programme which was punched on to the PACE programme card and used throughout treatment. The following parameters of treatments were logged by the CAPS:

1 Avoidance latency
2 D trials, where the patient's avoidance response is delayed for up to 7¹/₂ seconds
3 NR trials, where the patient cannot avoid until after the shock has occurred
4 Number of CR2s (requests for female relief slide)
5 Latency to first CR2
6 Proportion of inter-trial period in which CR2 responses were made

Treatment

Six weeks after the initial presentation the patient's mood was judged markedly improved and Anticipatory Avoidance aversion therapy commenced. On presentation his SOM score (Sambrooks and MacCulloch, 1973) was 48 for interest in males, and 36 for interest in females, and his sexual preference with regard to homosexual stimuli appeared to be for older men in general rather than younger boys. For the next five months the patient was given twenty-five sessions of Anticipatory Avoidance aversion therapy at approximately weekly intervals. During this time he showed some improvement in his homosexual activity in that it decreased in frequency from, on average, once every six weeks on presentation to virtually nil. After twenty-three treatments his SOM male score was 27, and his female score was 48.

Six months after presentation the patient stated that he was free from any abnormal sexual interest in general, although he was still emotionally relating to the younger person to whom he had been previously attached. However, as the boy had just received an extended prison sentence, this problem showed signs of being resolved. His heterosexual interest had increased, although he was having prolonged intercourse (*ejaculatio tarda*) and pain on ejaculation during masturbation, which was thought to have been a side effect of the tricyclic drug which he was taking. During the five-month period of treatment his mood was, in general, well maintained although he had a tendency to be labile. However, there were no marked mood problems during the treatment period and he was maintained on Amitriptyline, Imipramine and Diazepam — the Trimipramine having been omitted due to a marked increase in the patient's weight and difficulty in maintaining an erection.

However, two months after the end of treatment, he was admitted to a mental hospital unit because of acute depression with weeping, sleeplessness, guilt and suicidal ideation. At this point it began to appear that he had a somewhat more abnormal personality than we had first thought, being decidedly weak-willed, albeit with the redeeming features of a 'warm-hearted' affability, sensitivity and some obsessional traits.

He was in hospital for two weeks and his medication was increased, but not altered. He was somewhat labile in mood as an in-patient and would express strong desires to return home which, on being given leave, would be changed to a desire to return to hospital. However, an acute behavioural flurry by a schizophrenic patient appeared to be the most effective anti-depressant available and improved his mood sufficiently for him to insist on being discharged. Following this he was seen for follow-ups and supportive therapy; he was quite well in general, although he still showed a marked tendency to be mood labile. Two months later he complained of 'black-outs' and dizziness, but neurological investigations did not reveal any organic cause and it was decided that the symptoms were due to tension. He was also investigated for the second time due to his fear of cancer of the rectum, but no physical disease was found. He was still maintained on psychotropic drugs as follows: Diazepam, 5 mg. t.d.s., Imipramine, 50 mg. b.d., and Amytriptyline, 25 mg. nocte. In November and December 1971 (six months after the end of treatment), he complained of slight depression and a return of interest for the brother of his previous juvenile affair, although this was in fantasy only. He had had no other homosexual or extra-marital heterosexual contact. His relationship with his wife was emotionally quite good, although he still found it difficult to obtain an orgasm on sexual intercourse with her. This latter problem appeared to be due to a lessening of sex interest in his wife, in particular due to her weight level (76 kg.) and generally obese appearance as compared to when they were married. This weight problem appeared to be a psychological one as the wife found dieting 'impossible', and still complained to him about his previous heterosexual affair. Twelve months after treatment commenced, he presented for follow-up stating that he was quite well, but then broke down, crying, and admitted that he was very concerned about his present sexual attraction for the young boy mentioned earlier, although this was still fantasy without a behavioural component despite the availability of the contact on parole. The patient was a very strong, conscientious Christian and found it very difficult to reconcile his homosexual behaviour with Christianity. He was extremely good at organising local clubs and obtaining children's confidence, but he was therefore in a position also to abuse it, a temptation which made him feel extremely guilty. He derived a great personal benefit from being the centre of youthful attraction; his activities included 'counselling' club members about their 'love lives'. He remained depressed for the next two months and was put on Isocarboxazid, a mono-amine oxidase inhibitor. Shortly after starting the new drug he appeared to develop a hypertensive reaction to the MAOI and was characteristically admitted as a nocturnal emergency to a general hospital for a period of 48 hours' observation. No evidence of hypertension was found, however, and no actual diagnosis can be made. A month later, he was changed to Diazepam, 10 mg. q.d.s., and Optimax, tab. 1 b.d.

It was at this point that the patient admitted for the first time, in fact, that his homosexual tendency was always strongest for young boys of fourteen to sixteen and *this had always been the case.* However, as it made him very guilty he had dissimulated on initial presentation for treatment and suggested that his interest was for older men. He also reported having masturbated one of his teenaged sons, in the bathroom at home. This behaviour had occurred about twelve times since the end of treatment, at approximately monthly intervals, and the patient had not been able to report it to us until this date because of extreme guilt feelings. At this point he also reported interest in another boy whom he had masturbated in his car on the way home from a local club. His sexual interest in his wife was declining and he used a fantasy (young female) during intercourse with his wife. At this time he could no longer reach a climax with a male fantasy and even if his fantasy started off as a younger boy he could not maintain this to climax and would always finish with a female fantasy. A month later, he was given a booster session of Anticipatory Avoidance aversion therapy using boys between 14 and 16 years as the conditioned stimulus. Two weeks later (in response to a marked improvement in mood) he had lost twelve pounds in eight days on a crash slimming diet. At this point he was still reporting some suicidal feelings because of family problems. His SOM scores at the beginning of the booster sessions were boys 48, females 48 (a paper and pencil version of the SOM using stems *'Boys* are sexually to me').

After nine treatments the patient reported marked improvement and cessation of the homosexual problem (male SOM score = 37) and he decided that there was no need for him to attend. However, he returned a month later and asked to continue the booster treatment and he had a further nine sessions which we called the second booster. After the nine sessions his homosexual SOM scores for boys (31) and females (48) were both well within normal range and it was agreed that his treatment cease. He was again supported at follow-up. For eighteen months after presentation he was being followed up at approximately six-weekly intervals; he was originally maintained on Optimax, 1 tablet q.d.s., and Diazepam, 5 mg. q.d.s., and although he was mood labile he was, in general, able to control his mood swings so that they did not get out of hand. If circumstances became difficult, for example, his job or difficulties in the family, then his mood took violent dips; he would immediately rush for help (usually by phone) showing a strong identification with the female therapist and decided lack of control over his own attention-getting behaviour. These 'flurries' however were rarely of more than 48 hours' duration. In general supportive psychotherapy at short intervals controlled his mood and no alteration of medication was necessary. Between 'flurries' of mood swings he was able to restrain his attention-seeking urges to make homosexual pick-ups during a depressive swing which would then cause him many guilt problems. After twenty-two months the patient reported no homosexual problems. He was still having some heterosexual difficulties with his wife which were partly an interpersonal problem.

It appeared to us that he did not find his wife sexually attractive and there existed a definite animosity between them which was confirmed at interview by his wife. A month later the patient again suffered a dip in mood, and, on questioning, he revealed that he was having a torrid affair with a 'mature' fifteen-year-old girl from his youth club. The general pattern was as before, that he would form a verbal relationship with the girl, and begin to give her lifts home in his car. In addition, she would call on him at his house. Sex play to the stage of heavy petting soon took place, and he then described her defloration in the back of his car. He reported this event with virtually no remorse (they both immensely enjoyed intercourse, he being now fully potent because of her 'activity'), and with a certain air of grand relish which we construed as attention-seeking. We gave general advice along 'logical' lines as follows:

1 Your behaviour is deemed unacceptable by much of society, and your church in particular.
2 Because of your identification with church the behaviour makes you feel guilty.

Three alternatives are possible:

1 Continue the behaviour with unchanged attitudes and continue to feel guilty and depressed.
2 Devalue the church's rules and therefore reduce your own dissonance, hence reducing the symptoms.
3 Give up the behaviour, and reduce the symptoms.

This dilemma eloquently highlighted the irresolute aspects of his personality; he insisted on keeping the relationship with the girl, and also continued to feel guilty and to appeal to us to do something.

We continued to follow him up with general supportive psychotherapy, and two years after initial presentation he was admitted to a medical unit complaining of chest pain and breathlessness. An ECG report suggested that he had had a bout of paroxysmal supra-ventricular tachycardia. At that time he was smoking 40+ cigarettes per day, and on discharge we felt that he looked ill. Further ECGs were inconclusive, but the strong possibility remains that he had had a minor coronary artery occlusion. He was not on tricyclic anti-depressants at the time of his dysrhythmia. Since then he has visited his sister in America maintained on Diazepam only. He has no homosexual intent towards men or boys, and his heterosexual affair continues, although his guilt feelings are now somewhat reduced as his partner is also considering relationships with boys nearer her own age, which makes the patient feel less responsible.

Objective in-treatment data

1 Sexual interest latencies

The technique of taking Sexual Interest Latencies (SILs) was not developed until Case 1 had undergone aversion therapy, using adult males as the C.S. and therefore SILs for adult men were only obtained after the first 25 sessions of Anticipatory Avoidance (AA). These data are presented in Figure 14·3.

Sixteen slides were rated (0 to 10) *before* treatment and contained 8 slides rated 8 or more. After 25 sessions of aversion to men all slides except one had a latency under 15 seconds, thus producing a flat curve (top left) in which high-rated slides achieved low-interest latencies approximating to those of low-rated slides.

The pre-treatment SILs for boys (top right) show high latencies for high-valency slides and low SILs for low-valency slides in clear contrast to the first curve in Figure 14·3. The next three curves for boys, prior to sessions 2, 3 and 6, show a tendency to reduction in SILs while maintaining the obvious positive relationship between rating and latency in seconds. Clearly the pre-session 6 curve suggests that little progress had been made in relation to the more attractive slides; this point is born out both by the clinical data and the avoidance latencies in session 9 (see Figure 14·5).

After an interregnum, as stated, we administered a second booster treatment to boys and the remaining SILs, in relation to these sessions, are shown in the bottom third of Figure 14·3. These curves show a reduction of SILs between the pre-treatment period and the pre-session 7 period.

The relationships between the slide ratings and the slide latencies were correlated and found to be significant (r values between 0·658 and 0·8677; $p = <0·001$) thus supporting our earlier findings that a slide's latency is an indicant of its interest level (MacCulloch and Sambrooks, 1974).

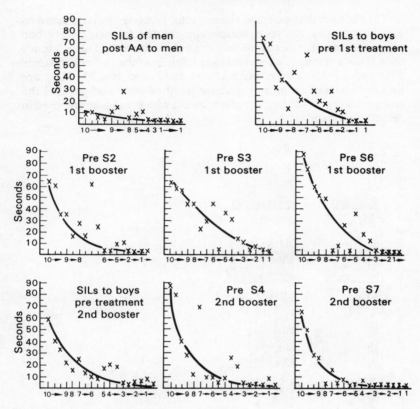

FIGURE 14·3   *Sexual interest latencies*
Ordinate = latency in seconds; *Abscissa* = rating of slide sexual
interest; *S* = sessions.

2   In-treatment avoidance latencies

In-treatment avoidance latencies were calculated as means as
follows: data were manipulated in relation to the slide used for
treatment. The sessions (S) per slide were S1-5 (on slide 12); S6-7
(on slide 11); S8-9 (on slide 8); S10-11 (on slide 4); S12 (on slide
13); S13-15 (on slide 5); S16-23 (on slide 13); S24-5 (on slide 14).
The latency of the first trial for each of S1 to 5 were added and
divided by 5, and the process was repeated to produce *mean*
latencies for trials 1 to n related to the slide used as the cs_1. These
data are presented in Figure 14·4 and show a tendency to 'S'-shaped
learning curves. Previous work (MacCulloch, Birtles and Feldman,

1971) showed that positive slopes, long latencies in later sessions and irregularity between temporally related latencies were bad prognosticants for outcome in AA aversion therapy. These latency data show a strong tendency to long latencies (above 4 seconds, see S12 and 13-25) and positive slopes (S12 and 16-25). They are therefore mixed from a prognostic point of view and parallel the stormy course of the first set of treatment which was administered in relation to men.

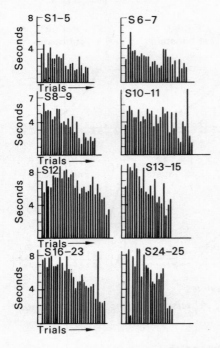

FIGURE 14·4   *Mean latencies by slides (Case 1)*

Figure 14·5 presents raw avoidance latency data on boys for sessions 1 and 2 (slide 12), S3-6 (slide19) and session 9 (slide 6) (the recording equipment being out of action for sessions 8 and 9). The latencies in relation to slide 12 show a clear tendency to decrement asymptotically to a time of 2 seconds. The cs_1 was then changed to slide 19 and session 3 and the first third of session 4 show the *expected* increase in latency related to the increased sexual valency of that slide. Therafter in sessions 5 and 6 the asymptotic learning curves develop. Slide 6 in session 9 shows resistance to learning and nearly half the trials show very long latencies (7 seconds).

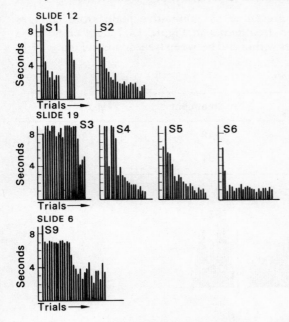

FIGURE 14·5   *Avoidance latencies (Case 1: boys; first booster)*

The SIL data (see Figure 14·3, pre-session 6, first booster) agree with these data, as did clinical interview. A second course of 8 aversion treatments to boys (second booster) was given and the data are presented in Figure 14·6. This shows smoother latency learning curves than the other two treatment courses. The last 5 sessions (slides 22 and 4) in particular show progressive smooth learning curves asymptotic to 1 second.

3 The sexual orientation method data

We were able to administer an automated version of the Sexual Orientation Method (SOM) by machine interface (Sambrooks and MacCulloch, 1973) before and after each of the first 25 treatment sessions. Table 14·2 presents data which show an overall fall in the male score of 38 points, and an overall increase in female score of 17 points. The SOM data were examined in two components:

1   The change in male and female scores *during* the course of treatment.

2   The change in these scores between treatments.

These data are presented as cumulative male score changes within and between treatments in Figure 14·7, and cumulative female score changes within and between treatments in Figure 14·8.

TABLE 14-2   *SOM scores*

	Pre-treatment	Post-treatment
Male score	48	10
Female score	31	48

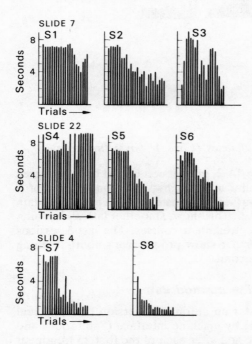

FIGURE 14·6   *Avoidance latencies (Case 1: boys; second booster)*

A striking feature of the raw data was their variability, there being marked score changes both in and out of treatment. The influence of treatment itself, and the between-treatment periods is well shown in Figures 14·7 and 14·8. Figure 14·7 shows that

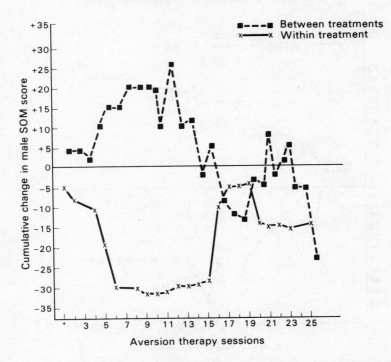

FIGURE 14·7 *Cumulative male SOM scores within treatments, and between treatments (Case 1)*

in-treatment cumulative male score changes are increasingly negative for the first 6 sessions. This means that the male SOM score was decreasing during the course of each of the 30-minute treatments; conversely the *between*-treatment male scores *increase* over the first 10 sessions. This second phenomenon could possibly be interpreted as extinction. However, from session 12 through to 25, the between-treatment cumulative changes scores fall, indicating that a significant attitude change is occurring *between* these treatment sessions. We would like to suggest that this might be interpreted as a response increment effect, or so called incubation (see Eysenck, 1968).

Returning to the in-treatment cumulative scores, after session 8 no further overall reduction takes place, but the scores *increase* in treatment. We are not fully able to interpret these findings at this point but if the two curves are considered together it appears that the second half of the *between*-treatment curve mirrors the

318   **Jean E. Sambrooks and Malcolm J. MacCulloch**

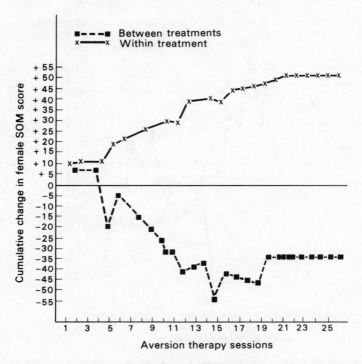

FIGURE 14·8   *Cumulative female SOM scores within treatments, and between treatments (Case 1)*

improvement of the first part of the *in*-treatment curve, and that the first part of the *between*-treatment curve anticipates the second half of the *within*-treatment curve. This last phenomenon could be explained as follows. When the patient first comes into treatment he is highly interested in the male slides and early sessions reduce his male scores; as treatment proceeds he succumbs less often at a behavioural level to homosexual temptations between treatments. Thus, at the start of the later sessions his SOM male score was depressed in value as a generalisation from his out of treatment improvement. Then in treatment he allows himself to examine slides for interest and realises that 'men' are more interesting than he had thought at the start of treatment. An alternative hypothesis might envisage a relearning effect due to repeated exposure of male slides with a reduced number of shock trials.

Figure 14·8 shows the cumulative female SOM changes within and between treatments. The former shows a steady increase in female scores which form a curve that becomes and remains horizontal at session 21. The latter curve shows an initially sustained between-treatment fall in female scores until session 11. At this point a between-treatment increase in female score occurs and then the initial trend is repeated until session 19 when a further rise occurs at which point the curve becomes horizontal because his female score is maximal at 48. There is a parallel in these female SOM data with the male data in that between-treatment female SOM decrement (or extinction) ceases after a significant number of sessions and the trend reverses to show a *between*-treatment improvement, perhaps explicable again in terms of incubation.

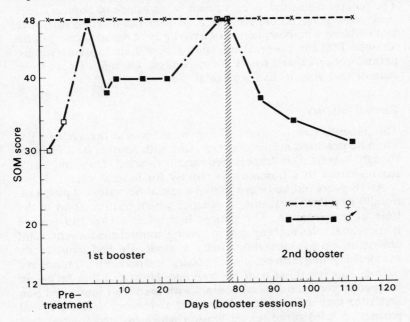

FIGURE 14·9   *SOM scores (Case 1: boys and women)*

Figure 14·9 shows the SOM data on 'boys' and 'women' in both booster sessions. (Pre- and post-measures were not continued as they are somewhat arduous for the patient.) Variability in the 'boys' score is apparent in the first booster but in the second booster session converts to a classical decremental curve (see Series Case I, Feldman and MacCulloch, 1971). We would infer here that it is likely that the 'boys' SOM in the second booster accurately reflects the *in vivo* situation.

This case can be regarded as an indicant of the value and interest of behavioural measures during treatment and also shows how, in such a complex case, many changes of treatment tactics are necessary by the therapists in order to make and maintain treatment progress.

We now present a second case which by contrast with the first case demonstrates that a diagnosis of 'homosexual behaviour' is *not* a unitary description of a clinical problem.

Case 2

The patient consulted us as a result of an attack of homosexually contracted gonorrhoea. He was a 36-year-old married man with two children who complained of irritability of mood because of his 'double' life; his venereal infection forced him to overcome his natural reticence and to ask for treatment. He said, 'I wish to be *normal* and able to live a normal life.'

Sexual history

The patient's first homosexual experience was at the age of 13½, when he practised mutual masturbation with another boy. He then thought about this experience and practised frequent auto-masturbation to a homosexual fantasy for several years.

At 18 years old he began to make casual homosexual pick-ups, usually in public lavatories, a practice which continued up to the time of presentation. The patient had taken active and passive homosexual roles and engaged in petting, mutual masturbation and anilinctus, on average about twice a week. He had consistently avoided any long term emotional 'affairs' and his age preference in a partner was for those near his own age. He stated that he would frequently come into social contact with men who interested him and after such an experience he would endeavour to find a casual partner to release the sexual tension which his first interest had created.

He first became interested in the opposite sex at about 14 and enjoyed petting and kissing with a small number of girls throughout his teens. His first experience of heterosexual intercourse was with his wife after his marriage in the late twenties. He reported that he enjoyed sexual intercourse, but he continued his homosexual pick-ups. His marriage was reasonably happy but he gradually became dissatisfied with the very passive general behavioural role which he had originally encouraged in his wife, and he began to wish that she would be more self-assertive. In addition, he disliked using a contraceptive sheath; his wife was reluctant to arrange alternative contraception, so that he found that he was increasingly disinclined to attempt intercourse because of the risk of an unwanted pregnancy. As this situation developed over a number of years it caused him increasingly to feel both irritated and sexually unsatisfied with his wife.

Family history

Both his parents were alive and his upbringing was unremarkable and 'happy'. However, he claimed that his mother was a very forceful, dominating character and that his father was content to let her make all the family decisions. He considered that this abnormality of parental roles may have influenced his relationship with his wife and contributed to his bisexual orientation and behaviour.

Personality

The patient was a tall, slender man, immaculately dressed, with a courtly manner, and at the initial interview he was very reserved and embarrassed in his manner; apart from stating his problem he was reluctant to discuss his home life or his sexual activities in any detail. He was successful in his career and in general was a sensitive but out-going person with social friends of both sexes. The main feature of his personality was his meticulousness. There was no evidence of lability of mood, attention-seeking or weak-willed personality traits (Schneider, 1959). He was assigned an '0' scale score of 0.

Pre-treatment assessment

This patient was repeatedly administered the automated form of the som before, during and after treatment. His pre-treatment scores were as follows:

Male = 48 (range 6-48 [max]) *Female* = 46 (range 6-48 [max])

On this prognosticant this patient, a 'secondary' homosexual, was predicted to do well with aversion therapy.

Personality assessment

The present patient was administered the Cattel 16 PF. His 'C' scale score was 4, the combined personality score was 4—0=4. On this measure the patient was predicted to have a better than evens chance of success. His pre-treatment EPI scores (Eysenck and Eysenck, 1964) were N,8; E,8; L,2.

Summary

We assessed this patient as a bisexual having a self-insecure personality abnormality with a 23-year history of homosexual behaviour of wide repertoire. As his pre-treatment female SOM was 46 and the combined personality scale score was 4 we therefore predicted, from reference to Feldman and MacCulloch (1971, p. 154), that the patient would be successful in aversion therapy as he was designated a secondary homosexual with a good personality.

Treatment method and in-treatment assessment

The patient was given ten sessions of anticipatory avoidance aversion therapy over ten weeks using 3 male and 2 female slides as shown in Table 14·3.

TABLE 14·3   *Sequence of stimuli for anticipatory avoidance aversion therapy*

Session no.	No. of trials	Male slide rating	Female slide rating	Hours treatment
1	33			
2	26			
3	19	*Slide no. 1 rated 3		2·5
4	20			
5	18		Slide no. 47 rated 10	
6	17			
7	21	Slide no. 2		
8	17	rated 6		2·0
9	15	Slide no. 3	Slide no. 48	
10	28	rated 7	rated 8	0·5
Total	214			

* Slide numbers refer to our stimuli bank.

Results

Clinical
The patient attended punctiliously for all his assessment and

treatment sessions and he was frankly sceptical about the potency of the treatment. After three sessions of aversion he said, 'I can see now how it is possible for this to work.' In the intervals of time prior to, and after, treatment we began to chat to him as a pair. He began to find that he could talk more freely and he began to pay the female therapist compliments. We talked to him about his wife and their relationship and it appeared that he felt himself to be much more competent and able than his wife (he seemed to be very able in his job) and he related how he had for years made out lists for the family shopping. It had been his 'job' to buy in the meat and green groceries. He said, 'I can balance money — my wife can't do it.'

If it had occurred that his wife had done the shopping and she had over spent or 'made an error', he would become touchy and irritable, whilst retaining an icily polite manner. This unbalanced relationship spilled over into their sexual relationship. He tended to be withdrawn and to avoid approaches to sexual intercourse, particularly because of their contraceptive difficulties. He had developed a life style by which it was possible completely to conceal his homosexual activities from his wife. He was remote and guarded. As sessions proceeded we suggested that sexual activity was a balance in terms of outlets and that although suppression of the unwanted (homosexual) approach behaviour was important and difficult, the fostering of heterosexual approach was equally crucial and probably more difficult.

We suggested that he begin to assess women in the street, and at work, and assign them scores for interest to him, that is, the judgment component of the exercise was stressed as in order to make a judgment one has to 'look at', and then consider the stimulus object. He reported that he was able to do this and did so with increasing interest as the sessions went by. At the same time we began to encourage him to think about the meaning of his marital relationship. One day he arrived and said, 'I think I've been too dominating with my wife, I've stopped her developing herself.' We discussed the idea of behaviour shaping which he readily grasped. During the Christmas recess he successfully shaped his wife to take a more assertive approach with the Christmas arrangements, and in particular with the handling of a children's party about which she was frankly phobic. Meanwhile, aversion sessions and in-treatment SOM and SIL assessments were proceeding. After ten sessions he announced that he was 'cured'; we questioned him closely and elicited that he had made no homosexual approach behaviour for four weeks, and more importantly, he had had *no* homosexual fantasy for the same period. He found that it was quite easy to resist looking at, and thinking about, men in a sexual connotation and even if such thoughts occurred he was able to terminate them immediately without regret.

We reluctantly stopped treatment after ten sessions as the patient's place of work was being difficult and followed him up 2, 6 and 8 weeks after treatment with a view to further sessions if necessary. However, his progress remained sure and steady and he described how he was able to pass his 'favourite' pick-up toilet, which was situated on a lonely country road, with ease. Formerly, if he saw a car stopped at this convenience he would be compelled to stop and visit the urinal to see who was there, and if they were interesting to indulge in homosexual activity. His emotional relationship with his wife continued to improve, he observed and understood her behaviour more readily and he was less irritable with her. Sexual intercourse to orgasm, which was satisfactory for both of them, continued once or twice per week. Six months after treatment he was re-assessed, still having no sexual problems, and his SOM score was: male = 30; female = 47. His wife was pregnant and he was very proud of this fact.

Objective in-treatment data

1 Sexual interest latencies

The patient was administered SILs and the relationship between slide rating and slide latency is shown in Figure 14·10.

The initial pre-treatment correlation between these parameters was significant ($r = 0·473$ $p<0·01$). However, for the two following SILs the slides were not re-rated and therefore the correlations between latencies and ratings were non-significant as treatment progressed. This is not an unexpected event as it would be predicted that, with successful treatment, slides and latencies should no longer correlate unless a re-rating procedure is followed. However, slides were re-rated pre S10 and produced a flat line, as expected, as all the slides were now of reduced interest.

We would also suggest that this subject found difficulty in assigning values of sexual interest to slides and also possibly allowed himself less 'looking at' time in relation to sexually arousing slides, because of the therapist's presence in the laboratory.

The contrast in SIL values between Cases 1 and 2 is of interest because we were repeatedly and forcibly reminded of the tendency of Case 1 to fantasise sexual material and actually to view male and female pin-ups.

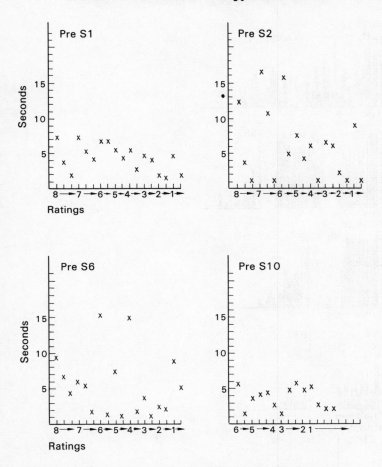

FIGURE 14·10   *Sexual interest latencies (Case 2: males)*

2 *Avoidance latencies*

Figure 14·11 presents the in-treatment avoidance latencies session by session. Slide 12 was used over the first five sessions where latencies show a gradual decrease asymptotic to 2-3 seconds.

There are a number of mixed length latencies. In session 6 at the change to slide 28 more latencies are long, showing that the patient has correctly identified the cs_1 hierarchy (that is, slide 28 was more interesting than slide 12) and also that he was following the instruction 'leave the slide on so long as it is sexually interesting to

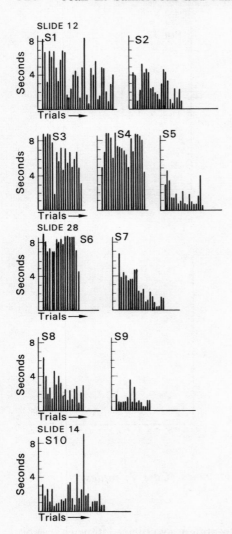

FIGURE 14·11   *Avoidance latencies by session (Case 2)*

you.' By session 9 the latencies in relation to slide 28 were mainly less than 2 seconds. Slide 14 (session 10) only provoked a mild increase in latencies. These ten sets of in-treatment latencies are classically of the success type (MacCulloch, 1969; Feldman and MacCulloch, 1971; MacCulloch, Birtles and Feldman, 1971).

3   SOM scores

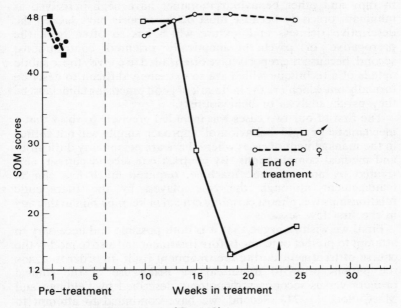

FIGURE 14·12   *SOM scores (Case 2)*

Figure 14·12 shows the male and female SOM scores for the three periods; pre-, in-, and post-treatment. The abscissa scale relates to real time in weeks. The graph shows a pre/post male score drop of 34 points from 48 down to 14. At two months follow-up his male score was 18 and at a six months follow-up was still at 30 points. His in-treatment female SOM score change was +2 from 46 to 48 and at two months follow-up was 47. At latest follow-up it remained at 47 points.

Discussion and conclusions

Franks and Wilson (1973) have pointed out that aversion therapy has played a central role in the development of behaviour therapy during the last decade. It has, however, received much criticism from both lay and professional groups, often on the grounds that it forces people to do things against their will (aversion therapists are people who seek to label people as abnormal and then 'cure' them!), or that it is distasteful and implies psychological abnormality on the part of the therapists. It is necessary and proper to attempt to redress the balance of attitudes to aversion therapy: first, aversion therapy and other behaviour therapies have been perceived as inhuman, precisely because most of the reports have lacked the descriptive richness and texture which has so often been the prerogative of psychotherapeutically oriented contributions; second, because the reports have often failed to convey those subtle details of a technique which are so extremely difficult to describe formally but which are the hallmark of good practising clinicians, be they psychoanalysts or behaviourists.

The first of our two cases was included precisely to show that a mechanistic or rigid 'behavioural' approach simply will not suffice in the management of cases where there are personality difficulties and medical complications. By contrast our second patient, also treated by an automatic machine, required much less clinical management although the role played by the therapeutic relationships was almost certainly crucial in keeping him in therapy in the first few sessions.

First, we wish to argue that it is both possible and necessary to attempt to predict outcome before treatment and also to modify the course of treatment during the treatment itself. In order to assess the patient prior to treatment we make use of the clinical primary-versus-secondary dichotomy described by Feldman and MacCulloch (1971). Second, we have continued to attempt to assess personality, realising that there are grave pitfalls at the clinical level, amply demonstrated by the first case and contrasted by the second case. Our in-treatment SOM data is in line with previously published work, however the facility for automatic presentation and scoring leads to the feasibility of repetitive testing which has demonstrated two interesting features in Case 1: (a) great score variability (previously suspected by MacCulloch, 1969, on the grounds of gross clinically detected mood swings), and (b) the change over time of the direction of score changes both within and between treatments. These changes merit further attention; it may be that the between-treatment male SOM score decrements in later sessions is evidence of response increment or incubation (Eysenck, 1968). If this is so we have demonstrated a biological function at a clinical level which is of crucial importance to both theorists and clinicians. The in-treatment increase of male SOM score late in treatment in Case 1 might reflect reactive inhibition; if this is so then the SOM or its equivalent might be seen as an important instrument to guide therapists in the spacing of their treatment sessions.

Sexual Interest Latencies seem to us to merit general consideration because they may be used in any kind of therapy which changes interest in subjects or objects which can be visually presented in a valid way. We would include all sexual objects (such as fetishes), also alcohol, food and so on. Further work may, in future, tell us about how different subjects perceive and evaluate visually presented materials. There would still appear to be interest in taking in-treatment latencies by using the AA technique, and we are currently evaluating computer techniques of predicting outcome and the form of treatment early on in therapy based on latencies taken in the first six sessions.

Clinical training and experience are not yet supplanted by measurements in this field. However, the inconsistencies in the avoidance latency data, the SILS and the SOM data which appeared early on in the treatment of the first case are, in retrospect, salutary because they were noted prior to that point in time at which we realised the full implications of this patient's personality disorder. We feel that measurable dependent variables which will help the clinician to diagnose, prognose and treat are of the greatest importance although their existence should never be taken to imply that a worker may ignore the interpersonal aspects of his or her work.

Conclusions

H. J. Eysenck

After reading through these very divergent fourteen accounts, one may rightly ask if they enable one to come to any general conclusions — other than that behaviour therapy makes use of many different methods, and is applied to a great many different behavioural problems. It may be possible to derive some general conclusions, although of course these are predicated to some extent on the hypothesis that the cases here considered are not too dissimilar from those which behaviour therapists routinely handle. There is good reason to believe that such an hypothesis is acceptable; behaviour therapists will themselves be able to judge from their own experience whether this is correct or not. Given, then, that these cases are not entirely unusual or biased, we may use them to discuss what to many psychologists has become an important target for criticism, namely the medical model of mental disorder.

When we observe people behaving in a manner which is apparently 'abnormal', self-destructive, or maladjusted, we have two very obvious and well-established ways of regarding their behaviour. The first is the *medical model*; according to this such people are ill. They suffer from some form of disease, and the observed behaviour is simply a symptom (or set of symptoms) of this disease. Treatment would consist of curing the underlying illness; this would make the symptoms disappear automatically. Trying to treat the symptoms would be useless — we do not try to treat a fever directly, but attack the cause of the fever. The acceptance of Freud's teaching by psychiatrists owes much to his clever use of the medical analogy — the patient's complaints are but symptoms, the underlying disease is the 'complex' which must be eradicated by 'interpretive' psychotherapy before the symptoms can disappear for good. 'Symptomatic' treatment, on this account, is useless; relapses and symptom substitutions will show the strength of the surviving 'complex'.

A good example of such a medical model, properly applied, is GPI (general paralysis of the insane), a disorder which used to be thought of as a functional psychosis produced by smoking, drinking, whoring and other behavioural excesses; no doubt, had personality questionnaires existed at the time, it would have been found highly correlated with extraversion! In actual fact, of course, the disease is a consequence of syphylitic infection; the behavioural correlates (smoking, drinking, whoring — and extraversion, which is causally linked with all these behaviours) are associated with this infection simply because people who frequent whores are more likely to contract syphylis than are non-smoking, non-drinking introverts who sit at home and read books on psychology. Porphyria, another physical disease which is frequently mistaken for a form of hysterical complaint, is another case in point; you cannot cure the disease by treating the symptom — in fact, barbiturate treatment, which might be appropriate for hysterical symptoms, is severely contra-indicated for porphyria!

But for the great majority of so-called 'mental diseases', in particular the functional psychoses (schizophrenia and manic-depressive illness) and the neuroses, no such simple 'cause' has been found, in spite of the great advances which biological psychiatry has made in recent years (Mendels, 1973). There are clear-cut genetic determinants, suggesting the importance of biological factors (Eysenck, 1973), but no single 'causes' such as would be presented by invading viruses or microbes. Most psychiatrists would be prepared for the possibility of such a single 'cause' being discovered in the field of the psychoses (although even there it would have to interact very much with environmental 'causes' without which it would be unlikely to act), but in the field of the neuroses even the possibility of finding such a 'cause' would be disputed by most experts. Freud's attempt to substitute a psychological 'cause' (the Oedipus complex) for a physical one, in order to preserve the medical model, is now seen to have failed; the experimental evidence is strongly against his theory (Eysenck and Wilson, 1973), and the application of his methods to neurotic and psychotic disorders has failed to show any advance over the rate of spontaneous remission observed when no psychiatric treatment of any kind is adminstered (Rachman, 1971).

In distinct contrast to the medical model we have the *behavioural model,* which forms the basis of behaviour therapy (Eysenck and Rachman, 1965). This model postulates very simply that all behaviour is *learned,* and that 'abnormal' behaviour is learned according to the same laws as 'normal' behaviour. The principles of learning and conditioning apply equally to both, enabling us to understand the genesis of both normal and abnormal behaviour. Thus the 'symptoms' the patient complains of are simply items of behaviour which the patient has learned; there is no underlying 'cause' or 'complex' which produces and sustains the 'symptoms', and makes them reappear once they have been eliminated by 'purely symptomatic' treatment. It also follows from this way of looking at the problem that behaviours, once learned, can also be unlearned, or 'extinguished', as the Pavlovian would say. Similarly, missing behaviours, that is, behaviours which have not been learned although for 'normal' behaviour they should have been learned (for example, socialized forms of conduct), can be conditioned once the lack becomes apparent. Human behaviour is plastic, although not infinitely so, and the psychologist can use his scientific skill and knowledge to the best advantage by changing behaviour for the better through learning and unlearning, conditioning and extinguishing forms of behaviour which are adjusted or maladjusted. Patients are not ill; psychologists often prefer the term 'clients' because of the medical overtones of the term 'patients', and like to think of maladapted conduct rather than of mental illness.

The reader may like to go through the case histories here presented and try to think, in each case, about the implications of the events recorded for the great debate between the adherents of the 'medical' and the 'behavioural' models. It seems likely that he will receive a powerful impression of the applicability of the behavioural model, and the relative uselessness of the medical model. If it is true that we are all neurotic, as some psychoanalytic writers have suggested, then even this makes sense in terms of the behavioural model; we all have failed to learn some useful forms of conduct, and have been conditioned into some maladapted forms of behaviour. But to say that we are *ill*, in a medical sense, clearly does not fit the bill. Of course the very term 'illness' is poorly defined in medical teaching; usually it is taken for granted. This makes discussion very difficult; where a term is ill-defined it is not easy to say whether it does or does not apply to a particular phenomenon. Certainly the usual meaning of the word is fairly clear to most readers, and it would be stretching this meaning beyond what is reasonable to say that the types of conduct here discussed constitute 'diseases' requiring medical treatment.

If this argument be correct, then one contention which has hindered the development of behaviour therapy for many years, and is still hindering it in countries such as Germany and France, immediately falls to the ground — the contention, namely, that all treatment of neurotic and other psychiatric patients is by definition medical, and should therefore only be undertaken by medically qualified physicians. A training in medicine qualifies the successful candidate to practise what he has learned — physical medicine; it does not qualify him to practise the application of psychological principles which have constituted no part of his training. Much the same is true of the psychiatrist; psychology does not constitute a notable part of his training (although it might be argued that it should), and he could certainly not claim any expertise in conditioning and learning theory, or its application. This suggests that clinical psychologists, trained in behaviour therapy, should be free to develop and practise the various methods involved in this discipline, without the need of having a medical degree in addition to their psychological training.

This is certainly the situation towards which we are travelling in Great Britain, where the Royal College of Psychiatry has recognized the value of behaviour therapy, and where specialist medical committees set up by the Department of Health and Social Security have recommended recognition of their independent professional status in the National Health Service. In America, too, the American Psychiatric Association has set up a Task Force on Behavior Therapy which reported favourably, stating that the principles 'developed largely from experimental psychology — have reached a stage of development where they now unquestioningly have much to offer informed clinicians in the service of modern clinical and social psychiatry'. Further, they suggest that 'departments of psychology and psychiatry have an opportunity to combine their individual talents for the benefit of the trainee in behavior therapy'. Such a combination of expertise and social function, in the service of the patient, is indeed the pattern which is developing more and more, in place of the sterile hostility and mutual backbiting which characterized the American development of clinical psychology, as a feared opponent and hated rival of orthodox medical psychiatry. This outright opposition has been largely avoided in Britian, and omens are favourable for the most friendly co-operation between psychology and psychiatry.

Perhaps the reader may wonder just where the general argument outlined above leaves a place for the psychiatrist. The answer is that many of the disorders which traditionally fall under the heading of psychiatry are purely medical, and leave little room for psychological intervention; epilepsy, degenerative geriatric disorders, and many other examples might be cited here. Treatment of functional psychoses is at the moment almost entirely medical, that is, involves the use of drugs which the psychologist would not be trained to prescribe, and which he would be legally unable to prescribe. Even in the case of the neurotic patient a medical examination is often necessary to rule out physical complications and causes; the example of porphyria has already been mentioned. There is a vast field where the psychologist would be completely out of his depth, and the boundary between this and his own field of expertise is not as clearly drawn as might be desired. Clearly, under the circumstances friendly co-operation on a basis of independent and equal professional status is the best policy for both sides — and for the patient to whose better health and adjustment both sides wish to contribute. The patient is not interested in internal debates of this kind; he wishes to get better, and if behaviour therapy can help him in this quest, then clearly it is up to psychiatry and psychology jointly to provide the necessary conditions which will make such help readily available to the majority of patients or clients. Far too little is being done at the moment to implement such a programme; there are fewer than 600 clinical psychologists in Britain, many of whom have had no training in behaviour therapy, and the number of psychiatrists properly trained in these procedures can hardly go into three digits. There is an urgent need for more and better behaviour therapists to be trained, and if this book can help, even in the smallest way, in speeding up this training, then the labour in putting it together will have been well rewarded.

Bibliographical Index

The figures in square brackets refer to the page numbers of this book.

ABEL, G.G, LEVIS, D.J., and CLANCY, J. (1970), 'Aversion therapy applied to taped sequences of deviant behavior in exhibitionism and other sexual deviations: a preliminary report', *J. Behav. Ther. & Exp. Psychiat., 1*, pp. 59-60. [46]

ALLEN, K.E., HART, B.M., BUELL, J.S., HARRIS, F.R., and WOLF, M.M. (1964), 'Effects of social reinforcement on isolate behavior of a nursery school child', *Child Dev., 35*, pp. 511-18. [7]

ARGYLE, M. (1967), *The Psychology of Interpersonal Behaviour*, Harmondsworth, Penguin. [123]

AVERILL, J.R. (1968), 'Grief: its nature and significance', *Psychol. Bull., 70*, pp. 721-48. [228-9]

AYLLON, T., and AZRIN, N.H. (1965), 'The measurement and reinforcement of behavior of psychotics', *J. Exp. Analysis Behav., 8*, pp. 357-83 [7]

AYLLON, T., and AZRIN, N.H. (1968), *The Token Economy: A Motivational System for Therapy and Rehabilitation*, New York, Appleton-Century-Crofts. [62, 64]

AYLLON, T., and HAUGHTON, E. (1964), 'Modification of symptomatic verbal behavior of mental patients', *Behav. Res. & Ther., 2*, pp. 87-97. [61]

AYLLON, T., and SKUBAN, W. (1973), 'Accountability in psychotherapy: a test case', *J. Behav. Ther. & Exp. Psychiat., 4*, pp. 19-30. [73]

AZRIN, N.H. (1972), personal communication. [75]

AZRIN, N.H., and HOLZ, W.C. (1966), 'Punishment' in W.K. Honig (ed.), *Operant Behavior*, New York, Appleton-Century-Crofts. [45]

BAER, D.M., WOLF, M.W., and RISLEY, T.R. (1968), 'Some current dimensions of applied behavioral analysis', *J. Appl. Behav. Anal., 1*, pp.91-7 [73, 276]

BANDURA, A. (1961), 'Psychotherapy as a learning process', *Psychol. Bull., 58*, pp. 143-59. [123]

BANDURA, A. (1969), *Principles of Behavior Modification*, New York, Holt, Rinehart & Winston. [89, 269]

BANDURA, A. (1971), 'Vicarious and self-reinforcement processes' in R.

Glaser (ed.), *The Nature of Reinforcement,* New York, Academic Press. [269]

BANNISTER, D. (1965), 'The rationale and clinical relevance of repertory grid technique', *Br. J. Psychiat., 111,* pp. 977-82. [124]

BANNISTER, D., and MAIR, J.M.M. (1968), *The Evaluation of Personal Constructs,* London and New York, Academic Press. [124, 129]

BARKER, J.C., THORPE, J.G., BLAKEMORE, C.B., LAVIN, N.I., and CONWAY, C.G. (1961), 'Behaviour therapy in a case of transvestism', *Lancet, 1,* p. 510. [45]

BARLOW, D.H. (1973), 'Increasing heterosexual responsiveness in the treatment of sexual deviation: a review of the clinical and experimental evidence', *Behav. Ther., 4,* pp. 655-71. [44]

BEECH, H.R. (1969), *Changing Man's Behaviour,* Harmondsworth, Penguin. [124]

BERGIN, A.E. (1966), 'Some implications of psychotherapy research for therapeutic practice' in G.E. Stollak, B.G. Guerney and M. Rothberg (eds), *Psychotherapy Research: Selected Readings,* Chicago, Rand-McNally. [1, 2]

BERGLER, E. (1947), 'Frigidity in the female: misconceptions and facts', *Marr. Hyg., 1,* pp. 16-21. [237]

BERGLER, E. (1951), *Neurotic-Counterfeit Sex,* New York, Grune & Stratton. [237]

BEVAN, J.R. (1960), 'Learning theory applied to the treatment of a patient with obsessional ruminations' in H.J. Eysenck (ed.), *Behaviour Therapy and the Neuroses,* Oxford, Pergamon, pp. 165-9. [175]

BIRTLES, C.J., SAMBROOKS, J., MacCULLOCH, M.J., and HOLLAND, P. (1971), 'An inexpensive computer assisted psychometric system', *Med. & Biol. Eng., 10,* pp. 145-52. [305]

BLAKEMORE, C.B., THORPE, J.G., BARKER, J.C. CONWAY, C.G., and LAVIN, N.I. (1963b), 'Follow-up note to: The application of faradic aversion transvestism', *Behav. Res. & Ther., 1,* pp. 29-34. [45]

BLAKEMORE, C.B., THORPE, J.G., BARKER, J.C., CONWAY, C.G., and LAVIN, N.I. (1963b), 'Follow-up note to: The application of faradic aversion conditioning in a case of transvestism', *Behav. Res. & Ther., 1,* p. 191. [45]

BOND, I.K., and HUTCHISON, H.C. (1964), 'Application of reciprocal inhibition therapy to exhibitionism' in H.J. Eysenck (ed.), *Experiments in Behaviour Therapy,* Oxford, Pergamon. [44, 93]

BOWLBY, J. (1961), 'Processes of mourning', *Int. J. Psychoanal., 42,* pp. 317-40. [228]

BOWLBY, J. (1963), 'Pathological mourning and childhood mourning', *J. Am. Psychoanal. Ass., 11,* pp. 500-41. [228]

BROADHURST, P.L. (1973), 'Animal studies bearing on abnormal behaviour' in H.J. Eysenck (ed.), *Handbook of Abnormal Psychology,* 2nd ed., London, Pitman, pp. 721-54. [177]

BURGESS, E.P. (1968), 'The modification of depressive behavior' in I.R. Rubin and C. Franks (eds), *Advances in Behavior Therapy,* New York, Academic Press. [229]

CARR, A.T. (1970), 'A psychophysiological study of ritual behaviour and decision processes in compulsive neurosis', unpublished Ph.D thesis, University of Birmingham. [175]

CASE, H.W. (1960), 'Therapeutic methods in stuttering and speech blocking' in H.J. Eysenck (ed.), *Behaviour Therapy and the Neuroses*, Oxford, Pergamon, pp. 207-20. [177]

CAUTELA, J.R. (1967), 'Covert sensitization', *Psychol. Rep.*, *20*, pp. 459-68. [53, 282, 283]

CAUTELA, J.R. (1970a), 'Covert reinforcement', *Behav. Ther.*, *1*, pp. 33-50. [205]

CAUTELA, J.R. (1970b), 'Covert negative reinforcement', *J. Behav. Ther. & Exp. Psychiat.*, *1*, pp. 273-8. [205]

CAUTELA, J.R. (1971), 'Covert extinction', *Behav. Ther.*, *2*, pp. 192-200. [205]

CAUTELA, J.R., and WISOCKI, P.A. (1969), 'The use of male and female therapists in the treatment of homosexual behavior' in I.R. Rubin and C. Franks (eds), *Advances in Behavior Therapy, 1968*, New York, Academic Press, pp. 165-74. [45]

CAUTELA, J.R., and WISOCKI, P.A. (1971), 'Covert sensitization for the treatment of sexual deviations', *Psychol. Rec.*, *21*, pp. 37-48. [45]

CHURCH, R.M. (1963), 'The varied effects of punishment on behavior', *Psychol. Rev.*, *70*, pp. 369-402. [45]

CLARK, D.F. (1963a), 'Fetishism treated by negative conditioning', *Br. J. Psychiat.*, *109*, pp. 404-7. [45]

CLARK, D.F. 1963b), 'Treatment of fetishism by negative conditioning – a further note', *Br. J. Psychiat.*, *109*, pp. 695-7. [45]

CLARK, D.F. (1965), 'A note on avoidance conditioning techniques in sexual disorder', *Behav. Res. & Ther.*, *3*, pp. 203-6. [46]

CLARK, D.F. (1966), 'Behaviour therapy of Gilles de la Tourette's syndrome', *Br. J. Psychiat.*, *112*, pp. 771-8. [177]

COHEN, M., LIEBSON, I.A., FAILLACE, L.A., and SPEERS, W. (1971), 'Alcoholism: controlled drinking and incentives for abstinence', *Psychol. Rep.*, *28*, pp. 575-80. [282]

COMFORT, A. (1972), *The Joy of Sex*, New York, Crown. [260]

COOPER, A.J. (1963), 'A case of fetishism and impotence treated by behaviour therapy', *Br. J. Psychiat.*, *109*, pp. 649-52. [45]

DAVIES, D.L. (1962), 'Normal drinking in recovered alcohol addicts', *Q. Stud. Alcohol*, *23*, pp. 94-104. [282]

DiLORETO, A. (1971), *Comparative Psychotherapy*, New York, Aldine-Atherton. [8, 9]

DUNLAP, K. (1932), *Habits, their Making and Unmaking*, New York, Liveright. [177, 182]

EDGINGTON, E.S. (1967), 'Statistical inference from N=1 experiments', *J. Psychol.*, *65*, pp. 195-9. [4]

EDWARDS, N.B. (1972), 'Case conference: asssertive training in a case of homosexual pedophilia', *J. Behav. Ther. & Exp. Psychiat.*, *3*, pp. 55-63. [45, 50, 58]

EVANS, D.R. (1968), 'Masturbatory fantasy and sexual deviation', *Behav.*

Res. & Ther., 6, pp. 17-19. [85]

EYSENCK, H.J. (ed.) (1960), *Behaviour Therapy and the Neuroses,* Oxford, Pergamon. [45]

EYSENCK, H.J. (ed.) (1964), *Experiments in Behaviour Therapy,* Oxford, Pergamon.

EYSENCK, H.J. (1965), *Fact and Fiction in Psychology,* London, Penguin. [7]

EYSENCK, H.J. (1968), 'A theory of the incubation of anxiety/fear responses', *Behav. Res. & Ther., 6,* pp. 309-21. [12, 101, 317, 328]

EYSENCK, H.J. (ed.) (1973), *Handbook of Abnormal Psychology,* 2nd ed., London, Pitman. [332]

EYSENCK, H.J., and BEECH, R. (1971), 'Counterconditioning and related methods' in A.E. Bergin and S.L. Garfield (eds), *Handbook of Psychotherapy and Behavior Change,* New York, Wiley. [270]

EYSENCK, H.J., and EYSENCK, S.B.G. (1964), *Manual of the Eysenck Personality Inventory,* London, University of London Press. [322]

EYSENCK, H.J., and RACHMAN, S. (1965), *The Causes and Cures of Neurosis,* London, Routledge & Kegan Paul. [12, 332]

EYSENCK, H.J., and WILSON, G.D. (1973), *The Experimental Study of Freudian Theories,* London, Methuen. [8, 12, 332]

FELDMAN, J.P., and MacCULLOCH, M.J. (1964), 'A systematic approach to the treatment of homosexuality by conditioned aversion: preliminary report', *Am. J. Psychiat., 121,* 2, pp. 167-71. [305]

FELDMAN, M.P., and MacCULLOCH, M.J. (1965), 'The application of anticipatory avoidance learning to the treatment of homosexuality: I, Theory, technique, and preliminary results', *Behav. Res. & Ther., 2,* pp. 165-83. [46]

FELDMAN, M.P., and MacCULLOCH, M.J. (1971), *Homosexual Behaviour: Theory and Assessment,* Oxford, Pergamon. [46, 303, 304, 305, 319, 322, 326, 328]

FELDMAN, M.P., MacCULLOCH, M.J., MELLOR, V., and PINSCHOF, J.M. (1966), 'The application of anticipatory avoidance learning to the treatment of homosexuality: III, The sexual orientation method', *Behav. Res. & Ther., 4,* pp. 289-99. [303]

FENICHEL, O. (1945), *Psychoanalytic Theory of the Neurosis,* New York, Norton. [185]

FERSTER, C.B. (1972), 'An experimental analysis of clinical phenomena' in S.W. Bijou and E. Ribes-Inesta (eds), *Behaviour Modification: Issues and Extensions,* London, Academic Press. [115]

FERSTER, C.B., and SKINNER, B.F. (1957), *Schedules of Reinforcement,* New York, Appleton-Century-Crofts. [73]

FOA, U.G., and FOA, E.B. (1973), *Societal Structures of the Mind,* Springfield, Illinois, Thomas. [50]

FOOKES, B.H. (1968), 'Some experiences in the use of aversion therapy in male homosexuality, exhibitionism, fetishism-transvestism', *Br. J. Psychiat., 115,* pp. 339-41. [45]

FRANKS, C.M., and WILSON, T.G. (1973), *Annual Review of Behavior Therapy: Theory and Practice,* New York, Brunner, Mazel. [327]

FREUD, S. (1917), 'Mourning and melancholia', *S.E.,* vol. 14 [228]

FREUD, S. (1938), *Basic Writings*, New York, Modern Library. [61]

FREUND, K. (1960), 'Some problems in the treatment of homosexuality' in H.J. Eysenck (ed.), *Behaviour Therapy and the Neuroses*, Oxford, Pergamon, pp. 312-26. [45]

FUCHS, S.S. (1960), 'Replication report: an attempt to obtain inhibition with reinforcement', *J. Exp. Psychol., 59*, pp. 343-4. [182]

GAUPP, L.A., STERN, R.M., and RATLIFF, R.G. (1971), 'The use of aversion-relief procedures in the treatment of a case of voyeurism', *Behav. Ther., 2*, pp. 585-8. [46]

GLEITMAN, H., NACHMIAS, J., and NEISSER, U. (1954), 'The S-R reinforcement theory of extinction', *Psychol. Rev., 61*, pp. 23-33. [177]

GLYNN, J.D. and HARPER, P. (1961), 'Behaviour therapy in a case of transvestism', *Lancet, 1*, pp. 619-20. [45]

GOLDIAMOND, I. (1965), 'Self-control procedures in personal behavior problems,' *Psychol. Rep., 17*, pp. 851-68. [223]

GOLDSTEIN, A., SERBER, M., and PIAGET, G. (1970), 'Induced anger as a reciprocal inhibitor of fear', *J. Behav. Ther. & Exp. Psychiat., 1*, pp. 67-71. [196]

GOTTMAN, J.M. (1973), 'N-of-one and N-of-two research in psychotherapy', *Psychol. Bull., 80*, pp. 93-105. [2, 4, 40]

GRAY, J.A. (1971), *The Psychology of Fear and Stress*, London, Weidenfeld & Nicolson. [100]

GRAY, J.J. (1970), 'Case conference: behavior therapy in a patient with homosexual fantasies and heterosexual anxiety', *J. Behav. Ther. & Exp. Psychiat., 1*, pp. 225-32. [45]

GRINGS, W.W., and LOCKHART, R.A. (1966), 'Galvanic skin response during avoidance learning', *Psychophysiology, 3*, pp. 29-34. [100]

GUTHEIL, E.A. (1959), 'Reactive depressions' in S. Arieti (ed.), *American Handbook of Psychiatry*, New York, Basic Books. [228]

HALEY, J. (1963), *Strategies of Psychotherapy*, New York, Grune & Stratton. [269]

HALLAM, R.S., and RACHMAN, S. (1972), 'Some effects of aversion therapy on patients with sexual disorders', *Behav. Res. & Ther., 10*, pp. 171-180. [46]

HASTINGS, D.W. (1963), *Impotence and Frigidity*, Boston, Little, Brown. [238]

HODGSON, R., and RACHMAN, S. (1970), 'An experimental investigation of the implosion technique', *Behav. Res. & Ther., 8*, pp. 21-7. [20]

HODGSON, R., RACHMAN, S., and MARKS, I.M. (1972), 'The treatment of chronic obsessive-compulsive neurosis: follow-up and further findings', *Behav. Res. & Ther., 10*, pp. 181-9. [18, 39, 203]

HOLTZMAN, W.H. (1963), 'Statistical models for the study of change in the single case' in C.V. Harris (ed.), *Problems Measuring Change*, Madison, University of Wisconsin Press. [4]

HOYER, W.J. (1973), 'Application of operant techniques to the modification of elderly behavior', *Gerontologist, 13*, pp. 18-22. [183]

HUNTER-BROWN, M. and LIGHTHILL, J.A. (1968), 'Selective anterior cingulotomy: a psychosurgical evaluation', *J. Neurosurg., 29*, p. 513. [203]

JACOBSON, E. (1938), *Progressive Relaxation,* University of Chicago Press. [282]

JENSEN, A.R. (1961), 'On the reformulation of inhibition in Hull's system', *Psychol. Bull., 58,* pp. 274-98. [177, 182]

JONES, H.G. (1960), 'Continuation of Yates's treatment of a tiqueur' in H.J. Eysenck (ed.), *Behaviour Therapy and the Neuroses,* Oxford, Pergamon, pp. 250-8. [128, 177]

JONES, H.G. (1971), 'In search of an ideographic psychology', *Bull. Br. Psychol. Soc., 24,* pp. 279-90. [123]

JOURARD, S.M. (1964), *The Transparent Self,* Princeton, Van Nostrand. [269]

KANFER, F.H., and KAROLY, P. (1972), 'Self-control: a behavioristic excursion into the lion's den', *Behav. Ther., 3,* pp. 398-416.

KANFER, F. and SASLOW, G. (1969), 'Behavioral diagnosis' in C.M. Franks (ed.), *Behavior Therapy: Appraisal and Status,* New York: McGraw-Hill. [209, 270]

KEEHN, J.D. (1959), 'More about inhibition of reinforcement', *Psychol. Rep., 5,* pp. 141-2. [177]

KEEHN, J.D., and SABBAGH, U. (1958), 'Conditioned inhibition and avoidance learning', *Psychol. Rep., 4,* pp. 547-52. [177]

KEGEL, A.H. (1952), 'Sexual functions of the pubococcygens muscle', *Western J. Obstet. & Gyn., 60,* p. 521. [248, 263]

KELLY, D. (1972), 'Physiological changes during operations on the limbic system in man', *Cond. Reflex, 7,* 127. [203]

KELLY, G.A. (1955), *The Psychology of Personal Constructs,* New York, Norton. [124, 270]

KENDRICK, D.C. (1958), 'Inhibition with reinforcement (conditioned inhibition)', *J. Exp. Psychol., 56,* pp. 313-18. [177, 182]

KENDRICK, D.C. (1960), 'The theory of "conditioned inhibition" as an explanation of negative practice effects: an experimental analysis' in H.J. Eysenck (ed.), *Behaviour Therapy and the Neuroses,* Oxford, Pergamon, pp. 221-35. [177, 182]

KING, L.W., LIBERMAN, R.P., and DeRISI, W.J. (1973), 'An evaluation of outcome effects of Personal Effectiveness Training (Assertion Training) in a community mental health centre', submitted to *J. Abnorm. Psychol.,* 1973.

KINSEY, A.C., POMEROY, W.B., and MARTIN, C.E. (1948), *Sexual Behavior in the Human Male,* Philadelphia, Saunders. [260, 269]

KINSEY, A.C., POMEROY, W.B., MARTIN, C.E., and GEBHARD, P.H. (1953), *Sexual Behavior in the Human Female,* Philadelphia, Saunders. [255]

KRAFT, T. (1967a), 'A case of homosexuality treated by systematic desensitization', *Am. Psychother., 21,* pp. 815-21. [45]

KRAFT, T. (1967b), 'Behavior therapy and the treatment of sexual perversions', *Psychother. & Psychosom., 15,* pp. 351-7. [45]

KUSHNER, M. (1965), 'The reduction of a long-standing fetish by means of aversive conditioning' in L.P. Ullmann and L. Krasner (eds), *Case Studies in Behavior Modification,* New York, Holt, Rinehart & Winston, pp. 239-42. [45]

LADER, M.H. (1969), 'Psychophysiological aspects of anxiety' in M.H. Lader (ed.), *Anxiety, Br. J. Psychiat.* special publication no. 3, pp. 53-61. [101]

LADER, M.H., and MATTHEWS, A.M. (1968), 'A physiological model of phobic anxiety and desensitisation', *Behav. Res. & Ther., 6,* pp. 411-21. [101]

LANG, P.J. (1968), 'Fear reduction and fear behavior: problems in treating a construct' in J.M. Shlieu (ed.), *Research in Psychotherapy,* Washington, American Psychological Association, vol. III. [101]

LARSON, D. (1970), 'An adaptation of the Feldman and MacCulloch approach to treatment of homosexuality by the application of anticipatory avoidance learning', *Behav. Res. & Ther., 8,* pp. 209-10. [46]

LAVIN, N.I., THORPE, J.G., BARKER, J.C., BLAKEMORE, C.B., and CONWAY, C.G. (1961), 'Behavior therapy in a case of transvestism', *J. Nerv. Ment. Dis., 133,* pp. 346-53. [45]

LAZARUS, A.A. (1965), 'The treatment of a sexually inadequate man' in L.P. Ullman and L. Krasner (eds), *Case Studies in Behavior Modification,* New York, Holt, Rinehart & Winston. [239]

LAZARUS, A.A. (1966), 'Behavior rehearsal vs. non-directive therapy vs. advice in affecting behavior change', *Behav. Res. & Ther., 4,* pp. 209-12. [270]

LAZARUS, A.A. (1968a), 'A case of pseudonecrophilia treated by behavior therapy', *J. Clin. Psychol., 24,* pp. 113-15. [45]

LAZARUS, A.A. (1968b), 'Learning theory and the treatment of depression', *Behav. Res. & Ther., 6,* pp. 83-9. [229]

LEHNER, G.F.J. (1954), 'Negative practice as a psychotherapeutic technique', *J. Gen. Psychol., 51,* pp. 69-82. [177]

LEITENBERG, H. (1973), 'The use of single-case methodology in psychotherapy research', *J. Abnorm. Psychol., 82,* pp. 87-110. [4, 7, 8]

LEVIN, S., HIRSCH. I., SHUGAR, G., and KAPCHE, R. (1968), 'Treatment of homosexuality and heterosexual anxiety with avoidance conditioning and systematic desensitization: data and case report', *Psychother.: Theory, Res. & Pract., 5,* pp. 160-8. [45]

LEWINSHOHN. P.M., WEINSTEIN, M.S., and SHAW, D.A. (1968), 'Depression: a clinical research approach' in R. Rubin and C. Franks (eds), *Advances in Behavior Therapy,* New York, Academic Press. [229]

LIBERMAN, R.P. (1972), *A Guide to Behavioral Analysis and Therapy,* New York, Pergamon. [212]

LIBERMAN, R.P. (1973), 'Applying behavioral techniques in a community mental health center', in R.D. Rubin, J.P. Brady, and J.D. Henderson (eds), *Advances in Behavior Therapy,* New York, Academic Press. [208]

LIBERMAN, R.P., DeRISI, W.J., KING, L.W., ECKMAN, T., and WOOD, D. (1974), 'Behavioral measurement in a community mental health center', in P.O. Davidson, F. Clark, and L Hamerlych (eds), *Evaluating Behavioral Programs in Community, Residential and Educational Settings,* Champain, Illinois, Research Press, pp. 103-39. [209]

LIBERMAN, R.P., KING, L.W., DeRISI, W.J., and McCANN, M. (1975), *Personal Effectiveness: Guiding People to Assert their Feelings and Improve their*

Social Skills, Champain, Illinois, Research Press. [209]

LIBERMAN, R.P., and RASKIN, D.E. (1971), 'Depression: a behavioral formulation', *Arch. Gen. Psychiat., 24,* pp. 515-23. [223, 229]

LIBERMAN, R.P., TEIGMAN, T., PATTERSON, R., and BAKER, V. (1973), 'Reducing delusional speech in chronic paranoid schizophrenics', *J. Appl. Behav. Anal., 6,* pp. 57-70. [61]

LIDZ, T. (1973), *The Origin and Treatment of Schizophrenic Disorders,* New York, Basic Books. [123]

LINDSLEY, O.R. (1956), 'Operant conditioning methods applied to research in chronic schizophrenia', *Psychiat. Res. Rep., 5,* pp. 118-39. [298]

LINDSLEY, O.R. (1960), 'Characteristics of the behavior of chronic psychotics as revealed by free-operant conditioning methods', *Dis. Nerv. Syst., 21,* pp. 66-78. [298]

LOBITZ, W.C., and LoPICCOLO, J. (1972), 'New methods in the behavioral treatment of sexual dysfunction', *J. Behav. Ther. & Exp. Psychiat., 3,* pp. 265-71. [237, 238]

LOCKE, E.A. (1971), 'Is "behavior therapy" behavioristic? (An analysis of Wolpe's psychotherapeutic methods)', *Psychol. Bull., 76,* pp. 318-27. [185]

LOCKE, H.J., and WALLACE, K.M. (1959), 'Short marital adjustment and prediction tests: their reliability and validity', *Marr. & Fam. Liv., 21,* pp. 251-5. [252]

LOOFT, W.R. (1973), 'Reflections on intervention in old age: motives, goals and assumptions', *Gerontologist, 13,* pp. 6-10. [183]

LoPICCOLO, J., and LOBITZ, W.C. (1972), 'The role of masturbation in the treatment of primary orgasmic dysfunction', *Archs Sex. Behav., 2,* pp. 163-71. [238, 255, 259]

LoPICCOLO, J., and LOBITZ, W.C. (1973), 'Behavior therapy of sexual dysfunction' in L.A. Hamerlynck, L.C. Handy, and E.J. Mash (eds), *Behavior Change: Methodology, Concepts and Practice,* Champain, Illinois, Research Press. [238]

LoPICCOLO, J., and STEGER, J.C. (1973), 'The Oregon Sex Inventory: an instrument for assessment of sexual dysfunction', unpublished MS, University of Houston. [252]

LoPICCOLO, J., STEWART, R., and WATKINS, B. (1972), 'Treatment of erectile failure and ejaculatory incompetence of homosexual etiology', *J. Behav. Ther. & Exp. Psychiat., 3,* pp. 233-6. [238]

LORAND, S. (1939), 'Contributions to the problem of vaginal orgasm', *Int. J. Psychoanal., 20,* pp. 432-8. [237]

LOVAAS, O.I., KOEGEL, R., SIMMONS, J., and LONG, J. (1973), 'Some generalization and follow-up measures on autistic children in behavior therapy', *J. Appl. Behav. Anal., 6,* pp. 131-66. [70]

LOVIBOND, S.H., and CADDY, K.G. (1970), 'Discriminated aversive control in the moderation of alcoholics' drinking behavior', *Behav. Ther., 1,* pp. 437-44. [282]

McAULEY, R., and QUINN, J.T. (1971), 'Behavioural analysis treatment and theoretical implications of a case of depression', paper presented at the Dublin Conference on Behavioural Modification. [229]

MacCULLOCH, M.J. (1969), 'Aversion therapy', MD thesis, Manchester University. [326, 328]

MacCULLOCH, M.J., BIRTLES, C.J., and FELDMAN, M.P. (1971), 'Anticipatory avoidance learning for the treatment of homosexuality: recent developments and an automatic aversion therapy system', *Behav. Ther.*, *2*, pp. 151-69. [313, 326]

MacCULLOCH, M.J. and FELDMAN, M.P. (1967a), 'The management of 43 homosexuals using aversion therapy', *Br. Med. J.*, *2*, pp. 594-7. [303, 304]

MacCULLOCH, M.J. and FELDMAN, M.P. (1967b), 'Personalities and the treatment of homosexuality', *Acta Psychiat. Scand.*, *43*, pp. 300-17. [305]

MacCULLOCH, M.J. and SAMBROOKS, J.E. (1974), 'Sexual interest latencies in aversion therapy: a preliminary report', *Archs Sex. Behav.*, *3* (in press). [305, 312]

McGUIRE, R.J., CARLISLE, J.M., and YOUNG, B.G. (1965), 'Sexual deviations as conditional behaviour: a hypothesis', *Behav. Res. & Ther.*, *2*, pp. 185-90. [81]

McGUIRE, R.J., and VALLANCE, M. (1964), 'Aversion therapy by electric shock: a simple technique', *Br. Med. J.*, *1*, pp. 151-2. [88]

MAHONEY, M.J. (1972), 'Reseach issues in self-management,' *Behav. Ther.*, *3*, pp. 45-63. [223]

MARKS, I.M. (1969), *Fears and Phobias,* London, Heinemann. [100]

MARKS, I.M. (1972), 'Perspective on flooding', *Semin. in Psychiat.*, *4*, pp. 129-38. [230]

MARKS, I.M., and GELDER, M.G. (1967), 'Transvestism and fetishism: clinical and psychological changes during faradic aversion', *Br. J. Psychiat.*, *113*, pp. 711-29. [8]

MARKS, I.M., GELDER, M.G., and BANCROFT, J. (1970), 'Sexual deviants two years after electric aversion', *Br. J. Psychiat.*, *117*, pp. 173-85. [45]

MARKS, I.M., and SARTORIUS, N. (1968), 'A contribution to the measurement of sexual meaning', *J. Nerv. Ment. Dis.*, *145*, pp. 441-51. [82]

MARQUIS, J.N. (1970), 'Orgasmic reconditioning: changing sexual object choice through controlling masturbation fantasies', *J. Behav. Ther. & Exp. Psychiat.*, *1*, pp. 263-71. [86]

MASTERS, W.H., and JOHNSON, V. (1970), *Human Sexual Inadequacy,* Boston, Little, Brown. [237, 238, 239, 245, 246, 254, 255, 269]

MATHER, M.D. (1970), 'Obsessions and compulsions' in C.G. Costello, *Symptoms of Psychopathology,* New York, Wiley, vol. II, pp. 302-19. [175]

MAXWELL, A.E. (1958), *Experimental Design in Psychology and the Medical Sciences,* London, Methuen. [40]

MENDELS, J. (ed.) (1973), *Biological Psychiatry,* New York, Wiley. [332]

MENDELSON, M. (1967), 'Neurotic depressive reaction' in A.M. Freedman and H.I. Kaplan (eds), *Comprehensive Textbook of Psychiatry,* Baltimore, Williams & Wilkins. [228]

METZNER, R. (1963), 'Some experimental analogues of obsession', *Behav. Res. & Ther.*, *1*, pp. 231-6. [175]

MEYER, V. (1967), 'Modification of expectations in cases with obsessional rituals', *Behav. Res. & Ther., 4,* pp. 273-80. [38, 175, 201]

MEYER, V. and LEVY, R. (1973), 'Modification of behaviour in obsessive-compulsive disorders' in H.E. Adams and I.P. Unikel (eds), *Issues and Trends on Behavior Therapy,* Springfield, Ill., Thomas. [165]

MILLS, K.C., SOBELL, M.B., and SCHAEFER, H.H. (1971), 'Training social drinking as an alternative to abstinence for alcoholics', *Behav. Ther., 2,* pp. 18-27. [282]

MOORE, B.E. (1961), 'Frigidity in women', *J. Am. Psychoanal. Ass., 9,* pp. 571-84. [237]

MOUNTJOY, P.T., EDWIN, A., and ROGERS, C.C. (1960), 'Response decrement under continuous reinforcement as a function of effort', *J. Scient. Labs Denison Univ., 45,* pp. 124-8. [182]

NAMBOODIRI, J.K. (1972), 'Experimental designs in which each subject is used repeatedly', *Psychol. Bull., 77,* pp. 54-64. [4]

NORDQUIST, V.M., and WAHLER, R.G. (1973), 'Naturalistic treatment of an autistic child', *J. Appl. Behav. Anal., 6,* pp. 79-87. [73]

NORRIS, F.M., and JONES, H.G. (1971), 'Conceptual distance indices as measures of alienation in obsessional neurosis', *Psychol. Med., 1, 5,* pp. 381-7. [123]

OBLER, M. (1973), 'Systematic disensitization in sexual disorders', *J. Behav. Ther. & Exper. Psychol., 4,* pp. 93-102. [237]

O'BRIEN, R., AZRIN, N.H., and HENSON, K. (1969), 'Increased communications of chronic mental patients by reinforcement and by response priming', *J. Appl. Behav. Anal., 2,* pp. 23-30. [7]

OSWALD, L. (1962), 'Induction of illusory and hallucinatory voices with considerations of behavior therapy', *J. Ment. Sci., 108,* pp. 196-212. [45]

PATTERSON, R., and TEIGMAN, J. (1973), 'Conditioning and post-hospital generalization of non-delusional responses in a chronic psychotic patient', *J. Appl. Behav. Anal., 6,* pp. 65-70. [61]

PHILLIPS, J.P.N. (1968), 'A note on the scoring of the sexual orientation method', *Behav. Res. & Ther., 6,* pp. 121-3. [303]

PROKASY, W.F. (1960), 'Postasymptotic performance decrements during massed reinforcements', *Psychol. Bull., 57,* pp. 237-47. [177, 182]

RACHMAN, S. (1971), *The Effects of Psychotherapy,* Oxford, Pergamon. [2, 4, 12, 332]

RACHMAN, S. (1974), 'Primary obsessional slowness', *Behav. Res. & Ther., 12,* pp. 9-18. [30, 40]

RACHMAN, S., HODGSON, R.J., and MARZILLIER, J. (1970), 'Treatment of an obsessional-compulsive disorder by modelling', *Behav. Res. & Ther., 8,* pp. 385-92. [203]

RACHMAN, S. HODGSON, R.J., and MARZILLIER, J. (1970), 'Treatment of an obsessional-compulsive disorder by modelling', *Behav. Res. & Ther., 8,* pp. 385-92. [203]

RACHMAN, S., MARKS, I.M., and HODGSON, R.J. (1973), 'The treatment of obsessive-compulsive neurotics by modelling and flooding in vivo', *Behav. Res. & Ther., 11,* pp. 463-71. [18, 33, 39]

RACHMAN, S., and TEASDALE, J. (1969), *Aversion Therapy and Behaviour*

Disorders: an Analysis, London, Routledge & Kegan Paul. [81]

RAMSAY, R. (1971), 'The social relations of phobic patients', paper read at the first EABT Conference, Liège, Belgium. [101]

RAYMOND, M.J. (1956), 'Case of fetishism treated by aversion therapy', *Br. Med. J., 2,* pp. 854-7. [45]

REINERT, R.E., and BOWEN, W.T. (1968), 'Social drinking following treatment for alcoholism', *Bull. Menninger Clin., 32,* pp. 280-90. [282]

REVUSKY, S.H. (1967), 'Some statistical treatments compatible with individual organism methodology', *J. Exp. Analysis Behav., 10,* pp. 319-30. [4]

ROGERS, C. (1961), *On Becoming a Person, a Therapist's View of Psychotherapy,* Boston, Houghton Mifflin. [61]

RUBIN, I. (1968), 'Sex and aging in man and woman' in C.E. Vincent (ed.), *Human Sexuality in Medical Education and Practice,* Springfield, Illinois, Thomas. [243, 269]

RYLE, A., and BREEN, D. (1971), 'The recognition of psychopathology on the repertory grid', *Br. J. Psychiat., 119,* pp. 319-21. [123]

SAMBROOKS, J.E., and MacCULLOCH, M.J. (1973), 'A modification of the sexual orientation method and an automated technique for presentation and scoring', *Br. J. Soc. & Clin. Psychol., 12,* pp. 163-74. [303, 308, 315]

SCHACHTER, S., and SINGER, J.E. (1962), 'Cognitive, social and physiological determinants of emotional state', *Psychol. Rev., 69,* pp. 379-99. [123, 269]

SCHNEIDER, K. (1959), *Psychopathic Personalities,* 9th ed., London, Cassell. [304, 321]

SCHOFIELD, W. (1950), 'Changes in response to the Minnesota Multiphasic Inventory following certain therapies', *Psychol. Monogr., 64,* no. 311. [2]

SERBER, M. (1970), 'Shame aversion therapy', *J. Behav. Ther. & Exp. Psychiat., 1,* pp. 213-15. [45]

SHAPIRO, M.B. (1961), 'The single case in fundamental clinical psychological research', *Br. J. Med. Psychol., 34,* pp. 355-64. [3]

SHAPIRO, M.B. (1964), 'The measurement of clinically relevant variables', *J. Psychosom. Res., 8,* pp. 245-54. [129]

SHAPIRO, M.B. (1966), 'The single case in clinical-psychological research', *J. Gen. Psychol., 74,* pp. 3-23. [3]

SHAPIRO, M.B. (1970), 'Intensive assessment in the single case: an inductive: deductive approach' in P. Mittler (ed.), *The Psychological Assessment of Mental and Physical Handicaps,* London, Methuen. [128]

SHARPE, R., and MEYER, V. (1973), 'Modification of "cognitive sexual pain" by the wife under supervision', *Behav. Ther., 4,* 2, pp. 285-7. [150, 151]

SHINE, L.C., and BOWER, S.M. (1971), 'A one-way analysis of variance for single-subject designs', *Educ. Psychol. Measur., 31,* pp. 105-13. [4]

SIDMAN, M. (1960a), 'Normal sources of pathological behavior', *Science, 132,* pp. 61-8. [275]

SIDMAN, M. (1960b), *Tactics of Scientific Research,* New York, Basic Books. [2, 275]

SIGGINS, L.D. (1967), 'Mourning: a critical survey', *Int. J. Psychiat., 3,* pp. 418-32. [229]

SKINNER, B.F. (1938), *The Behavior of Organisms,* New York, Appleton-Century-Crofts. [275]

SKINNER, B.F. (1953), *Science and Human Behavior,* New York, Macmillan. [275]

SKINNER, B.F. (1969), *Contingencies of Reinforcement,* New York, Appleton-Century-Crofts. [75]

SLATER, P. (1965a), 'The use of the repertory grid technique in the individual case', *Br. J. Psychiat., 111,* pp. 965-75. [125]

SLATER, P. (1965b), *The Principal Components of a Repertory Grid,* London, Andrews. [125]

SLATER, P. (1967), *Notes on* INGRID *67,* London, Institute of Psychiatry, Maudsley Hospital. [125]

SLATER, P. (1968), *Summary of the Output of* DELTA, London, Institute of Psychiatry, Maudsley Hospital. [136]

SOBELL, M.B., and SOBELL, L. (1972), 'Individualized behavior therapy for alcoholics: rationale, procedures, preliminary results and appendix', *State of California, Department of Mental Hygiene Research Monograph,* no. 13. [282]

SOLOMON, R.L. (1964), 'Punishment', *Am. Psychol., 19,* pp. 239-53. [45]

SOLOMON, R.L., and WYNNE, L.C. (1953), 'Traumatic avoidance learning acquisition in normal dogs', *Psychol. Monog., 67,* p. 4. [178]

SOLOMON, R.L. and WYNNE, L.C. (1954), 'Traumatic avoidance learning: the principles of anxiety conservation and partial irreversibility', *Psychol. Rev., 61,* pp. 353-85. [178]

SOLYOM, L., GARZA-PEREZ, J., LEDWIDGE, B.L., and SOLYOM, C. (1972), 'Paradoxical intention in the treatment of obsessive thoughts: a pilot study', *Comp. Psychiat., 13,* pp. 291-7. [175, 182]

SOLYOM, L., and MILLER, S. (1965), 'A differential conditioning procedure as the initial phase of behavior therapy of homosexuality', *Behav. Res. & Ther., 3,* pp. 147-60. [46]

SOLYOM, L., ZAHMANZADEH, D., LEDWIDGE, B., and KENNY, F. (1969), 'Aversion relief treatment of obsessive neurosis' in R. Rubin and C.M. Franks (eds), *Advances in Behavior Therapy,* New York, Academic Press, pp. 93-109. (176]

STEVENSON, I., and WOLPE, J. (1960), 'Recovery from sexual deviations through overcoming non-sexual neurotic responses', *Am. J. Psychiat., 116,* pp. 737-42. [45, 50, 58]

STUART, R.B. (1969), 'Operant-interpersonal treatment for marital discord', *J. Consult. & Clin. Psychol., 33,* pp. 675-82. [75]

STUART, R.B. (1972), *Slim Chance in a Fat World,* Champain, Illinois, Research Press. [223]

TAYLOR, J.G. (1963), 'A behavioural interpretation of obsessive-compulsive neurosis', *Behav. Res. & Ther., 1,* pp. 237-44. [175, 178]

THORPE, J.G., SCHMIDT, E., BROWN, P.T., and CASTELL, D. (1964), 'Aversion-relief therapy: a new method for general application', *Behav. Res. & Ther., 2,* pp. 71-82. [176]

TODD, F.J. (1972), 'Coverant control of self-evaluative responses in the treatment of depression: a new use for an old principle', *Behav. Ther., 3,* pp. 91-4. [223]

ULLMANN, L.P., and KRASNER, L. (1969), *A Psychological Approach to Abnormal Behavior*, Englewood Cliffs, Prentice-Hall. [45, 58]

WAHLER, R.G. (1969), 'Setting generality: some specific and general effects of child behavior therapy', *J. Appl. Behav. Anal.*, *2*, pp. 239-46. [70]

WALTON, D. (1960), 'The relevance of learning theory to the treatment of an obsessive-compulsive state' in H.J. Eysenck (ed.), *Behaviour Therapy and the Neuroses*, Oxford, Pergamon, pp. 153-64. [175]

WALTON, D. and MATHER, M. (1964), 'The application of learning principles for the treatment of obsessive-compulsive states in the acute and chronic phases of illness' in H.J. Eysenck (ed.), *Experiments in Behaviour Therapy*, Oxford, Pergamon. [30, 175]

WATERS, W.F., and McCALLUM, R.N. (1973), 'The basis of behavior therapy, mentalistic or behavioristic? A reply to E.A. Locke', *Behav. Res. & Ther.*, *11*, pp. 157-64. [185]

WATSON, D.L., and THARP, R.G. (1972), *Self-directed Behavior: Self-modification for Personal Adjustment*, Monterey, California, Brooks-Cole. [223]

WICKRAMASEKERA, I. (1968), 'The application of learning theory to the treatment of a case of sexual exhibitionism', *Psychother.: Theory, Res. & Pract.*, *5*, pp. 108-12. [45]

WINCE, J.P., LETTENBERG, H., and AGRAS, W.S. (1972), 'The effects of token reinforcement and feedback on the delusional verbal behavior of chronic paranoid schizophrenics', *J. Appl. Behav. Anal.*, *5*, pp. 247-62. [62]

WOLPE, J. (1958), *Psychotherapy by Reciprocal Inhibition*, California, Stanford University Press. [52, 84, 89, 175, 185, 239]

WOLPE, J. (1962), 'Isolation of a conditioning procedure as the crucial psychotherapeutic factor: a case study', *J. Nerv. Ment. Dis.*, *134*, pp. 316-29. [206]

WOLPE, J. (1969), *The Practice of Behavior Therapy*, New York, Pergamon. [52, 238, 255, 269]

WOLPE, J. (1971a), 'Dealing with resistance to thought-stopping: a transcript', *J. Behav. Ther. & Exp. Psychiat.*, *2*, pp. 121-5. [176]

WOLPE, J. (1971b), 'Neurotic depression: experimental analog, clinical syndromes, and treatment', *Am. J. Psychother.*, *25*, pp. 362-8. [229, 235]

WOLPE, J. (1973), *The Practice of Behavior Therapy*, 2nd ed., New York, Pergamon. [191, 192, 193, 206]

WOLPE, J. and LAZARUS, A.A. (1966), *Behavior Therapy Techniques: a Guide to the Treatment of Neuroses*, Oxford and New York, Pergamon. [132, 133, 175, 237]

WOLPE, J., and RACHMAN, S. (1960), 'Psychoanalytic "evidence": a critique based on Freud's care of Little Hans', *J. Nerv. Ment. Dis.*, *130*, pp. 135-48. [5]

YAMAGAMI, T. (1971), 'The treatment of an obsession by thought-stopping', *J. Behav. Ther. & Exp. Psychiat.*, *2*, pp. 133-5. [175]

YATES, A.J. (1958), 'The application of learning theory to the treatment of tics', *J. Abnorm. & Soc. Psychol.*, *56*, pp. 175-82. [177, 178, 182]

YATES, A.J. (1970), *Behavior Therapy*, New York, Wiley. [3, 4]

General Index

DATE DUE

DEMCO NO. 38-298